Curriculum Development

Curriculum Development

A Guide to Practice

Second Edition

Jon Wiles
Joseph C. Bondi

University of South Florida

Charles E. Merrill Publishing Company
A Bell & Howell Company
Columbus   Toronto   London   Sydney

Published by
Charles E. Merrill Publishing Company
A Bell and Howell Company
Columbus, Ohio 43216

This book was set in Bodoni Book.
Designer: Matthew Lederman
Cover designer: Tony Faiola

Library of Congress Catalog Card Number: 83-62532
International Standard Book Number: 0-675-20170-5
Printed in the United States of America

2 3 4 5 6 7 8 9 10—91 90 89 88 87 86 85

This second edition is dedicated to our families: Margaret, Amy, and Michael Wiles; and Patsy, Pam, Beth, and Brad Bondi. We also dedicate this book to those educational leaders encountered in school settings, throughout our nation, who are striving to improve educational experiences for schoolchildren.

Table of Contents

Preface

During the five years since the initial edition of *Curriculum Planning: A Guide to Practice,* we have noted sweeping changes in the methods by which schools and districts improve instructional programs. Competency-based educational targets, multi-media commercial learning systems, and the advent of the personal computer, to name a few of the changes, have impacted upon the process of curriculum development. We have developed our second edition with such changes in mind.

Two threads run throughout this book: (1) curriculum development is truly a value-laden task with important decisions at every turn, and (2) the process of curriculum development is consistent despite major changes in roles and responsibilities in education. The authors feel that knowing the process and understanding the issues of curriculum are important to successful practice.

The 1980s and 1990s will not be easy times for educational leaders. Therefore, we have included chapters on the political dimensions of curriculum development and alternative futures for curriculum development to assist the reader in an orientation to these areas.

Finally, while working in some forty states during the past five years, we have repeatedly observed the importance of planning in curriculum development. In particular, long-range planning that focuses on desired ends and manages the improvement of curriculum to achieve these ends seems to differentiate successful schools and districts from unsuccessful ones. Curriculum development is a complex process that requires time, and there can be no lasting change and improvement of school curriculum without careful planning and execution.

It is hoped that the reader will find this book to be an overview of the process of curriculum development as well as a source of "handles" for practice in specific school environments. We sincerely thank William C. Heeney, Stephen F. Austin State University, and

Larry Wald, Central Washington University, for their helpful and constructive review of the manuscript and we are indebted to all of those
individuals and districts who have shared products of their curriculum
development process for your review and study.

Curriculum Development

Part One
Curriculum Perspectives

Chapter One
The Field of Curriculum

A curriculum is a plan for learning consisting of two major dimensions, vision and structure. Vision in a curriculum is the product of a set of assumptions about people and the world at large and takes the form of some conceptualization of reality. Formally called a philosophy, this "reality" interprets the role of education through certain lenses. Because there are many differing views of reality in our society, there are also many conceptions of the role of education and many plans for educating. Any curriculum, or plan for learning, will always contain a set of value-laden assumptions about the purpose of education in our society.

The curriculum also contains a structure or basic organization for translating the visionary aspects of the plan into experiences for the learner. This methodology or organization is actually the way in which the intentions of the plan are to be implemented. In the past decade, the process of structuring the curriculum in our schools has been greatly refined, and represents a significant advance in our ability to design and implement improved school programs. While the visionary value questions posed sixty years ago by early curriculum theorists still remain open or unanswered, the process of developing school programs is approaching a science.

The structure of the curriculum development process consists of a basic four-step cycle: (1) analyze, (2) design, (3) implement, and (4) evaluate. This book seeks to illuminate the many ramifications of that cycle as they apply to improving educational experiences for schoolchildren. The visionary aspects of developing a learning plan for schools are addressed in the following section as well as in other parts of the book where appropriate.

Historical Perspectives of Curriculum _____

Formal education has always served as an adaptive mechanism for human cultures. Education represents one of the primary means by which cultures preserve their past and prepare for the future. Formal education, or schooling, is often a vehicle for social reconstruction and, in the United States, education has changed as our society has developed.

In the earliest days of this nation, schools were established in religious institutions to develop a literate membership capable of reading the Bible and withstanding the temptations of the devil.[1] By 1830, the first tax-supported public elementary schools were being established in Massachusetts to cope with an initial wave of immigrants who had to be assimilated into that region.[2] Until the outbreak of the Civil War, a major mission for the schools was the development of literacy; reading, 'riting and 'rithmetic.

Following the Civil War, during a period in which public schools were in a state of disorganization, a major private school movement occurred in the United States under the general name of "academies." The academies drew their purpose from Thomas Jefferson's conception of a highly educated Renaissance man; a person with wide interests and expertise in a number of areas. The curriculum of the academies was classical, including Latin, Orthography, and Grammar. Until the establishment of public-supported secondary schools in 1874,[3] the academies served to prepare students for later learning in colleges and universities.

In the 1870s and 1880s, our nation was engaged in the conquest and development of the North American continent. The need for educated civil servants and leaders became obvious in the new states and territories, as did the need for an educated populace to participate in a democratic form of government. Public education was made universal, extending through the secondary grades, and the curriculum was broadened to accommodate a wider range of students. By the early 1890s, the historic chain between the private academies and the colleges and universities was breaking down. During this period, secondary education was defined and quantified by formal committees of educators and government officials.

In the first quarter of the twentieth century, the nation experienced an industrial revolution characterized by mechanization, urbanization, and mobility. Millions of immigrants entered the United States and were assimilated into our culture. The secondary school became popular[4] and took on new tasks like teaching English as a subject and offering vocational preparation. Later, physical education, art, and music entered the curriculum to meet the needs of individuals and society.

During the past half-century, the program of the school has been altered on numerous occasions to adjust to a changing society or to serve special groups of learners. Wars, depressions, revolutions in transportation and communication, and a growing body of knowledge about learners themselves have acted to stretch the curriculum of the school in America. Schools have established programs to promote literacy, preserve and utilize knowledge, develop the society, and aid in the personal growth and development of individuals. The plan for educating in America has been altered each time new visions of the school purpose have been proposed.

Curriculum, as a special area of study within education, emerged from the need to arrange, organize, and translate such visions into educational programs of study. Although the first formal book in the area of curriculum was not produced until 1918,[5] serious study of options in education were well underway in the nineteenth century. A logical point of departure for the study of curriculum can be found in the 1890s when highly visible committees were formed to organize American education into a predictable sequence of learning sometimes referred to as the "educational ladder." During the meetings of these "great committees," true curriculum concerns were voiced in the form of issues, and true curriculum development occurred as structure was given to the elementary and secondary programs of the public schools.

Prior to the 1880s, there was no formal conception of the "common school experience" for all persons in our society. The various curricula of the elementary and secondary schools, both public and private, were varied, and colleges and universities experienced the problem of students entering with uneven preparation. In 1888, Charles W. Eliot, President of Harvard University, was invited to speak to the National Education Association (NEA) and subsequently delivered a talk entitled "Can School Programs Be Shortened and Enriched?" Eliot's speech called for taking two years away from the traditional eight-year elementary school program and applying them toward a secondary school with six years of education. Hence, the elementary school would be shortened and the high school program enriched.

Eliot's speech stirred considerable interest and resulted in the appointment of three prestigious study committees: The Committee of Fifteen on Elementary Education, The Committee of Ten on Secondary Education, and the Committee on College Entrance Requirements. A fourth committee, The Committee on Economy of Time in Education, also met during this period to discuss major issues and make recommendations on the purpose and organization of public education in America.

While, in fact, these committees never really discussed anything but the reorganization of existing educational structures, they did initiate a scrutiny of the programs in education. Questions raised during these formal inquiries formed the foundation for the emergence of the area of curriculum—an area of inquiry concerned with the conceptualization, design, implementation, and assessment of educational programs. Nearly one hundred years later, curriculum development stands as an essential area of study in education and as a critical function in a nation experiencing rapid change.

An Evolving Definition

Although the first use of the term curriculum can be found in Scotland as early as 1820, the first modern use of the term in the United States came nearly a century later. The term curriculum comes from the Latin word "currere" which means "to run." The course of the race, with time, came to mean the "course of study." Not surprisingly, then, the traditional definition of curriculum is a course of study or training leading to a product or education. For most lay persons, curriculum today is equated with course guides, syllabi, or textbooks that establish the "course." Such a classic definition of the term also reflects the meaning of curriculum for the most conservative or structured educators in the field. The following definitions of curriculum are indicative of how conservative philosophies of education see or "envision" school programming:

> The curriculum should consist of permanent studies—the rules of grammar, reading, rhetoric and logic, and mathematics (for the elementary and secondary school), and the greatest books of the western world (beginning at the secondary level of schooling).[6]

> The curriculum must consist essentially of disciplined study in five great areas: (1) command of mother tongue and the systematic study of grammar, literature, and writing, (2) mathematics, (3) sciences, (4) history, (5) foreign language.[7]

> The curriculum should consist entirely of knowledge which comes from the disciplines. . . . Education should be conceived as a guided recapitulation of the process of inquiry which gave rise to the fruitful bodies of organized knowledge comprising the established disciplines.[8]

The definition of curriculum as a product or as an experience that is contained proved unsatisfactory to many educators involved in the development of school programs. For one thing, the early years of this century witnessed an enormous growth in knowledge and for the first time knowledge was not contained in a print form. Information came to learners through media like the radio and was interpreted by the individual without the direct aid of a teacher. With the dissemination of such new knowledge, identifying "essential" knowledge became more difficult and packaging knowledge became a problem of maintaining relevance and updating material.

In addition, the composition of schools changed considerably during this period in our history. Secondary schools, no longer the preserve of a small number of students who would attend college, became a universal experience. In some cases, basic skills of citizenship took precedence over classical knowledge and new courses and experiences had to be devised for learners. As more subjects were added to the school plan, and as the differences among individual learners forced accommodation by teachers, the definition of "curriculum" began to stretch. Specialists in curriculum began to speak of a difference between a planned program of studies and the program actually experienced by the learner (the so-called "hidden curriculum"). A watershed break with the traditional definition of the curriculum as a product came in 1935 when two leading curriculum specialists, Caswell and Campbell, acknowledged the "socializing" function of the schooling experience. The curriculum, they said, "is composed of all of the experiences children have under the guidance of the teacher."[9] Other writers in this century have followed Caswell and Campbell in seeing the curriculum as an experience rather than a product of study:

> A sequence of potential experiences is set up in the school for the purpose of disciplining children and youth in group ways of thinking and acting. This set of experiences is referred to as the curriculum.[10]
>
> The curriculum is now generally considered to be all of the experiences that learners have under the auspices of the school.[11]

By the mid-1950s, it became increasingly evident that schools had a tremendous influence on students' lives. Some of those influences were structured, while others were due to the congregation of youth. It was recognized that students also had experiences not planned by the school. During this period, definitions were dominated by those aspects of the curriculum that were planned, as opposed to simply the content or general experiences of students.

> The curriculum is all of the learning of students which is planned by and directed by the school to attain its educational goals.[12]
>
> A curriculum is a plan for learning.[13]
>
> We define curriculum as a plan for providing sets of learning opportunities to achieve broad goals and related specific objectives for an identifiable population served by a single school center.[14]

Finally, beginning in the 1960s and continuing in the 1980s, there has been a concern for the performance of educational programs. This focus, often referred to as "accountability" in schools, has pushed the definition of the curriculum toward an emphasis on ends or outcomes:

> Curriculum is concerned not with what students will do in the learning situation, but with what they will learn as a consequence of what they do. Curriculum is concerned with results.[15]
>
> (Curriculum is) the planned and guided learning experiences and intended outcomes, formulated through systematic reconstruction of knowledge and experience, under the auspices of the school, for the learners' continuous and willful growth in personal-social competence.[16]

While the definition of curriculum has been altered in response to social forces and expectations for the school, the process of curriculum development has remained constant. Through analysis, design, implementation, and evaluation, curriculum developers set goals, plan experiences, select content, and assess outcomes of school programs. These constant processes have contributed to the emergence of structure in curriculum planning.

Emerging Structure in Curriculum Development ___

While definitions of curriculum and visions of the purpose of education have been expansive during the past century, the structure of curriculum development has been a "filling-in process." The principles that exist in the field of curriculum have evolved more from practice than from logic or enlightenment. In such instances, the theory of curriculum has followed the practice found in school environments.

The focus of most curricular principles is specific rather than global. As Tanner and Tanner have noted, "In the absence of a holistic conception of curriculum, the focus is on piecemeal and mechanical functions . . . the main thrust in curriculm development and reform over the years has been directed at microcurricular problems to the neglect of macrocurricular problems."[17]

Principles of curriculum have evolved as "core" procedures rather than theoretical guidelines. Maccia has called this the "proxiological approach" to theorizing as opposed to a more philosophical or theoretical approach.[18] The cause for this evolution of principles is a combination of the absence of systematic thinking about curriculum planning; the vulnerability of curriculum planning to social, political, and economic forces; and the constantly changing priorities of education in the United States.

Because of this situation, identification of curricular principles is difficult. Taba describes the almost unmanageable condition of curriculum approaches in this way:

> Decisions leading to change in curriculum organization have been made largely by pressure, by hunches, or in terms of expediency instead of being based on clearcut theoretical considerations or tested knowledge. The scope of curriculum has been extended vastly without an adequate consideration of the consequence of this extension on sequence or cumulative learning. . . . The fact that these perplexities underlying curriculum change have not been studied adequately may account for the proliferation of approaches to curriculum making.[19]

Prior to the major curriculum reforms in the late 1950s and early 1960s, most curriculum development in school settings was oriented toward producing content packages. In developing courses of study, curriculum specialists sought to refine school programs by redesigning essential topic areas and updating older programs on a scheduled basis. This rather static role for curriculum practitioners in the field resulted in the evolution of both theoretical constructs for developing curriculum and operational procedures that changed little over time.

An early observation by John Dewey that "the fundamental factors in the educative process are 1) the learner, 2) the society, and 3) organized subject matter"[20] set the stage for defining curriculum parameters. Bode, an early curriculum theorist and student of Dewey, renewed this theme in 1931 when he wrote, ". . . the difference in curriculum aims stems from three points of view: 1) the standpoint of subject-matter specialists, 2) the standpoint of the practical man and, 3) the interests of the learner."[21]

By 1945 these three general concerns were finding acceptance in most curriculum literature. Taba, for instance, discussed the three sources of data in curriculum planning as 1) the study of society, 2) studies of learners, and 3) studies of subject matter content.[22] By the early 1960s Taba had further refined the study of society to mean "cultural demands . . . a reflection of the changing social milieu of the school."[23]

Gaining acceptance as a fourth important planning base for curriculum in the mid-1950s and early 1960s was the study of learning itself. Studies from various schools of psychology and the advent of sophisticated technology in school settings raised new possibilities and choices for educators who were planning programs.

These four major areas of concern for curriculum planners, known as the foundations or "bases" of planning, remain today the basis of most analysis, design, implementation, and evaluation of school programs. These vital areas of concern are addressed in depth in the following chapter.

The importance of these planning bases as organizers for thinking about the development of educational programs is best summarized by Hilda Taba, a curriculum specialist concerned with the development aspects of curriculum:

> . . . semantics aside, these variations in the conception of the function of education are not idle or theoretical arguments. They have definite concrete implications for the shape of educational programs, especially the curriculum. . . . If one believes that the chief function of education is to transmit the perennial truths, one cannot but strive toward a uniform curriculum and teaching. Efforts to develop thinking take a different shape depending on whether the major function of education is seen as fostering creative thinking and problem solving or as following the rational forms of thinking established in our classical tradition. As such, differences in these concepts naturally determine what are considered the 'essentials' and what the dispensable frills in education.[24]

Paralleling the conceptual "mapping out" of the field of curriculum concerns was the evolution of operational procedures. Early curriculum development focused on subject content, which was a mechanical and rather simple operational technique developed in the 1920s and continued as the dominant operational concern until the early 1960s. Writing in the 1926 National Society for the Study of Education Yearbook, Harold Rugg outlined the operational tasks of curriculum development as a three-step process: 1) determine the fundamental objectives, 2) select activities and other materials of instruction, and 3) discover the most effective organization and placement of this instruction.[25]

By 1950, the technique of "inventory, organize, and present" had reached refinement in Tyler's widely read four-step analysis:

1. What educational purposes shall the school seek to attain?
2. What educational experiences can be provided that are likely to attain those purposes?
3. How can these educational experiences be effectively organized?
4. How can we determine whether these purposes are being attained?[26]

By addressing the assessment of curriculum development, Tyler introduced the concept of the curriculum development cycle whereby evaluation led to a reconsideration of purpose. Such a cycle in schools illuminated the comprehensiveness of the planning activity and later gave birth to refinements such as systems analysis and taxonomies of learning. Tyler's four-step model also rekindled a fifty-year-old effort to develop manageable behavioral objectives in education.[27]

The ordering of the development procedure also encouraged a mechanistic approach to curriculum development. Such approaches, long practiced in schools, are thoroughly represented in curriculum literature through various definitions:

> Curriculum development . . . it is basically a plan of structuring the environment to coordinate in an orderly manner the elements of time, space, materials, equipment and personnel.[28]
>
> The function of curriculum development is to research, design, and engineer the working relationships of the curricular elements that will be employed during the instructional phase in order to achieve desired outcomes.[29]

Perhaps the most refined version of Tyler's procedure for developing school curriculum was outlined by Taba in 1962. Seven major steps of curriculum development were identified:

1. diagnosis of needs
2. formulation of objectives
3. selection of content
4. organization of content
5. selection of learning experiences
6. organization of learning experiences
7. determination of what to evaluate and means of doing it

Within each step, substeps were provided which identified criteria for action. For example, in the selection of learning experiences it is important that the curriculum developer consider the following:

1. validity and significance of content
2. consistency with social reality
3. balance of breadth and depth of experiences
4. provision for a wide range of objectives
5. learnability-adaptability of the experience to life of student
6. appropriateness to needs and interests of learners[30]

Modern lists of these steps differ from Taba's in that they see curriculum as a more comprehensive process which may or may not be tied to a content product. In the following example, for instance, Feyereisen presents curriculum development as a problem-solving action chain:

1. Identification of the problem
2. Diagnosis of the problem
3. Search for alternative solutions
4. Selection of the best solution
5. Ratification of the solution by the organization
6. Authorization of the solution
7. Use of the solution on a trial basis
8. Preparation for adoption of the solution
9. Adoption of the solution
10. Direction and guidance of staff
11. Evaluation of effectiveness[31]

The broader focus of the Feyereisen description reflects a growing concern in curriculum development with planning for change in school environments from a macro-perspective. Curriculum development is increasingly a process with systemic concerns.

While other examples of the basic structure of the curriculum cycle could be provided at this point, it should be clear to the reader that a regular review process developed and was widely practiced in American schools between 1920 and 1960. It is certain that this process reflected the historical dominance of subject matter content as the focus of curriculum renewal:

Certainly, a review of the plans made and implemented today and yesterday leaves no doubt that the dominant assumption of past curriculum planning has been the goal of subject matter mastery through a subject curriculum, almost inextricably tied to a closed school and graded school ladder, to a marking system that rewards successful achievement of fixed content and penalizes unsuccessful achievement, to an instructional organization based on fixed classes in the subjects and a time table for them.[32]

Progress in the so-called "substantive dimension" of curriculum development continues today. Since the early 1960s curriculum specialists have employed systems thinking to incorporate most facets of school life in their planning. There have also been major developments in managerial techniques used to "engineer" program development in schools. Finally, the evaluation cycle of curriculum development has become a primary force in addressing change in school design. The process of curriculum development, from the inception of an idea or problem to the final assessment of the reconstruction effort, has become a highly skilled area of educational leadership.

In sharp contrast to these developments, the visionary or theoretical dimensions of curriculum development in schools have not progressed substantially since the 1960s. In the 1960s a growing body of social problems and issues, a more complete knowledge of human development, a geometric expansion of our knowledge base, and new approaches to learning all acted to stimulate thinking about a curriculum for the future. During the 1960s and the early 1970s, alternative education models flourished and visions of educational programming soared to new heights. These theoretical expansions of the field of curriculum were abruptly curtailed by changing conditions in our society including a depressed economy, general political conservatism, and an inability of educators to gain consensus for major value-laden changes. In the 1980s, the primary focus of curriculum development has returned to the mechanistic aspects of planning and developing isolated courses and programs of study.

Roles and Issues for Curriculum Specialists _____

Changes in the American society since 1970 have contributed significantly to the complexity of curricular concerns in schools. The public has generally become more sophisticated in understanding the value dimensions underlying decisions by educational planners and, with such understanding, has become more active in the decision-making process in schools. Important decisions affecting the lives of schoolchildren are being made in the 1980s and such decisions reflect the problems and issues of our society at large. These new pressures on educational decision-making affect the role of the curriculum developer and present those who plan school programs with the difficult task of defining the school's mission.

In its literature, the various areas of concern and influence in curriculum planning are known as "domains." At least five major domains currently affect curriculum planning and decision-making: philosophy and goal development, instructional systems, materials development, management of instruction, and teacher training. (These may be seen in Figure 1.1.)

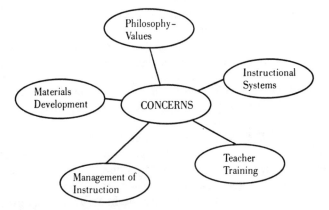

Figure 1.1 Curriculum Domains

In each of these domains, treated fully in other sections of this book, curriculum planners must make normative decisions which reflect values and choices. The type of role assumed by the curriculum specialist in approaching these decisions, and how the curriculum developer includes or excludes the public in such decision-making is a major issue in the field. The extreme positions on this question of role are reflected in the following statements:

> Curriculum planning lies at the heart of educational planning—dealing with the definition of educational ends and the engineering of means for achieving them.[33]
>
> Curriculum theory should be a subordinate of total educational theory.[34]

Arguments for which of the above role definitions is most suitable for curriculum workers are complex. The argument for an assisting technical role is that curriculum theory and practice have traditionally been far apart. So-called "blue sky" curriculum designs rarely achieve fruitful application in the real world of schools. If curriculum developers are to be useful, so the argument goes, they must meet the real needs of education. This can be done best by maintaining a "tractive" or static orientation, being specific in operations and serving where needed.

Arguments which hold that curriculum developers should provide leadership by being both dynamic and intellectual, and by achieving a global orientation to education, are multiple. Bruce Joyce provides the strongest argument against the traditional posture:

> In the past, educational planners have been technically weak (unable often to clarify ends or engineer means) and morally or technically unable to bring about a humanistic revolution in education . . . curriculum workers have defined themselves as helpers, not leaders, letting

the community and teachers make decisions and then assisting in the implementation of those decisions.

By focusing on schools and teachers in schools, curriculum is being forced to operate within the parameters of the institution . . . by far the most paralyzing effect of the assumptive world in which the curriculum specialist lives is that it tends to filter out all ideas which might improve education but which fit awkwardly into the school pattern.[35]

Because of the traditional orientation, say those calling for an active role for the curriculum specialist, the field of curriculum has continued to speak the language of sequence, prerequisites, academic achievement, and mastery. Learning theories that do not fit the existing school program, or are not seen as feasible in terms of current teacher practices, are neglected.

The perception of a curriculum specialist as a thinker, designer, leader, and projectionist goes back to the writings of Dewey, Counts, and other progressives of the early twentieth century. George Counts, for instance, observed that "the goals of education must be determined by philosophical and analytical concepts of the good life.[36]

Among those perceiving curriculum development as a dynamic operation there is a great fear that the gravitational pull of bureaucracy in education has won out. With each consolidation of schools, with each new piece of legislation, with each new regulation, the school becomes more closed to change, more self-perpetuating and product-oriented. This trend is in direct conflict with the desire of some curriculum theorists to see education as a process. Berman, for instance, calls for a process-oriented person who has opportunities in school to plan for the future; a planning that involves process skills and competencies. Such "communicating, loving, decision-making, knowing, organizing, creating, and valuing" persons will never evolve without strong curriculum leadership.[37]

Finally, it is worth noting that these differences in the perception of the role of the curriculum specialist reflect a differing time-image point of reference. Those seeing curriculum work as a support function are generally concerned with the here-and-now of the present. Those who seek a more dynamic role for curriculum development are more concerned with what schools can become. These role expectations illuminate the great philosophical range among curriculum developers.

The question of role definition in curriculum is made more difficult because of the condition in schools today. Environmental factors which are to some degree situational from district-to-district are:

The absence of clear goals
Unpredictable entry of power sources from outside
A consistent dependence on "money" as the moving force
Structural line and staff relationships in the district
The absence of "systems" thinking in problem-solving

An operational orientation to the present rather than future
Decentralized decision-making and policy implementation
The absence of evaluative feedback in policy renewal
An incomplete linkage to vital research
Inadequate training and understaffing of personnel
Administrative turnover
Lack of authority in program development
An overreliance on administrative arrangements for change
Responsibility for decisions without adequate guidelines
A lack of functional training in basic planning skills

In most school districts, curriculum directors appear in a staff role on organizational charts that describe administrative relationships. This means that curriculum specialists have basic responsibilities without clear authority. Often, curricular decisions will affect other dimensions of school organization such as legal, financial, and personnel. Curriculum workers must maintain lines of communication with all such offices and campaign for support of desired objectives. In many school districts, administrative policy and instructional activity are dictated by administrative concerns, rather than by curriculum goals.

Related to the act of "borrowing" authority from administrators is a continual reliance on administrative action to implement curriculum change. Designing school structures, procuring materials and staff, informing the public, and activating programs are all beyond the immediate control of the curriculum specialist.

The professional organization for curriculum development, The Association for Supervision and Curriculum Development (ASCD), describes the role of the curriculum director as an improver of instruction, but in a 1982 statement identifies primarily static tasks for the position: developing materials, writing curriculum content, conducting research, writing grant proposals, preparing courses of study.[38] It is obvious that, at that time, the ASCD statement endorsed a supporting role for those in curriculum positions.

From the list below, the reader will note that some roles performed by curriculum personnel are active and change-oriented while others reinforce existing conditions in the schools:

expert	adviser	retriever
linker	manager	advocate
counselor	trainer	data collector
diagnoser	modeler	referrer
instructor	observer	confrontor
demonstrator	evaluator	analyzer

The authors believe that the visionary aspects of curriculum development are essential to a rational process of improving school programs. We see curriculum development as a process of promoting desired change through purposeful activities, producing a condition where environmental variables are controlled and behavior is directional. When these things occur, quality programs can be designed, implemented, and evaluated by educational leaders.

Like the role of the curriculum specialist, the mission or end sought by those acting in a program development capacity is not always certain. The open nature of public schools, the diversity of value structures in the United States, the press of socioeconomic conditions, and the inability of educators to control change all contribute to a degree of murkiness in school planning.

To a degree greater than most educational planners like to admit, change occurs in school settings in spite of planning. Macdonald has summarized the difficulty in this manner:

> The development of the curriculum in the American public schools has been primarily an accident. A description of what curriculum exists is essentially a political and/or ethical document rather than a scientific or technical one. It is a statement which indicates the outcomes of a very complex interaction of groups, pressures, and events which are most often sociopolitical in motivation and which result in decisions about what ought to be.[39]

The uneven and sometimes unpredictable flow of change in school environments is the result of increased public attention to education, media coverage, political activism, legal assessments of educational activity, and the discovery of education as a business market. All of these forces, and others, have led to a decrease in the control over change experienced by school planners.

The absence of a systematic means of developing, reviewing, and selecting curricula on a national basis has contributed to the unclear mission of the curriculum worker. Despite strong convictions and development skills, the professional curriculum worker is only one of many forces vying for the control of change in the educational environment.

Some curriculum theorists look at the degree of change in education as a recurring phenomenon and propose a sort of "wave theory" for change based upon factors such as the national economy, political overtones, and other stressful events. One such position is held by Goodlad who believes that the control of the curriculum planning process leaves the curriculum specialist in stressful times:

> In periods of unusual political, economic, or social stress, curriculum change is likely to be more counter-cyclical in relation to the past, to occur rapidly, and to be led by persons not identified with earlier curriculum change, or, for that matter, with the schools.[40]

In the 1980s we have experienced intense social pressure from economic and political forces resulting in a conservative definition of schooling and a mechanistic orientation from curriculum developers. In some states, such as Florida and Connecticut, curriculum development has become a quasi-legal act which is mandated by state laws. In other states, a lack of mandate and the high cost of education have made education a complex political phenomenon. Regardless of the cause, in many of the nation's 14,000 school districts there is continuous turmoil and a residue of programs leftover from the 1960s. These conditions translate into curriculum concerns such as imbalance, lack of continuity, and a general fuzziness in the goals-outcomes relationship. There have been few times in the nation's history when schools were more in need of strong curriculum leadership to provide direction and minimize distortions in educational improvement.

In this text the authors will be speaking of a general curriculum development process, but it is important to note that at least five levels of focus are now regularly identified in the study of curriculum: the classroom, the school, the district, the state, and the national levels. The primary concerns of each level of focus are presented in Figure 1.2 to orient the reader's thinking about the process of curriculum development:

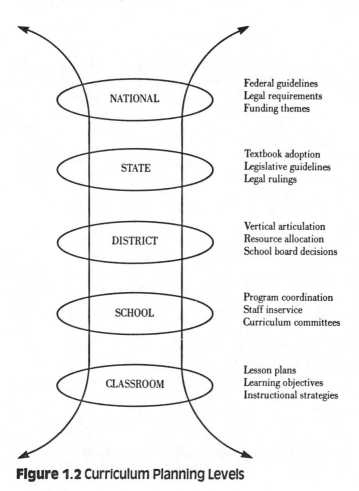

Figure 1.2 Curriculum Planning Levels

Curriculum development, clearly, tends to be more mechanistic at the classroom and school levels, while district, state, and national concerns are more often addressed to major value issues and themes for educating.

The Development Process

Regardless of the level of focus in the study of curriculum development, the process of improving school programs will be similar. The promotion of quality education programs requires organization. In all cases, goals (vision) must be clear. A design or plan must be understood and accepted. Conditions must be established for the implementation of a plan. Finally, achievements or anticipated accomplishments must be measured and recorded to mark progress. A basic cycle: analysis, design, implementation, and evaluation guides the program improvement process regardless of the level of focus or operation. Each step is described below:

Analysis

Often in curriculum development activities there is an absence of philosophic consensus which detracts from the spirit and efficiency of the development effort. Because the goals of public education are multiple and ever-changing, maintaining philosophic consensus is difficult. The process of clarifying values and setting goals, because of its regularity, can be perceived as both time-consuming and redundant. Yet, without such a basic operation, curriculum development remains largely unstructured and directionless. Without clear communication about the destination of development activities, relationships such as those alluded to in *Alice in Wonderland* are both possible and probable:

> *Alice:* "Will you tell me, please, which way I ought to go from here?"
> *Cat:* "That depends a good deal on where you want to get to."
> *Alice:* "I don't much care where . . ."
> *Cat:* "Then it doesn't matter which way you go."
> *Alice:* "So long as I get somewhere . . ."
> *Cat:* "Oh, you're sure to do that if only you walk long enough."[41]

In order to make clear and correct decisions in planning curriculum development, the situation must be analyzed and the ultimate goals identified. Organizing development must be rationalized in terms of objectives.

Design

Once the intentions of the curriculum improvement effort are clear, relevant data about desired changes must be organized and placed into the form of an action plan. Such a plan clearly identifies what is to be done, the order of changes to be made, a time estimate for changing, various responsibilities for parts of the plan, and the anticipated results of these efforts. Collectively, these parts of the plan serve to communicate to all persons involved what is to happen.

Implementation

The activation of the curriculum design often calls for some sort of management system which takes the basic plan for changing or improving the curriculum and "drives" it toward completion. Involved in this step are things such as the application of resources and training for those in need of skills. Most curriculum development efforts at this stage are a basic "time, distance, and rate" problem with the resources applied being the primary variable.

Evaluation

The evaluation of a curriculum development effort monitors the progress of the effort toward achievement of desired goals. Actually, this stage is usually a "validation" of progress rather than an "evaluation" or judgment of results, to make sure that changes are occurring as desired, that the improvements are directional, and that the results are as anticipated by the improvement design.

The curriculum development cycle is outlined in Table 1.1 to show application at the classroom level:

Summary ———————————————————————————

A curriculum is a plan for learning. All educational plans consist of a vision that interprets social values and a structure that translates those values into experiences for learners. Curriculum development is the process whereby values are interpreted and arranged into learning experiences.

Over time, the purpose of education in the United States has changed. Modern curriculum study in this country dates from the early 1890s, when major committees debated the form and structure of public schooling. Today, curriculum development is an essential component of professional education.

Definitions of curriculum have evolved as the purpose of American education has changed. These definitions vary according to the degree of structure desired in the learning experience.

Curriculum development, as a process, is today a basic cycle: analysis, design, implementation, and evaluation. This process is applicable at all levels of conceptualization and undergirds all efforts to improve school programs.

Table 1.1
An Outline for Curriculum Development — Classroom Level

Operation	Focus	Activity	Resource Base
Analyze	Clarify values Set goals	Identify purposes Set parameters Outline program Select content Order content	Environmental forces Information sources
Design	Establishing programs	Develop lessons Select materials Choose instruction strategy Establish management pattern	Knowing about the learning process
Implement	Training for interaction	Integrate learning Individualizing instruction	Knowledge of human development
	Application and manage- ment of resources	Delivery systems, grouping, space, time, focus of learning, climate, personnel roles	Change theory Knowledge of the act of learning
Evaluate	Assessment	Evaluative criteria Student and teacher assessment	All of the above

Notes

1. These earliest schools were known as Latin Grammar Schools established in 1647, only twenty-seven years after the landing of the Mayflower.
2. When Irish Catholics arrived in Massachusetts in large numbers, the Protestant government passed legislation to have tax-supported public schools for "socialization" purposes.
3. The Kalamazoo case established the precedent of public-supported secondary education in Michigan.
4. The enrollment of the American secondary school soared from about 200,000 pupils in 1890 to nearly four million pupils in 1925.
5. Franklin Bobbitt, *The Curriculum* (Boston: Houghton-Mifflin, 1918).
6. Robert M. Hutchins, *The Higher Learning in America* (New Haven, Connecticut: Yale University Press, 1936), p. 82.
7. Arthur Bestor, *The Restoration of Learning* (New York: Alfred A. Knopf, 1956) 48–49.
8. Phillip H. Phenix, "The Disciplines as Curriculum Content," in A. Harry Passow, ed., *Curriculum Crossroads* (New York: Teachers College Press, 1962), p. 64.

9. Hollis L. Caswell and Doak S. Campbell, *Curriculum Development* (New York: American Book Company, 1935), p. 66.

10. B. Othanel Smith, William O. Stanley, and J. Harlen Shores, *Fundamentals of Curriculum Development* (New York: Harcourt Brace Jovanovich, 1957), p. 3.

11. Ronald Doll, *Curriculum Improvement,* 2nd ed. (Boston: Allyn and Bacon, 1970).

12. Ralph W. Tyler, "The Curriculum Then and Now," in proceedings of the 1956 Conference on Testing Problems (Princeton, New Jersey: Educational Testing Service, 1957), p. 79.

13. Hilda Taba, *Curriculum Development: Theory and Practice* (New York: Harcourt Brace Jovanovich, 1962), p. 11.

14. J. Galen Saylor and William M. Alexander, *Curriculum Planning for Schools* (New York: Holt, Rinehart & Winston, 1974), p. 6.

15. Mauritz Johnson, "Appropriate Research Directions in Curriculum and Instruction," *Curriculum Theory Network* 6 (Winter 1970–71): 25.

16. Daniel Tanner and Laurel Tanner, *Curriculum Development: Theory into Practice* (New York: Macmillan, 1975), p. 45.

17. Tanner and Tanner, *Curriculum Development: Theory into Practice,* preface.

18. Elizabeth S. Maccia, "Curriculum Theory and Policy," a paper presented at American Educational Research Association, Chicago, 1965.

19. Hilda Taba, *Curriculum Development: Theory and Practice* (New York: Harcourt Brace Jovanovich, 1962), p. 9.

20. John Dewey, *The Child and the Curriculum* (Chicago: University of Chicago Press, 1902), p. 4.

21. Boyd H. Bode, "Education at the Crossroads," *Progressive Education* 8, pp. 543–544.

22. Hilda Taba, "General Techniques of Curriculum Planning," American Education in the Postwar Period, *44th Yearbook,* Part I, National Society for the Study of Education (Chicago: University of Chicago Press, 1945), p. 85.

23. Taba, *Curriculum Development: Theory and Practice,* p. 10.

24. Taba, *Curriculum Development: Theory and Practice,* p. 30.

25. Harold Rugg, "Curriculum-Making: Past and Present," *26th Yearbook,* Part I, National Society for the Study of Education (Chicago: University of Chicago Press, 1926), p. 22.

26. Ralph W. Tyler, *Basic Principles of Curriculum and Instruction* (Chicago: University of Chicago Press, 1949).

27. Robert F. Mager, *Goal Analysis* (Belmont, California: Fearon Publishers, 1972).

28. Kathryn V. Feyereisen, A. John Fiorino, and Alene T. Nowak, *Supervision and Curriculum Renewal: A Systems Approach* (New York: Appleton-Century-Crofts, 1970), p. 204.

29. A. Dean Hauenstein, *Curriculum Planning for Behavioral Development* (Worthington, Ohio: Charles A. Jones, 1975), p. 6.

30. Taba, *Curriculum Development: Theory and Practice,* p. 12.

31. Feyereisen, *Supervision and Curriculum Renewal,* p. 61.

32. William M. Alexander, "Curriculum Planning As It Should Be," an address to Association for Supervision and Curriculum Development Conference, Chicago, October 29, 1971.

33. Bruce Joyce, "The Curriculum Worker of the Future," *The Curriculum: Retrospect and Prospect,* 71st Yearbook, National Society for the Study of Education, Part I (Chicago: University of Chicago Press, 1971), p. 307.

34. George Beauchamp, *Curriculum Theory* (Wilmette, Illinois: Kagg Press, 1968).

35. Joyce, "The Curriculum Worker of the Future."

36. George Counts, "The Curriculum: Retrospect and Prospect," 71st Yearbook, Part I, National Society for the Study of Education (Chicago: University of Chicago Press, 1971), p. 10.

37. Louise Berman, *New Priorities in the Curriculum* (Columbus, Ohio: Charles E. Merrill, 1968).

38. Draft Statement, *1982 Yearbook* (Alexandria, Virginia: Association for Supervision and Curriculum Development).

39. James B. Macdonald, "Curriculum Development in Relation to Social and Intellectual Systems," *The Curriculum: Retrospect and Prospect,* 71st Yearbook, National Society for the Study of Education (Chicago: University of Chicago Press, 1971), p. 95.

40. John I. Goodlad, "The Changing American School," *66th Yearbook,* National Society for the Study of Education (Chicago: University of Chicago Press, 1966), p. 32.

41. Lewis Carroll, *Alice's Adventures in Wonderland* (London: Macmillan & Co., 1932).

Suggested Learning Activities _____

1. Develop a time line of major events which have influenced education and altered the definition of the term "curriculum."

2. Describe what is meant by the term "curriculum structure."

3. Identify some ways in which curriculum workers regularly analyze, design, implement, and evaluate school programs.

4. Now that you have completed this chapter, write your own personal definition of curriculum development. Which words suggest an active definition? A static definition?

Books to Review _____

Association for Supervision and Curriculum Development. *Considered Action for Curriculum Improvement.* Alexandria, Virginia: ASCD, 1980.

Bobbitt, Franklin. *The Curriculum.* Boston: Houghton Mifflin, 1918.

Caswell, Hollis, and Campbell, Doak. *Curriculum Development.* New York: American Book Company, 1935.

NSSE. *The Curriculum: Retrospect and Prospect.* Chicago: National Society for the Study of Education, 71st yearbook, University of Chicago Press, 1971.

Pratt, David. *Curriculum Design and Development.* New York: Harcourt Brace Jovanovich, 1980.

Taba, Hilda. *Curriculum Development: Theory and Practice.* New York: Harcourt Brace Jovanovich, 1962.

Torres, Gertrude. *Curriculum Processes: A Guide to Curriculum Development.* Englewood Cliffs, New Jersey: Prentice-Hall, 1982.

Chapter Two
Foundations of Curriculum Planning

Throughout this century educational planners have been faced with an ever-growing number of choices in constructing school programs. Such choices reflect our increased sophistication in understanding how people develop and learn. To be an effective educational planner, curriculum specialists must become familiar with, and put into an effective order, an extensive body of data about human development and the realms of learning.

Our increased knowledge about human ability and capacity for learning results from organized inquiry and from general experience. In historical perspective, it is difficult to ascertain whether our current beliefs about the learning process preceded, or resulted from, critical inquiry. What is clear, however, is that certain issues about what can be learned and how we learn have encouraged resolution through basic research and demonstrated practice. These issues have encouraged the collection and ordering of primary data in a number of well-defined areas, and these areas form the basic foundation for all curriculum planning.

Issues That Stimulate Inquiry _____

During the latter half of the nineteenth century and the first quarter of the twentieth American education was bombarded by new thoughts and findings relevant to the process of school planning. Basic sources of data came from educational thought and practices in Europe, from experimental programs, and from the early efforts of the field of psychology in this country. By 1925, this influx of ideas had fragmented American education into schools of thought that held very different premises about the purpose and procedures of education.

Major differences of opinion about planning educational programs revolve around these primary questions: Education for what? Education for whom? Education by what means? What is the role of the formal education programs and to what ends are they to be directed? Who is to be served by these programs, and should their focus be broad or narrow? How are these programs to be designed and what is the best way to promote effective learning? The scope of these and other such foundational questions is demonstrated by a list of unknowns compiled by Briggs over fifty years ago:

1. What are the desired ends of education?
2. What is the good life?
3. To what extent shall education modify the character and actions of future citizens?
4. For what ends are the schools responsible?
5. What subject areas are most vital in attaining these ends?
6. What should be the content of these subject arrangements?
7. How should the material be organized?
8. What is the responsibility of each level of schooling?

181500

9. What is the relative importance of each course of study?
10. How much time should be allotted for each subject?
11. How long should education be continued at public expense?
12. What is the optimum length of the school day? School year?
13. What is the optimum work load for each pupil?
14. What are the most probable future needs of the pupil?[1]

Questions such as those posed by Briggs encouraged debate, inquiry, and experimentation in school environments. These activities began to produce information that educational planners could use to defend school practices. This information also suggested considerable changes in the form of schooling, as observed by Tanner and Tanner:

> The need for a radically new conception of curriculum was the inevitable result of a number of forces—changes in our conception of knowledge, particularly scientific knowledge; changes in our knowledge of the learning process as a result of the child-study movement; and the need to link formal school studies with the life of the learner and the changing demands of the larger social scene.[2]

It can be observed that the field of curriculum as a specialized area of education has developed in an effort to study these questions and translate what is known about these concerns into viable school programs. Four major areas of study have become recognized: social forces affecting schools, treatments of knowledge, human growth and development, and learning as a process. These four areas comprise the basic foundations of curriculum planning.

Social Forces

There has been an unprecedented amount of change in the United States during the twentieth century. Revolutionary changes have occurred in the ways in which we live as the result of advancements in transportation, communication, and manufacturing. In a single lifetime an agrarian culture has been transformed into a highly mobile, complex, urban society.

The relationship of this nation's education system to these changes is a dynamic one. Public education in this country is an open system, susceptible to all currents of political, economic, and cultural change. Public education also possesses a unique historical role in our nation as the adaptive mechanism for change. If change is to occur in an orderly manner, the school is generally perceived to be the correct vehicle for such controlled change.

Adapting to changes in the social milieu, and assuming the responsibility for leading orderly change in the society, has placed great stress on the American school. Communication mediums and changing social values serve as prime examples of social forces that have had an impact on school planning.

At the beginning of the twentieth century, communication was fairly primitive by today's standards. There was a great dependence, of course, on the printed page. The telegraph existed, the telephone was in infant stages of development, and motion pictures were a promising medium. Mass communication, however, was both scarce and inefficient. Communication, such as the result of a presidential election, took considerable time to disseminate. Three mass communication devices appeared within a fifty-year period to alter this pattern: radio, television, and the computer.

Radio was the first communication medium to broaden the scope of the organized knowledge that had previously been in the domain of schools. Large amounts of information could be distributed quickly, and by mid-century could be broadcast to other countries.

> The effect of radio on expansion of nonrelated and non-applied knowledge is analogous to the distribution of seed by a grass spreader, creating in effect a 'carpet of knowledge' by cultivating a lawn so thick that single blades became indistinguishable. Regarding the interrelationships between segments of knowledge, the nuances and vagaries of the unusual become entwined with the simplicity and ordinariness of the mundane. Prospectives of knowledge are clouded and often obfuscated entirely by their lack of definition. Conjecture becomes fact.[3]

Television added another means by which we gained information and was even more influential in one respect. Beaming into 97 percent of all homes an average of six-and-one-half hours daily by 1970, this medium influenced the values and standards of American society. In *Crisis in the Classroom*, Silberman observed:

> Television has taken over the mythic role in our culture; soap operas, situation comedies, Westerns, melodramas, et al., are folk stories or myths that convey or reinforce the values of the society. . . . The trouble is that television does not enable its audience to see things the way they really are. On the contrary, while more current and realistic than schools, television nonetheless presents a partial and, in important ways, distorted view of contemporary society.[4]

By the late 1970s, concern for controlling the impact of television, particularly as a medium affecting the thoughts and perceptions of children, was intense. Congressional hearings, campaigns by parent-teacher organizations, and criticism by members of the television industry were common.* A line from a widely acclaimed movie, *Network*, summarized the impact of television as a communication medium:

*For an unusually thorough treatment of this problem see *The National Elementary Principal* 56, 3, Jan./Feb., 1977.

This tube can make or break presidents, popes, prime ministers. This
tube is the most awesome goddamned force in the whole godless world.
And woe is us if it ever falls into the hands of the wrong people![5]

A third communication innovation of the twentieth century that
has had a major effect on both society and schools is the *computer*.
Although the impact of the computer is perhaps more subtle than that of
either radio or television, due to its inaccessibility and mystique for the
average citizen, the implications of computer usage are more powerful.

Thirty years ago the comical product of the 'mad cap' scientists' noc-
turnal devisements, today computer science is as much a part of our
lives as our favorite breakfast cereal, and with every day that passes
encroaches ever so more fitfully into the domain of human life, human
decisions, and human behavior.

Partly akin to the television in its mechanical wizardry, whereas
the television indoctrinates, the computer coerces us into action through
its assumed infallibility in making decisions and plotting paths of action
necessary to our living in comfort. While the computer habituates the
pinnacle of man's intellectual genius, it is likewise the jailer who holds
the key to our intellectual freedom. With his piece-by-piece orientation
to information and knowledge application, man is, quite simply, presented
with an unchallengeable opponent in the computer. The variance in
speed in processing knowledge posits man in the impossible position of
receiving computation as *fait accompli* from the computerized savant. In
creating the computer, man has performed the heretofore-thought impossible task of devising a being superior to himself in intellectual capacity,
a being who can theoretically 'outthink' all men combined, a being who
in fact is a god.[6]

In terms of data processing and the generation of cross-referenced
knowledge systems, in terms of long-distance, high-speed transmission
of data, and most recently in terms of home-delivered programming
through personal computers, the computer age has presented a momen-
tous challenge to our society. We have become accustomed to, and in
some cases dependent upon, satellite-aided, direct-dial communication,
instantaneous news updating, and machine monitoring of our complex
and growing communication needs. These mediums are also having a
significant impact on the way that school planners think about the role
of formal schooling.

A century ago, schooling was almost exclusively a knowledge-
focused activity. Students and teachers interacted to "master" intellectual essentials such as Virgil's *Aeneid*, Xenophon's *Anabasis*, Orthography, and Latin prose. In the 1980s, computers have called into
question this historic role. Steve Wozniak, founder of Apple Computers,
states the case in this manner:

It's healthy to learn basic concepts such as arithmetic and logic, but there is just no point in having to solve the problems over and over again every day. It's a waste of time. . . . machines can do that stuff and leave us to think about more important things . . . personal computers are going to free people from the mundane things . . . they will allow people's minds to work at a higher level.[7]

Today, because of advances in our communication capabilities, radical advances in a very short period of time, some fundamental issues about schooling have been revived. If, for instance, knowledge is being generated, disseminated, and delivered at a pace beyond our capacity to absorb it, what is the point in organizing schools around the mastery of essential data? If there is too much to be known today, what essential data knowledge should all of our citizens possess? Or, if radio, television, and personal computers can serve as the disseminators of fundamental information about the society in which we live, at a cost a fraction of the schooling process, what should be the new role of the formal educating medium?

Another force that acts upon schools and the planning of school programs is the ever-changing value structure of our society. Primary concerns for educational planners are the assessment of social values, the identification of comprehensive values, and the development of educational programs in which values are relevant to the time.

The twentieth century has seen massive changes in both personal and social value structures in the United States. Such changes have resulted from the interaction of economic, social, political, and technological forces over a period of time. Contrasting two time periods twenty years apart, such as 1950 and 1970, indicates the scale of value alteration within a generation.

In 1950, the United States was in a process of renewal following World War II. There was a desire to return to simpler, more normal times, and the American people looked to social institutions for structure in their lives. The family, the church, the government, the law— all were respected without question. In 1950, people held strong beliefs in the work ethic, pursued materialism relentlessly, and saw formal education as the means to a better life. Religion, patriotism, tradition, privacy, and conformity were cherished. There was a high degree of predictability in everyday life.

By 1970, only twenty years later, the American society had undergone tremendous changes. Two wars, a space race, the racial integration of the society, a host of technological triumphs, and a major redefinition of the role of the individual in society had altered the face of America. Gone was the blind allegiance to social institutions, replaced by a basic cynicism about government, church, and other social agencies. Gone was the dedication to the work ethic and the foundational belief in formal schooling as the means to the "good life." Gone was the ready acceptance of tradition, patriotism, conformity, and roles. Gone, in many cases, was the predictability of everyday existence.

Replacing the primary values of 1950 was a set of beliefs which held individuality in esteem, defended the rights of persons and groups, accepted a broader pattern of behavior and moral codes, sought the preservation of natural resources, honored good health, and recognized mobility and temporary relationships as normal.

As we approach the mid–1980s, there appears to have been yet another change in the national mood. A period of fundamental conservatism in politics, economics, and religion has "locked" both government and education into a period of severe retrenchment. Those new patterns of behavior and the new values of the 1970s have seemingly submerged for the time being.

School planners from 1950–1980 have been deluged with data input and projections of probable change in our society. Schools, during this period, have been criticized for being obsolete, discriminatory, irrelevant, unresponsive, and nonproductive. What is clear, after thirty years of reactive curriculum development, is that ours is a plural culture and that to serve such a culture educators must adopt a multifaceted posture on the purpose of education and schooling. Among the major roles of the school in the 1980s are the preservation of cherished wisdom and tradition, meeting social needs via governmental mandates, and providing services to individual learners. As we study the many laws, school programs, and innovation adoptions since 1950, we can explain the absence of clarity in purpose in terms of educators' efforts to serve all of the plurality.

In serving the past, the present, and the future simultaneously, educational planners are confronted with major value decisions concerning the role of schooling. Is the school's primary function to be the preservation of society, to assist in meeting pressing social needs, or to design the future society? These three purposes for the school present curriculum designers with potential value screens through which they can sift input data.

Treatment of Knowledge

The kinds of societal changes outlined in the previous section had an important effect on curriculum planning. Organized information was more plentiful and accessible, but its proliferation also made it less manageable. Value-laden decisions that might govern the selection, organization, relevance, presentation, and evaluation of information were difficult, if not impossible, to make. Arno Bellack, writing in the midst of curriculum reforms of the early 1960s, outlined the planner's dilemma:

In current debates about what should be taught in schools, the 'conventional wisdom' long honored in pedagogical circles about the nature of knowledge and the role of knowledge in the curriculum is being called into question. The enemy of conventional wisdom, Professor Galbraith (the originator of that felicitous term) tells us, is the march of events. The fatal blow comes when conventional ideas fail to deal with new conditions and problems to which obsolescence has made them inapplicable. The march of events in the world at large that is placing new demands on the schools, and in the world of scholarship that is making new knowledge in great quantities, is forcing us to reexamine our ideas about the nature of knowledge and its place in the instructional program.[8]

The scope of information available to scholars, and to school children, was immense. Estimates of the rate at which organized knowledge doubled its volume ranged from every seven years in the mid–1960s to every two years by the mid–1970s. Traditional curriculum tasks such as reviewing and updating the subject content became unmanageable.

Related to the problems of scope and volume of organized knowledge was one of organization. Cases of knowledge overload were plentiful, conjuring visions of a nation choking on the proliferation of its own wisdom:

The American crisis, then, seems clearly to be related to an inability to act. It is not that we do not will action but that we are unable to act, unable to put existing knowledge to use. The machinery of our society no longer works or we no longer know how to make it work.[9]

Educational planners, in general, reacted to the glut of data that related to traditional school subjects by refocusing on the structure of information rather than on information itself. One of the best-known leaders of this reorganization movement was Jerome Bruner. Bruner rationalized the shift away from mastery of essential data to the study of representative data structures in this way:

Teachers ask me about the 'new curricula' as though they were some special magic potion. They are nothing of the sort. The new curricula are based on the fact that knowledge has an internal connectedness, a meaningfulness, and that for facts to be appreciated and understood and remembered, they must be fitted into that internal meaningful context.[10]

Another problem related to the organization of knowledge sources for the school curriculum was the advent of "new" fields of knowledge created from crossing standard disciplines of study. Knowledge in the sciences, such as biochemistry, and in the social sciences, such as demography, gave rise to new structures of organization. The incorporation and management of such new areas posed difficult problems for school planners due to the compactness of traditional knowledge organizations.

With the dramatic increase in the volume of knowledge, and the corresponding questions of how to meaningfully organize it, came even more pressing inquiries about the purpose of knowledge in organized learning. Although challenges to the knowledge-based curriculum weren't novel, the regularity with which educators questioned the traditional motif of educating in public schools during this period was surprising. Defining education in a new way, Earl Kelley wrote:

> The only man who is educated is the man who has learned how to learn; the man who has learned how to adapt and change; the man who has realized that no knowledge is secure, that only the process of seeking knowledge gives the basis for security.[11]

Futurist Alvin Toffler, in assessing the onrush of the knowledge explosion as it related to the role of schooling, observed:

> Instead of assuming that every subject taught today is taught for a reason, we should begin from the reverse premise: nothing should be included in the required curriculum unless it can be strongly justified in terms of the future. If this means scrapping a substantial part of the formal curriculum, so be it.[12]

By the mid–1980s, the delivery of knowledge direct-to-the-student was increasing. Among the most important mediums bypassing the traditional schooling format were the many capabilities of the personal computer. Using the Apple, Commodore, TRS-80, Texas Instruments, ATARI, IBM, and a host of competing brands, students in public schools could learn music, art, languages, reading, geography, math, science, social studies and many other subjects without direct teaching or tutoring. Students who possessed their own personal computer at home, of course, had a most unfair edge in access to learning.

The reaction of educational planners to the problem of organization of knowledge was to place emphasis on the identification of goals and objectives of educating, which would serve as guidelines for content selection. This orientation placed knowledge in a new and different role in educational planning:

> The education received in school is not meant to perpetuate an academic discipline, prepare students for college, or train bricklayers. All these things may be accomplished, but its chief mission is to produce graduates who are capable of becoming active, participating, contributing members of society. To achieve this goal the individual must learn to live with himself and others and must have a system of values to guide him. Therefore, if this is the ultimate purpose of education, we must start by defining the needs of the individual, the nature and needs of

society, and the system of values from which we can derive the objectives of the curriculum.

The means should not determine the ends. For example, if the
areas of knowledge are used to determine the objectives, they will in all
probability prejudice the objectives. In addition, the inclusion of a variable
such as knowledge areas would also predestine the content, curricular
organization, scope, and sequence variables. . . .[13]

Another consideration for educational planners that related to
treatments of knowledge was the way in which individual learners
reacted to information. In particular, research efforts studying the
effects of attitude, emotion, and feelings toward learning (affect), and
the process of information manipulation, storage, and retrieval (cognition), linked reception and retention of learning with readiness and
attitudes toward learning. The question of form of knowledge thus
became a concern.

Mario Fantini, widely recognized advocate of change in urban
educational environments, stated the relationship this way:

Although educators have hinted at the relationship between affect and
cognition, the functional linkage is seldom made. Too often, the school
severely limits the relationship between the two with its definition of
affect. It considers affect only in terms of play, interests, classroom
climate, readiness, teacher-pupil interaction, motivation, and the like, all of
which it can use to induce the child to accept prescribed academic content.

Yet it is obvious that knowing something cognitively does not
always result in behavior that follows on that knowing. This is because
knowledge alone cannot influence total behavior. Moreover, all kinds of
knowledge are not equally influential. The missing ingredient in this
equation seems to be knowledge that is related to the affective or emotional world of the learner.

What most often prompts action or behavior is a feeling or emotion about something rather than knowledge per se. It may be that
'knowing about' can prompt feeling, but it is feeling that generates
behavior. Unless knowledge relates to feeling, it is unlikely to affect
behavior appreciably.[14]

Closely related to the relationship of affect and knowledge were
two other concerns of educational planners, language usage and the
medium of delivery. When curriculum planners attempted to bring
knowledge to the schools, they had to deal with school populations that
represented many cultures. This situation meant that planners were confronted with both nonstandard English and a problem in communication.

Communication is a funny business. There isn't as much of it going on
as most people think. Many feel that it consists in saying things in the
presence of others. Not so. It consists not in saying things but in having
things heard. Beautiful English speeches delivered to monolingual Arabs

are not beautiful speeches. You have to speak the language of the audience—of the whom in the who-says-what-to-whom communications diagram. Sometimes the language is lexical (Chinese, Japanese, Portuguese), sometimes it is regional or personal (125th Street-ese, Holden Caufield-ese, anybodyese). It has little to do with words and much to do with understanding the audience. . . .[15]

In addition to language patterns and word usage, planners discovered the medium of delivery to have special effect on the interpretation and utilization of knowledge. McLuhan, in particular, opened the eyes of planners to the effects of electronic communication, describing information delivery systems in such terms as "hot," "cool," and "slick." In its extreme form, according to McLuhan, the medium can be both the "message" and the "massage."[16] *How* knowledge is delivered may be more important than *what* knowledge is delivered.

A final input that affected the planning of knowledge utilization in schools was the advent of serious forecasting of the future. As educators reviewed past utilization of knowledge and studied the present knowledge explosion, the wisdom of continuing with a content-dominated curriculum was questioned. After all, facts, by definition, were phenomena of the past and present rather than of the future. In some respects traditional knowledge placed blinders on our ability to escape the pull of the present and open our minds to the real possibilities of the future. The call for creative, nonlinear thinking presented an interesting challenge.

Related to a futuristic treatment of knowledge was the concept of programming. In viewing school curriculums it becomes clear that the knowledge taught to children *programs* their ability to meet the future. If education's image of the future is inaccurate, or if the knowledge given our students does not prepare them for the future, then the schools have betrayed those they teach.

In summary, the questions raised in assessing organized knowledge as a planning foundation are significant: What is to be taught? What should be the role of organized knowledge? What is the relative importance of knowledge bodies? What is the correct organization of information? What is the best form for bringing knowledge to students? All of these questions must be addressed by educational planners.

Human Growth and Development

A third foundational consideration important to educational planners has been the growing body of information related to human development. These data have been critical in such regular school activities as placement and retention, counseling, and planning curricular content and activities. Knowledge about human development has also provided the impetus for the development of a host of new programs in schools such as early childhood education, special education, compensatory education, and middle school education. Perhaps most important, our understandings about patterns of growth and development have caused educators to perceive formal educational planning from the perspective of the individual student.

Contributions to our understanding of human development have been gradual throughout this century. As information about human development has accumulated, various schools of thought have emerged in an effort to organize the data. These interpretations of our knowledge about human growth provide the basis for the difference in learning theories found among educators. Such differences can most clearly be understood in relation to several basic issues related to human development.

One issue revolves around the question of what constitutes normal development. Record keeping on the physical maturation of schoolchildren over extended periods has made available to educators fairly predictable ranges of growth for chronological age. It appears, in general, that children in the United States are achieving physical maturation at an ever-earlier age. Such findings are attributed to better health and nutritional care during childhood.

Our knowledge of intellectual, social, and emotional development during the school-age years is considerably less precise. However, organized inquiry has developed significant studies that guide our present decision making about development-related factors in these areas.

In the area of intelligence, considerable documentation exists regarding student performance on intelligence measuring devices such as the Stanford-Binet Scale. Little concrete evidence exists, however, to support hypotheses about intellect or intellectual capacity. What we currently operate with are models of how people are believed to develop and normal ranges of development in the capacity to think.

Without question, the dominant model in this area is one developed by Swiss educator Jean Piaget nearly sixty years ago. Piaget hypothesized four distinct but chronologically successive models of intelligence: (a) sensorimotor, (b) preoperational, (c) concretely operational, and (d) formal operational. Piaget's model of continual and progressive change in the structure of behavior and thought in children has assisted educators in preparing intellectual experiences in schools.

In the areas of social and emotional development there exists even less precise data about human development, although there has been considerable educational research into these areas over the past thirty years. Studies such as Project Talent,[17] Robert Havighurst's "Growing Up in River City,"[18] and James Coleman's study of equality of educational opportunity[19] have provided planners with documented long-term studies of the social development of certain populations. Such studies have been supplemented by lists of social concerns such as those developed by Stratemeyer.[20]

Data related to emotional development have been compiled by the National Institute of Health and other health-related agencies. At best, our vision of what constitutes normal emotional development is a rough estimate.

For educational planners, the question of normal development is largely unresolved, particularly in areas of expectation relating to such questions as capacity and creativity.[21] Our data base regarding human development grows daily.

Another issue relating to human development is whether such growth can be or should be controlled or accelerated. Primary research with infants and children by White and associates[22] suggests that development can indeed be accelerated through both experience and environment. The work of behaviorist B.F. Skinner,[23] on the other hand, is conclusive in its demonstration that behavior can be shaped. These two options leave the curriculum developer with significant value decisions about both the anticipated outcome of an education and the more mechanical aspects of planning learning experiences.

Two final issues are indicative of the many planning considerations which relate to foundational data in human development. First, there is the mind-boggling question of the type of person schools should create. All developmental theorists agree that human growth is, to some degree, malleable. Medical research and practice suggest that a bright future is in store for the manipulation of gene pools, the alteration of chromosomes to overcome heredity, and the transplantation of artificial organs. Diet and direct stimulation of mind and body seem capable of uncovering talents and developing more fully functioning individuals. Experience with thought control and extrasensory perception, as well as studies in deprivation would suggest that human growth can be purposefully expanded or stunted. Schools appear to be increasingly in the unique position of defining and controlling human development.

Perhaps even more interesting for planners is the question, "What is the role of affect in education?" Here the command of basic human emotions seems possible. The works of Kohlberg and Mayer suggest that our understanding of moral development in students has only begun.[24]

Issues such as the definition of normal growth, the means by which we promote growth and development, the type of growth we seek, and our growing understanding of affective development in human beings make the study of human development a necessary foundation for school planning.

Learning as a Process

New understandings of human development, new perspectives of the role of knowledge in learning, and new social values related to the schooling process have meant that a variety of learning approaches have become fashionable and acceptable in schools. Specifically, school planners must begin to incorporate the following planning data into their design of educational programs: 1) the biological basis of development can be altered, 2) physical maturation can be retarded or accelerated through diet and stimulation, 3) intellectual growth can be stimulated and directed, and 4) cultural influences on learning can be controlled or encouraged. These "new realities" suggest that schools can promote multiple types of learning in the classroom and therefore facilitate different types of development in students. The learning theory and the instructional approach selected by the curriculum planner are a function of the desired goals of student growth.

At the philosophical level, a topic to be treated more fully in the following chapter, educators differ considerably regarding the type of development schools should promote. Three major approaches to learning have evolved: a behavioral approach, an approach incorporating drive theories, and an environmental approach. While these basic approaches to learning have numerous identifiable subtheories, they are presented here, in this form, to indicate the range of learning theory which exists among school planners.

The *behavioral approach* is characterized by an external perspective of the learning process, viewing learning as a product of teacher behavior. Under this approach to learning, educational planners and teachers who deliver such plans study the student to ascertain existing patterns of behavior and then structure specific learning experiences to encourage desired patterns of behavior.

Armed with terms such as *conditioning* (repetitive response), *reinforcement* (strengthening behavior through supportive action), *extinction* (withdrawing reinforcement), and *transfer* (connecting behavior with response), the behavioral learning theorist seeks to shape the student to a predetermined form. Common school practices under this learning approach are fixed curriculums, didactic (question-answer) formats, and programmed progression through materials. Perhaps the most interesting and controversial use of this learning approach in schools today is in the practice of behavior modification.

Behavior modification is a simple cause-effect programming of observable behavior. The procedure uses a four-step technique: identifying the problem, recording baseline data, installing a system to alter behavior, and evaluating the new condition. As an external system of behavior control, behavior modification is not concerned with the attitudes or motivations of students under such a system, but rather with the results of the modification system. According to this learning approach, behavior that is rewarded will continue while behavior that goes unrewarded will extinguish.

A second learning theory is the *need-structured approach,* which is concerned with the needs and drives of students and seeks to use such natural motivational energy to promote learning. Teachers will often analyze and utilize the interests and needs of students as instructional vehicles when following this approach.

Key terms used with the needs/drives approach are *readiness, identification, imitation,* and *modeling.* Taking a cue from Freudian psychology, this theory orders the curriculum to coordinate with developmental readiness. Students learn through pursuit of unfulfilled needs, often modeling behaviors of others or developing predictable identification patterns.

Drive theories rely heavily on findings of human growth and development in planning curricular activities. This set of theories is dependent on student growth in planning school experiences.

The *environmental approach* to learning is concerned with the restructuring of the learning environment or the students' perceptions so that they may be free to develop. Unlike the static definition of growth presented by the behavioral approach or the dependent theories of need-structured approaches, the environmental approach is dynamic in nature. It acknowledges human diversity, believes in human potential, and promotes both uniqueness and creativity in individuals.

The basis of the environmental approach is the belief that behavior is a function of perception, and that human perceptions are the result of both experiences and understandings. When students have positive experiences that are self-enhancing, their perception and understanding of themselves and the world around them is altered. These new perceptions, in turn, allow for additional growth experiences. Student potential for development, under this learning approach, is limitless.

These three primary approaches to the structuring of learning in schools, approaches which might be labeled "push," "pull," and "restructure," are very different in their assumptions about people and possibilities for human development. They differ, for instance, in their beliefs about human potential. They differ in terms of their vantage point in describing learning (external vs. internal). They differ in their beliefs about the source of academic motivation.

To select any one of these approaches to learning would mean that basic classroom considerations such as the design of learning spaces, the choice of materials, and the roles of participants would have a distinct form. The learning theory of the planner is crucial to decision-making and projection. As such, learning as a process represents a strong fourth planning foundation.

The area of educational foundations is highly complex. It is an effort to bring order to a rapidly changing world that has an increasing number of relevant variables. Throughout the treatment of foundations of curriculum planning, there is an element of choice: which input to select, which data to validate, which decisions to make.

Ultimately, the choices and decisions related to the selection, activation, and evaluation of educational designs are normative matters. Before educational planners can be effective and consistent in their work they must understand their personal belief systems and formulate a philosophy of education that complements that system. The following chapter introduces some established philosophies of education and assists you in determining your priorities for schools.

Summary _____

Educational planners have been forced to assimilate and organize extensive data related to the development of school programs. Key issues about the purpose of schooling have led to the ordering of such data into four major areas: social forces, treatments of knowledge, human growth and development, and learning as a process. These four areas serve as primary organizers for the foundations of curriculum planning.

Our growing knowledge in these areas suggests that curriculum planning is increasingly normative in nature; there are value-laden decisions to be made about crucial issues that affect school programs. To be able to make such choices, curriculum planners must understand their own beliefs and form them into a consistent philosophy of education.

Notes _____

1. Thomas H. Briggs, *Curriculum Problems* (New York: Macmillan, 1926).
2. Daniel Tanner and Laurel N. Tanner, *Curriculum Development: Theory Into Practice* (New York: Macmillan Co., 1975), pp. 9–10.
3. Jon Wiles and John Reed, "Quest: Education for a Technocratic Existence" (Unpublished manuscript, 1975), p. 58.
4. Charles Silberman, *Crisis in the Classroom* (New York: Random House, 1970), pp. 33–34.
5. Paddy Chayefsky, *Network*, released by United Artists, 1977.
6. Wiles and Reed, *Quest*, pp. 61–62.
7. Mike Malone, "Getting Personal," *Apple Magazine* 2,1, 1981.
8. Arno A. Bellack, "Conceptions of Knowledge: Their Significance for Curriculum" in William Jenkins, ed., *The Nature of Knowledge: Implications for the Education of Teachers* (Milwaukee: University of Wisconsin—Milwaukee, 1962), p. 42.
9. Charles A. Reich, abstract from "The Greening of America," *New Yorker* (September 26, 1970), pp. 43–44.
10. Jerome S. Bruner, "Structures in Learning" *NEA Journal* 52 (March, 1963), p. 26.
11. Earl C. Kelley, *Education For What Is Real* (New York: Harper, 1947).
12. Alvin Toffler, *Future Shock* (New York: Random House, 1970).
13. Kathryn V. Feyereisen, A. John Fiorino, and Arlene T. Nowak, *Supervision and Curriculum Renewal: A Systems Approach* (New York: Appleton-Century-Croft, 1970), p. 138.

14. Mario Fantini, "Reducing the Behavior Gap," *National Education Association Journal* 57 (January, 1968), pp. 23-24.
15. John M. Culkin, "A Schoolman's Guide to Marshall McLuhan," *Saturday Review* 50, 11 (March 18, 1967), p. 71.
16. Marshall McLuhan and Quentin Fiore, *The Medium Is the Massage* (New York: Bantam Books, 1967).
17. John C. Flanagan, *The Identification, Development, and Utilization of Human Talents: The American High School Student*, Cooperative Research Project No. 635 (University of Pittsburgh, 1964).
18. Robert J. Havighurst, et al., *Growing Up In River City* (New York: J. Wiley and Sons, 1962).
19. Frederick Mosteller and Daniel P. Moynihan, eds., *On Equality of Educational Opportunity* (New York: Vintage Books, 1972).
20. Florence B. Stratemeyer et al., *Developing A Curriculum for Modern Living* (New York: Teachers College, Columbia University, 1947), p. 155.
21. Jon Wiles and Joseph Bondi, "The Care and Cultivation of Creativity," *Early Years* 12, 1 August/September 1981,: 34-37, 46, 108.
22. Burton L. White, *Experience and Environment: Major Influences on the Development of the Young* (Englewood Cliffs: Prentice-Hall, 1973).
23. B.F. Skinner, *Beyond Freedom and Dignity* (New York: Bantam/Vintage Books, 1972).
24. Lawrence Kohlberg and Rochelle Mayer, "Development as an Aim of Education," *Harvard Educational Review* 42 (November 1972): 452-453.

Suggested Learning Activities _____

1. Identify recent developments in our understanding of curriculum foundations that have implications for schools of the future.

2. Prepare a one-page reaction to data presented in this chapter for each of the bases of curriculum planning: social forces, utilization of knowledge, human growth and development, and learning as a process.

3. Analyze the impact the personal computer is having on your school district. What are some of the problems or concerns this "force" will present to the district by 1990?

4. What new changes in the four planning areas can we anticipate in the period 1985-2000 A.D.?

Books to Review _____

Bowles, Samuel and Gintis, Herbert, *Schooling in Capitalist America.* New York: Basic Books, Inc., 1976.
Eisner, Elliot. *The Educational Imagination: On the Design and Evaluation of School Programs.* New York: Macmillan, 1979.

Hunkins, Frances. *Curriculum Development: Program Improvement.* Columbus: Charles E. Merrill, 1980.

Lawn, Martin and Barton, Len, eds. *Rethinking Curriculum Studies: A Radical Approach.* London: Halstead Press, 1981.

Maker, Jane. *Curriculum Development for the Gifted.* Rockville, Md.: Aspen Systems Corp. 1982.

Postman, Neil. *Teaching As A Conserving Activity.* New York: Delecorte Press, 1979.

Wexler, Phillip. *Cultural and Economic Reproduction in Education.* London: Routledge and Kegan Paul Publishers, 1981.

Chapter Three
The Role of Philosophy in Curriculum Planning

At the heart of purposeful activity in curriculum development is an educational philosophy that helps leaders to answer value-laden questions and make decisions from among many choices. To John Dewey, this philosophy was a general theory of education. One of Dewey's students, Boyd Bode, saw the philosophy as "a source of reflective consideration." Ralph Tyler, an early leader in curriculum, likened the philosophy to "a screen for selecting educational objectives." Philosophies, then, serve curriculum leaders in many ways: to suggest purpose in education, to clarify objectives and activities in schools, to suggest learning theories, to define the roles of persons working in curriculum, and to guide the selection of strategies for curriculum change. Philosophy is essential as a prerequisite to serious curriculum improvement.

In arriving at an educational philosophy, curriculum specialists are forced to make value-laden choices. It is clear that there are many ways to operate schools, and curriculum decisions ultimately reflect differing beliefs and values about the nature and capacity of man. If curriculum specialists are aware of the range of beliefs about education, and if they have solidified their professional values, they will be better able to make consistent everyday decisions.

The need for a curriculum leader to have a strong philsophy of education has become increasingly obvious over the past thirty years because of the degree of change in schools. Public education has seen wave after wave of innovation, reform, new themes, and other signals of dissatisfaction with the status quo. Indicative of the calls for reformation of the schools is the following statement issued by the President's Advisory Committee on Science:

> When school was short, and merely a supplement to the main activities of growing up, the form mattered little. But school has expanded to fill time that other activities once occupied, without substituting for them. . . . Every society must somehow solve the problem of transforming children into adults, for its very survival depends on that solution. In every society there is established some kind of institutional setting within which the transformation is to occur, in directions predicated by societal goals and values. . . . In our view, the institutional framework for maturation in the United States is in need of serious examination. The school system, as it now exists, offers an incomplete context for the accomplishment of many important facets of maturation.[1]

Although it is certain that there is a desire for change in public education today, there is no strong mandate for the direction of such change in the United States. In the absence of centralized public planning and policy formation, local school boards rely on input from pressure groups, expert opinion, and various forces in the societal flow. Often, decisions about school programs are made in an isolated, piecemeal fashion, without serious consideration of the pattern of decision making. When goals are unclear, when there is no public concensus on value-laden decisions, or when curriculum specialists are unable to clearly articulate positions on controversial issues, then schools slip into the all-too-common pattern of reactive thinking and action.

The absence of direction often results in a curriculum that includes nearly everything but which accomplishes little. Given the public nature of American education, the dynamic nature of public school decision-making forums, and the dependence of school boards and superintendents on curriculum specialists for direction, the beliefs and values of the curriculum leader must be clear.

The Search for a Philosophical Attitude _____

Although there has been a steady interest in educational philosophies for nearly a century, the use of philosophical attitudes in planning school programs has been severely limited in the United States. With the exception of the "progressive" schools of the 1920s and 1930s, few educational programs have emerged that reflect strong philosophical understanding and commitment. As McClure has stated:

> With depressingly few exceptions, curriculum design until the 1950's was a process of layering society's new knowledge on top of the hodge-podge accumulation of society's old knowledge and arranging for feeding it, in prescribed time units, to students who may or may not have found it relevant to their own lives.[2]

The dependence of school leaders on public acquiescence for the development of school programs explains, in large part, the absence of philosophic consistency and the standardization of school programs over time. Without public demand for or approval of change, often interpreted in the public forum as no opposition, elected school leaders have failed to press for more distinct school programs.

Equally, the mandate of public education to serve all learners has acted to restrict the specification of educational ends and the development of tailored programs. The role of the schools as the assimilator of diverse cultures, from the turn of the century until the mid-1960s, contributed to the general nature of public school education.

Another factor in the absence of educational specificity in programs has been the lack of strong curriculum leadership at state and local levels. With the exception of university-based theorists, few curriculum specialists have had an understanding of philosophy, the clarity of vision, and the technical skills to direct school programs toward consistently meaningful activity. Although this condition is rapidly improving due to the greatly increased number of persons trained in curriculum development, the presence of a highly skilled curriculum leader often separates the successful school district from the mediocre school district.

The development of a clear and consistent set of beliefs about the purpose of education requires considerable thought, for there is a great amount of information to consider and strong arguments for the many philosophical positions which have developed. Perhaps the most important point to be made for the reader is to underscore Saylor and Alexander's observation that schooling is always a "moral enterprise":

> A society establishes and supports schools for certain purposes; it seeks to achieve certain ends or attain desired outcomes. Efforts of adults to direct the experiences of young people in a formal institution such as the school constitutes preferences for certain human ends and values.
>
> Schooling is a moral venture, one that necessitates choosing values among innumerable possibilities. These choices constitute the starting point in curriculum planning.[3]

To illustrate the diversity of beliefs about the purpose of formal education and approaches to educating, consider the two following statements by Robert Hutchins and A. S. Neill. These statements are representative of two established educational philosophies, *perennialism* and *existentialism*. First Hutchins:

> The ideal education is not an ad hoc education, not an education directed to immediate needs; it is not a specialized education, or a preprofessional education; it is not a utilitarian education. It is an education calculated to develop the mind.
>
> I have old-fashioned prejudices in favor of the three R's and the liberal arts, in favor of trying to understand the greatest works that the human race has produced. I believe that these are permanent necessities, the intellectual tools that are needed to understand the ideas and ideals of our world.[4]

Now Neill:

> Well, we set out to make a school in which we should allow children to be themselves. In order to do this, we had to renounce all discipline, all direction, all suggestion, all moral training. . . . All it required was what we had—a complete belief in the child as a good, not evil being. For almost forty years, this belief in the goodness of the child has never wavered; it rather has become a final faith. My view is that a child is innately wise and realistic. If left to himself without adult suggestions of any kind, he will develop as far as he is capable of developing.[5]

Such differences of opinion about the purpose and means of educating are extreme, but they illustrate the range of choices to be made by curriculum planners. These statements also indicate the trends of education which various philosophies favor. The perennialists who favor a highly controlled curriculum, strict discipline, and uniform treatment for students can easily identify with trends such as "back to the basics, and accountability." The existentialists who see a nonschool environment for personal growth, an environment with highly individualized activities and low degrees of formal structure, can identify with "alternative programs," "student rights" movements, and other nonstandard choices.

Critical Questions to Be Answered ⸺⸺⸺⸺⸺

Each curriculum planner must face and answer some difficult questions about the purpose and organization of schooling. The answers to such questions are critical to school planning, and establish the criteria for future decision-making and action. As Saylor and Alexander state the condition, it is one of defining responsibility:

> In selecting the basic goals which the school should seek to serve from among the sum total of ends for which people strive the curriculum planner faces the major issue: In the total process of human development what parts or aspects should the school accept responsibility for guiding?[6]

Tanner and Tanner observe that three major ends for schooling have been suggested repeatedly in the past:

> Throughout the twentieth century educational opinion and practice have been sharply divided as to whether the dominant source and influence for curriculum development should be the body of organized scholarship (the specialties and divisions of academic knowledge), the learner (the immature developing being), or society (contemporary adult life). . . .[7]

The decision of the curriculum leader to either relate to the knowledge bases of the past and present or to focus on the present and future needs of the learner and society is critical. Among other things, this decision will determine whether the role of the curriculum specialist is to restructure or only to refine the existing system of education.

Most often, curriculum development in schools is a mechanical, static function because the content base is accepted as the main criterion for curriculum work:

In the absence of reflective consideration of what constitutes the good man leading to the good life in the good society, the curriculum tends to be regarded as a mechanical means of developing the necessary skills of young people in conformance with the pervading demands of the larger social scene. Under such circumstances, the school does not need to bring into question the existing social situation, nor does it need to enable pupils to examine through reflective thinking possible alternative solutions to social problems. Instead, the school is merely expected to do the bidding of whatever powers and forces are most dominant in the larger society at any given time.[8]

If, however, the curriculum planner accepts the needs of learners as a criterion for planning school programs, such as in the early child-hood and middle school programs of the 1970s, the purpose of the formal education program is altered. The same is true if social reform or improving the society is chosen as the purpose of schools. In accept-ing an alteration of the traditional criterion for developing school pro-grams, curriculum developers "cross-over" into an advocacy role for change as they attempt to restructure the existing curriculum. The effectiveness of such a position in curriculum work is often determined by the clarity of the new objectives being worked for.

A number of primary questions override the value choices of all major educational philosophies: What is education for? What kind of citizens and what kind of a society do we want? What methods of instruction or classroom organization must we provide to produce these desired ends?

McNeil poses eight questions that are useful in developing the philosophical assumptions needed to screen educational objectives:

1. Is the purpose of school to change, adapt to, or accept the social order?
2. What can a school do better than any other agency or institution?
3. What objectives should be common to all?
4. Should objectives stress cooperation or competition?
5. Should objectives deal with controversial issues, or only those things for which there is established knowledge?
6. Should attitudes be taught? Fundamental skills? Problem-solving strategies?
7. Should teachers emphasize subject matter or try to create behavior outside of school?
8. Should objectives be based on the needs of the local com-munity? Society in general? Expressed needs of students?[9]

The reader is encouraged to take a position on these questions by selecting one or more of the following options and providing a rationale for such choice:

I Believe that Schools _____

1. a.   should accept the existing social order
   b.   should adapt to the social order as it changes
   c.   should seek to change or improve the social order because

   _____

   _____

2. can do the following things better than any other existing institution or agency _____

   _____

3. should promote the following common objectives for all students _____

   _____

   _____

4. should have program objectives that stress
   a.   competition
   b.   cooperation
   because _____

   _____

5. should have objectives that
   a.   deal with controversial issues
   b.   deal only with things supported by established knowledge
   because _____

   _____

6. should teach
   a.   attitudes
   b.   fundamental skills
   c.   problem-solving strategies
   because _____

   _____

7. should emphasize the following through teaching:
   a.   subject matter
   b.   behavior found beyond the classroom and school
   because _____

   _____

8. should have objectives based on
   a.   needs of the local community
   b.   the society at large
   c.   the expressed needs of students
   because _____

   _____

The Struggle to Be a Decisive Leader _____

While few educators would deny the importance of a philosophy in directing activity, few school districts or teachers relish discussions on the topic. Even well-known educators have confessed a dislike for such discourse:

> It is well to rid oneself of this business of "aims of education." Discussions on this subject are among the dullest and most fruitless of human pursuits.[10]
>
> A sense of distasteful weariness overtakes me whenever I hear someone discussing educational goals and philosophy.[11]

Part of the problem with discussing educational philosophies in earnest, in the past, has been the pervasiveness of the subject-dominated curriculum in American schools. This problem has been further compounded by "expert opinion" on the topic by college professors who, being products of the system, possess monumental conflict-of-interest in rendering such opinion. In school districts where inquiry into the purpose of educating has been quickly followed by retrenchment of the subject-matter curriculum, there has been little payoff in conducting philosophical discussions. But, where inquiry into educational purpose is honest, open, and leads to meaningful change, philosophical discussions are among the most exciting endeavors.

Charles Silberman, in his book *Crisis in the Classroom,* expresses the meaning of philosophical understandings for the learning programs of the school.

> What educators must realize, moreover, is that how they teach and how they act may be more important than what they teach. The way we do things, that is to say, shapes values more directly and more effectively than the way we talk about them. Certainly administrative procedures like automatic promotion, homogeneous grouping, racial segregation, or selective admission to higher education affect "citizenship education" more profoundly than does the social studies curriculum. And children are taught a host of lessons about values, ethics, morality, character, and conduct every day of the week, less by the conduct of the curriculum than by the way schools are organized, the ways teachers and parents behave, the way they talk to children and each other, the kinds of behavior they approve or reward and the kinds they disapprove and punish. These lessons are far more powerful than verbalizations that accompany them and that they frequently controvert.[12]

Two major benefits can be derived from an exploration of philosophical attitudes. First, major problem areas and inconsistencies in the school program can be identified:

Many contemporary educational principles and practices are something of a hodgepodge rooted in premises about the nature of man and his relationship with his physical-social environment that frequently are incompatible with one another.[13]

Second, areas of common ground among those responsible for educational leadership can be discovered. Common values which overlap individual beliefs form the most fertile ground for curricular collaboration and the development of successful projects and programs.

Before curriculum specialists can work with parents, teachers, administrators, and other educators to explore educational values, they must complete an examination of their own attitudes. During this process, the curriculum worker is seeking to identify a value structure which can organize and relate the many aspects of planning.

To clarify the values and beliefs that will tie together curriculum organization, instructional procedures, learning roles, materials selection, and other components of school planning, curriculum leaders must identify themes that seem true to them. While this process may be time-consuming, the investment is necessary. Curriculum leaders, in order to be both decisive and effective in their roles, must combat the urge to ignore the value implications of the job or reduce all aruguments to "thoughtful uncertainty."

Determinants of an Educational Philosophy _____

Major philosophies of life and education have traditionally been defined by three criteria: What is good? What is true? What is real? Individual perceptions of goodness, truth, and reality differ considerably, and an analysis of these questions reveals unique patterns of response. When such responses are categorized and labeled, they become formal philosophies.

In the language of philosophy, goodness is referred to as *axiology,* truth as *epistemology,* and reality as *ontology.* Axiological questions deal primarily with values, and in a school context philosophical arguments are concerned with the ultimate source of values to be taught. Questions of an epistemological nature in a school context are directed toward the mediums of learning or the best means of seeking truth. Ontological questions, in search of reality, are most often concerned with the substance of learning or content of study. Thus, the standard philosophic inquiries concerning goodness, truth, and reality are translated into questions concerning the source, medium, and form of learning in a school environment.

These queries are not simple, for there are many ways to select ideas, translate them into instructional patterns, and package them into curriculum programs. Those possibilities are forever increasing as our knowledge of the world becomes more sophisticated. Essential questions arise, questions that must be answered prior to planning learning experiences for students. Why do schools exist? What should be taught? What is the role of the teacher and the student? How does the school deal with change?

Five Educational Philosophies

There are many kinds of educational philosophies, but for the sake of simplicity it is possible to extract five distinct ones. These five philosophies are perennialism, idealism, realism, experimentalism, and existentialism. Collectively, these philosophies represent a broad spectrum of thought about what schools should be and do. Educators holding these philosophies would create very different schools for students to attend and learn in. In the following section, each of these standard philosophies is discussed in terms of their postures on axiological, epistemological, and ontological questions.

Perennialism

The most conservative, traditional, or inflexible of the five philosophies is perennialism, a philosophy drawing heavily from classical definitions of education. Perennialists believe that education, like human nature, is a constant. Since the distinguishing characteristic of humans is the ability to reason, education should focus on developing rationality. Education, for the perennialist, is a preparation for life, and students should be taught the world's permanencies through structured study.

For the perennialist, reality is a world of reason. Such truths are revealed to us through study and sometimes through divine acts. Goodness is to be found in rationality itself. Perennialists would favor a curriculum of subjects and doctrine, taught through highly disciplined drill and behavior control. Schools for the perennialist exist primarily to reveal reason by teaching eternal truths. The teacher interprets and tells. The student is a passive recipient. Since truth is eternal, all change in the immediate school environment is largely superficial.

Idealism

Idealism is a philosophy that espouses the wisdom of men and women that has been refined. Reality is seen as a world within a person's mind. Truth is to be found in the consistency of ideas. Goodness is an ideal state, something to be strived for.

Idealism would favor schools teaching subjects of the mind, such as is found in most public school classrooms. Teachers, for the idealist, would be models of ideal behavior.

Idealists would see the function of schools as being to sharpen intellectual processes, to present the wisdom of the ages, and to present models of behavior which are exemplary. Students in such schools would have a somewhat passive role, receiving and memorizing the reporting of the teacher. Change in the school program would generally be considered an intrusion on the orderly process of educating.

Realism

For the realist, the world is as it is, and the job of schools would be to teach students about the world. Goodness, for the realist, would be found in the laws of nature and the order of the physical world. Truth would be the simple correspondences of observation.

The realist would favor a school dominated by subjects of the here-and-now world, such as math and science. Students would be taught factual information for mastery. The teacher would impart knowledge of this reality to students or display such reality for observation and study. Classrooms would be highly ordered and disciplined, like nature, and the students would be passive participants in the study of things. Changes in school would be perceived as a natural evolution toward a perfection of order.

Experimentalism

For the experimentalist, the world is an ever-changing place. Reality is what is actually experienced. Truth is what presently functions. Goodness is what is accepted by public test. Unlike the perennialist, idealist, and realist, the experimentalist openly accepts change and continually seeks to discover new ways to expand and improve society.

The experimentalist would favor a school with heavy emphasis on social subjects and experiences. Learning would occur through a problem-solving or inquiry format. Teachers would aid learners or consult with learners who would be actively involved in discovering and experiencing the world in which they live. Such an education program would focus on value development, but in terms of group consequences.

Existentialism

The existentialist sees the world as one personal subjectivity, where goodness, truth, and reality are individually defined. Reality is a world of existing, truth subjectively chosen, and goodness a matter of freedom.

For existentialists, schools, if they existed at all, would be places that assisted students in knowing themselves and learning of their place in society. If subject matter existed, it would be matter of interpretation such as the arts, ethics, or philosophy. Teacher-student interaction would center around assisting students in their personal learning journeys. Change in school environments would be embraced as both a natural and necessary phenomenon.

The five standard philosophies are compared in Table 3.1 in terms of attitudes on significant questions.

Philosophies as Found in Schools

During this century, schools in America have evolved from highly standardized content-focused institutions to less structured and diverse forms of education. Our understandings of human development and the learning process, and the pressures on our rapidly changing society, account for these alterations of the schooling form.

All schools are designed to promote an education but, as philosophies differ, so do the design of school curriculums. Schools represent a blueprint or plan to promote learning but, because the ends sought by planners differ, all schools are not alike. This section introduces the reader to fifteen dimensions of school design; dimensions by which schools can be compared and contrasted. Each dimension has been prepared to illuminate the various philosophic continuums within schools. While these continuums do not match our five philosophies precisely, the reader can begin to see a rough parallel between these philosophies and the various dimensions of the school setting.

The intentions of schooling might be thought of as a continuum of choices. On one end of such a continuum is the belief that education is the process of shaping raw human talent into something definitive and useful to society. This classic view of education sees schools shaping and refining human thought and behavior through an increasingly controlled program of study. Such control, in the legitimate sense of the word, is accomplished by structuring the learning environment to facilitate highly predictable ends.

On the other end of that same choice continuum is the belief that human talents are best managed by allowing the natural capacities of individuals to develop through the removal of growth barriers. This definition of education would have schools acting to release the student from behaviors and perceptions which limit personal development. Thus, the institution of the school would formally seek the expansion of human potential in the process of learning.

Strong arguments can be made for either of these positions, as well as for the many intermediate stances on such a continuum. The crucial concept to be understood is that schools are institutions created by society to accomplish certain ends. Since there are many possible goals for the institution of the school, there are many legitimate forms of schooling. To the degree that the organization of the school corresponds with the objectives of the school, the school can effectively educate students.

The range of possible intentions for a school program, bordered on one end by a school seeking maximum control and on the other by a school promoting maximum freedom, can be translated into the universal variables of structure versus flexibility. These two variables, structure and flexibility, are used to facilitate the analysis of fifteen major dimensions of schooling. These fifteen dimensions are all ones that can be readily observed by a visitor to a school:

Table 3.1
Five Major Educational Philosophies

	Perennialism	Idealism	Realism	Experimentalism	Existentialism
Reality Ontology	A world of reason and God	A world of the mind	A world of things	A world of experience	A world of existing
Truth (Knowledge) Epistemology	Reason and revelation	Consistency of ideas	Correspondence and sensation (as we see it)	What works What is	Personal, subjective choice
Goodness Axiology	Rationality	Imitation of ideal self, person to be emulated	Laws of nature	The public test	Freedom
Teaching Reality	Disciplinary subjects and doctrine	Subject of the mind—literary, philosophical, religious	Subjects of physical world—math, science	Subject matter of social experiences— social studies	Subject matter of choice—art, ethics, philosophy
Teaching Truth	Discipline of the mind via drill	Teaching ideas via lecture, discussion	Teaching for mastery, of information— demonstrate, recite	Problem-solving, project method	Arousing personal responses— questioning
Teaching Goodness (Values)	Disciplining behavior (to reason)	Imitating heroes and other exemplars	Training in rules of conduct	Making group decisions in light of consequences	Awakening self to responsibility

Why Schools Exist	To reveal reason and God's will	To sharpen the mind and intellectual processes	To reveal the order of the world and universe	To discover and expand the society we live in to share experiences	To aid children in knowing themselves and their place in society
What Should Be Taught	Eternal truths	Wisdom of the ages	Laws of physical reality	Group inquiry into social problems and social sciences, method and subject together	Unregimented topic areas
Role of the Teacher	Interprets, tells	Reports, person to be emulated	Displays, imparts knowledge	Aids, consultant	Questions, assists student in personal journey
Role of the Student	Passive reception	Receives, memorizes	Manipulates, passive participation	Active participation, contributes	Determines own rule
School's Attitude Toward Change	Truth is eternal, no real change	Truth to be preserved, anti-change	Always coming toward perfection, orderly change	Change is ever-present, a process	Change is necessary at all times

1. Community involvement
2. School buildings and grounds
3. Classroom spaces
4. Organization of knowledge
5. Uses of learning materials
6. Philosophy of education
7. Teaching strategies
8. Staffing patterns
9. Organization of students
10. Rules and regulations
11. Discipline measures
12. Student progress reporting
13. Administrative postures
14. Teacher roles
15. Student roles

Examining the school by such criteria, in a systematic manner, will help the reader see a school in its totality. The underlying beliefs about educating will become more obvious and the program congruence or inconsistencies will be more visible. In short, the reader will be able to analyze the dimensions of a school setting in a selective and regular way and to understand the philosophic intent of the curriculum.

The Learning Environment

It is clear that environments, both real and perceived, set a tone for learning. What people feel about the spaces they occupy or interact with causes them to behave in certain ways. Churches, for instance, call for discrete behavior while stadiums elicit a different behavior.

Traditionally, schools have been solitary, sedate, and ordered environments. This atmosphere was the result of many forces: a narrow definition of formal education, a limited public access to knowledge, a didactic (telling-listening) format for learning.

In contrast, many innovative schools seem to be the organizational opposite of the traditional, structured school. They are often open, noisy, and sometimes seemingly chaotic activity centers. These changes in schools are the result of both a changing definition of education and a new understanding of the environmental conditions that enhance learning.

Three measures of the learning environments of schools are the relationship of the school and the surrounding community, the construction and utilization of buildings and grounds, and the organization of learning spaces within buildings. Within each of these three areas, selected dimensions have been identified which may assist in understanding the learning environment of the school.

Community Involvement

Individual schools differ according to the degree and type of interaction they enjoy with the immediate community. Schools that perceive their role as shaping the behavior and thoughts of students into acceptable patterns normally seek to limit community access and involvement in the school program. By limiting community access, the school also limits community influence on the school program and thus insures more predictable outcomes for students.

Conversely, schools intent on expanding student responses to the educational process generally encourage community access and involvement in school activities. By encouraging community access the school encourages community influence, thus insuring the divergent input characteristic of most communities.

Measures of community access and involvement with a school are plentiful. A simple measure readily available to the observer is to note how many and what kinds of nonschool personnel are in a school building on a given day. Perhaps a more analytic approach to the assessment of involvement, however, is to observe the school operation in terms of physical, legal, participatory, and intellectual access.

In a physical sense, community involvement can be measured by the amount of quasi-school related activity occurring in the school building. Activities such as school-sponsored visits to the building, community-sponsored functions in the building, parental participation in school-sponsored activities, and school programs being conducted in the community are indicative of interchange and involvement.

On the other hand, schools where the public is never invited to visit, where classes never leave the building, where the public is fenced out or locked out, held at the office when visiting, not welcome after school hours, or discouraged from mobility within the spaces of the school indicate limited access and involvement.

Legally, the community is allowed to become involved with the school at varying levels. In a tightly structured or closed school, legal access is normally restricted to setting limits and voting on school bonds. Increasing participation is measured by electing school officials and the chief administrative officer of the school district. Further access is indicated by school-building-level committees (such as a textbook selection committee) which allow community members to play an active role in policy formation. The ultimate access, not surprisingly called "community schools" in educational literature, has parents and the community-at-large serving in governance roles over school operation and activity.

In terms of participation in the daily operation of the school program, the community can be ignored, informed, included at an advisory level, or asked to participate wholly. Whether a school chooses to include the community in the type of school program that is being experienced by the students depends on whether such participation is seen as contributing to or detracting from the mission of the school.

Finally, there is an intellectual dimension to community involvement with the school that is indicated by access to goal setting, resource allocation, and program development. To the degree that the community is excluded from thinking about the substance of what is taught and the method of instruction, the school is characterized by limited intellectual access or high structure. If the school encourages programmatic and instructional participation from parents and members of the community, then access or high flexibility is evidenced.

There are great differences in the degree of access and community involvement with individual school buildings. As such, community involvement represents one salient dimension of the learning environment. The following descriptive continuums suggest the potential range of alternatives present in schools:

1.1 Access-Physical

No contact	Community functions in the school buildings	Scheduled community visits to the school	Regular community participation in school building activities	School learning activities in the community

S - -+- - - - - - - -+- - - - - - -+- - - - - - - - -+- - - - - - - - -+- - - F

1.2 Access-Legal

Voting for bonds	Electing school officials	Serving on official committees	Policy boards at school building level	Operational control over school programs

S -+- - - - - - -+- - - - - - - -+- - - - - - - - -+- - - - - - - - -+- - - F

1.3 Access-Participatory

Ignored	Informed	Advisory	Planning	Participatory

S -+- - - - - - - -+- - - - - - - -+- - - - - - - -+- - - - - - - -+- - F

1.4 Access-Intellectual

Never consulted about program content	Advisory in goal-setting	Set goals and parameters of school programs	Involved in planning implementation	Actively involved in implementing at classroom level

S - - -+- - - - - - -+- - - - - - -+- - - - - - -+- - - - - - -+- - - F

1.5 Access-General

Media access (the news)	Legal access (voting bonds)	Physical access (visitations)	Participatory access (school programs)	Intellectual access (goal-setting)

S - - + - - - - - - - - + - - - - - - - - + - - - - - - - - + - - - - - - - - + - - F

School Buildings and Grounds

The physical nature of school buildings and school grounds may be subtle indicators of the school's perceived mission and therefore useful measures for a visitor or interested observer. Features such as access points, building warmth, traffic control inside the building, and space priorities may reflect the intended program of the school.

Architects have observed that buildings are a physical expression of content. A dull, drab, unexciting building may reflect a dull, drab, unexciting educational process. An exciting, stimulating, dynamic building may reflect an active, creative learning center. A building not only expresses its interior activity, but may also reflect, and even control, the success of these functions. If school corridors, for example, are colorful, well lighted, and visually expansive, then this excitement and stimulation directs the individual in such a space. It is for this reason that most new airports have extremely wide and brightly colored corridors. The environment "sets up" the participant dispositionally.

School buildings have changed a great deal during this century, and those changes in architecture and construction reflect more subtle changes in the programs of schools. A stereotypic evolution of school buildings in the United States would show a progression from a cellular lecture hall (many one-room school houses together) to an open and largely unstructured space as illustrated in Figure 3.1.

While many of these changes might be explained by evolutions in architecture and cost effectiveness demands, it can be observed that a primary force behind the diminishing structure in school buildings has been the dissemination of knowledge through other mediums. As the "essential" curriculum of the turn of the century gave way to a more broadly-focused academic preparation, buildings were designed to incorporate diversity. Because spaces had multiple uses, the construction was necessarily flexible in design.

Just because a school building is traditional or open-space in design, however, tells the visitor little about the current philosophy of the school. Many flexible programs are found in old "egg crate" buildings and, equally, highly structured programs are sometimes found in modern open-space schools. Returning to our analytic tools, the degree of access, the warmth of the building, traffic control patterns inside the building, and space priorities, we can approach knowing the real program in the building.

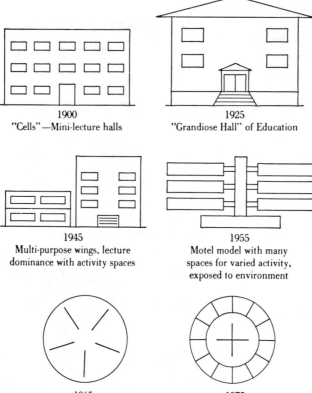

1900
"Cells"—Mini-lecture halls

1925
"Grandiose Hall" of Education

1945
Multi-purpose wings, lecture
dominance with activity spaces

1955
Motel model with many
spaces for varied activity,
exposed to environment

1965
Open spaces, multi-purpose rooms,
maximum flexibility

1975
Structured internal space,
closed to outside

Figure 3.1

Degree of Access

Many schools, because of genuine danger in the immediate neighborhood, limit the number of access points to the school building.
Other schools deliberately limit public access as a means of controlling
the environment and personnel in the building. Signs of extreme control in school buildings are a single entrance for all entering the building, constantly locked spaces such as bathrooms and auxiliary spaces,
and purposeful physical barriers to movement such as long unbroken
counters in school offices.

Cues such as these tell visitors, students, and even teachers in the
building that there are acceptable and unacceptable ways to enter the
building and move in the building. Highly controlled access and mobility
in school buildings indicate a belief that only certain types of movement in a building are conducive to successful education.

Building Warmth

Related to physical access is the concept of building warmth. The size of spaces, shape of space, scale of the environment (relationship between size of the people and objects in the environment), coloration, and use of lighting all affect the warmth of a school building. Generally speaking, a combination of extreme space (large or small), extreme light (bright or dim), extreme coloration (too drab or too bright), repelling shapes, (not geometrical or too geometrical), or disproportionate scale (too big or too little) can cause discomfort to the occupant.

In the past, small classrooms with oversized furniture, drab coloration, and square walls have been used purposefully to control environmental stimulation and direct attention to the teacher. Such a discomforting setting presupposed that teacher behavior was the significant action in the learning environment.

More recently, schools have used bright colors, curved walls, large expansive spaces, and acoustical treatments to encourage student mobility and mental freedom. Such an environment presupposes that education is an act which is highly individual and conducted through exploration. Control under such environmental conditions is often difficult.

While few school buildings are constructed to promote an identifiable pattern of instruction, the effect of environmental warmth is great on instructional procedure. Failure to consider this factor has led to many unsuccessful and inefficient teaching episodes.

Traffic Control Patterns

Traffic control within a school building, made famous by Kaufman's book *Up The Down Staircase,*[14] is also a reflection of the school's belief about the nature of education. Many schools go to great lengths to communicate *order* to inhabitants of the building. Adhesive strips dividing hallways into acceptable paths, turnstiles, fences, and children marching single file along walls are indicative of such structure in a building.

In buildings where flexibility is encouraged, the observer will see curved sidewalks, entrances to learning spaces without doors, seating spaces where occupants can stop and rest enroute to their destination, and multiple patterns of individual progression from point to point in the building.

Space Priorities

Finally, space usage and priorities reflect the learning environment in school buildings. Priorities are indicated by both the size of spaces in the building and the location of spaces in the building. In some schools, old and new, a significant portion of total available space is dominated by single-event spaces such as auditoriums, gymnasiums, swimming pools, and central office suites. In terms of construction costs and utilization, these spaces speak subtly of the priorities of the resident educators.

The number, kind, and quality of spaces can be a measure of the definition of educational priority in a school building.

A second, and perhaps more accurate, measure of space priority in a school building is the location of various areas. Studies of school buildings have indicated that the longer a teacher is in a building, the better his or her resource base becomes relative to other teachers. How much space, for instance, does the English department have? Where is the fine arts complex located? What new additions have been made to the building and which program do they serve?

Grounds.   Beyond the structural walls of the school building lie the school grounds. Sometimes these spaces will reveal the attitude of the school toward learning. One interesting measure of the school yard is whether it is being utilized at all. Some schools are located on ten-acre sites and never plant a bush or add a piece of equipment to make the grounds useful to the school. Other schools, by contrast, use the grounds extensively and perceive them as an extension of the formal learning spaces.

Another question to be asked about the school grounds is whether they are generally used for student loitering, casual recreation, physical education, or comprehensive educational purposes. Equipment and student behavior will indicate which, if any, uses are made of this valuable resource.

There are great differences in the way individual schools utilize their buildings and grounds. As such, the use of these resources represents another relevant dimension of the school environment. The following descriptive continuums suggest the potential range of alternatives present in schools.

2.1 Building-Access

Highly visible control of access exterior building	Access control visible interior only-high regimentation	Access control visible exterior only	Order visible but not excessive	Access not controlled exterior or interior

S – – – – + – – – – – – – – – –|– – – – – – – – + – – – – – – – –|– – – – – –|– – F

2.2 Building-Warmth

Spaces drab, overwhelming, repulsive, cold	Spaces ordered and monotonous	Spaces neutral, neither pleasant nor unpleasant	Spaces pleasant, light, clean, attractive	Spaces inviting, cheery, colorful

S – – + – – – – – – – – + – – – – – – – – – –|– – – – – – – – –|– – – – – – + – F

2.3 Building-Traffic control

Movement in building highly controlled	Movement patterns structured by arrangement	Traffic patterns established	Traffic patterns not specified; options available to individuals	Movement patterns not discernible

S -- + -------- |- -------- + -------- -|- ------- -|-- F

2.4 Building-Space priorities

Space allocation grossly distorted	Space allocation highly disproportioned in building	Some priorities via space allocation obvious	Space equally allocated to various components, location key	No space priority observable by size or locale

S --- |- -------- |- -------- -| -------- |- ------- -|- -- F

2.5 Building-Grounds

Grounds not in active use	Grounds used for informal activity	Grounds used for specific activity	Grounds use variable	Grounds use extensively for multiple activity

S -- |- ------- + -------- |- -------- + -------- + --- F

Classroom Spaces

Just as the school learning environment may be revealed in school dimensions such as community involvement and building use, the organization, movement, and ownership of physical space in the classroom is often indicative of the intentions of the school. In viewing these characteristics of the classroom, it is again obvious that all schools are not alike.

One way of viewing the classroom spaces is in terms of the organization for instructional effectiveness. A traditional pattern would be to order the room in such a way that all vision and attention is on the teacher. Figure 3.2 shows that there is little opportunity for lateral communication. Activity is "fixed" by the arrangement of furniture. The conditions are perfect for teacher lecture but little else.

Another possibility in organization of classroom spaces is to create multi-purpose spaces with the focus of attention generally in the center of the classroom (as shown in Figure 3.3). This style permits increased student involvement, mobility, and varied learning activities simultaneously. It does not focus attention solely on the teacher and cannot easily be controlled in terms of noise or lateral communication among students.

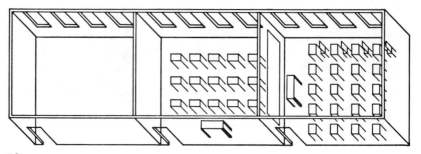

Figure 3.2

The extreme degree of flexibility in organization of classroom spaces is, of course, to perceive the classroom as simply a place where learners meet to prepare for educational experiences both in the school building and in the community.

Pupil movement within the classroom may be another subtle indicator of the structure or flexibility present in the learning environment (see Figure 3.4). Movement in some classrooms is totally dependent upon the teacher. Students in such a classroom must request

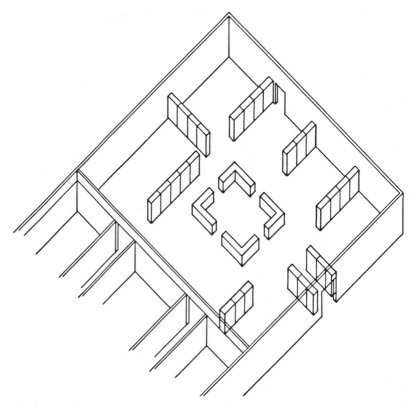

Figure 3.3

permission to talk, go to the washroom, or approach the teacher. Such structure usually minimizes noise and confusion but restricts activity to only verbal exchange. Movement in such classrooms, when it occurs, is generally to and from the teacher's desk.

In a less stationary classroom, movement is possible within controlled patterns monitored by the teacher. Movement is usually contextual depending upon the activity being engaged in. During teacher talk, for instance, movement may not be allowed, while at other times students may be able to sharpen pencils, get supplies, or leave the room for water without complete dependence on teacher approval.

Pupil movement is sometimes left to the complete discretion of the student. Even during a lesson or a teacher explanation a student may leave to use the washroom. In open-space buildings with high degrees of program flexibility, students are often seen moving unsupervised from one learning area to the next. Parents who have attended more structured, traditional programs often view such movement as questionable since it is believed that the teacher must be in direct contact with students for learning to occur. Yet, self-directed unsupervised movement is an integral part of any open, activity-centered curriculum.

A third consideration in viewing classroom spaces is what might be considered *ownership* or *territoriality* of the area. In most classrooms this dimension can be seen by both the spaces the teacher and student occupy, and by items that belong to those persons inhabiting the classroom.

At the most structured end of an ownership continuum in a classroom is the situation where the teacher has total access to any area or space in the room while the student "owns" no space. In some classrooms, particularly in elementary schools, teacher ownership of space can even extend into the desks, pockets, and thoughts of students.

In somewhat less structured environments, students have zones where they can locate without being inspected or violating the teacher's territoriality. The average classroom is divided about two-thirds for students and one-third for the teacher (as illustrated in Figure 3.5).

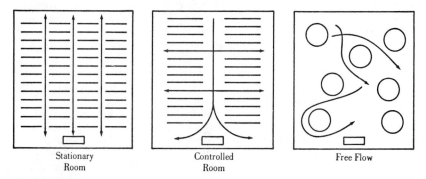

| Stationary | Controlled | Free Flow |
| Room | Room | |

Figure 3.4

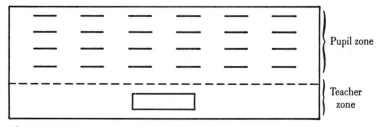

Figure 3.5

The most flexible pattern of ownership is the classroom where no overt symbols of territoriality exist. Either the teacher's desk is accessible for all purposes or, in newer schools, the teacher has a private place somewhere else in the building. Furniture in such classrooms is uniform for students and teachers alike.

Another measure of ownership available to the observer are personal items on display in the room. In particular, the display of student work or student art is a useful indicator. When student work is displayed, for example, are samples drawn from the work of all students, or simply a few? Are the samples on display uniform (everyone colors the same picture the same color) or diverse?

Other questions related to ownership would be concerned with the kind of teaching visuals on display (standard or tailored), the presence or absence of living objects, and any signs of reward for creative or divergent thinking. A highly structured classroom will generally be bland and uniform, while a highly flexible room will be nearly chaotic in appearance.

There are great differences in school classrooms, and these differences reflect the intentions of the school in educating students. As such, classroom spaces represent another important dimension of the learning environment. The following descriptive continuums suggest the potential range of alternatives present in schools:

3.1 Classroom Organization

Uniform seating arrangement dominates room	Classroom furniture uniform but not symmetrical	Furniture arranged for each activity	Multi-purpose spaces in room	Space out of classroom used for instruction

S - - -|- - - - - - - - - - -|- - - - - - - -|- - - - - -|- - - - - - - +- -F

3.2 Classroom Movement

Movement totally restricted by teacher	Total teacher control with noted exception	Pupil movement contextual	Pupil has freedom of movement within limit	Pupil movement at pupil discretion

S - - -+- - - - - - - - - -|- - - - - - - -|- - - - - - -|- - - - - - -|- -F

3.3 Classroom Ownership

Classroom space is dominated by teacher	Teacher dominates— some student zones	Classroom has areas of mutual free access	Territory only at symbolic level—open to all	All classroom spaces totally accessible to all persons

S --┠---------┨---------┠---------┨---------┨--F

Programs of Study ──────────────────

Schools differ to a great extent in the way in which they organize and utilize knowledge in the programs of study. In highly structured schools knowledge is, for all practical purposes, the curriculum and ordering knowledge represents the major activity of curriculum development. In highly flexible schools, by contrast, knowledge can be a simple medium through which processes are taught.

The Organization of Knowledge

The organization of knowledge can best be understood by viewing it in several dimensions: the pattern of its presentation, the way it is constructed and ordered, its cognitive focus, and the time orientation of the content.

In most schools, knowledge is presented as an essential body or set of interrelated data (as in the first circle of Figure 3.6). In some schools, however, this essential knowledge is supplemented by other useful learnings which may appear as unequal satellites around the main body of information (as in the second circle of Figure 3.6).

To the degree that student needs and interests are considered in planning the program of study, the satellites, or electives are expanded and become a more important part of the program. In some schools, electives are equal in importance to essential knowledge areas and consume up to one-half of school time (the paired circles in Figure 3.6). Once the school acknowledges the value of student-related content, it may find that it can teach the "essential" content in a form that accounts for student needs and interests (as in the next pair of circles in the figure).

As the interrelatedness of essential "subcourses" is verified, cross-referencing of coursework may occur. Finally, a maximum of flexibility in the ordering and utilization of knowledge may occur when a problem-oriented activity is the common denominator for organizing knowledge (the final circle in Figure 3.6).

Another distinguishing dimension of the organization of knowledge is to be found in the way it is constructed or ordered. Most programs of study employ one of three standard curriculum designs: the building blocks design, branching designs, or spiral designs. It is

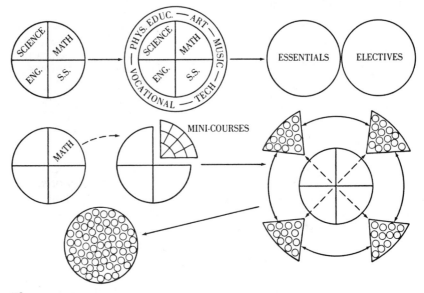

Figure 3.6

also possible, however, to order knowledge in school programs in terms of task accomplishment or simple learning processes.

The building blocks design takes a clearly defined body of knowledge and orders it into a pyramid-like arrangement. Students are taught foundational material which leads to more complex and specialized knowledge. Deviations from the prescribed order are not allowed because the end product of the learning design (mastery) is known in advance. Also, activities that do not contribute to this directed path are not allowed due to the efficiency of this model. Building blocks designs are the most structured of curriculum organizations.

Another common learning design found in schools is a branching pattern. Branching is a variation of the building blocks design but incorporates limited choice in the knowledge to be mastered. Branching designs recognize the value of foundational knowledge in learning, but allow choice within prescribed areas beyond the common experience. Like the building blocks, branching prescribes the eventual outcomes of the learning program, although the prescription is multiple rather than uniform. The branching design allows for some variability in learning but only within tightly defined boundaries of acceptance.

A third common organization of knowledge in programs of study is the spiral curriculum. In this design, knowledge areas are continually visited and revisited at higher levels of complexity. While this design does have some flexibility, it still controls what it taught and learned, and even predetermines the time it is to be received by the student.

A fourth possible organization of knowledge could occur if knowledge were organized to accomplish specified tasks. In such a case, the purpose of the learning experience would be predetermined, but the student interaction with data in terms of both content and order of content would be flexible. Competency-based skill continuums are an example of this design.

A final organization of knowledge in a school program of studies might use knowledge as simply a medium for teaching processes. Thus, reading could be taught regardless of the particular material used by the student. Such a process pattern would feature great flexibility in terms of the knowledge utilized, its order in learning experiences, and the expected outcomes for its selection and use.

The five patterns of knowledge construction are symbolized in Figure 3.7.

Still another dimension of the treatment of knowledge is the cognitive focus of instruction. In addition to a focus on factual material, such as learning important dates in history, is an organization of knowledge that teaches generalizations. Sometimes conceptual treatments of information are related to the lives of students. Maximum flexibility in the treatment of knowledge is gained by focusing on the personal world of the students, drawing concepts and facts from their experiences.

A final area related to knowledge in school settings is the time orientation of the instructional material. In some classrooms, all information is drawn from past experiences of mankind. In other rooms, information from the past is mixed with that from the present. Some classrooms will be strictly contemporary and deal only with the here-and-now. Beyond the present-oriented instructional space are those that mix current knowledge with projected knowledge, and some that deal only in probabilities. With each step from the known (past) to the speculative (future) content flexibility increases.

The following descriptive continuums suggest the potential range of alternatives found in schools:

4.1 Pattern of Presentation

Essential courses only	Essentials plus some satellite courses	Essentials and co-equal elective courses	Cross-referenced courses	Integrated courses

S – ┼ – – – – – – – –├ – – – – – – – – – ┤ – – – – – – – – – ┤ – – – – – – – ┼ – F

4.2 Constitution of Knowledge

Building blocks	Branching	Spiral	Task focused	Process pattern

S – ┼ – – – – – – – –┤ – – – – – – –├ – – – – – – – –┤ – – – – – – – – – ┤ – – – F

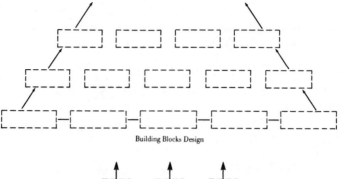

Building Blocks Design

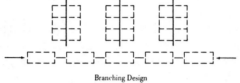

Branching Design

Spiral Design

Specific Tasks Design

Process-Pattern Design

Figure 3.7

4.3 Cognitive Focus

Related facts	Series/set of facts	Conceptual organization	Concepts via world of the students	Concepts via personal life of individual

S –|– – – – – – – –|– – – – – – – – –+– – – – – – – – –+– – – – – – – –+– – F

4.4 Time-Focus of Curriculum

Past only	Past and present	Present only	Present and future	Future only

S –+– – – – – – – – –|– – – – – – – – – –|– – – – – – – – –|– – – – – – – –|– F

Uses of Learning Materials

The ways in which learning materials are used or not used in classroom spaces varies tremendously from room to room. In some settings, no materials are visible to the observer except perhaps a single textbook. In other classroom spaces, the volume and variety of learning materials gives the impression of clutter. Three measures of the use of learning materials are the degree of sensory stimulation present, the diversity of learning mediums found, and the location of usable learning materials.

On the most structured end of a continuum, the stimulation from learning materials can be fixed and absolute, as when all material is written or programmed. Sometimes stimulation from learning materials is prescribed or controlled as during lectures. A slightly more flexible version of stimulation is available when the materials are interpreted, such as during an animated film or game playing. Still greater stimulation occurs when the learner is in physical proximity to the materials and has a tactile experience. Finally, stimulation that immerses the learner in multi-sense experiencing represents the greatest degree of stimulation to the learner.

Another measure of the effect of learning materials is found in the diversity of mediums present. While some classrooms have only textbooks, others have printed matter, audiovisual aids, games, displays, and interactive materials. An important question is, "How many types of learning mediums are interacting with the learner at any moment?"

Finally, the location of usable learning materials is a variable in classroom settings. In some schools, all learning materials are contained in standard classrooms. Still others have special purpose spaces where students may interact with materials. A third, and more flexible possibility, is that the school possesses areas (Instructional Materials Centers) where learning materials are clustered. An even more flexible pattern would be to identify and select learning materials both in the school and outside the school. Maximum flexibility, of course, would perceive all objects as being possible learning materials for instruction.

The following descriptive continuums suggest the potential range of alternatives found in schools:

5.1 Degree of Sensory Stimulation

Stimulation fixed	Stimulation prescribed	Stimulation interpreted	Stimulation experienced	Stimulation immersion

S – –|– – – – – – – – –|– – – – – – – – –+– – – – – – – –+– – – – – – – – –F

5.2 Diversity of Learning Mediums

Single medium	Two mediums	More than two mediums	Multiple concerted mediums	Infinite learning mediums

S -- -|- - - - - - - - - - -|- - - - - - - - - -|- - - - - - - - -|- - - - - - -|- - F

5.3 Location of Usable Learning Mediums

Classroom contained	Special purpose spaces	Clustered in special spaces	Found in school and out-of-school	All objects perceived as materials

S - -|- - - - - - - - - +- - - - - - - - -|- - - - - - - -+- - - - - - - - -|- - F

Instructional Orientation

In some classes, learning is absolutely structured. The teacher controls the flow of data, communication, and assessment. Such a condition is characterized by drill. Slightly more flexible is a pattern of didactic teaching whereby the teacher delivers information, controls the exchange of ideas, and enforces the correct conclusions through a question-answer session. A balance between complete structure and flexibility in the learning process is for the teacher to allow the free exchange of ideas in the classroom, but to enforce a standardized summation of the process. Even more flexible would be a pattern where students are allowed to experience a learning process and then draw their own conclusions about meaning. Most flexible is an instructional process that is not uniformly structured for all students, allows an exchange of ideas, and leaves the process open-ended.

Yet another measure of philosophy in the classroom is the acceptance of diversity among students. Sometimes this is observable in norms relating to dress or speech enforced by the teacher. Sometimes such a measure can be assessed by the appearance of the learning space. The key to this variable is whether students are made to act in standardized ways, or whether differences are allowed. On the most extreme end of structure would be a classroom where no individuality is allowed. In a classroom with maximum flexibilty, diversity among students in appearance and behavior would be significant.

The following descriptive continuums suggest the potential range of alternatives found in schools:

6.1 Instructional Format

Teacher drills	Didactic format with cloture	Free exchange with summation	Experience learning with individual summation	Non-structured learning with no summation

S --|- - - - - - - -|- - - - - - - -+- - - - - - -|- - - - - - - - -|- - F

6.2 Acceptance of Diversity Among Students

Teacher enforces conformity	Teacher communicates expectations for conformity	Teacher tolerates limited diversity	Teacher accepts student diversity	Teacher encourages student diversity

S – ┤ – – – – – – – – – – ├ – – – – – – – – ┤ – – – – – – – – ├ – – – – – – – ┤ – – F

Teaching Strategies

Like the actions that suggest educational philosophies, the teaching strategies found in classrooms often give clues regarding the degree of structure in the learning program. Such strategies can often be inferred from teacher behaviors and organizational patterns. For instance, some teachers behave in ways that allow only a single learning interface with students as in the case of the didactic method. Other times, teachers will provide multiple ways for students to interact and communicate during instruction.

Two behaviors that speak louder than words about the learning strategy employed in the classroom are the motivational techniques being used and the interactive distances between the teacher and student. By watching these phenomena, the observer can anticipate a pattern of structure or flexibility in other instructional areas.

There are a range of motivational techniques available to classroom teachers, and all are situationally legitimate. Some techniques, however, seek to control and structure learning while others encourage flexibility. Teachers using threats or fear as a motivator generally seek maximum structure in the classroom. Coercion, as a rule, arrests behavior and encourages conformity to previous patterns of behavior. Extrinsic rewards, immediate or deferred, also encourage structure by linking desired behavior with reward. Intrinsic rewards, whether immediate or deferred, have an opposite effect. Intrinsic rewards encourage student participation in the reward system and thereby a wider range of acceptable behaviors. If the motivational technique is observable, the overall learning strategy to constrict or expand student behavior is also understood.

Another dimension of the learning strategy in a classroom setting is the interactive distance between the teacher and students. To the degree that it is important to have two-way communication in the classroom, and to the degree that the instructional strategy values multiple learning styles among students, the teacher will make adjustments for differences.

In his book, *The Silent Language,* Edward Hall made observations about the appropriateness of certain distances between persons for certain activities.[15] Some distances (25 feet and beyond) were appropriate for broadcasting, while other distances (6 inches and under)

were reserved for intimate moments. In a classroom setting, it is possible to observe if the teacher makes adjustments in interactive distances during instruction or chooses to treat all situations alike.

The following descriptive continuums suggest the potential range of alternatives found in schools:

7.1 Motivational Techniques Used

Teacher threatens students, forces conformity	Teacher reinforces immediate conformity	Teacher reinforces eventual conformity	Teacher allows student to decide to conform	Teacher hopes student will eventually conform

S − − − ┤− − − − − − − − − ┤− − − − − − − ┤− − − − − − − − ┤− − − − − − − ┼− − F

7.2 Interactive Distances

Teacher operates at constant interactive distance	Teacher uses varied interactive distances	Teacher interacts at multiple distances	Teacher tailors distance to needs	Teacher uses full range of interactive distances effectively

S − − − ├− − − − − − − − − ├− − − − − − − ┤− − − − − − − ┤− − − − − − − ┼− − F

Staffing Patterns

A final indicator of structure versus flexibility in schools, in terms of instruction, is found in the staffing patterns observed. Two staffing indicators are the role of teachers in staffing, and the organization of teachers in the school building.

In some school buildings, all teachers are hired and assigned on the basis of subject-matter preparation. Such teachers are perceived as solitary craftsmen with the highly structured task of teaching a subject to students. In other schools, a teacher might be hired as a subject specialist, but assigned to a team which is interdisciplinary in nature. A more flexible pattern would be to staff a school with teachers having two or more subject specialties. It might even be possible to have one teacher (as in the elementary grades) responsible for all subjects. Or, a teacher could be hired to teach students at a certain level, rather than subjects.

Another staffing pattern is the organization of teachers in the building. Are all teachers isolated in self-contained classrooms? Do the isolated teachers have instructional aides? Do the classroom teachers meet together to plan activities? Are there ever combined teaching units? Do the teachers teach in teams or other cooperative arrangements?

The following descriptive continuums suggest the potential range of alternatives found in schools:

8.1 The Role of the Teacher

Solitary subject specialist	Subject specialist on team	Subject specialist in multiple areas	Subject specialist all areas	Specialist in teaching at a level

S – ├ – – – – – – – ┼ – – – – – – – – – –┤– – – – – – – – – –├– – – – – – – –┤– – F

8.2 Organization of Teachers

Teachers isolated in self-contained classrooms	Teacher and aide isolated	Teacher isolated except for planning	Two or more teachers work cooperatively	Teachers in formal teams for instruction

S – – ┼ – – – – – – – – ┼ – – – – – – – ┼ – – – – – – – – ├ – – – – – – – – – –┤– – – F

Administrative Conditions _____

Organization of Students

The way in which a school organizes students can give an observer some measure of the degree of structure in the school. Two different measures of student organization are the criteria for organization and the actual grouping patterns found in the school.

Most schools in the United States group students according to their age since most schools in the United States admit children into schools according to age. Schools use a more flexible criterion when students are organized by subject taught. Still greater flexibility is evidenced in schools that group students within grades and subjects according to capacity. Even greater organizational flexibility is found in schools that group students by needs and by student interests.

Beside criteria for grouping, the actual organization pattern of students can indicate the degree of structure or flexibility in the school. Perhaps the most structured situation exists when the size of the room determines the number of students present. A uniform number of students for all activities is also a highly structured condition. When a school begins to recognize that some activities should have large or small classes, a degree of flexibility is in evidence. Assignment of students based on the tasks to be accomplished and the individualization of instruction wherever possible represent the most flexibility in organization of students.

The following descriptive continuums suggest the potential range of alternatives found in schools:

9.1 Criteria for Organizing Students

By age/grade	By subject taken	By student capacity	By student needs	By student interest

S – – ┼ – – – – – – – – ┤– – – – – – – –┤– – – – – – – – –┤– – – – – – – –├– – F

9.2 Grouping Pattern of Students

By room size	By uniform number	By large and small designation	By task to be performed	Stressing individuali-zation where possible

S – ├ – – – – – – – ├ – – – – – – – – – ├ – – – – – – – – – ┤ – – – – – – – ┤ – – F

Rules and Regulations

Within schools and within individual classrooms, rules and regulations vary. Perhaps the most structured situations are those in which an excessive number of regulations exist based on historical precedent. Slightly less structured is the school with numerous and absolute regulations. A more flexible condition is when there are a few rules which are formal and enforced. When there are few rules and the rules are negotiable, or when no formal or informal regulations are stated, maximum flexibility is indicated. The following descriptive continuum suggests the potential range of alternatives in schools:

10.0 Rules and Regulations

Numerous rules with historical basis	Numerous and absolute rules	Few but absolute rules	Few and negotiable rules	No formal or informal rules

S – – – ├ – – – – – – – – – ┤ – – – – – – – ┼ – – – – – – ┤ – – – – – – – – ┤ – – F

Disciplinary Measures

Discipline techniques used in schools to influence student behavior cover a wide range of actions. In some schools, all infractions are given the same treatment regardless of severity. In more flexible schools, there is a hierarchy of discipline measures to deal with differing discipline problems. Sometimes, the pattern found in schools will be to deal only with the severe or recurrent discipline problems. In schools where great flexibility is found, the pattern for discipline is sometimes unclear due to the uneven application of discipline measures. There are schools where no discipline measures are observable.

The following descriptive continuum suggests the potential range of alternatives for discipline in schools:

11.0 Disciplinary Measures

All infractions same treatment	Hierarchy of discipline actions	Discipline activity only in severe cases	Unpredictable pattern of discipline	No observable discipline measures

S – – – ├ – – – – – – – – – ┼ – – – – – – – – ├ – – – – – – – – ┼ – – – – – – – ├ – F

Reporting Student Progress

The reporting of student progress in the most structured schools and classrooms is a mechanical process whereby students are assessed in mathematical symbols such as "83" or "upper quartile." A generalization of such preciseness is a system whereby student progress in learning is summarized by a symbol such as a "B" or "U." Increased flexibility in reporting student progress is evidenced by narrative descriptions which actually describe student work, and by supplemental reporting by other interested parties such as the student or the parent. Maximum flexibility in reporting student progress is found when such reporting is informal, verbal, and continuous.

The following descriptive continuum suggests the potential range of alternatives for reporting student progress found in schools:

12.0 Reporting Student Progress

Numerical symbolism	General symbols	Descriptive narrative supplements	Descriptive supplements from several parties	Informal verbal evaluation

S - -|- - - - - - - -|- - - - - - - -|- - - - - - - - -|- - - - - - - -|- - F

Roles of Participants _____

Administrative Attitudes

Administrative style, more than any other single factor, determines the atmosphere of a school building. It is certain that the way others in the school building perceive the administrator affects both teacher and student behavior. For this reason, clues about the structure or flexibility of a school or classroom can be gained by observing the administrator.

Administrators often assume one of five attitudes that characterize their pattern of interaction with others. At the most structured end is a "warden" who rules by intimidation. Closely allied to this model is the "benevolent dictator" who maintains absolute control while giving the impression of involvement. A more flexible posture for the administrator is to act as the "program manager," reserving key decisions for the only person with the comprehensive viewpoint. Still more flexible is the "collegial" leader who shares all decision-making with the teaching faculty. Finally, there is a leadership style which is nondirective, or "laissez faire."

A second interesting variable for studying administrative attitudes is the medium used to communicate with students. In some schools, the lead administrator is a phantom, known only by the presence of his portrait in the foyer. Such an administrator generally leaves communication with parents or students to an intermediary such as a vice-principal. Another impersonal medium is the intercom which is often used to communicate to students. Slightly more personal is a "live" address at assemblies. Finally, some administrators communicate with students by coming into the classrooms, and even sometimes by individual conferences.

The following descriptive continuums suggest the potential range of alternatives for administrative behavior found in schools:

13.1 Administrative Decision-Making Role

Makes all decisions unilaterally	Makes all key decisions unilaterally	Shares decision-making on specific items	Shares all decision-making on all items	Abdicates all key decision-making

S --|--------------+---------------+----------------+---------------+- F

13.2 Administrative Communication With Students

Unknown to students	Communicates through an intermediary	Speaks through intercom or at assemblies	Visits classes for discussion	Holds individual conferences

S --+---------------|----------------+----------------+----------------+-- F

Teacher Roles

The role of a classroom teacher in a school can vary from being an instructional unit who teaches a prescribed set of facts to students to a multi-dimensional adult who interacts with students and others in the building. For the most part, such perceptions are self-imposed. A key observation can be made from teacher responses to the question, "What do you teach?"

The following descriptive continuum suggests the potential range of responses to that question:

14.1 Teacher's Role Perception

Teacher deals with prescribed data only	Teacher deals with all knowledge in his field of expertise	Teacher deals with school knowledge and related matters	Teacher deals with both school and non-school items	Teacher teaches whatever he deems valuable

S ---|---------------+----------------+---------------+------+- F

Student Roles

Like teachers, students in schools hold a role perception of what they are and what they can do in a classroom setting. Sometimes such perceptions are self-imposed, but more often they are an accurate reflection of expected behavior for students. A question that usually receives a telling response for an observer in a school is, "How do students learn in this classroom?"

The following descriptive continuum suggests the potential range of responses to such a question:

15.1 How do Students Learn in Class

They recite and copy from board	They listen, take notes, take tests	They listen, read, question, take tests	They work on things, read	They do things that interest them

S – – –|– – – – – – – – –|– – – – – – – –|– – – – – – – –|– – – – – – – –|– – F

The value of viewing school components on a continuum, such as the degree of structure/flexibility, is that program congruence or inconsistencies can be identified. In schools where the program intent (philosophy) is clear, the degree of structure or flexibility should be relatively constant. Said another way, if the fifteen dimensions were plotted across the five degrees of structure/flexibility, strong schools would have reasonably vertical columns. A zigzag pattern in such a school profile would indicate an inconsistency in the learning design.

What Is Your Philosophy?

It should be noted by the reader that few educators hold a pure version of any of these philosophies, for schools are complex places with many forces vying for prominence. These schools of thought have evolved as distinctive forms of philosophy following the examination of beliefs on pertinent issues. When an educator chooses not to adopt a single philosophy, or blends philosophies for experience, or selectively applies educational philosophies in practice, it is called an *eclectic* position. Most classrooms and public schools come closest to an eclectic stance, applying philosophic preferences as conditions demand.

Whatever the educator's philosophy or beliefs about schools, and each of the five philosophies presented here are legitimate beliefs, it is critical that these values be clarified and understood in terms of their implications. To this end, the reader is invited to participate in a self-assessment that has been developed to show preferences on value-laden educational questions.

Philosophy Preference Assessment _____

Directions: For each item below, respond according to the strength of your belief, scoring the item on a scale of 1–5. A one (1) indicates strong disagreement, a five (5) strong agreement. Use a separate sheet of paper.

1. Ideal teachers are constant questioners.
2. Schools exist for societal improvement.
3. Teaching should center around the inquiry technique.
4. Demonstration and recitation are essential components for learning.
5. Students should always be permitted to determine their own rules in the educational process.
6. Reality is spiritual and rational.
7. Curriculum should be based on the laws of natural science.
8. The teacher should be a strong authority figure in the classroom.
9. The student is a receiver of knowledge.
10. Ideal teachers interpret knowledge.
11. Lecture-discussion is the most effective teaching technique.
12. Institutions should seek avenues towards self-improvement through an orderly process.
13. Schools are obligated to teach moral truths.
14. School programs should focus on social problems and issues.
15. Institutions exist to preserve and strengthen spiritual and social values.
16. Subjective opinion reveals truth.
17. Teachers are seen as facilitators of learning.
18. Schools should be educational "smorgasbords."
19. Memorization is the key to process skills.
20. Reality consists of objects.
21. Schools exist to foster the intellectual process.
22. Schools foster an orderly means for change.
23. There are essential skills everyone must learn.
24. Teaching by subject area is the most effective approach.
25. Students should play an active part in program design and evaluation.
26. A functioning member of society follows rules of conduct.
27. Reality is rational.
28. Schools should reflect the society they serve.
29. The teacher should set an example for the students.
30. The most effective learning does not take place in a highly structured, strictly disciplined environment.
31. The curriculum should be based on unchanging spiritual truths.

32. The most effective learning is nonstructured.
33. Truth is a constant expressed through ideas.
34. Drill and factual knowledge are important components of any learning environment.
35. Societal consensus determines morality.
36. Knowledge is gained primarily through the senses.
37. There are essential pieces of knowledge that everyone should know.
38. The school exists to facilitate self-awareness.
39. Change is an ever-present process.
40. Truths are best taught through the inquiry process.

Philosophy Assessment Scoring ─────────

The following sets of test questions relate to the five standard philosophies of education:

Perennialist—6, 8, 10, 13, 15, 31, 34, 37
Idealist—9, 11, 19, 21, 24, 27, 29, 33
Realist—4, 7, 12, 20, 22, 23, 26, 28
Experimentalist—2, 3, 14, 17, 25, 35, 39, 40
Existentialist—1, 5, 16, 18, 30, 32, 36, 38

Scoring Steps

1. Taking these questions by set (e.g., the eight perennialist questions), multiply each question by the value of the answer given (i.e., strongly disagree = 1). Total the numerical value of each set. In a single set of numbers, the total should fall between 8 (all 1s) and 40 (all 5s).
2. Divide the total score for each set by five (Example: 40/5 = 8).
3. Plot the scores on the graph shown in Figure 3.8.

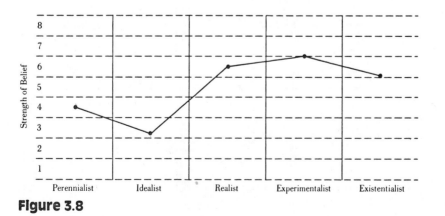

Figure 3.8

Interpretation

Having scored and plotted your responses on the grid provided, you now have a profile which is distinctive to your own beliefs about schools. It can be noted that some patterns are common and therefore subject to interpretation. The pattern already on the grid, for instance, is a composite response by over/800 students, both graduate and undergraduate, at five universities.

Pattern #1 (Figure 3.9). If your profile on the response grid is basically flat, reflecting approximately the same score for each set of questions, an inability to discriminate in terms of preference is indicated.

Pattern #2 (Figure 3.10). If your pattern is generally a slanting line across the grid, then you show a strong structured or nonstructured orientation in your reported beliefs about schools.

Pattern # 3 (Figure 3.11). If your pattern appears as a bimodal or trimodal distribution, (two or three peaks), it indicates indecisiveness

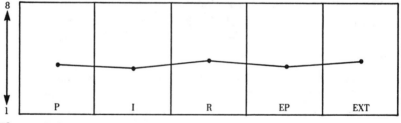

Figure 3.9

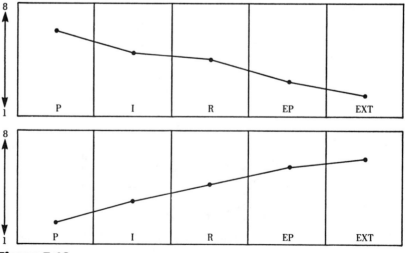

Figure 3.10

on crucial issues and suggests the need for further clarification. The closer the peaks (adjacent sets) the less contradiction in the responses.

Pattern #4 (Figure 3.12). If the pattern appears U-shaped, as in either of the pictures below, a significant amount of value inconsistency is indicated. Such a response would suggest strong beliefs in very different and divergent systems.

Pattern #5 (Figure 3.13). Finally, a pattern which is simply a flowing curve without sharp peaks and valleys may suggest either an eclectic philosophy, or a person only beginning to study his or her own philisophy.

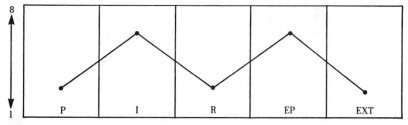

Figure 3.11

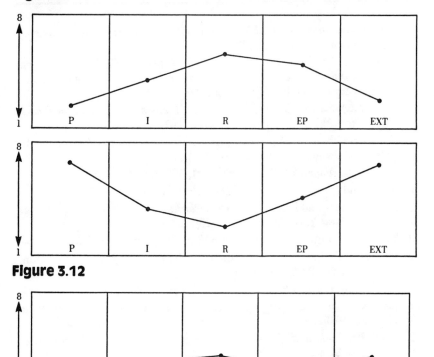

Figure 3.12

Figure 3.13

Summary

Educational philosophies are the heart of purposeful activity in curriculum development. Philosophies serve as value screens for decision-making. Because educators today are confronted by multiple choices, it is vital that curriculum specialists understand their own values and beliefs about schooling.

Over the years, the American school has evolved from a highly structured and traditional institution to one that possesses considerable flexibility. The degree of structure or flexibility found in the learning design of a school is a reflection of the undergirding philosophy of education being practiced. Whatever the philosophy, consistency in the design is the key to effectiveness of the curriculum.

In this chapter, five major educational philosophies were presented to the reader, along with a Philosophy Assessment Inventory to assist the reader in clarifying his or her posture on key issues. The authors believe that in order to be a decisive leader, curriculum specialists must be aware of their own values and be able to accurately assess the value systems found in today's schools.

Notes

1. *Youth: Transition To Adulthood,* A report of the President's Advisory Commission on Science, 1973.
2. Robert M. McClure, "The Reforms of the Fifties and Sixties: A Historical Look at the Near Past," *The Curriculum: Retrospect and Prospect,* National Society for the Study of Education, 1971, p. 51.
3. Galen Saylor and William M. Alexander, *Planning Curriculum for Schools* (New York: Holt, Rinehart & Winston, 1974), pp. 144–145.
4. Robert Hutchins, *On Education* (Santa Barbara, California: Center for the Study of Democratic Institutions, 1963), p. 18.
5. A. S. Neill, *Summerhill* (New York: Hart, 1960), p. 4.
6. Saylor and Alexander, *Planning Curriculum for Schools,* p. 146.
7. Daniel Tanner and Laurel N. Tanner, *Curriculum Development: Theory Into Practice* (New York: Macmillan, 1975), p. 95.
8. Tanner and Tanner, *Curriculum Development: Theory into Practice,* p. 64.
9. John D. McNeil, *Designing Curriculum: Self-Instructional Modules* (Boston: Little, Brown, 1976), pp. 91–92.
10. Martin Mayer, *The Schools* (New York: Harper & Row, 1961).
11. James B. Conant, as reported in *Crisis in the Classroom* (New York: Random House, 1970).
12. Charles E. Silberman, *Crisis in the Classroom* (New York: Random House, 1970), p. 9.
13. Morris L. Bigge, *Learning Theories for Teachers* (New York: Harper & Row, 1971), viii.

14. Bel Kaufman, *Up The Down Staircase* (Englewood Cliffs, New Jersey: Prentice-Hall, 1965).
15. Edward Hall, *The Silent Lanugage* (New York: Doubleday, 1959).

Suggested Learning Activities _____

1. Using the philosophy assessment inventory found in this chapter, analyze your beliefs about the roles of schools. If your profile does not correspond to what you think you believe, explain this discrepancy.
2. Using the scales found in this chapter, visit a school with which you are familiar and analyze its profile. What observations can you make about this type of analysis of a school?
3. Using Figure 3.1, describe the type of instructional program most likely to be implemented in the various structures. Where would you like to work? Why?

Books to Review _____

Bank, Adrianne. *A Practical Guide to Program Planning: A Teaching Models Approach.* New York: Teachers College Press, 1981.

Bigge, Morris. *Learning Theories for Teachers.* New York: Harper & Row, 1971.

Bode, Boyd. *Modern Educational Theories.* New York: Macmillan, 1927.

Cay, Donald. *Curriculum: Designs for Learning.* New York: Bobbs-Merrill, 1966.

Dewey, John. *Democracy and Education.* New York: Macmillan, 1916.

Goodlad, John. *Curriculum Inquiry: The Study of Curriculum Practice.* New York: McGraw-Hill, 1979.

Guttchen, Robert, and Bandman, Bertram. *Philosophical Essays on Curriculum.* New York: Lippincott, 1969.

Herman, Therese. *Creating Learning Environments.* Boston: Allyn and Bacon, 1977.

Joyce, Bruce, and Morine, Greta. *Creating the School.* New York: Little, Brown, and Company, 1976.

Kneller, George. *Existentialism and Education.* New York: John Wiley and Sons, 1958.

Rogers, Frederick A. *Curriculum and Instruction in the Elementary School.* New York: Macmillan, 1975.

Seeley, David. *Education Through Partnership: Mediating Structures and Education.* Cambridge: Ballinger, 1981.

Part Two
Curriculum Procedures

Chapter Four
Basic Tasks of Curriculum Development

Curriculum development, at its best, is a comprehensive process that (1) facilitates an analysis of purpose, (2) designs a program, (3) implements a series of related experiences, and (4) aids in the evaluation of this process. At its worst, curriculum development is an activity that does none of the above. Clearly, there are basic tasks which distinguish quality curriculum development from simple program change. It is also evident that modern curriculum development involves much more than the implementation of new courses of study.

Establishing the Philosophy

A philosophy, the clarification of beliefs about the purpose and goals of education, is essential to curriculum development. Without direction, school programs meander, become targets for social pressure, or operate in a state of programmatic contradiction. The development of a philosophy of education is a prerequisite to assuming a leadership function in school program development.

Curriculum specialists can assist others with whom they work in the clarification of their beliefs and goals. This can be done in three basic ways:

1. Others can be asked to review existing statements of philosophy or related documents and restate them in terms of desired changes.

2. Others can be asked to transfer their own personal philosophy of living into a school context, setting goals for school from general life goals.

3. Others can be asked to look for patterns in current behavior in society that might suggest goals for schools.

Methods that can be used to help others achieve goal clarity and consistency include writing personal goal statements, assigning priorities to various items, surveying existing documents, and analyzing school programs. One widely practiced method of clarifying philosophic positions is to have persons develop belief statements. These statements rest on a simple premise: each time a person acts, there is a rationale for action. Without a formalization of such rationales, it is impossible to coordinate or manage individual activities.

Belief statements can be organized in numerous ways, and the correct way for any individual district is dependent upon the planning format. Below are listed examples of belief statements organized around students, learning, teaching roles, grouping of students, and educational programs in general. The generic philosophy from which these are drawn is that the school exists to meet the needs and interests of students:

Students

1. WE BELIEVE that students are individuals with unique characteristics and interests.
2. WE BELIEVE that each student should have an equal opportunity to learn, based on his/her needs, interests, and abilities.

Learning

1. WE BELIEVE that students learn best when content is relevant to their own lives.
2. WE BELIEVE that students learn best in an environment that is pleasant and one in which the democratic process is modeled.

Teaching

1. WE BELIEVE that the role of the teacher in the classroom is primarily that of a facilitator of learning.
2. WE BELIEVE that student learning may be affected more by what teachers do than by what they say.

Grouping

1. WE BELIEVE that a more effective program of instruction can be provided for students if they are grouped according to maturation level and similar interest.
2. WE BELIEVE that a high school should include those students who are mature enough to participate in a program that is more specialized than the middle school and those students beyond the age of 18 who have a need to complete the requirements for a high school diploma.

The Educational Program

1. WE BELIEVE that all special programs should incorporate specific educational objectives that complement the total school program.
2. WE BELIEVE that evaluating and changing programs to more effectively meet the needs and interests of students should be a continuous process.

Once the school district or school has identified its philosophy and stated such a philosophy in easy-to-understand belief statements, it is ready to develop goals that will serve to guide development. Such goals are drawn from the philosophic orientation of the district, the needs of the school population, and the unique characteristics of the community.

As curriculum specialists clarify their own beliefs about the purpose of education and assist others in finding their value systems, the odds for meaningful curriculum development increase. Shared values can form the bond of commitment to change. The time spent in assessing group philosophies has significant payoff in areas such as continuity in school programs and articulation among school levels, developing relationships and roles among school faculties, the selection of learning activities and materials, evaluation of school programs, and the redesign of basic curriculum offerings.

Most important, however, is the connection of philosophy to leadership and decision-making in education. To be decisive leaders, and consistent decision makers, the curriculum specialists must know their values and those of the persons around them.

Formulating Goals

Educational goals are statements of the outcomes of education. The scope of the entire educational program of a school can be found in the goals of that school. Goals are the basic elements in educational planning. The reflection of societal needs in educational goals usually results in statements describing categories of human behavior. Goals relating to "maintaining health," and "carrying out the activities of a citizen in a democratic society" are examples of societal needs.

Goals may be stated at several levels of generality or specificity. Goals that are general or broad reflect a philosophical base and are not concerned with a particular achievement within a period of time.

Perhaps the most familiar goals were defined by the Commission on Reorganization of Secondary Education in 1918. Those goals were: (1) health, (2) command of fundamental processes, (3) worthy home membership, (4) vocation, (5) citizenship, (6) worthy use of leisure time, and (7) ethical character. These became widely known as the Seven Cardinal Principles of Secondary Education.

The second attempt at defining the purposes of secondary education was expressed in 1938 by the Educational Policies Commission of the National Education Association and the American Association of School Administrators. The group developed a number of goals under the four headings of (1) self-realization, (2) human relationships, (3) economic efficiency, and (4) civic responsibility.

Most recently, the ASCD Working Group on Research and Theory identified a set of valued learning outcomes "that reflected the 'holistic' nature of individuals." Hundreds of organizations, including state departments of education and regional research and development centers, were requested to share their goals with the group. The group identified ten major goals for youth:[1]

1. Self-Conceptualizing (Self-Esteem)
2. Understanding Others
3. Basic Skills
4. Interest and Capability for Continuous Learning
5. Responsible Member of Society
6. Mental and Physical Health
7. Creativity

8. Informed Participation in the Economic World of Production and Consumption
9. Use of Accumulated Knowledge to Understand the World
10. Coping with Change

The scope of all of the above goals indicates that they are general goals aimed at an entire unit of organization such as the elementary school, middle school, or senior high school.

In the following sections we should consider steps and procedures involved in clarifying goals and objectives. A discussion of the processes involved in defining various levels of goals and objectives is designed to assist the curriculum planner whether in the classroom or at the school or district level.

Clarifying Goals and Objectives _____

The following news item illustrates the need for formulating goals and objectives in a clear manner.

READING CROSS-EYED MIGHT HELP

HOUSTON—The parent of a Houston high school pupil received a message from the principal about a special meeting on a proposed educational program. It read:

"Our school's cross-graded, multi-ethnic, individualized learning program is designed to enhance the concept of an open-ended learning program with emphasis on a continuum of multi-ethnic, academically enriched learning using the identified intellectually gifted child as the agent or director of his own learning. Major emphasis is on cross-graded, multi-ethnic learning with the main objective being to learn respect for the uniqueness of a person."

The parent wrote the principal:

"I have a college degree, speak two foreign languages and four Indian dialects, have been to a number of county fairs and three goat ropings, but I haven't the faintest idea as to what the hell you are talking about. Do you?"

Goals provide a philosophically unified structure that undergirds and relates all aspects of the learning situation from the development of an overall curriculum plan to lesson plans in the classroom.

There appears to be a lack of organized coherence in many of the goals and objectives found in curriculum plans. Often, goals are not clearly stated and there is confusion when various levels of goals and objectives are indiscriminately grouped together. Educators have been accused of using their own language in describing programs to the public. That language is not only confusing to the public, but to educators themselves. The following exercise illustrates this point.

Instant Educator

To play the Instant Educator game, select in any order one word from Column A, one from Column B, and one from Column C. Now copy them on scratch paper in the order they were selected.

A	B	C
1. social	1. involvement	1. objectives
2. perceptual	2. motivation	2. activity
3. developmental	3. accelerated	3. curriculum
4. professional	4. cognitive	4. concept
5. homogeneous	5. effectiveness	5. evaluation
6. interdependent	6. maturation	6. processes
7. exceptional	7. integration	7. approach
8. instructional	8. orientation	8. articulation
9. individual	9. guidance	9. utilization
10. sequential	10. creative	10. resources
11. environmental	11. culture	11. adjustment
12. incremental	12. relationship	12. capacity

Examples: (A-10) sequential; (B-1) involvement; (C-2) activity; (B-4) cognitive; (A-3) developmental; (C-7) approach.

Now that you have the hang of it, enjoy your new status by sprinkling a few common words between the phrases like this:

> Social involvement objectives in today's schools are realized by combining an accelerated development curriculum with professional effectiveness utilization and creative instructional evaluation.

> The motivation of interdependent activity in an environmental adjustment culture is not easy when one takes into account the perceptual maturation processes of the individual.

> The utilization of instructional guidance resources will enable students to employ a sequential orientation approach to social integration.

After you have mastered this creative incremental approach to educationalese, you will realize that happiness is social effectiveness through concept articulation. Infectious, isn't it?

Classifying Goals and Objectives _____

Educational goals inherently reflect to some degree a philosophical position of the writer. Each objective reflects the philosophical, sociological, and cultural peculiarities of the writer and the immediate school community of which he or she is a part.

The statement of goals leads to general or broad objectives that are more specific than the goal statements, but still stated in broad terms.

Finally, specific behaviorally stated objectives evolve from the goals and general objectives. Activities or strategies and a means of evaluation are included in statements of behavioral objectives. The process found in development of all school programs is illustrated as follows: Philosophy———→Goals———→Broad Objectives———→Specific Objectives.

Learning objectives should be designed at more than one single level of operation. Table 4.1 illustrates three levels—Level I, Level II, and Level III.

Level I objectives are stated in very general terms. They are usually found at the system level. Those responsible for writing Level I objectives sometimes refer to them as purposes or goals. These statements are found in school board publications, district publications, and at state levels. An example of a goal statement is found in the following resolution of the West Virginia Board of Education:

RESOLUTION

Resolution Identifying the Teaching
of Reading as the Highest Curricular
and Instructional Priority in the
Schools of West Virginia

WHEREAS, The West Virginia Board of Education adopted seventeen (17) Education Goals for West Virginia on February 14, 1975, which give the highest priority to the mastery of skills needed for reading, writing, speaking, perceiving, and using numbers; and

WHEREAS, In order to eliminate functional illiteracy which stands at approximately 20% of the adult population over sixteen years of age; and

WHEREAS, Efficiency in reading and the communication skills is the basic prerequisite for school achievement and for becoming an informed, productive, and active participant in our culture and society; and

WHEREAS, There currently exists a strong interest among professional educators and parents in the State of West Virginia in increasing both time and resources that are devoted to the teaching of reading and the other basic communication skills;

BE IT THEREFORE RESOLVED THAT, Beginning January 1, 1976, the teaching of reading shall become the highest priority in the curriculum of the schools in West Virginia. The West Virginia Department of Education, working cooperatively with both local and regional educational agencies, shall begin immediately to pursue a plan for implementing curricular and instructional practices which concentrate on reading and the other basic communication skills, for providing programs to be utilized by parents to become knowledgeable regarding the reading development of children, for enabling teachers and prospective teachers to improve their skills in the teaching of reading, and for providing for the assessment and evaluation of reading achievement in the schools of West Virginia.

BE IT FURTHER RESOLVED THAT, County boards of education be encouraged to adopt this or similar resolutions declaring the teaching of reading and the other basic communication skills to be the highest curricular and instructional priority beginning January 1, 1976, and that the necessary resources be committed to a plan to implement this resolution.

Level I objectives should be accompanied by a related and complementary policy statement. The West Virginia statement describes how the teaching of reading is to be met and upon whom the various responsibilities fall. Generally, a statement about how the educational program is to be evaluated is included.

Level II objectives are stated in broad or general terms, but are somewhat more specific than Level I statements. They are, however not behaviorally stated as in the case of Level III learning objectives. Level II objectives support Level I objectives. They reflect the same philosophy and are directed toward the realization of the Level I goals or purposes.

Level III objectives are found at the classroom level and are behaviorally stated. These specific objectives support Level II and Level I objectives.

Behavioral objectives are statements describing what the learner is doing when he or she is learning. Teachers need to describe the desired behaviors well enough to preclude misinterpretation. Thus, the key to writing successful objectives is to use action verbs to describe specific behaviors. Words such as "knowing" and "understanding" are

Table 4.1
The Relationships Between Levels I, II, and III Learning Objectives

Level of Objective	Type	Origin	Features
Level I	Broad goals or purposes	Formulated at district level by councils or school board	Seldom revised
Level II	General but more specific than Level I	Formulated at school or department level	Contains an outline of process to accomplish Level I objectives
Level III	Behaviorally stated	Formulated by teams of teachers or single teacher	Describe expected outcome, evidence for assessing outcome, and level of performance

not explicit enough to describe what the learner is doing to demonstrate learning.

An acceptable objective lets the student know what is expected of the learner. It also enables the teacher to measure the effectiveness of his or her own work.

Behaviorally stated objectives contain essential elements:

1. The terminal behavior must be identified by name. An observable action must be named that shows that learning has taken place.
2. The important conditions under which the behavior is expected to occur should be described.
3. The criteria of acceptable performance should be specified.

A simple method of developing a complete behavioral objective is to apply the A, B, C, D rule. "A" stands for the audience, "B" for the behavior, "C" for the condition, and "D" the degree of completion. A behavioral objective containing all of these elements will be a complete objective.

The advocacy of behavioral objectives by those seeking to clarify educational purposes has met resistance from those who believe describing learner outcomes in this fashion is too simplistic and ignores the interrelatedness of human activity.

In the rush to write clear, precise statements, teachers often chose simple objectives that required little thinking on the part of their students. Those teachers actually were writing objectives in the lowest levels of cognitive behavior. Through inservice training, teachers can master the skill of writing objectives requiring higher forms of thinking on the part of their students. In addition, teachers should write objectives leading to affective and psychomotor behaviors.

The three taxonomies of educational objectives are best illustrated in Tables 4.2, 4.3, and 4.4.

Taxonomies are classification schemes developed by educators to define educational goals. The reader is especially encouraged to review the following three sources for a detailed discussion of the three taxonomy schemes.

> Benjamin S. Bloom, ed., *Taxonomy of Educational Objectives, The Classification of Educational Goals—Handbook I: Cognitive Domain* (New York: David McKay Company, Inc., 1956).
>
> David Krathwohl, Benjamin Bloom, and Bertram Masia, *Taxonomy of Educational Objectives, The Classification of Educational Goals—Handbook II: Affective Domain* (New York: David McKay Company, Inc., 1964).
>
> Anita J. Harrow, *A Taxonomy of the Psychomotor Domain—A Guide for Developing Behavioral Objectives* (New York: David McKay Company, Inc., 1972).

Table 4.2
Levels of Cognitive Behavior

	Comprehension (ability to comprehend what is being communicated and make use of the idea without relating it to other ideas or material or seeing fullest meaning)	Application (ability to use ideas, principles, theories in new particular and concentrated situations)	Analysis (ability to break down a communication into constituent parts in order to make organization of the whole clear)	Synthesis (ability to put together parts and elements into a unified organization or whole)	Evaluation (ability to judge the value of ideas, procedures, methods, using appropriate criteria)
Knowledge (ability to recall; to bring to mind the appropriate material)	Requires knowledge	Requires knowledge	Requires knowledge	Requires knowledge	Requires knowledge
Comprehension		Requires comprehension	Requires comprehension	Requires comprehension	Requires comprehension
Application			Requires application	Requires application	Requires application
Analysis				Requires analysis	Requires analysis
Synthesis					Requires synthesis

Source: From *TAXONOMY OF EDUCATIONAL OBJECTIVES: The Classification of Educational Goals: HANDBOOK I: COGNITIVE DOMAIN* by Benjamin S. Bloom et al. Copyright © 1956 by Longman Inc. Reprinted by permission of Longman Inc., New York.

Table 4.3
Levels of Affective Behavior

	Receiving	Responding	Valuing	Organization	Characterization
	(attending; becomes aware of an idea, process, or thing; is willing to notice a particular phenomenon)	(makes response at first with compliance, later willingly and with satisfaction)	(accepts worth of a thing, an idea or a behavior; prefers it; consistent in responding; develops a commitment to it)	(organizes values; determines inter-relationships; adapts behavior to value system)	(generalizes certain values into controlling tendencies; emphasis on internal consistency; later integrates these into a total philosophy of life or world view)
					Requires organization of values
				Requires development of values	Requires development of values
			Requires a response	Requires a response	Requires a response
		Begins with attending	Begins with attending	Begins with attending	Begins with attending

Source: From *TAXONOMY OF EDUCATIONAL OBJECTIVES: The Classification of Educational Goals: HANDBOOK 2: AFFECTIVE DOMAIN* by David R. Krathwohl et al. Copyright © 1964 by Longman Inc. Reprinted by permission of Longman Inc., New York.

Table 4.4
Levels of Psychomotor Behavior

Observing	Imitating	Practicing	Adapting
(watches process; pays attention to steps or techniques and to finished product or behavior; may read directions)	(follows directions; carries out steps with conscious awareness of efforts, performs hesitantly)	(repeats steps until some or all aspects of process become habitual, requiring little conscious effort, performs smoothly)	(makes individual modifications and adaptations in the process to suit the worker and/or the situation)
	Requires observation, or reading of directions	Requires imitation	Requires practice
		Requires observation, or reading of directions	Requires imitation
			Requires observation, or reading of directions

Source: From *A Taxonomy of the Psychomotor Domain: A Guide for Developing Behavior Objectives* by Anita J. Harrow. Copyright © 1972 by Longman Inc. Reprinted with permission of Longman.

If we are committed to identifying valued learning outcomes that reflect the "holistic" nature of individuals, then we must insist that goal statements, whether found in state departments or classrooms, reflect a balance of objectives in all three domains of behavior.

Relating Goals and Objectives to Curriculum Development

Anyone familiar with curriculum documents is probably aware that there is a discrepancy between curriculum planned and curriculum implemented. Curriculum workers using curriculum materials know that statements of goals and objectives accompanying those materials are not always reflected in the curriculum as it becomes operative in the classroom. Since most curriculum development projects are cooperative endeavors involving people, it is sad that goals and objectives of curriculum documents are not reflected in classroom practice. Such a condition often reveals the absence of a knowledgeable curriculum specialist on the scene.

The authors are concerned about a general reluctance on the part of curriculum leaders to come to grips with the various existing processes and influences that shape and decidedly determine the final curriculum programs in our schools. It is the position of the authors that until these variables in the political realm of education are acknowledged and confronted openly, curriculum theory will continue to be superfluous to practice and curriculum development will continue to be a largely unpredictable phenomenon characterized by an ever-present gap between theory and practice.

The Behavioral Objective

Following the development of goals and general descriptors of direction, long-range planning requires the specification of objectives that will guide the creation of school programs. Objectives are written operational statements which describe the desired outcome of an educational program. Without such objectives, the translation of general goals into programs is likely to be haphazard.

The objectives developed by a school district should be derived from existing goal statements. If objectives are developed that do not directly relate to a goal area, they may suggest goals which need to be addressed by the district. The major purpose of identifying objectives, from a planning perspective, is so that the population to be served, timing, and expected outcomes can be managed and evaluated.

Many school districts become "bogged down" in an attempt to translate goals into objectives due to the behavioral aspect of stating objectives. In general, objectives attempt to communicate to a specific group the expected outcomes of some unit of instruction. When such objectives are stated in behavioral terms, identifying both the capability learned and the performance the capability makes possible, the process can become mechanical and sometimes threatens individualized programs. If the emphasis of the school program is on experiencing rather than on being able to exhibit behaviors, such specificity may be altogether inappropriate for curriculum planning. Advantages of using behavioral objectives:

1. Helps to identify the specific behaviors to be changed.
2. Increases interschool and intraschool communication.
3. Directs instructional activities in the classroom.
4. Provides a meaningful basis for evaluation.

Disadvantages of using behavioral objectives:

1. Is sometimes simplistic; human behavior is more than the sum of the parts.
2. Behavioral objectives disregard the interrelatedness of human activity.
3. Often will limit choice, remove or prohibit alternatives.
4. In the classroom can limit concomitant learning.

In terms of working through understandings about a desired educational program, it is believed that general or conceptual descriptors can serve as planning objectives. School districts may, however, wish to pursue instructional objectives which are behaviorally stated, and many guides are available to assist such a task. Examples of planning objectives in the area of science are shown below:

Have scientific observation and description skills
a. Observe and identify phenomena, objects, and their properties.
b. Observe and identify changes in physical and biological objects.
c. Order a series of observations.
Have scientific hypothesis formation skills
a. Distinguish among hypothesis, prediction, inference, and opinion.
b. Formulate a simple hypothesis, and give explanations for various phenomena on the basis of known information and observations.
Understand the content and concepts of advanced science
a. Understand concepts about the life of man.
b. Understand the concepts relating to physical science.
c. Understand the concepts relating to ecology.

Curriculum Mapping

A final step in sorting out the objectives of a school program is a curriculum mapping process illustrated in Figure 4.1. In this process, major concepts, general and specific learning skills, and subject matter content are identified for each grade level. In performing this critical step, school planners can gain an oversight of what is intended in each subject at each grade level. Such subject matter intentions can be checked against the more general goals and objectives for education to determine relevance.*

There are two major benefits in this mapping process which connects goals and objectives to programs. First, by viewing the intentions for students in totality, school planners can often identify redundancy in both the scope (breadth) and the sequence (order) of the general curriculum. Second, such an overview can help planners see commonality among parts of the curriculum. Understanding the interrelatedness of the curriculum can have payoff in both instructional coordination and in a maximum utilization of district resources.

Once objectives have been generated for each desired goal and placed in a format that allows a review of the total blueprint for educating students in the district, it is necessary to identify program concepts which will give form to instruction. Program concepts are, in essence, sets of instructional and organizational strategies that are philosophically based.

The program concept phase of curriculum development is perhaps the most difficult step in building school programs. Although the need is to develop programs that are compatible with the district philosophy; there is always a tendency to return to what is familiar to us. Hence, the conceptual objectives often end up being translated into school programs with standard characteristics such as a textbook-dominated six-period day. At this stage, the educational philosophy adopted before specific objectives were developed can assist in answering the question of how to best teach to achieve the desired ends.

Schools and school districts differ tremendously in how they interact with students to accomplish desired goals and objectives. Generally speaking, however, schools vary according to how much structure they demand in the instructional program (see chapter 3). Structure, as opposed to flexibility in instructional organization, is a reflection of the anticipated conciseness of the desired outcomes. School districts that desire highly predictable outcomes for all students who experience their program should not encourage instructional flexibility, for each variable encourages diversity of outcome.

In schools where there is a philosophy focusing on the student as an individual, there is a wider choice for instructional patterns. The program concept, when translated into instructional arrangements indicates to school planners how desired outcomes should be approached.

---

*It is also possible to do a time analysis of content by this mapping process. See Fenwick English, *Quality Control in Curriculum Development* (Arlington, Virginia: American Association of School Administrators, 1978), pp. 35–45.

In the following example, a school district identifies seven concepts that are felt to reinforce their desire to develop a program focused on the individual child.

Philosophy Statement. We desire in each school, kindergarten through adult education, a program that will focus on the individual student to provide learning experiences in the affective, cognitive, and psychomotor areas.

Program Concepts

1. A program of individualized instruction will be implemented.
2. A basic diagnostic-prescriptive approach to teaching will be utilized.
3. A variety of materials, both commercial and teacher-made, will be used.
4. A flexible schedule will be implemented.
5. Instructional assistants will perform teaching, planning, and clerical tasks.
6. Instructional leaders (teachers) will serve as facilitators of program planning and implementation.
7. A facility that provides as much flexibility in programming as possible will be promoted.

In summary, there is a planning "flow" from philosophy to goals to objectives. Within this sequence of logic there should be consistency; if we believe this, then our objectives should be thus and so.

A final step prior to actually designing and implementing the learning experiences for students is the needs assessment. The needs assessment provides planning data about the target of our efforts and often suggests the methodology of our instructional plan.

The Needs Assessment

Basic to all curriculum development is an assessment of present conditions. The needs assessment technique represents a comprehensive inquiry into the educational status of a school district and starts with the avowed goals for education. The major intent of a needs assessment is to determine the degree to which a school district is implementing a stated philosophy of education and the degree to which goals are being met by existing programs.

Where possible, the needs assessment utilizes the most objective methods possible of data collection and analysis. The type and quality of data available, and the time available for collecting and processing data will place limits on the scope of the study, the number and types of instruments used, and the statistical procedures applied. Unlike the

Figure 4.1 Curriculum Mapping in the Sixth Grade

Content	Concepts	Skills	(Skills Cont.)
American Neighbors ___ Canada ___ Mexico and Central America ___ South America (choose one country from both Central and South America) *Europe* ___ Eastern Europe ___ Western Europe (choose at least one country from each) *Non-Western* ___ China, Japan, or India ___ The Middle East	*Culture* ___ Physical Environment (geography, resources) ___ Art, Music, Dance ___ Cultural Environment (food, clothing, shelter) ___ Social Structure ___ History (political, archaeological, anthropological) ___ Technology ___ Values, Beliefs, Religion *Conflict* ___ Ideological ___ Social ___ Economic *Rights and Responsibilities* (Government, Law) *Change* ___ Urbanization ___ Physical Environment ___ Technological ___ Social ___ Political	*Reading* ___ Analyzing and evaluating information by interpreting pictures, graphs, and tables ___ Drawing conclusions, separating relevant from unrelated idea ___ Vocabulary ___ Recognizing terms ___ Application of terms ___ Skimming and summarizing ___ Placing related events in chronological order ___ Developing numerical chronology ___ Recognizing geographical facts ___ Recalling facts *Writing* ___ Creative Writing ___ Recognizing main ideas ___ Selecting facts and ideas	*Geographical* ___ Reading maps and globes ___ Using a map key ___ Making maps, charts, graphs, etc. ___ Map types ___ Classifying map chronology ___ Using an atlas ___ Using a world almanac ___ Using parallels and meridians *Discussion* ___ Leading ___ Supporting others' views ___ Clarifying ___ Summarizing ___ Evaluating ___ Drawing conclusions ___ Debating ___ Listening *Speaking* ___ Voice projection ___ Argumentation ___ Concluding

_____ Cultural
_____ Economic

Cooperation
_____ Cultural
_____ Economic
_____ Political (alliances, treaties)
_____ Scientific

Scarcity
_____ Money
_____ Natural Resources
_____ Production

Power and Authority
_____ Military
_____ Economic
_____ Political
_____ Social

Competition
_____ Economic
_____ Technological
_____ Recreational
_____ Political
_____ Cultural

_____ Using an introduction
_____ Using a topical listing

Essay Writing
_____ Main ideas
_____ Grouping related ideas
_____ Notetaking
_____ Making outlines
_____ Making bibliographies

Thinking
_____ Problem-Solving
_____ Analyzing
_____ Hypothesizing
_____ Classifying information
_____ Sequencing events
(cont. next column)

_____ Interviewing skills
_____ Answering
_____ Questioning
_____ Extemporaneous

Interpersonal Relations and Group Participation
_____ Leading and identifying leaders
_____ Problem-solving
_____ Supporting others' views
_____ Building on others' ideas
_____ Completing tasks
_____ Evaluating
_____ Taking turns
_____ Seeing rights as a majority rule principle
_____ Comparing problems from previous experiences
_____ Suggesting solutions
_____ Giving and accepting criticisms
_____ Listening to others

Affective
_____ Clarifying values
_____ Understanding/tolerating others
_____ Choosing friendships
_____ Responding to authority

accreditation review and the school survey, a needs assessment will always be somewhat subjective in nature, incorporating in a purposeful manner the perceptions of students, parents, and educators.

Needs assessments presuppose a commitment to maximum involvement of the school community. The plan provides for the collection of data from parents, students, and school personnel, and for the review of data by representatives from each group. This involvement process utilizes an important factor in the educational validity of needs assessment data—an attitude of "ownership" on the part of the school community.

The needs assessment represents a critical step toward the development of a curriculum management plan (see chapter seven) because it reduces a philosophy of educating to decision-making data used in planning. The willingness of a school district to identify its deficiencies and select its goals in full view of public scrutiny paves the way for rational and orderly program development in the future.

The Needs Assessment Framework _____

The conduct of a needs assessment in a school district is flexible. The dimensions of school operations considered and the data to be gathered are dependent on the mandate for change in the district and the openness and honesty of those initiating such assessment. In general, however, it is possible to identify the primary needs assessment framework that supplies critical planning data to a school district. The following outline represents a typical needs assessment approach:

I.   General Information
    a.   Location of school district
    b.   Demographic characteristics of immediate area
    c.   Natural resources of region
    d.   Commercial—industrial data
    e.   Income levels of area residents
    f.   Special social-economic considerations

II.   General Population Characteristics
    a.   Population growth patterns
    b.   Age, race of population
    c.   Educational levels of population
    d.   Projected population

III.   School Population Characteristics (Ages 3–19)
    a.   School enrollment by grade level
    b.   Birth rate trends in school district
    c.   In-migration, out-migration patterns
    d.   Race/sex/religious composition of school district
    e.   Years of school completed by persons over 25 years of age
    f.   Studies of school dropouts

Figure 4.2 Some Symptoms of School Problems

1. Improvement of Basic Academic Achievement

( ) Pupils perform below real ability.
( ) Students not prepared for grade level.
( ) Students consider curriculum irrelevant.
( ) Instructional materials are too difficult.
( ) Advanced course offerings not available in some subjects.
( ) Low standardized test scores.
( ) Students do poorly on daily work.
( ) Graduates seem unprepared for job market or higher education.
( ) High rate of student failure.
( ) Students cannot apply basic skills.

2. Continued Commitment to Reduction of Racial Isolation

( ) Student polarization along racial lines.
( ) Division among faculty along racial lines.
( ) Student-teacher antagonism along racial lines.
( ) Racially-motivated hostility in the community.
( ) Unequal status roles for minorities in curriculum materials.
( ) Transported students feel unwelcome.
( ) Racial groups establish certain areas of the school as their "territory."
( ) School lacks unified approach to reducing racial isolation.
( ) Parents of transported students are not involved in the school.
( ) Avoidance of problem situation by school personnel.

3. Improvement in Staff Attendance and Continued Upgrading of Staff Performance

A. *Attendance*
( ) Frequent staff absences.
( ) Habitual staff tardiness.
( ) Patterns of staff absences and tardiness.

B. *Performance*
( ) Low expectations for student achievement and behavior.
( ) Apparent lack of productive teaching techniques and methods.
( ) Instruction not geared to student needs.
( ) Resistance to progressive change and professional growth.
( ) Learning experiences seem passive.
( ) Lack of positive learning environment.
( ) Poor classroom management.
( ) Lack of staff cooperative effort.

4. Improvement in School Morale and Community Relations

A. *School Morale*
( ) School administration viewed as cold and detached from student concerns.
( ) Administrator and staff feel isolated, lack of mutual support.
( ) Low status of some subject areas in teacher's view.
( ) Extensive vandalism.

Figure 4.2 (continued)

( ) Negative student attitude toward learning.
( ) Students are uninvolved, unmotivated.
( ) Lack of harmonious staff relationships.

B. *Community Relations*
( ) Inadequate efforts to involve students in community, or the opposite.
( ) Lack of parent interest.
( ) Lack of teacher involvement in the community served by the school.
( ) Principals and teachers do not try to involve parents and community in the school program.
( ) Lack of communication between school and community.

5. **Student Attendance, Behavior, and Discipline**

A. *Attendance*
( ) Frequent truancy.
( ) Frequent tardiness.
( ) Frequent class-cutting.
( ) High absentee rate.
( ) High dropout rate.
( ) High rate of student mobility.

B. *Behavior and Discipline*
( ) Vandalism.
( ) Violence.
( ) Disruptive classroom behavior.
( ) Students' use of illegal drugs.
( ) Disruptive behavior on campus or playground.
( ) Frequent referrals of students to office for disciplinary action.
( ) Disruption caused by outsiders.
( ) Excessive noise level and confusion throughout the school.
( ) Disrespect for authority.

IV.   Programs and Course Offerings in District
    a.   Organization of school programs
    b.   Programs' concept and rationale
    c.   Course offerings
    d.   Special program needs
V.   Professional Staff
    a.   Training and experience
    b.   Awareness of trends and developments
    c.   Attitudes toward change
VI.   Instructional Patterns and Strategies
    a.   Philosophical focus of instructional program
    b.   Observational and perceptual instructional data
    c.   Assessment of instructional strategies in use
    d.   Instructional materials in use
    e.   Decision-making and planning processes
    f.   Grouping for instruction

Conducting the Needs Assessment

Using a needs assessment pattern to gather data essential to curriculum planning is advantageous in that most of the process is carried out by the people closest to the subject of study. While accreditation studies and formal school surveys usually use "expert" opinion to judge or evaluate the school district, a needs assessment format enables such districts to use parents, teachers, and students in the same process. The key to understanding this distinction is to be found in the idea that needs assessments address relative progress toward goals rather than absolute conditions. The emphasis in a needs assessment is not so much on what presently exists, but rather on what the present condition is compared to identified goals and objectives.

Usually, needs assessments are initiated because it is believed that present conditions in a school district can be improved upon. Such a position sees curriculum development as a continuum, and the needs assessment is begun to gain clarity of direction.

The first step of a needs assessment is to decide what data are needed for decision-making, and to develop a strategy for data gathering. A typical needs assessment in a school district will utilize citizens groups or study teams comprised of a mixture of persons from the school community. Sometimes such teams are formed by schools or according to school level, but it is often of benefit to have the teams study areas such as student achievement or facilities vertically through all grade levels. The following are some guidelines for teams organized according to the outline presented earlier.

General Information

It is important that any needs assessment be put in perspective so that findings of such a study will have meaning to the particular community under review. Each of the more than 14,000 school districts in the United States have different and significant variables that affect the type of schools which can be planned. Failure to understand these situational variables or to put findings into an appropriate context can lead to misunderstanding and, sometimes, to false aspirations.

A needs assessment should include an accurate but brief description of the school district setting. The size of the district, its population, and the natural resources that might affect school operation should be included. So, too, should information about local commerce and industry which may indicate the tax support for schools in the area as well as the relative wealth of the parents of schoolchildren.

Special social or economic conditions in an area should also be noted. For instance, if a nearby military base is served by the district, or if there is a seasonal migrant population to plan for, it is important that these variables be acknowledged.

General data about the community, regardless of location, is available in public libraries in standard census reports. Current information dating from the last census data can generally be gained from the local chamber of commerce.

General Population Characteristics

In gathering information about the people who inhabit the area served by the school district, there is an attempt to understand the educational and cultural levels of the community, general attitudes about schools, and expectations for education in the area.

Some of the most important information to be gathered about the people who are served by the school district is that which indicates the cultural heritage and set of traditions in the community. In areas where populations are stable, both in terms of turnover and composition, there is usually minimal social or cultural change. Because schools tend to reflect the communities they serve, one would expect to find a comparable stability in school data. In communities that have experienced considerable growth or turnover of population, however, school planning data tend to be more varied and expectations for change in the schools increased.

Along with information about population changes, data about economic development in the community will often indicate anticipated population changes which will affect schools. The closing of key industries, declining farm populations, closing of military bases, or seasonal industries can signal new patterns for school districts. Out-migration of urban population, regional economic prosperity, or the development of new industries based on natural resources can also affect school planning.

In looking at the composition of the population to be served, a number of variables are important indicators for school planners. Birth rate projections, population stability patterns, racial and economic composition, and special social and cultural characteristics such as languages spoken or national origin of parents all have planning implications for school leaders.

Another influential variable to assess in a formal needs assessment is the educational level of parents and persons in the community over twenty-five years of age. Data about the educational achievement levels of the community will often indicate the amount of belief in, and support for, education. Knowledge of such a factor can also help planners to develop strategies for a school bond election, elect school officials, or initiate a new school program in the community.

School Population Characteristics ⎯⎯⎯⎯⎯⎯⎯⎯⎯

The 1980s are a decade in which most school districts in the United States have experienced a steady or declining enrollment. This natural phenomenon is of vital importance to school planners for two reasons: (1) school enrollment is the basis of program funding in most school districts, and (2) enrollment changes may indicate a change in the type of population being served by the school program.

Among the most stable and useful data available to school planners are birth rate trends in the district and school enrollment patterns by grade level. With high consistency, school planners can anticipate enrollment in schools and within grade levels in schools. Closer analysis of population increases and declines within schools can even provide information about dropout and retention patterns, as well as alert school planners to new populations of students who must be accommodated by the curriculum. Up-to-date information about birth rates is usually available through county records, while data about grade level enrollment are readily available through school attendance records in most districts.

The racial, ethnic, religious, and sexual composition of a school district is also important to school planners. Due to the mobility of populations within the United States today, primary characteristics of communities can change rapidly, and with such change, cause an alteration in the purpose of education in the district. Often, school districts will offer curriculum programs for the populations who lived in the community twenty-five years earlier.

Perhaps the most important planning data that can be gained from an assessment of the school age population is the information that deals with dropouts. Most school districts in the United States have an alarming number of students who, for a variety of reasons, terminate their schooling (shown in Table 4.5). The community and the school system should be particularly concerned by students who walk out of school never to return by personal choice. Not only can such an exodus indicate that something is lacking in the general school program, but dropouts present the community with a social problem rarely understood.

Students who quit school prior to graduation are usually faced with employment difficulties, limited job opportunities, low earning

Table 4.5
Sample Dropout Grid

Year	Number of Dropouts	Number 16 Years and Older	Dropout Percentage
1978–79	34	258	13%
1979–80	38	253	15
1980–81	44	239	18
1981–82	30	234	13
1982–83	48	277	17
Total	194	1,261	15

power, lessened opportunity for promotions, and emotional stress from social and cultural pressures. These realities for the dropout often translate into social problems for the community which find form in greater need for law enforcement, mental health services, welfare assistance, and public works projects. To accept a high dropout rate as a normal occurrence in schooling is shortsighted indeed.

Studies of dropouts often provide school planners with a profile of students not benefiting from existing school programs. Causation factors such as the need to work, home problems, pregnancy, or poor scholarship can indicate to planners those areas of the curriculum in need of review and renewal.

Without question, the single leading cause of school dropouts is academic failure.* Included in this broad category are students who lack interest in school, students who rebel against failure and are expelled, students who choose less threatening environments in which to interact, and students who are incapable of competing with other students. School districts that have a substantial number of dropouts must decide where the fine balance between academic excellence and social conscience resides.

Data about dropouts are often available through school attendance records, while follow-up data are easily obtained from social agencies in the community. A valuable technique in assessing the school dropout is the interview.

Programs and Course Offerings

The general scope and depth of an educational program can be best identified by reviewing the number and types of courses and special activities offered by individual schools. Of importance in understanding the programs of a school district are the organization of school programs, the rationale for such organization, the breadth and scope

*While school records show academic failure to be the leading cause of school dropouts, the relationship is considerably more complex. The cause of dropping out of school may vary with age, sex, race, social background, etc.

of course offerings, and the degree to which special education needs are met.

Many school districts conceptualize schooling according to levels of attainment and reference programs such as primary school, elementary school, middle school, and high school. In such an organization, students advance through the program by grades rather than by age, maturation, achievement, readiness, or interest.

In such programs, content and skill development are dominant organizers; there is little consideration for individual differences, and curriculum planning focuses on the sequencing of experiences. Such programs are usually organized in quantitative units with teachers, students, classrooms, and textbooks assigned by a predetermined formula. Supplemental activities, enrichment experiences, and student services are added to the core program as resources allow.

Some school districts perceive schooling as an evolution of development (as shown in Table 4.6) with school organization acting to facilitate passage through a predetermined development profile. In such districts, grade lines are not as clearly drawn, and district resources are applied as necessary for successful completion of the pattern.

Still other school districts focus on the individual learner and provide experiences thought beneficial to all learners. In such educational programs, expectations for performance are less uniform and structure is less rigid.

Perhaps less important than the actual organization in a needs assessment is the rationale of the school district for the schooling pattern that exists. Needs assessments analyze school programs in nonjudgmental ways according to how well they are accomplishing their stated objectives. Such objectives can often be found in formal philosophies or statements of purpose. Where such official documents are absent, the purpose of schooling can be inferred by those assessing the district with opportunity for reaction from school leaders.

Regardless of the avowed purpose of schooling and the primary organization of the educational program, the heart of the assessment process should address the course offerings and experiences had by the students. Most school districts in the United States, because of history and state and local requirements, arrange school into subject areas. Nearly all schools provide a core of activities that includes mathematics, science, English, and social studies. Most districts also provide supplemental programs in physical education, art, music, and vocational arts. Beyond such basic programs, courses and experiences are offered that reflect the capacity of the district to address individual differences. Often, the degree to which a school district "tailors" such offerings is an indication of the awareness of school leaders of the needs of students.

In recent years, due to research and legislation, school districts in the United States have become sensitive to the needs of special groups

Table 4.6
Developmental Profile

DEVELOPMENTAL PROFILE

Santa Clara Inventory
of
Developmental Tasks

Name _____   Birthdate _____

School _____ Teacher _____ Grade ____

Testing Dates: Scoring:

C.D. _____

L.D. _____

A.M. _____

A.P. _____

V.M. _____

V.P. _____

V.M.P. _____

M.C. _____

0 — Almost never

1 — Some of the time

2 — Most of the time

												Auditory Memory			
												0	1	2	
									Auditory Perception			discriminate between com. sounds 5-5			
									0	1	2	0	1	2	
						Visual Memory			recall animal pictures 4-4			name objects from memory 4-5			
						0	1	2	0	1	2	0	1	2	
			Visual Perception			match color objects 3-3			match form objects 3-4			match size objects 3-5			
			0	1	2	0	1	2	0	1	2	0	1	2	
Visual Motor Performance			follow target with eyes 2-2			string beads 2-3			copy a circle 2-4			copy a cross 2-5			
0	1	2	0	1	2	0	1	2	0	1	2	0	1	2	
Motor Coordination creep 1-1			walk 1-2			run 1-3			jump 1-4			hop 1-5			

PRE-SCHOOL

Table 4.6
(continued)

DIRECTIONS TO THE TEACHER: This is the record form on which each child's performance is recorded. The column for Testing Dates allows the teacher to measure each category up to three times; however, if the student exhibits mastery when first observed, only one date is entered. The abbreviations mean: M.C. — Motor Coordination, V.M.P. — Visual Motor Performance, V.P. — Visual Perception, V.M. — Visual Motor, A.P. — Auditory Perception, A.M. — Auditory Memory, L.D. — Language Development, C.D. — Conceptual Development. The scoring criteria for each task are listed in the Observation Guide.

	0 1 2	0 1 2	0 1 2	0 1 2	0 1 2	0 1 2
Conceptual Development	assign number value 8-8	identify first, last, top, middle, bottom 8-9	tell how 2 items are alike 8-10	sort objects 2 ways 8-11		
Language Development	give personal information 7-7	describe simple objects 7-8	relate words and pictures 7-9	define words 7-10	language usage 7-11	
	perform 3 commands 6-6	repeat a sentence 6-7	repeat a tapping sequence 6-8	repeat 4 numbers 6-9	recall story facts 6-10	repeat 5 numbers 6-11
	identify common sounds 5-6	locate source of sound 5-7	match beginning sounds 5-8	hear fine diff. between similar words 5-9	match rhyming sounds 5-10	match ending sounds 5-11
	recall a 3-color sequence 4-6	recall 2 items in a sequence 4-7	reproduce design from memory 4-8	recall 3 items in a sequence 4-9	recall 3-part design 4-10	recall word forms 4-11
	match size and form on paper 3-6	match numbers 3-7	match letters 3-8	match direction on design 3-9	isolate visual images 3-10	match words 3-11
	copy a square 2-6	cut with scissors 2-7	tie shoes 2-8	copy letters 2-9	copy a sentence 2-10	copy a diamond 2-11
	balance on one foot 1-6	use of hands and arms 1-7	skip 1-8	balance on walking beam 1-9	jump rope assisted 1-10	jump rope unassisted 1-11
	5-5½ YRS.		**6-6½ YRS.**		**7 YRS.**	

of students found in the school. While a list af all such special students would be lengthy, addressing programs to serve special education, career education, and adult education can illuminate course offerings outside of the general curriculum.

In every community there are children and youth who have special educational needs that cannot be met within the operation of the general program of instruction. There are many definitions of students with special needs in existence, and most include those children with emotional, physical, communicative, or intellectual deviations which interfere with school adjustment or prevent full attainment of academic achievement. Included in such a broad classification would be the intellectually gifted, the mentally retarded, physically handicapped, speech handicapped, behaviorally disordered, multi-handicapped, homebound, autistic, hospitalized, and visually or hearing impaired. School districts vary in how they organize themselves in order to serve these special learners. Legislation at the national level (Public Law 94-142) has set strong guidelines for "special education" programs which affect about one child in eight. Table 4.7 illustrates how planners might "see" such students needing additional programming in the curriculum.

Career and vocational education is fast becoming a major curriculum component of many school districts in the nation. While the impetus for this trend comes from many sources, career and vocational education still represents the major alternative for secondary school students who choose a non-college preparatory program.

Student interest in vocational programs is generally high among all types of students. The mandate for school districts to provide quality vocational experiences is heightened when it is recognized that the majority of all students graduating from secondary schools do not go on as full-time students in postsecondary institutions.

A valuable resource for those assessing student vocational interests is the *Directory of Occupational Titles* produced by the United States Department of Labor.[2] This directory identifies over 21,000 job titles which may be of interest to students. Using instruments such as the *Ohio Vocational Interest Survey,* areas in which vocational experiences might be developed can be identified. Student questionnaires which seek to pinpoint plans for following graduation can also provide school leaders with rough indicators of need.

A third type of special education program provided by some school districts is adult education. A program for adults will depend on their level of educational attainment, the skills and knowledge needed by adults in the community, and whether interests are occupational or for personal development. School districts can effectively use adult education programs to increase community involvement as well as to build bridges to parents of schoolchildren.

Table 4.7
Students with Special Education Needs

	Elementary School			Middle School			High School			Total		
Year	80–81	81–82	82–83	80–81	81–82	82–83	80–81	81–82	82–83	80–81	81–82	82–83
Educable mentally retarded	24	26	28	26	28	31	20	23	25	70	77	84
Trainable mentally retarded	4	5	7	2	3	4	1	2	3	7	10	14
Behavioral disorders	4	7	8	9	10	12	2	5	6	15	22	26
Visually impaired	0	4	5	0	1	2	0	2	3	0	7	10
Hearing impaired	2	4	5	0	1	2	0	0	1	2	5	8
Speech impaired	18	20	21	16	19	20	0	2	3	34	41	44
Multi-handicapped	1	2	2	1	1	1	0	0	0	2	3	3
Hospital/homebound	5	6	6	3	4	4	2	2	2	10	12	12
Gifted	14	15	15	13	13	13	14	14	14	41	42	42
Learning Disability	15	18	20	30	34	35	31	31	31	76	83	86
									Total	257	302	329

For adults in the community who have less than a high school education, offerings may be geared to meet basic education needs. Such programs often lead to completion of a high school equivalency test. Other adults may be interested in education for job opportunities. Still other adults in the community may participate in education for personal improvement. Popular items are such topics as family-oriented courses, household mechanics, child development courses, and recordkeeping.

Schools providing educational experiences for adults in the community can use questionnaires and other devices to effectively assess needs and interests. The list below is illustrative of the types of offerings regularly requested by adult learners:

Job-Oriented	Personal Development
a. Typing	a. Reading improvement
b. Bookkeeping	b. Arts crafts
c. Shorthand	c. Horticulture
d. Office machines	d. Slimnastics
e. Income tax	e. Self-protection
f. Electric wiring	f. Home improvement
g. Brick masonry	g. Photography
h. Cosmetology	h. Interior decorating
i. Sales clerking	i. Leisure activities
j. Carpentry	j. Basic sewing

The Professional Staff

A thorough needs assessment also reviews the professional staff in the school district. Among primary concerns are the training and experience of teachers, supervisors and administrators, the balance among the various teaching positions, and anticipated staff needs. Also subject to analysis is the awareness of the staff to recent trends and developments in the field as well as attitudes toward change.

A review of staff training often will indicate a dominance of age, race, or sex among school faculties. These patterns are important in terms of the goals of the district and the specific programs being promoted in the buildings. Such an assessment will sometimes reveal an excessive number of graduates from a single university or a pattern of inbreeding among teachers. While the latter situation is sometimes unavoidable in remote regions, a diversity among teaching backgrounds is desirable in terms of the experiences teachers bring to the classroom.

A district-wide assessment of allocated teaching positions will often reveal overstaffing in particular subject areas at the expense of other equally important areas. Such a district-wide review will also indicate trends in staffing that can assist planners in projecting future staffing needs.

An analysis of faculty familiarity with new trends and developments in subject areas, and new innovative concepts, is important if the district anticipates new programs. Such a review can often pinpoint staff development needs that can be addressed in inservice sessions.

Finally, school districts can find extremely useful the analysis of professional staff attitudes toward change in general and toward specific curriculum alterations in particular. Such attitudes are the result of many factors, and experience has shown that age and experience of teachers are poor predictors of readiness to change.

Data for Instructional Planning _____

Instructional Patterns and Strategies

By far the most important segment of a needs assessment in schools is the part that focuses on instructional patterns and strategies. Such teacher behaviors should reflect uniformly the intentions of the district to deliver quality programs to students. The types of instruction found in classrooms should result from an understanding of the goals of the district, and an assessment of strategies and techniques can occur only following a clarification of the district philosophy.

In some districts, the predominant goal of instruction is to have all students master the essential data that will distinguish them as an educated person. Other school districts place greatest emphasis on the needs, interests, and abilities of students. A key distinction in these two extreme positions is the role of the student in the learning process. Since needs assessments tend to utilize subjective perceptual data about schools, they are most useful in districts favoring a student-centered curriculum.

Two major techniques can be used to assess instructional patterns and strategies: the observation technique and the administering of perceptual instruments. The perceptual approach is by far the most common method of reviewing instruction in the needs assessments.

The perceptual data technique, commonly referred to as the opinionnaire, requires the administration of instruments to teachers and, in some cases, students and parents. This perceptual survey is based on findings of phenomenological psychology which holds that people behave in terms of personal meanings which exist for them at a given moment. In short, behavior is based on perception because we behave and react to that which we believe to be real. A personal perception may or may not be supported by facts, but such perceptions serve as facts to each of us.

Perceptual instruments are useful in needs assessments because they possess several distinct advantages. First, they are quick to administer and tally. Second, they are easily managed and are less time-consuming than interviews or quantitative measures. Most important, however, is the fact that such perceptual techniques allow all teachers

in the district to participate in the data-gathering stage. Such involvement is critical if programmatic responses to such findings are to be
credible and supported.

In the example below, school planners wished to learn if teachers
in the district supported a child-centered instructional program in the
middle grades. In order to reduce this philosophical posture to planning data, a needs assessment was administered to some 700 intermediate teachers, as well as to principals and parents.* Figure 4.3 shows
a sample page of the original questionnaire with item 10 asking the
critical question. Figure 4.4 shows the computer printout of responses;
in item 10 approximately 85 percent of teachers responding felt this
item was important. Finally, in Figure 4.5, Teacher Questionnaire
item 10 is reported to the Board as documentation of teacher support
for a child-centered approach in the middle grades. Hence, the needs
assessment has translated philosophy and goals into hard data for
planning analysis.

One such perceptual instrument currently in use is the experimental *Sims-Nallia Inventory of Instructional Strategies.* This instrument
is comprised of sixty-five strategies commonly found in school classrooms (such as individualizing instruction or grouping students by
achievement level). The Sims-Nallia feeds back to teachers a composite
profile of instructional practices in use by all teachers in a percentage
form. Such a "mirror" serves to alert classroom teachers to the practices of others in the district and does so without judgment about the
meaning of the heavily-used practices.

Another instructional pattern worthy of assessment is the use
of materials in the classroom. While most schools utilize textbooks
as a medium for learning, others use a variety of instructional materials and still others attempt to individualize the instructional materials
used by students.

Needs assessments also regularly look at the type of planning and
decision-making that occurs in classrooms and schools. Are students
(and teachers) involved in decisions that affect their learning and
related experiences? Are students (and teachers) involved in the assignment of activities and tasks? The selection of content? The construction of courses?

Needs assessments generally gather data on the types of grouping
patterns found in the school district. Are students grouped for instruction by interest or needs? Are they grouped in classroom settings by
ability or age? Are students' content grouped with each subject being
taught separately? How are decisions about student grouping arrived at?

Classroom management is usually reviewed by a needs assessment. Although all teachers use some system of classroom management, formal or informal, some patterns are more common than others.

*Our thanks to the East Baton Rouge Parish School District for per-
mission to use these needs assessment examples.

Student prescriptions, contracts, tutors, furniture arrangement, classroom rules, and communication patterns are all valuable indicators of the prevailing management system. Sometimes such analysis will reveal problem areas common to many teachers and fertile ground for staff development activities.

Figure 4.3 Middle School Opinionnaire (Principal-Teacher Form A)

Please rate each of the following statements in terms of *their importance to you for the middle school*. Choose the answer that tells how you feel about each one and blacken the bubble below the letter of that choice on the separate computer answer sheet. *Use a Number 2 pencil only.* Use the following key to show your feelings.

A	B	C	D	E
Very Important	Important	Fairly Important	Not Very Important	Not Important At All

1. Specialized guidance and counseling services should be available.

2. Both teachers and counselors should be involved in guidance.

3. Emphasis should be on group guidance.

4. Emphasis should be on individual guidance.

5. Each student should have at least one teacher who knows him/her personally.

6. Each student should meet with that teacher individually.

7. Opportunities for social activities for students (dances, athletic games, boosters, etc.) should be provided.

8. Club activities should be scheduled during the day to provide opportunities for group work in areas of common interest.

9. School-wide opportunities should be provided to help students develop good attitudes and standards for themselves.

10. The middle school program should be more child-centered than subject-matter centered.

11. The middle school program should be a unique program bridging the gap between the elementary schools and the secondary schools.

12. Provisions should be made for students to explore their individual interests through exploratory elective courses.

13. Provisions should be made for short-term exploratory/enrichment activities in addition to the regularly scheduled electives.

14. Behavior problems of students should be handled, when possible, by teachers and parents without the involvement of the administrators.

15. An alternative program to suspension should be provided for students having behavior problems (In-school Suspension Program).

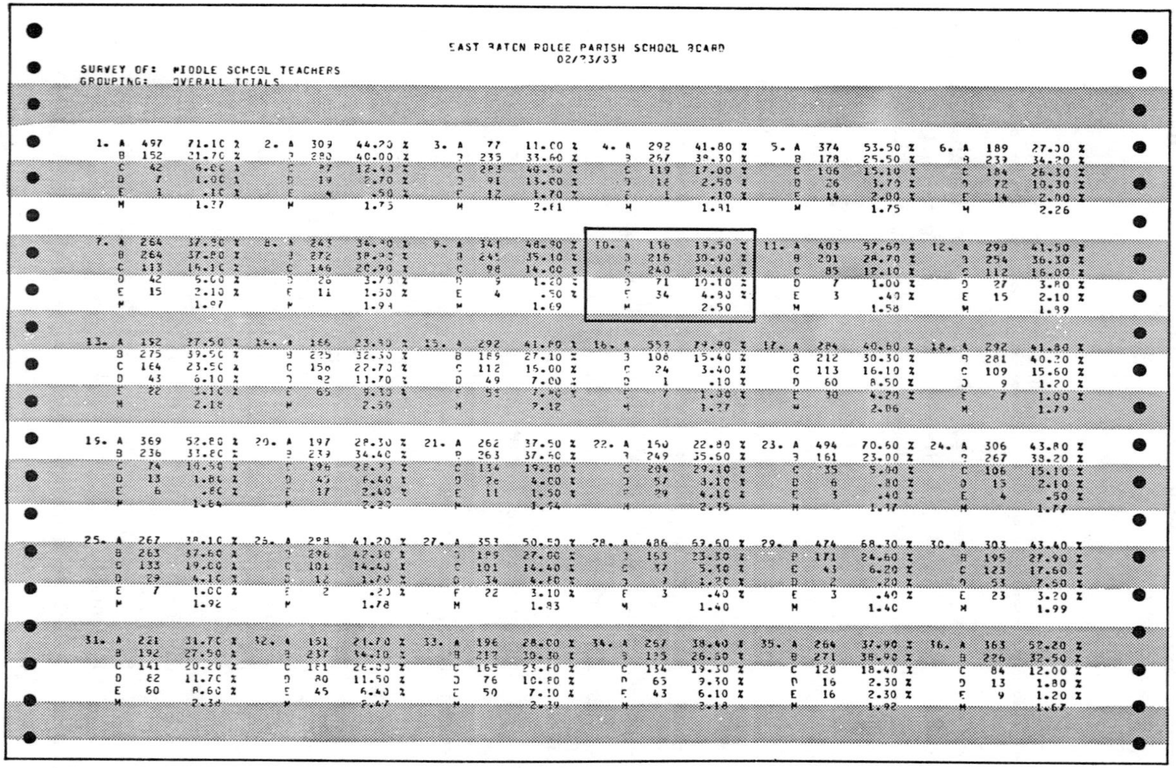

EAST BATON ROUGE PARISH SCHOOL BOARD
02/23/83

SURVEY OF: MIDDLE SCHOOL TEACHERS
GROUPING: OVERALL TOTALS

1.	A	497	71.10 %	2.	A	309	44.20 %	3.	A	77	11.00 %	4.	A	292	41.80 %	5.	A	374	53.50 %	6.	A	189	27.00 %
	B	152	21.70 %		B	280	40.00 %		B	235	33.60 %		B	267	38.30 %		B	178	25.50 %		B	239	34.20 %
	C	42	6.00 %		C	87	12.40 %		C	283	40.50 %		C	119	17.00 %		C	106	15.10 %		C	184	26.30 %
	D	7	1.00 %		D	19	2.70 %		D	91	13.00 %		D	18	2.50 %		D	26	3.70 %		D	72	10.30 %
	E	1	.10 %		E	4	.50 %		E	12	1.70 %		E	1	.10 %		E	14	2.00 %		E	14	2.00 %
	M		1.37		M		1.75		M		2.61		M		1.31		M		1.75		M		2.26
7.	A	264	37.90 %	8.	A	243	34.90 %	9.	A	341	48.90 %	10.	A	136	19.50 %	11.	A	403	57.60 %	12.	A	290	41.50 %
	B	264	37.80 %		B	272	38.90 %		B	245	35.10 %		B	216	30.90 %		B	201	28.70 %		B	254	36.30 %
	C	113	16.10 %		C	146	20.90 %		C	98	14.00 %		C	240	34.40 %		C	85	12.10 %		C	112	16.00 %
	D	42	5.00 %		D	26	3.70 %		D	9	1.20 %		D	71	10.10 %		D	7	1.00 %		D	27	3.80 %
	E	15	2.10 %		E	11	1.50 %		E	4	.50 %		E	34	4.80 %		E	3	.40 %		E	15	2.10 %
	M		1.97		M		1.94		M		1.69		M		2.50		M		1.58		M		1.99
13.	A	192	27.50 %	14.	A	166	23.30 %	15.	A	292	41.80 %	16.	A	559	79.90 %	17.	A	284	40.60 %	18.	A	292	41.80 %
	B	275	39.50 %		B	225	32.30 %		B	189	27.10 %		B	108	15.40 %		B	212	30.30 %		B	281	40.20 %
	C	164	23.50 %		C	156	22.70 %		C	112	15.00 %		C	24	3.40 %		C	113	16.10 %		C	109	15.60 %
	D	43	6.10 %		D	82	11.70 %		D	49	7.00 %		D	1	.10 %		D	60	8.50 %		D	9	1.20 %
	E	22	3.10 %		E	65	9.30 %		E	55	7.80 %		E	7	1.00 %		E	30	4.20 %		E	7	1.00 %
	M		2.18		M		2.39		M		2.12		M		1.27		M		2.06		M		1.79
19.	A	369	52.80 %	20.	A	197	28.30 %	21.	A	262	37.50 %	22.	A	160	22.80 %	23.	A	494	70.60 %	24.	A	306	43.80 %
	B	236	33.80 %		B	239	34.40 %		B	263	37.60 %		B	249	35.60 %		B	161	23.00 %		B	267	38.20 %
	C	74	10.50 %		C	196	28.20 %		C	134	19.10 %		C	204	29.10 %		C	35	5.00 %		C	106	15.10 %
	D	13	1.80 %		D	45	6.40 %		D	28	4.00 %		D	57	8.10 %		D	6	.80 %		D	15	2.10 %
	E	6	.80 %		E	17	2.40 %		E	11	1.50 %		E	29	4.10 %		E	3	.40 %		E	4	.50 %
	M		1.64		M		2.23		M		1.74		M		2.35		M		1.37		M		1.77
25.	A	267	38.10 %	26.	A	288	41.20 %	27.	A	353	50.50 %	28.	A	486	69.50 %	29.	A	474	68.30 %	30.	A	303	43.40 %
	B	263	37.60 %		B	296	42.30 %		B	189	27.00 %		B	163	23.30 %		B	171	24.60 %		B	195	27.90 %
	C	133	19.00 %		C	101	14.40 %		C	101	14.40 %		C	37	5.30 %		C	43	6.20 %		C	123	17.60 %
	D	29	4.10 %		D	12	1.70 %		D	34	4.80 %		D	9	1.20 %		D	2	.20 %		D	53	7.50 %
	E	7	1.00 %		E	2	.20 %		E	22	3.10 %		E	3	.40 %		E	3	.40 %		E	23	3.20 %
	M		1.92		M		1.78		M		1.83		M		1.40		M		1.40		M		1.99
31.	A	221	31.70 %	32.	A	151	21.70 %	33.	A	196	28.00 %	34.	A	267	38.40 %	35.	A	264	37.90 %	36.	A	363	52.20 %
	B	192	27.50 %		B	237	34.10 %		B	212	30.30 %		B	185	26.50 %		B	271	38.90 %		B	226	32.50 %
	C	141	20.20 %		C	181	26.00 %		C	165	23.60 %		C	134	19.30 %		C	128	18.40 %		C	84	12.00 %
	D	82	11.70 %		D	80	11.50 %		D	76	10.80 %		D	65	9.30 %		D	16	2.30 %		D	13	1.80 %
	E	60	8.60 %		E	45	6.40 %		E	50	7.10 %		E	43	6.10 %		E	16	2.30 %		E	9	1.20 %
	M		2.38		M		2.47		M		2.39		M		2.18		M		1.92		M		1.67

Figure 4.4 Printout of Teacher Response

Grading practices and grade-level placement of students is also an area addressed by a needs assessment. In particular, analyses of grade distribution by level, in schools and across the district, can indicate strengths and weaknesses. The construction of tables of overagedness in the school district can also be helpful to school planners.

In some needs assessments, student independence is an area that is analyzed. Particularly in districts where goals indicate a desire to foster independence, measures of how much students are dependent on teachers for direction and decisions can prove insightful. Student responsibility, for instance, is essential for the successful operation of an individualized curriculum.

Figure 4.5 Report to School Board on Support of Major Middle School Components

___

I. Rationale

The middle school, a child-centered program representing grades six through eight, is a continuation of basic education in fundamental skills and an introduction to specialized and exploratory opportunities based on individual needs. It is a sensitive, supportive learning environment that will provide those experiences that assist the transient adolescent in making the transition from childhood dependency to adult independence, thereby helping each individual to bridge the gap between the self-contained structure of the elementary school and the departmental structure of the high school. Thus, the middle school program is designed to foster the intellectual, social, emotional, and moral growth of children in keeping with the characteristics of their development.

	Principals	Teachers	Parents
The Middle School Program should be more child-centered than subject matter-centered. (T.10)	100%	85%	—
The Middle School Program should be a unique program bridging the gap between elementary schools and the secondary schools. (T.11)	100%	98%	—

II. Academic Program

The academic program emphasizes basic skills development (remediation and extension) through science, social studies, reading, English, and mathematics courses. A well-defined skills continuum is used as the basic guide in all schools in each area including physical education, health, and other required courses. A variety of teaching strategies is utilized.

A. *Curriculum (Scope and Sequence)*			
A well-defined scope and sequence should be available for each discipline. (T.36)	100%	97%	—

A final measure of instructional strategy is the method by which instructional effectiveness is evaluated. Do teachers and building faculties make programmatic assessments on a regular basis and use such findings to "adjust" the curriculum? Is classroom supervision perceived as an assisting behavior that upgrades instructional practices or is it an irregular and feared activity?

Student Data

In school districts where there is an attempt to serve the individual needs of learners, as opposed to giving all students the same academic treatment, it is important to gather student data. Data relating to student experiences is valuable for preplanning input, while information about student feelings and achievement can assist school planners in making adjustments to the existing curriculum.

In reviewing student experiences, a number of variables are useful indicators of both the breadth and depth of the student's world. A questionnaire that assesses student travel, recreational, aesthetic, and cultural backgrounds can provide teachers with invaluable points of reference for instruction. Examples of such questions might be:

1. Have you ever seen an ocean?
2. Have you ever flown on an airplane?
3 Have you ever been to a band concert?
4. Have you ever been in a public library?
5. Have you ever visited a foreign country?

Questionnaires that deal with assessments of experiences, at the secondary as well as the elementary levels, give teachers insights into students' backgrounds and levels of sophistication. When tallied as a percentage, the general level of experience for entire schools can be developed. Another equally valuable assessment device that might provide the same type of experience is a projection technique that would ask students how to spend extra money, or to plan travel trips.

Information about student attitudes, particularly those relating to self-esteem, can assist school planners in personalizing the instructional program. Beyond learning of student interest, motivation, and attitudes toward learning itself, such assessments often give clear portraits of student confidence in the instructional setting. Research over the past twenty years has shown consistently that individuals who feel capable, significant, successful, and worthy tend to have positive school experiences. In contrast, students who have low self-esteem rarely experience success in school settings.[3]

Measures of self-esteem, a personal judgment of worthiness the individual holds toward himself, are plentiful. Two measures used regularly in needs assessments are the *When Do I Smile* instrument (grades K–3) and the *Coopersmith Self-Esteem Inventory* (grades 4–12). *When Do I Smile* is a twenty-eight item instrument that can be administered to nonreaders. Students respond by marking faces that are happy, blank, or sad. By this means, school planners can gain insight into attitudes about school, peers, and general self.

The Coopersmith Self-Esteem Inventory, a fifty-item instrument, assesses student attitudes about themselves, their lives at home, and school life. Students respond to statements such as "I can make up my mind without too much trouble" or "I'm pretty happy" with either a "like me" or "unlike me" response. Such instruments can tell school planners a great deal about student confidence, support from home, and attitudes toward the existing curriculum.

Assessments of student achievement can be either broad or narrow in focus. The measure of this essential category is really a reflection of the school district's definition of education. When an educational program is perceived as primarily the mastery of skills and cognitive data, standardized achievement tests can be used exclusively to determine progress. When *education* is defined more broadly, measures of achievement become personal and more affective in nature.

Standardized achievement testing is carried out in most school districts in the United States on a scheduled basis. Tests such as the *California Achievement Test* can provide computer-scored analyses in areas such as math, language arts, and reading. Such standardized tests give school districts an assessment of relative progress in terms of validated national norms. Achievement tests compare a student's progress with what is considered to be normal progress for students in the nation of approximately the same age and/or grade level. These tests *do not* address a student's ability to perform.

It is useful for school planners to know if students in a district or particular school are achieving above or below grade level, for such information might suggest the retention or elimination of a specific curriculum program. More important, however, are general trends revealed by such tests. A continuing decline in reading scores, for instance, may pinpoint a level of schooling where curriculum review is needed. In Table 4.8, students in a district are displayed according to whether they are achieving above or below grade level in reading according to three commonly used standardized tests: *Gates McGinitie* (lower elementary), *Iowa Test of Basic Skills* (middle grades), and *Test of Academic Progress* (secondary grades).

In school districts where education is defined in terms of comprehensive criteria, assessments of student achievement are generally multiple. Sometimes such assessments have multiple dimensions, such as achievement in knowledge utilization, skill acquisition, and personal development. Sometimes such assessments are criterion-referenced, matching student achievement against goals rather than norms. Almost always the evidence of student achievement is multi-dimensional, supplementing standardized tests with samples of student work, teacher observations, and other such measures of growth.

Table 4.8
Summary of Reading Achievement in One School District

///// Indicates Below Grade Placement

GRADE LEVEL	NUMBER OF STUDENTS BY GRADE							TOTAL
	2	3	4	5	6	8	11	
14.0–14.9								
13.0–13.9							6	6
12.0–12.9							6	6
11.0–11.9						1	8	9
10.0–10.9						5	16	21
9.0–9.9						6	21	27
8.0–8.9					1	14	16	31
7.0–7.9				1	7	9	9	26
6.0–6.9				2	16	29	7	54
5.0–5.9		3	7	9	29	27		75
4.0–4.9		5	27	25	43	13		113
3.0–3.9	3	14	28	55	26	2		128
2.0–2.9	16	40	30	21	9			116
1.0–1.9	75	41	3	11	0			130
0.0–0.9								
TOTAL	94	103	95	124	131	106	89	742

Facilities

A final area considered by most needs assessments are the educational facilities used by the district to accomplish its program goals. Ideally, such facilities should be designed on the basis of program concepts.

An indepth study of facilities seeks to answer the following critical questions:

1. What is the overall pattern of facilities in the district?
2. How adequate is each plant and site for educational use?
3. How are the facilities currently being utilized?
4. What is the net operating capacity of each facility?

Assessments of facilities and sites attempt to analyze the adequacy and capacity ratings of all plants and grounds for maximum benefit to the educational program. A basic principle of most such studies is that flexible, multi-use facilities are more beneficial than those that limit programs to a single instructional pattern. A facility (school building) is considered adequate and modern if it provides for a variety of grouping patterns, the utilization of educational media, guidance, health and food services, special interest instruction (music, art, home economics, science, horticulture, etc.), large group assembly, and administrative functions.

One commonly used criterion for assessing school facilities is the *Linn-McCormick Rating Form for School Facilities* developed by the Institute of Field Studies, Teachers College, Columbia University. The Linn-McCormick scale uses a point system that systematically evaluates school buildings from classrooms through custodial facilities. Facilities are then rated on a scale from "excellent" to "poor." Such a scale does not consider the financial capability of the district to provide such facilities.

The value of such a building-by-building analysis, for educational planning, is that it allows school planners to see facilities in terms of the desired educational program. School plants can be compared and priorities for new building programs identified. If additional school sites are projected, lead time is available for survey and acquisition. Remodeling, where needed, can be scheduled.

In the assessment of facilities, an important phase is the identification and analysis of special facilities. In most school districts, special facilities are perceived as supplemental to regular instructional spaces and thus are a luxury. School districts must choose among a host of special rooms and spaces such as gymnasiums, art rooms, teacher offices, and so forth. Additionally, many schools have had to plan special rooms to deal with special students such as the physically handicapped. The decision as to which kinds of special rooms and spaces are present should be based on school planning rather than convenience or familiarity.

When school facilities are assessed, considerable attention should be directed to the utilization of such facilities. Detailed study of plant utilization can often lead to more efficient use of existing buildings and sites. Such study also will often reveal multi-use spaces in areas where only single use is presently in operation, i.e., the "cafetorium."

The assessment of school facilities and sites, including special areas and utilization patterns, should assist school planners in developing long-range facilities planning. Such planning can eliminate an undesirable pattern of building schools and acquiring sites after housing needs are in a critical state. Under such conditions, educational facilities are rarely adequate or appropriate to the needs of the instructional program.

Who Should Be Involved in Curriculum Development? _____

Curriculum development is a cooperative endeavor. Perhaps Figure 4.6 best illustrates the results of cooperation. It has to involve many groups, agencies, and individuals from both the school and community. The teacher, who must carry out the curriculum, will largely determine the success of any curriculum change. The recipients of the curriculum, students, must be a part of the process of curriculum development. Parents and members of the community who must support curriculum change should be involved in curriculum development work from the very start.

Administrators, supervisors, and other curriculum workers in leadership roles have to be involved in curriculum improvement.

The more persons and groups who can identify themselves with a curriculum, the more likely that curriculum will be successful. All curriculum decisions have direct consequences for the students, school personnel, and community persons involved.

COOPERATION

Figure 4.6

Providing the Leadership for Curriculum Development _____

The Role of the Curriculum Worker/Leader

The term *curriculum worker* applies to most educators-teachers, central office administrators, or principals. The term *curriculum leader* applies to those persons in leadership roles who have the primary responsibility for planning, coordinating, and/or managing curriculum activity in a school district. Curriculum leaders may be teachers chairing departments or committees, supervisors, and/or school administrators.[4]

There is a growing emphasis on curriculum development at the school or district level. The identification of curriculum leaders who can facilitate curriculum development is essential to the success of any change process. Many competencies have been compiled for the curriculum leader. Since the success of a curriculum leader depends on good human relations, the following competencies have been identified that will help the curriculum leader coordinate the activities of an educational staff related to curriculum planning and development. The curriculum leader should be able to:

- Produce and implement a year-long plan focused upon curriculum planning and the development of problems involving staff, parents, students, and support personnel, indicate their specific assignments and responsibilities, and provide a schedule of steps toward completion.
- Coordinate at a variety of levels and areas (locally as well as regionally) programming for instructional development.
- Define, with staff, common problems and help staff with the solution of these problems.
- Develop, with staff, behavioral objectives, which will be measurable and compatible with the content area.
- Schedule periodic interdepartmental meetings within a school or a school system to define common curricular problems and to seek solutions.
- Help and encourage teachers to be innovative and to accept different methods as long as they produce the desired outcomes.
- Develop a program for continuous curriculum development.
- Accept the individual differences of adults in conducting workshops for the development of curriculum.
- Be a primary resource person.
- Help determine integration of subject areas into total overall curriculum.
- Evaluate the current educational trends and know the philosophical basis for these trends.

- Recognize the dangers to educational development inherent in each of these trends.
- Assist the group to pursue various possible solutions to a problem.
- Summarize clearly and concisely various solutions.
- Assist the group in coming to decisions based on the alternative choices.
- Follow through on a course of action decided.
- Evaluate the effects a course of action may have on those affected by the program change.
- Disseminate information on current innovations to staff members directly involved in a specific area of innovation.
- Promote and encourage the direct involvement and participation of teachers in planning, implementing, and evaluating curricular innovations and adjustments.
- Describe the various points of view and the proper relationships of different subject areas to each other.
- Coordinate curriculum planning and development for the local district, K–12.
- Open channels of communication within professional staff that will allow crossing grade levels, ability levels, and individual discipline structures.
- Develop an attitude of commitment to local, district, state, and national curriculum development and improvement programs.
- Determine the needs of the community and of individual pupils in planning and developing programs at all levels of instruction to fulfill these needs.
- Plan budgetary allocations to ensure that curriculum plans can be inaugurated.
- Improve his ability to communicate positively and influentially with many different personalities.
- Offer, by example, his own philosophy of education.
- Provide vision for long-range plannings.
- Seek help and cooperation from staff members in setting up programs of curriculum development and/or improvement.
- Use research on child development and learning in selecting and sequencing concepts for curriculum development.
- Communicate progress, plans, and problems between staff members and curriculum-making bodies.
- Speak competently before faculty and critically appraise their efforts.
- Understand both elementary and secondary education (with a strong background in one of the levels).
- Establish a philosophy or a frame of reference (from which he operates and acts in a manner consistent with such a philosophy or frame of reference).

- Appoint cross-sectional committees (K–12) to establish in writing common goals for all levels.
- Approach all curriculum change with a concern for communication, both horizontal and vertical.
- Produce, in printed form, a description of the district's organization for curriculum improvement (which accounts for both human and material resources).
- Identify, accept and anticipate the needs of teachers (who are engaged in planning for curriculum innovation).
- Identify, and accept the needs of teachers in planning and development.
- Set up a system for the exchange of information among teachers.
- Provide a means for continuous evaluation of existing programs.
- Identify and solve instructional problems that hinder improvement of teaching-learning situations in the classroom.[5]

Summary

Curriculum development in recent years has shifted from primarily developing and implementing new courses of study to a complicated process of determining total programs for learners. Establishing a working philosophy, formulating goals at a number of conceptual levels, and relating objectives to program development are all tasks of modern curriculum development.

Basic to all educational planning is an assessment of what exists. From such an assessment should come an understanding of the strengths and weaknesses of the educational program, as well as goals for development.

School districts approach the assessment of learners who experience school programs in a number of ways. Of the comprehensive reviews of school programs, the needs assessment approach seems to provide the broadest profile to school planners. Using generic categories such as general information, population characteristics, school population characteristics, programs and course offerings, instructional patterns and strategies, student data, professional staff, and facilities, the needs assessment thoroughly analyzes the school program. Such analyses provide school planners with a comprehensive set of data for future school development.

The needs assessment provides school planners with a vehicle for involving the public in the development of school programs. Such an inclusion strategy is thought by the authors to have maximum payoff in the long-range development of public school programs. Curriculum development is a cooperative endeavor with many groups involved including teachers, students, parents, and consultants. Curriculum planning groups must have competent leaders to direct them.

Notes

1. Report to the Executive Committee of A.S.C.D. (mimeograph), Research and Theory Working Group. October 15, 1977.
2. *Directory of Occupational Titles,* 3rd ed. United States Department of Labor, Bureau of Employment Security (Washington, D.C. 1965).
3. Wallace La Benne and Bert Greene, *Educational Implications of Self-Concept* (Pacific Palisades: Goodyear Publishing, 1969).
4. Working Group on the Role, Function and Preparation of the Curriculum Worker, Donald Christensen, Chairperson, *Curriculum Leaders: Improving Their Influence* (Washington, D.C.: A.S.C.D., 1976), p. 5.
5. Francis Ciurczak, ed. "The Future Role of the Curriculum Worker," IMPACT on Instructional Improvement 9, No. 1, 1973, 13–15.

Suggested Learning Activities

1. Develop an outline of events that would lead a school district from no clear philosophy to a state of logical internal consistency in program development.
2. Develop a list of "quality indicators" that a district might want to review in conducting a needs assessment.
3. State in your own words how a needs assessment contrasts with general review studies for accreditation.

Books to Review

Benjamin, Harold. *The Saber Tooth Curriculum.* New York: McGraw-Hill, 1972.

Bloom, Benjamin, ed. *Taxonomy of Educational Objectives—Handbook I: Cognitive Domain.* New York: McKay, 1956.

Harrow, Anita J. *A Taxonomy of the Psychomotor Domain.* New York: McKay, 1972.

Krathwohl, D. R.; Bloom, Benjamin; and Masia, Bertram. *Taxonomy of Educational Objectives—Handbook II: Affective Domain.* New York: McKay, 1964.

Larson, Robert. *Goal-Setting in Planning: Myths and Realities.* Burlington: Center for Research, 1980.

Mager, Robert. *Preparing Instructional Objectives.* Palo Alto, California: Fearon Publishers, 1962.

McAshon, H. H. *The Goals Approach to Performance Objectives.* Philadelphia: W. B. Saunders, 1974.

Oliver, Albert I. *Curriculum Improvement,* 2nd ed. New York: Harper & Row, 1971.

Saylor, J. Galen and Alexander, William. *Planning Curriculum for Schools.* New York: Holt, Rinehart & Winston, 1974.

Smith, B. Othanel; Stanley, William; and Shores, J. Harlan. *Fundamentals of Curriculum Development,* rev. ed. New York: World Book, 1957.

Stenhouse, L. *Curriculum Research and Development In Action.* London: Heinemann, 1980.

Chapter Five
Instructional Considerations in Curriculum Development

Since curriculum is a plan for learning and objectives determine what learning is important, it follows that good curriculum planning will involve the selection and organization of both content and learning experiences. Instructional considerations in curriculum development require curriculum planners to move beyond a theoretical framework of curriculum to the implementation of curriculum plans at the classroom level. The most significant part of any curriculum plan is the organized classroom plan. Parents see this aspect of curriculum development as the cornerstone of the school. Instructional considerations in curriculum development at the classroom level include teachers making daily decisions about content, grouping, materials, pacing and sequencing of activities, and assessing how well students have learned. Each of these decisions directly affects student learning. This chapter will explore curriculum development as it interfaces with classroom instruction. The selection of curriculum experiences, organizing for instruction, resources for learning, and teaching strategies will be analyzed from a planning perspective.

In chapter two we learned that certain foundational information sources help curriculum leaders to analyze and plan the curriculum. These "bases of curriculum planning" are filtered through a philosophic stance to form general and then more specific objectives. Such objectives are the framework or tapestry from which instructional plans are developed. Figure 5.1 illustrates the relationship of these planning variables:

In developing instructional experiences, there are some indicators of a good curriculum that might be considered:

1. A good curriculum provides experiences that are rich and varied and designed for culturally diverse students.
   a) Content is in tune with social and cultural realities of the times.
   b) Subject matter has meaning for the learner and an importance the student accepts and understands.
   c) Classroom activities are arranged to provide a balanced program of learning opportunities.
2. A good curriculum is organized flexibly to serve the educational objectives of the school.
   a) Grouping practices do not discriminate against students because of their sex, race, or socioeconomic status.
   b) Both formal and informal grouping methods are used to promote individualization of instruction.
   c) Variable time allotments and schedules are provided for individual and group activities.
3. A good curriculum utilizes resources that are appropriate to the needs and interests of learners.
   a) Resources are selected that are relevant to the goal-seeking activities involved.
   b) Materials are used that are free from biases of sexism and racism.

Bases of the Curriculum

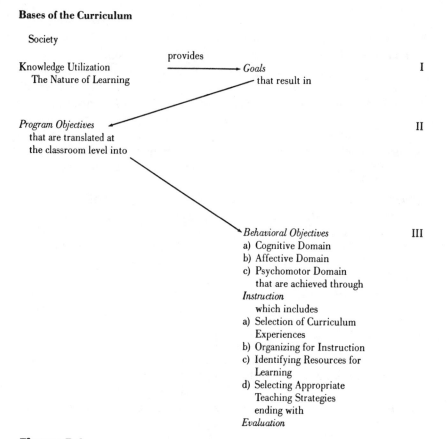

Society

Knowledge Utilization
   The Nature of Learning

          provides

→ *Goals*   I
  that result in

Program Objectives   II
  that are translated at
  the classroom level into

Behavioral Objectives   III
a) Cognitive Domain
b) Affective Domain
c) Psychomotor Domain
   that are achieved through
Instruction
   which includes
a) Selection of Curriculum
   Experiences
b) Organizing for Instruction
c) Identifying Resources for
   Learning
d) Selecting Appropriate
   Teaching Strategies
   ending with
Evaluation

Figure 5.1

    c)   Students are provided with necessary skills for sorting out messages provided by mass media.
4. A good curriculum includes appropriate teaching strategies to carry out learning objectives.
    a)   Teaching strategies take into consideration characteristics of learners.
    b)   Cooperative teaching and planning are encouraged so teachers can share learning resources and special talents.
    c)   Classroom practices give attention to the maturity and learning problems of each student.

Selection of Curriculum Experiences

    Selection of curriculum experiences has always been a problem in curriculum development. Today's schools have inherited responsibilities for instruction that go well beyond the basic instruction provided by schools fifty years ago. There is more for students to learn than there is time available in school. Because of the back-to-the-basics movement in recent years, there is less time available for those learning experiences not classified as "basic instruction." Yet the needs of society have made the school assume more of the responsibilities formerly assumed by other institutions. How to reconcile the push for more time for basics and more time for the personal development of children is a major problem facing the modern curriculum leader.

At the classroom level, the push and pull of pressure groups becomes even more critical. Here, the teacher is often faced with a school board mandate to provide a certain number of minutes of reading per day for every child. This is often accompanied by a push for so many class periods a week of mathematics. Many school districts have requirements that certain subjects be taught in certain years in a prescribed manner. Curriculum planners must realize that the classroom teacher must ultimately carry out the instructional program and must have some flexibility in selecting curriculum experiences.

Providing Balance in the Instructional Program

In the past, most curriculum experiences were grouped as "curricular" or "extracurricular." Furthermore, they were almost universally grouped or described within subject fields. The broadening of the definition of curriculum today has diminished somewhat the distinction between curricular or extracurricular experiences.

Within a school program all learning experiences can be classified under the following headings:

1. The personal development of the individual
2. Skills for continued learning
3. Education for social competence

The above classification can serve as the basis for planning a school program, and provides direction for instruction at the classroom level. Clear attention can be given to each of the three phases of the school program while still recognizing that the three phases are related.

Using such a classification system, curriculum planners can develop a plan that will provide a great variety of rich learning opportunities in each area. The personal development phase would include exploratory and enrichment experiences in a broad range of human activities. There can be activities leading to a better understanding of one's self, health and physical activities appropriate to levels of maturity, and various school services that would involve the learner's family and home. The skills for the continued learning phase can include diagnosis of learning needs with cognitive learning experiences so structured that students can master critical skills and progress in an individualized manner. The social competence phase might include courses of study in the sciences and mathematics, social studies, humanities, languages and literature, and the vocational fields.

Although such a classification system would be primarily a check on the scope of the school program, it might also provide teachers with a guide for determining balance in the curriculum as they develop lesson plans or participate in writing curriculum guides. The classroom instructor would also use different means of organizing for instruction as he or she provides learning experiences in the different phases of the curriculum. For instance, there might be more organized group instruction in the social competence phase than in the personal development phase. Group sizes could also vary with respect to the particular phase of the curriculum.

Providing for Culturally Diverse Students

In selecting curriculum experiences, teachers today must take into consideration the needs of culturally diverse students. Individualizing instruction for culturally and ethnically diverse students does not mean these students are deficient and need individual help to catch up with their fellow students. The burden should not be on the child to adjust to a monocultural school (basically white, Anglo, and middle class in orientation). Rather, school personnel must realize that we live in a polycultural society and must develop a sensitivity to the cultural orientations of each child.

Recent authors of texts and articles have emphasized the need to recognize the individuality of children. Ernest Garcia in an ERIC document wrote, "Cultural differences that need the attention and sensitivity of the teacher are going to come with individuals."[1] Teachers need to recognize and accent cultural differences and be able to respond with the types of teacher behaviors designed to instill a feeling of pride, not shame, on the part of students.

The Association for Supervision and Curriculum Development Commission on Multicultural Education has suggested all educational content and processes be examined for evidence of realistic treatment of cultural pluralism. They offer the following recommendations:

1. Examine text materials for evidence of racism, classism, sexism, and realistic treatment of cultural pluralism in American society.
2. Develop new curricula for all levels of schooling—curricula that enhance and promote cultural diversity.
3. Provide opportunities to learn about and interact with a variety of ethnic groups and cultural experiences.
4. Include the study of concepts from the humanistic and behavioral sciences, which are applicable for understanding human behavior.
5. Organize curricula around universal human concerns, which transcend usual subject-matter disciplines; bring multicultural perspectives to bear in the study of such issues.

6. Broaden the kinds of inquiry used in the school to incorporate and facilitate the learning of more humanistic modes of inquiry.
7. Create school environments that radiate cultural diversity.
8. Maximize the school as a multicultural setting, with the idea of utilizing the positive contributions of all groups to accomplish common tasks and not just to reduce deficiencies for the deprived.
9. Recognize and utilize bilingualism as a positive contribution to the communication process, and include bilingual programs of instruction of monolingual children.
10. Examine rules, norms, and procedures of students and staff with the purpose of facilitating the development of learning strategies and techniques that do not penalize and stigmatize diversity, but rather encourage and prize it.
11. Institute a system of shared governance in the schools, in which all groups can enter equally in the learning and practice of democratic procedures.
12. Organize time, space, personnel, and resources to facilitate the maximum probability and flexibility of alternative experiences for all youngsters.
13. Institute staffing patterns (involving both instructional and noninstructional positions) that reflect our culturally pluralistic and multiracial society.
14. Design and implement preservice and inservice programs to improve staff ability to successfully implement multicultural education.[2]

Rational Selection of Content

Today, the problems of rational selection of content are especially crucial. There is a growing trend to exclude from the curriculum certain courses of study. The M.A.C.O.S. controversy, the banning of certain books in schools, has left educators confused about the criteria by which to decide the content of curriculum.* Many school districts have adopted strict guidelines for the inclusion or exclusion of curriculum content. In an effort to gain acceptance of certain programs of study, school superintendents and Boards of Education have appointed citizens to committees to evaluate content, select textbooks, and perform other duties formerly exclusively the domain of school personnel. It is early yet to see how far this trend will go and whether parents and citizens can make any better selection of content than teachers, administrators, and supervisory personnel. The danger of militant groups

*M.A.C.O.S.—Man A Course of Study, a social studies curriculum project for upper elementary grades which has been attacked by ultraconservative elements for its value orientations.

taking extreme steps to include or exclude content by influencing textbook selection dictates a strong stand by professional educators to repudiate bigotry and alienation in our society.[3]

Relevancy of Subject Matter

Content should be relevant and significant. To be relevant and significant, content must constantly be examined to see that it reflects not only recent scientific knowledge, but also reflects the social and cultural realities of the times.

In the advanced technological age in which we are living, subject matter in school curricula many times becomes obsolete before it reaches the printed or audiovisual form. Publishers and other producers of school materials are faced with not only the growing body of knowledge itself, but the growing complexity of that knowledge. The minimum level of understanding of mathematics and science that an ordinary person must develop to live comfortably in a technical society has increased dramatically in recent years. What is "basic" today was not even imagined fifty years ago.

Similar problems of significance exist in social studies and language arts. What social studies text can keep up with the changes in government experienced in recent years? What literature book can compete with television for the attention of schoolchildren? Certainly, there will be a need for texts that deal with fundamental concepts underlying each of the disciplines. Distinguishing what is fundamental or basic knowledge is not an easy task for curriculum planners. The more fundamental a concept, the greater will be the breadth of application, for the concept is fundamental because it has a broad and powerful applicability. In those districts and states where there is mandated mastery of certain "fundamentals," students run the risk of being exposed to information that will have very little applicability outside the classroom.

If content is to be useful, it must be in tune with the social and cultural realities of the times. American education tends to be overly responsive to immediate social pressures as evidenced by the emphasis on science and mathematics during the Sputnik era and the current back-to-the-basics movement. Although public education must be responsive to society, taking cues from the demands of an immediate situation sometimes leads to an imbalance of curriculum experiences that poorly prepare students for the future. An example was the increased emphasis on science and mathematics in elementary schools after Sputnik was launched because there was supposedly a shortage of technically trained personnel. By the time elementary-grade youngsters became employable, that shortage no longer existed.

Selecting the curriculum experiences that are critical in developing a future generation that can exist in an ever-shrinking world means the curriculum planner must be in tune with a changing world. Independence has changed to interdependence in today's world. Our curriculum can no longer perpetuate the degree of provincialism and ethnocentricity it had in the past. Understanding our own diverse society is important, but we must also have comparative materials and experiences to understand other cultures as well as our own.

Developing loyalty to democratic human values remains a major task of curriculum planners. The breakdown of the great institutions of our society, most especially the family, has led to an alienation of the individual from the basic sources on which to build a value orientation. Modern technology also tends to influence social institutions in directions that are inimical to democratic human values. The challenge of selecting curriculum experiences for today's curriculum planners is to maintain the balance between intellectual proficiency and intelligent social perspective. It is ironic to note that Hilda Taba vividly pointed this out in 1962 as she discussed the impact of technology on American education.

> Some educators take a simple view of the needs arising from a technological society and combine this view with the traditional concept of education. . . . they believe that a technological society simply requires technically prepared people. . . . that the task of the school is to increase and to improve the training in mathematics and science for everyone. . . .[4]

Instructional Organization in Curriculum Development

If curriculum development is a plan for learning, learning experiences need to be organized so that they serve the educational objectives of a school. This section will examine some of the ways schools are organized so that instruction can be provided. Classroom organization will also be examined to identify ways of organizing curriculum experiences to make learning more efficient.

Individualizing instruction means a child can truly progress at his or her own rate, that he or she can pursue interests in great depth, and that independence and responsibility for learning are fostered. Often a curriculum is ineffective not because its content is ineffective, but because learning experiences are organized in a way to prevent learning. For years, some schools have operated under the following fallacious assumptions:

1. A classroom group size of 30 to 35 students is the most appropriate for a wide variety of learning experiences.
2. The appropriate amount of time for learning a subject is the same uniform period of length, 40 to 60 minutes in length, 6 or 7 periods a day, for 36 weeks out of a year.

3. All learners are capable of mastering the same subject matter in the same length of time. For example, we give everyone the same test on chapter 7 on Friday. We pass everyone from level one of Spanish to level two when June comes.
4. We assume the same material is appropriate to all members of a group. For example, we give the same assignment to the entire group.
5. We assume once a group is formed the same group composition is equally appropriate for a wide variety of learning activities.
6. We assume the same classroom is equally appropriate for a wide variety of learning activities. Conference rooms are not provided for teacher-pupil conferences. Large group facilities are not provided for mass dissemination of materials. Small group rooms are unavailable for discussion activity, etc.
7. We assume the same teacher is qualified to teach all aspects of his subject for one school year.
8. We assume all students require the same kind of supervision.[5]

Operating on these assumptions we lock students into an educational egg-crate, 25 students to a cubicle, from 8 or 9 A.M. to 3 or 4 P.M., 5 days a week for 12 or 13 years. We stand up in front of the students, talking 90 percent of the time, asking them questions which we have deemed appropriate for their formal education. In short, it might be suggested that our present education system is designed more for the convenience of teaching than it is for the facilitation of learning.

Schools need to break this lockstep approach to instruction. Rigid class sizes, inflexible classroom facilities, and fixed schedules should be challenged by curriculum planners. Organizing schools for instruction is not an easy task. We need to apply all we know about the nature of knowledge, human growth and development, and learning styles of children in formulating a plan for instructional organization.

The logic of curriculum development that leads to sound instructional organization can be seen in the Instructional Paradigm (Figure 5.2).

Organizing for Individualized Instruction _____

There are very few educational plans that do not have as a major goal the individualization of instruction. Individualized instruction remains, however, largely an unfulfilled goal.[6] The topic of individualization is not a new one, nor has it been ignored in the literature. Indeed, we can go back to the 1925 yearbook of the National Society for the Study of Education (NSSE) and find the title of their yearbook to be *Adapting the Schools to Individual Differences*. NSSE also published a 1962 yearbook entitled *Individualizing Instruction*. The literature and work on which those two volumes drew went back over one hundred years. Our addition to whole-class instruction within a graded framework has been strong and some doubt whether we can ever bring about any other forms of instruction.

Instruction focuses upon the teacher's behaviors and the delivery system being used. Perhaps we should use the term "individualized learning" to illustrate that this is the phenomenon we are trying to influence. All teaching must ultimately be construed in terms of the effect of teaching on learning. There is no single instructional approach that can be advocated for all types of learners. Eclectic systems that utilize a number of diverse approaches seem likelier to succeed than systems of limited variety.

The following are assumptions for organizing a school for individualized instruction:

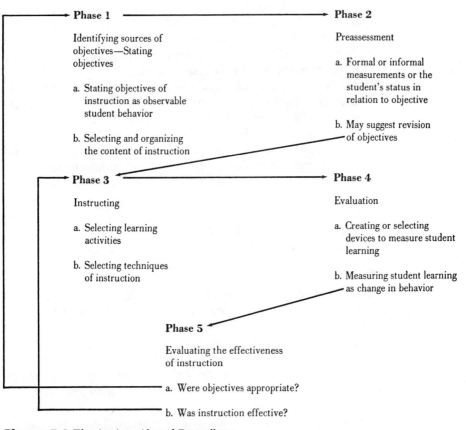

Figure 5.2 The Instructional Paradigm

Source: Jon Wiles and Joseph Bondi, *Supervision: A Guide to Practice* (Columbus: Charles E. Merrill, 1980), p. 53. Reprinted with permission.

1. The organization of the school should not only encourage but require varied rates of pupil progress.
2. Reporting and marking procedures should convey a clear idea of the pupil's rate of progress with respect to his particular developmental norms and standards.
3. Subject matter—i.e., substantive content—must have meaning for the learner and an importance which he both understands and accepts.
4. Administrative policies that govern pupil progress should not be based on a grade-level concept but on a continuum of cumulative experience along which children and youth move at personalized and uneven rates.
5. Provisions for program enrichment and for related school activities should be developed to encourage willing and psychologically sound participation of children moving toward maturity at diverse and uneven rates.
6. The nature of social activities encouraged by the school should not tend to exclude children who are more or less mature than or "different" from their age mates.
7. Reliance should not yet be placed on any single grouping plan, however ingenious it may appear to be.
8. The instructional staff should be sufficiently large, competent, and diversified to permit every child to be well known by at least one faculty member-counselor at a given time.
9. Instructional aids should not be allowed to supersede a basic reliance on the human element in the teaching-learning process. Large-group instruction must be counterbalanced by small, close-knit groups and guided individualized experience.

Formal and Informal Approaches to Individualized Instruction

Attempts at individualization fall into two general categories: *informal* and *formal*. In the informal approach, the teacher attempts to stay alert to the fact that some learners need more time and attention to master a particular skill, concept, or body of knowledge, while other learners need less time and attention. Extra practice is given the slow learner while the faster learner is provided with additional challenges. Teachers will use different resources and teaching strategies to reach students of different abilities. Good teachers have followed those practices for years.

In formal systems of individualized instruction, there is an attempt to provide a unique program of studies for every child. This is accomplished by a sequence of diagnosis, prescription, and evaluation. Pretests are used in the diagnosis stage to identify what a student can do in each learning area. A prescription follows which includes the materials necessary to teach the particular skill. Finally, an evaluation procedure called the posttest is administered. The child works through a rather rigid sequence of activities achieving mastery in one level before moving to the next level.

There are several formal systems that are widely used in today's schools. All are found in elementary schools, although these systems have been modified for use in middle schools and high schools. Formal systems have several advantages in practice. They force a school to define clearly what is to be learned and provide a monitoring process to see that it is done. They also demand that mastery of one unit of work be accomplished before the student moves on to the next unit.

Three formal systems that are widely used in elementary schools are Individually Prescribed Instruction (IPI), Program for Learning in Accordance with Needs (PLAN), and Individually Guided Education (IGE), or the Wisconsin Design. IPI was developed by the University of Pittsburgh and Research for Better Schools. PLAN was developed by the Westinghouse Learning Corporation. PLAN utilizes a computer hookup for assessment and involves a series of teacher-learner units (TLU's).

IGE was developed by the University of Wisconsin and later used by the Institute for Development of Educational Activities (IDEA). IGE is a comprehensive system of organization and management of instruction and learning environments. It represents an alternative to schools organized in either age-graded, self-contained classrooms or in subject-centered departments.[7]

Along with the advantages of formal systems, there are disadvantages. In comparison with total class instruction, systems like IPI and PLAN reduce the time pupils and teachers are in contact. Students sometimes move from unit to unit or packet of materials to packet of materials without much contact with an adult or other students. Another problem involves the amount of paperwork required in such programs. Unless teacher aides or parent volunteers are available, teachers sometimes are overwhelmed by recordkeeping. PLAN does utilize a computer for this task, but at considerable expense. In IPI and IGE the teacher or aide must keep the records.

It is difficult to determine whether formal or informal systems of individualized instruction result in greater learning on the part of students. It is not guaranteed that individualized instruction, formal or informal, results in greater learning. There are many variables influencing the success of an instructional program, such as the training and support given teachers, the Hawthorne effect, and the enthusiasm of teachers who volunteer for special programs. We should not get so involved with the cult of individualized instruction that we lose sight of the fact that individualizing instruction is a means, not an end, in education.[8]

Graded vs. Nongraded Instruction

The organizational plan used by a majority of schools is the graded plan. Some schools have dropped the artificial barriers of grades and adopted a nongraded organizational plan. There is more evidence of a nongraded structure in the elementary school, especially in the primary years, than any other school level. In recent years schools have been constructed to accommodate a nongraded structure.

Some schools have implemented ability or achievement grouping within grades. Such an arrangement "nongrades" a curriculum, but allows children of the same age level to remain together. An interesting method of cutting across grade lines has been the grouping of students according to physical or social maturity rather than relying on the single criterion of achievement in subject matter. Some middle schools have implemented physical or social grouping arrangements. Others have used exploratory and enrichment courses as a means of breaking down grade barriers. The criterion for grouping in this arrangement is not age or years in school, but an interest in a particular field of study.

A way of appraising graded and nongraded patterns of organizing for instruction can be seen in Table 5.1.

Scheduling Instructional Groups

A number of formal plans for scheduling instructional groups have been developed over the years. The Trump plan and the nongraded high school are two organizational plans that have influenced the secondary school. The Trump plan advocates variable schedules for individual and class activities. It attacks the traditional class period of 50–60 minutes. Periods of variable length provide for greater flexibility in organizing the instructional program. In variable scheduling, the school day is divided into time frames (modules) of 15–20 minutes each. The grouping of the modules allows for shorter or longer periods of time. The nongraded high school received the most attention from the plan implemented at the Melbourne (Florida) Senior High School.[9] In the Melbourne school, the content and learning units, except for some nonacademic subjects, are divided into five phases rather than into the traditional subject pattern:

Phase One: Subjects designed for students needing special attention in small classes.

Phase Two: Subjects designed for students needing more emphasis on the basic skills.

Phase Three: Materials designed for average ability in the subject matter.

Phase Four: Subject matter designed for capable students seeking education in depth.

Phase Five: Challenging new courses available to students with exceptional ability who are willing to assume responsibility for their own learning and go beyond the requirements of the normal high school.

Phase Six: Nonacademic subjects offered that do not permit student mobility; for example, typing and physical education are upgraded but unphased.

Other plans of scheduling instructional groups such as core instruction, interdisciplinary instruction, and the previously mentioned IGE plan have been applied to elementary, middle, and high schools. Whether instructional groups are scheduled by content, at grade level, or across grade levels, classroom teachers still must be able to schedule instructional groups within a single classroom. Elementary teachers have met with greater success in scheduling within a classroom than high school teachers. Through the use of skill groups, interest groups, and learning centers, elementary teachers have been able to shift groups or the nature of pupil activities. Middle school teachers have adopted many of the elementary techniques of organizing for instruction and have added core arrangements and interdisciplinary units of instruction to provide for even more flexibility. Unfortunately, very few high schools have moved beyond the traditional type of scheduling that requires that all subjects be taught the same length of class time and the same number of days a year.

Homogeneous vs. Heterogeneous Grouping

Homogeneous grouping refers to the practice of assigning students to instructional groups on the basis of their similarity, presumed ability, or achievement. This is sometimes called *tracking*. The major argument in favor of homogeneous grouping is that pupils of equal ability can be taught more efficiently than children of varying abilities. There are many arguments against grouping children homogeneously. They include research data indicating that homogeneous ability grouping tends to sort pupils into somewhat socioeconomic groups, that errors in placement of pupils are often made, and that designated "smart" or "slow" children do not perform any better or worse because of the way they are grouped. Another serious objection is that the process of labeling "slow" children can have serious consequences in their lives, because they accept and ultimately internalize the school's judgment of them.

Heterogeneous grouping allows students of varying abilities, interests, and achievement to interact together in an instructional group. It is interesting to note that parents do not object to homogeneous grouping as long as their children are in a "high" track.

Recent federal court decisions and legislation have resulted in decisions and regulations barring tracking of elementary and secondary students on the basis of ability or sex. Title Nine federal regulations

Table 5.1
Dimensions of Graded and Nongraded Instruction

Dimension	Graded Pattern	Transitional Pattern (Pseudo-Nongraded)	Nongraded Pattern
1. Grouping (Operational practices and/or factors considered)	1. Age 2. Grade achievement 3. Academic progress in relation to grade standards 4. Homogeneity in subjects 5. Intelligence quotients	1. Reading ability 2. Reading levels 3. Homogeneity 4. Multi-grade for homogeneity 5. Academic progress on basis of level standards 6. Subject groups—planned for homogeneity	1. Multi-factors 2. Multi-age for diversity 3. Intra-class grouping for individual and group needs 4. Multi-age skills groups—planned for individual needs 5. Multi-age interest groups—planned for individual interest 6. Interclass grouping—for individual and group needs
2. Pupil progress (Operation practices and/or factors considered)	1. Grade requirements 2. Reading ability 3. Group standards 4. Annual promotion	1. Level requirements 2. Reading ability 3. Traditional marks 4. Modification in marking and reporting narrative reports and/or parent conferences	1. Multi-factors 2. Collective decision based on extensive data 3. Mobility to new organizational block after two or three years (no special promotion period) 4. Continuous progress on basis of the individual's potential

5. Marks as reflected on report card	5. Promotion upon completion of level requirements (short periods for some students, longer for others)	

3. Teacher (Operational practices and/or factors considered)

1. Selects curriculum materials on basis of grade	1. Selects curriculum materials on basis of levels (levels equivalent to grades, example: Level 1-We Read Pictures, etc.)	1. Selects curriculum materials on the basis of individual need, interest, and potential
2. Long-range plans based on books, topics, or units required for specific grade	2. Long-range plans based on completion of books, topics, or skills to be introduced at a specific level	2. Identifies concepts, attitudes, and skills which are to be a part of a longitudinal program
3. Groups for instruction on the basis of progress in reading texts (Usually three groups)	3. Groups for instruction on basis of skills to be introduced at a specific level	3. Long- and short-range goals determined by individual potential and proficiency
4. Tends to ignore range of reading ability in content area (same text for all in spelling, science, social studies, health, etc.)	4. Tends to ignore range of reading ability in content areas	4. Encourages open-ended pursuits and in-depth study
5. Gives uniform assignments	5. Gives uniform assignments	5. Frequently plans individual conferences sessions, seminars, and small group skill sessions

Table 5.1
(continued)

Dimension	Graded Pattern	Transitional Pattern (Pseudo-Nongraded)	Nongraded Pattern
	6. All pupils exposed to same materials—at different periods during the school year	6. All pupils exposed to same materials. Pacing based on completion of materials planned for specific levels	6. Group membership changes frequently (often from period to period and day to day)
	7. Pupil success equated with grade requirements	7. Pupils' success equated with level requirements	7. Open-ended goals—no superimposed limitations. Limitations determined by individual in academic potential and level of proficiency
	8. Group progress of primary concern	8. Group progress of primary concern	8. Gives personalized assignments including homework
	9. Teacher success based on coverage of graded materials	9. Increased teacher freedom in the selection of materials	9. Utilizes a variety of materials. Only a few copies of any one instructional source utilized
	10. Sex differences, cultural differences, and learning styles ignored	10. Sex differences, cultural differences, and learning styles ignored	10. Considers individual differences in all curriculum areas
	11. Considers graded manual, curriculum as the perfect guide to instruction success	11. Increased utilization of multi-level materials	11. Works with individuals over an extended period of time
			12. Utilizes team learning and cooperative teaching whenever feasible

4. Curriculum content (Operational practices and/or factors considered)		
1. Graded textbooks	1. Graded textbooks with levels	1. Recognition of a body of knowledge in each curriculum area
2. Graded course of study	2. Graded course of study translated into levels	2. Emphasis upon individual potential in regard to mastery of skills
3. Emphasis upon covering designated content within a specific period	3. Emphasis upon covering content designated for each level	3. Introduction, teaching and refinement of content varies with individual learners
4. Emphasis upon mastering designated skills for each grade	4. Emphasis upon covering content designated for each level	4. Curriculum content organized on a continuous and recurring scheme
5. Mastery of graded content expected of all pupils	5. Mastery of level requirements expected of all pupils—but at a different rate of progress	5. Introduction, teaching, and reteaching of concepts and skills based on analysis and diagnosis
		6. Success and mastery relative—viewed in relation to individual differences
		7. Continuity based on understanding and mastery of skills and concepts at lower proficiency levels

have barred grouping practices based on sex of students. For instance, home economics and industrial arts classes must provide equal opportunity for the enrollment of both boys and girls. Sports programs cannot be limited to just boys. The Federal District Court of Washington, D.C. ruled in 1976 that the practice of ability grouping was unconstitutional because it was discriminatory and resulted in the denial of equal protection of the laws for children from varying racial and socioeconomic backgrounds. That decision and others led many school administrators to reexamine their grouping practices.

Selecting Appropriate Teaching Strategies

Strategies or methods of teaching include all those techniques, procedures, manipulations, and facilitations of content and learning environments that are performed by teachers. There are seven functions that are of vital importance to effective teaching. Teachers must be able to:

1. identify and separate the contributing elements constituting a given teaching-learning situation
2. conceptualize the relationships between those interacting elements
3. select and plan appropriate instructional strategies
4. develop and sharpen suitable skills in order to translate the selected strategies into practice
5. acquire reliable and meaningful feedback in the form of empirical and objective data
6. evaluate the effectiveness of the selected strategies
7. modify and revise strategies for future improvement.

Preliminary to developing curriculum plans, the teacher must answer the following questions:

Who are my students?
What should they learn?
How should they learn it?
When should they learn it?

Teaching strategies, then, are preceded by a determination of the characteristics of the learners, including physical and intellectual characteristics, age level, maturity, reading ability, I.Q., and performance evaluations. Other data including attitudes, learning styles, and cultural backgrounds provide valuable clues to teachers and other curriculum planners.

Determining what the student should learn involves establishing criteria for the selection of content. Those criteria include determining whether the content is valid, significant, and consistent with social realities.

While questions of content may be difficult to answer, determining how and when to present content is an easier task if data regarding students form the basis for instructional decisions. Once curriculum planners determine needs and interests of learning, the next step is the selection of appropriate strategies to help achieve stated objectives. Different students do learn at different rates and in different ways. Some methods are more appropriate than others. Some are more effective. The selection of teaching strategies is but one step in a complicated teaching-learning process that begins with a thorough knowledge of the learner.

Popham and Baker have identified a series of instructional activities to promote the learner's attainment of instructional objectives. They include:

1. Appropriate Practice—allowing the learner opportunities to practice the behavior implied by the instructional objective.
2. Knowledge of Results—the teacher allowing a pupil to discover whether his responses are adequate.
3. Analyzing and Sequencing Learner Behaviors—identifying and sequencing learner behaviors to be mastered en route to the achievement of an educational objective.
4. Perceived Purpose—identifying the methods used to develop a learning set where learners perceive the worth of what they are studying.
5. Evaluation—includes pre-assessment of learner competencies, test construction, item sampling, and interpretation of student-performance data.[10]

Selecting appropriate teaching strategies, then, is a key element in the instructional process. Some common strategies found in today's schools are:

1. **Comparative Analysis**—A thought process, structured by the teacher, that employs the description, classification, and analysis of more than one system, group, or the like in order to ascertain and evaluate similarities and differences.
2. **Conference**—A one-to-one interaction between teacher and learner where the individual's needs and problems can be dealt with. Diagnosis, evaluation, and prescription may all be involved.
3. **Demonstration**—An activity in which the teacher or another person uses examples, experiments, and/or other actual performance to illustrate a principle or show others how to do something.
4. **Diagnosis**—The continuous determination of the nature of learning difficulties and deficiencies, used in teaching as a basis for the selection, day by day or moment by moment, of appropriate content and methods of instruction.

5. **Directed Observation**—Guided observation provided for the purpose of improving the study, understanding, and evaluation of that which is observed.
6. **Discussion**—An activity in which pupils, under teacher and/or pupil direction, exchange points of view concerning a topic, question, or problem to arrive at a decision or conclusion.
7. **Drill**—An orderly, repetitive learning activity intended to help develop or fix a specific skill or aspect of knowledge.
8. **Experimentation**—An activity involving a planned procedure accompanied by control of conditions and/or controlled variation of conditions together with observation of results for the purpose of discovering relationships and evaluating the reasonableness of a specific hypothesis.
9. **Field Experience**—Educational work experience, sometimes fully paid, acquired by pupils in a practical service situation.
10. **Field Trip**—An educational trip to places where pupils can study the content of instruction directly in its functional setting, e.g., factory, newspaper office, or fire department.
11. **Group Work**—A process in which members of the class, working cooperatively rather than individually, formulate and work toward common objectives under the guidance of one or more leaders.
12. **Laboratory Experience**—Learning activities carried on by pupils in a laboratory designed for individual or group study of a particular subject-matter area, involving the practical application of theory through observation, experimentation, and research, or, in the case of foreign language instruction, involving learning through demonstration, drill, and practice. This applies also to the study of art and music, although such activity in this instance may be referred to as a studio experience.
13. **Lecture**—An activity in which the teacher gives an oral presentation of facts or principles, the class frequently being responsible for note-taking. This activity usually involves little or no pupil participation by questioning or discussion.
14. **Manipulative and Tactile Activity**—Activity by which pupils utilize the movement of various muscles and the sense of touch to develop manipulative and/or perceptual skills.
15. **Modeling and Imitation**—An activity frequently used for instruction in speech, in which the pupils listen to and observe a model as a basis upon which to practice and improve their performance.
16. **Problem Solving**—A thought process structured by the teacher and employed by the pupils for clearly defining a problem, forming hypothetical solutions, and possibly testing the hypothesis.

17. **Programmed Instruction**—Instruction utilizing a workbook or mechanical and/or electronic device which has been programmed by (a) providing instruction in small steps, (b) asking one or more questions about each step in the instruction and providing instant knowledge of whether each answer is right or wrong, and (c) enabling pupils to progress at their own pace.

18. **Project**—A significant, practical unit of activity having educational value, aimed at one or more definite goals of understanding and involving the investigation and solution of problems.

19. **Reading**—Gathering information from books, periodicals, encyclopedias, and other printed sources of information, including oral reading and silent reading by individuals.

20. **Recitation**—Activities devoted to reporting to a class or other group about information acquired through individual study or group work.

21. **Role-Play**—An activity in which students and/or teacher take on the behavior of a hypothetical or real personality in order to solve a problem and gain insight into a situation.

22. **Seminar**—An activity in which a group of pupils, engaged in research or advanced study, meets under the general direction of one or more staff members for a discussion of problems of mutual interest.

Resources for Learning

Learning resources are not limited to textbooks and traditional teaching materials. Learning resources are now so varied, plentiful, and powerful that they are sometimes confusing to the teacher. The recent extensive application of technology to education has created a critical need to establish criteria for the selection of learning resources. Curriculum planners need to give much consideration to the selection and use of learning resources as more and more commercial materials are produced for schools.

Guidelines for Selection of Learning Resources

Perhaps the most important characteristic to be considered in selecting any resource for learning is its relevancy to the goal-seeking activity involved. The use of an outdated textbook or films without relation to the subject at hand certainly indicates that a teacher has ignored the obvious criterion of relevancy.

A second criterion to be used in the selection of learning resources is accuracy. For years, texts and other materials depicted all children in pictures as white. Sex roles were obvious in those same materials.

Recently, a national awareness of cultural pluralism and changing sex roles has caused publishers and other producers of school materials to eliminate sexist and racist types of references in materials. Teachers need to help pupils identify particular biases, such as those used for advertising, and use materials showing different viewpoints.

Resources for learning should be selected that are appropriate to the needs and interests of the learners. Relevant materials are available on almost any topic to fit any level of student ability or maturity. Teachers must select a wide range of resources sufficient to provide for each individual. Student interests, though, do not dictate that only materials of interest to students should be included in the curriculum. The danger of organizing all resources around the current interests and needs of children, except perhaps in the primary grades, has long been recognized. George Counts in the 1926 Yearbook of the National Society for the Study of Education (NSSE) stated, "Nothing should be included in the curriculum merely because it is of interest to the children, but whatsoever is included should be brought into the closest possible relation with their interest."[11] The entire act of planning for instruction can be seen to be an extension of general curriculum development efforts. In Table 5.2, curriculum development operations (the basis cycle) are shown interfacing with the developing plan for teaching.

Table 5.2
Curriculum and Instruction Related

Operation	Focus	Activity
Analysis	Value clarification Goal setting	Objectives determined Mapping of scope & sequence Content determined
Design	Establishment of the curriculum	Develop lesson plans Select Instructional Strategy Select Materials Identify Management System
Implementation	Planning for Interactive Learning Experiences	Integrate learning for students Individualizing instruction Grouping of students
	Application of Resources	Activate delivery system Establish learning climate Establish learning roles Manage time
Evaluation	Assessment of Effectiveness	Select Evaluation Criteria Collect Sample Evidence Assess in terms of goals and objectives for learning

Sources of Instruction-Center Materials _____

A. **Teachers** are a prime source of instructional materials. Knowing his or her own students and their capabilities and interests, teachers can develop individualized materials with which to reach their students.

B. **Schools** are centers of materials development. Often curriculum guides, guidance materials, and other useful materials are produced by curriculum committees established at the school level. Again, the closeness to students makes these materials especially relevant for the students using materials developed at the school level.

C. **School districts** produce numerous materials that are often disseminated across district lines. Curriculum guides in the subject areas, interdisciplinary booklets, skill continuums, and total curriculum packages that include sources of materials, suggested activities, and skill checklists are found at the district level. The *Savvy Curriculum Project* of the Memphis City Schools is an excellent example of the latter. Many of the inservice activities conducted at the district level include the development of instructional materials.

D. **State departments of education** make use of the services of school personnel, consultants, and staff persons to develop numerous instructional materials. State guides for the elementary, middle, or high school are produced as well as guides in the subject areas. Topics such as team teaching and learning centers often are the source of booklets published by departments of education.

E. **Regional agencies** funded by private and government grants turn out many instructional materials. Often, several school districts will fund a regional agency for purposes of evaluation, research, or to foster innovations. Materials generated by such agencies become the property of the member districts. The development of Leagues of Middle Schools in the past ten years has resulted in the sharing of instructional materials. The Florida League of Middle Schools, established in 1973 as an association for mutual aid, had as one of its stated purposes, "To serve as a clearinghouse for the exchange of ideas, materials, and personnel needed for middle school development."

F. **National networks,** such as the Kettering Foundation, IGE, and the National Middle School Resource Center, are funded by government or foundation grants and provide materials, programs, and consultants. Materials development is usually contracted out to state departments, school systems, and universities. The ERIC network, housed at different universities and other educational agencies, provides for wide dissemination of instructional materials. A similar agency that produced instructional materials for teacher education was the Protocol Center, housed at the University of South Florida in Tampa.

G. **Professional associations** produce numerous instructional materials. Some of the national organizations that produce materials are:

1. The Association for Supervision and Curriculum Development (ASCD)
2. The National Education Association (NEA)
3. Phi Delta Kappa (PDK)
4. The National Association of Elementary School Principals (NAESP)
5. The National Association of Secondary School Principals (NASSP)
6. The American Educational Research Association (AERA)
7. The National Middle School Association (NMSA)

State affiliates of these organizations also produce instructional materials. Annual meetings of state and national organizations usually feature extensive displays of instructional materials.

H. **Commercial publishers and other businesses** produce textbooks that represent the major source through which students gain formal knowledge about the subjects studied at school. Commercial publishers also produce audio and visual materials. Big business has not ignored the education market and such giants as IBM, Westinghouse, and RCA are actively engaged in producing "software" and "hardware" for schools.

I. **Professional journals** usually have a listing of materials that can be obtained free or at nominal costs. Many materials are found on the pages of such journals. Two journals that contain a wealth of such information are *The Instructor* and *Teacher*.

Other sources of instructional materials are found in Appendix B of this text.

Types of Instructional Materials

In this section we shall examine several of the traditional kinds of instructional materials found in most classrooms. We will also discuss some of the newer kinds of instructional materials that are finding their way into our schools.

Textbooks

Textbooks certainly represent the traditional and possibly the major source of formal knowledge acquired by students. Although the use of textbooks has come under increasing attack, teachers have refused to discard them in the classroom. Textbooks are useful and provide a way of organizing information into a meaningful structure. "Base textbook series" in reading are still adopted by school districts although numerous other reading materials and systems are in use. The "back to the basics" movement has strengthened the use of "base" textbooks in schools.

Today's textbooks are well written and more attractive than they were in the past, but with emphasis on individualized instruction, they can only be a part of the repertoire of the classroom teacher. Many textbooks, when examined for readability level, reveal that they seldom are geared for the age or grade group they are intended for in schools. That, coupled with the fact that age or grade level is a poor indicator of mastery of skills, mandates the use of flexible materials of varying difficulty in the classroom. Textbooks are just one of the resources a teacher should use in carrying out instruction.

Other Printed Materials Used in Instruction

These are aimed at individualizing instruction. One form of textual material is called *programmed instruction.* The concept of programmed instruction has fared better than the "teaching machine" advocated by Skinner although many of the same operant conditioning principles are found in programmed instruction.

Self-Pacing Materials

Such materials as "Uni-Pacs," Learning Activity Packages (LAPS), and curriculum units are becoming a part of the vocabulary of students and teachers. Self-pacing materials are materials developed to individualize instruction and are usually found in school settings where the following features are typically found:

Concept-centered curriculum
Some type of provision for flexible scheduling
Continuous progress
Team teaching
Independent study

Self-pacing materials are designed to teach a single idea or concept and are structured for use in a continuous progress school program.[12] Such materials generally include a statement of a major concept, subconcepts, behavioral objectives, a pretest, sequential and diversified learning activities, multi-level content, quest study, posttest, evaluation of materials, teaching suggestions, and identifying information. Behavioral objectives are written at all levels of the cognitive, affective, and psychomotor domains.

Games and Simulation

Classrooms are becoming areas where not only teacher-made, but commercial materials are being innovatively employed. Games and simulation devices have been used to stimulate interest in students in all subject areas.

Games are grounded in the belief that learning ought to be fun—and a conviction that allowing youngsters to find joy in learning bears fruit throughout the rest of their lives.

The attitude of learners toward an activity is important because it so crucially affects how well they will learn that activity.

The use of gaming and simulation devices provides students with an opportunity to learn by doing, and emphasizes the maximum of discovery through activity. Examples of academic games and simulations in use in schools today are found in Table 5.3.

Audiovisual Materials of Instruction _____

The term *audiovisual materials* includes a broad range of materials, but typically excludes textbooks and other printed materials. The distinction becomes less clear when audiovisual materials are accompanied by written materials.

Computer-Assisted Instruction (CAI)

An entrant into the field of instructional materials for several decades, it is just now reaching its potential as a learning tool. The development of a home computer that can be purchased at a reasonable cost and can be used in conjunction with a television set raises the possibility of a dramatic breakthrough in the teaching-learning process.

Educational Films

These can be projected in the classroom or over educational television channels. Films today are produced by government agencies, private companies specializing in educational materials, corporations, and by school districts. An exciting trend of schools today finds students producing films. Availability of cameras and other film equipment in schools today opens up this dimension of instruction for many students.

Educational Television

TV became the subject of criticism in its infancy because it was used as a total instruction program by some educators. Educational television stations, as a part of the public television network, are now producing both in-school programs and out-of-school programs. Government support of public television has resulted in a vast improvement in the quality of programs.

Table 5.3
Academic Games and Simulations

Name of Game	Description
Napoli	Students act as legislators in a fictional House of Representatives, and each represents a region and a party. Each student exercises one vote after each of eleven issues has been discussed and debated. The student's reelection depends upon satisfactorily representing both the *region* and the party.
Plans	The student acts as a member of an Interest Group which uses its influence to produce changes in American society. Each group has specific goals.
A Simulation of American Government	This game utilizes the roles played by national government officials such as President, Cabinet, Senate, and the pressures exerted by interest groups and news media.
Simsoc	Students participate as citizens in a simulated society, in which each person's goals depend on other people in the society for their achievement.
Life Career Game	Designed to simulate the kinds of choices and decisions each of us must make throughout life. Each player is given various basic facts about the hypothetical person and must then make decisions relative to education, employment, marriage, etc. Each round of the game represents a year in the person's life.
Galapagos	Focuses on the evolution of Darwin's finches on the Galapagos Islands. It aids in teaching the concepts of speciation and adaptive evolution.
Structural Linguistics	Game of English
Emergency Preparedness Simulation Game	Game of health and physical education.
Equations	This game of creative mathematics provides a situation for learning some of the elementary operations of mathematics—addition, subtraction, multiplication, division, and exponentiation.

Cassettes, Slides, and Tapes

These are a part of the audiovisual equipment in today's schools. Slide-tape productions are used in learning centers and students are using and producing audiovisual materials. Peer-produced materials are adding to the quality of instruction in many classrooms.

The impact of television on curriculum content has drawn increasing attention from educators who view television as both a threat and a promise. Research indicating that school age youth view television an average of twenty-five hours a week has caused concern about the quality of television programming. A number of groups over the last decade have been organized to aid in the development of television as a medium for positive learning experiences.

1. The AIT (Agency for Instructional Television) is a nonprofit American-Canadian organization formed in 1973 from the parent organization, National Instructional Television. The stated purpose of AIT is to strengthen education through television and other technologies. The AIT, in a joint effort with state agencies, develops and distributes program projects. Schools may write to the main office to request their being placed on the AIT mail list to receive the quarterly newsletter and program information:

   > Agency for Instructional Television
   > Box A
   > Bloomington, Indiana 47401
   > (812) 339-2203

2. PTST (Prime Time School Television) is a nonprofit organization dedicated to "making television work for teachers and teachers work for television." Teachers are encouraged to recommend and use the evening television as part of their classroom resources. Guides and program materials produced through PTST are made available through the programs' commercial sponsors.

   > PTST
   > 120 South LaSalle Street
   > Chicago, Illinois 60603

Finally, teachers are able to enrich instructional delivery through the use of a variety of teaching activities, materials, and methodologies. A partial list of these techniques is found in Table 5.4.

Analyzing Instructional Personnel _____

While instructional supervision is not normally considered a function of those responsible for curriculum development, the authors believe that it should be. The truth is that any curriculum program is only as good as the instructor who delivers it. By any logic, the classroom teacher is a part of the curriculum and therefore should be a concern of curriculum planners. Until recently, educational researchers have had a fairly long history of not being of much help to educational practitioners. Other than a general checklist of teacher competencies, a supervisor was armed with little else to judge the effectiveness of a particular teacher. Since about 1960, however, systems and instruments have been developed to help us look at classroom instruction in a more systematic way.

The concept of systematic observation is certainly one of the more widely publicized of these recent innovations. By its very nature and basic construct, an observational system represents an effective

Table 5.4
Partial List of Teaching Activities and Materials

Learning centers
Collages
Models
Films
Bulletin boards
Small group discussion
Exhibits or displays
Games
Scrapbooks
Notebooks
Speeches
Plays or skits
Large group discussion
Filmstrips
Observations
Panel discussions
Assigned readings
Slides
Puppets
Role playing
Resource people
Field trips
Interviews
Debates
Newspaper articles (want ads)
Brainstorming
Research projects
Simulated work activities
Writing letters
VTR (Video taping)
Unipacs or LAPS
Committee work
Overhead and/or opaque projectors
Demonstrations
Problem solving
Decision-making problems
Radio and television programs

means for providing objective empirical data describing specific teacher and student variables that are found to interact in a given teaching-learning situation. Data of this kind have been found to be quite helpful in helping teachers analyze and improve their individual teaching effectiveness.

Currently, several manageable observational systems are available for teacher use. Each is specifically designed to assess a different and particular dimension of the classroom situation. Originally developed by Flanders, interaction analysis is designed to assess the verbal dimension of the teacher-pupil interaction in the classroom.[13]

Flanders developed a category system that takes into account the verbal interaction between teachers and pupils in the classroom. The system enables one to determine whether the teacher controls students in such a way as to increase or decrease freedom of action. Through the use of observers or by using audio or video tape equipment, a teacher can review the results of a teaching lesson. Every three seconds an observer writes down the category number of the interaction he or she has just observed. The numbers are recorded in sequence in a column. Whether the observer is using a live classroom or tape recording for his or her observations, it is best for the observer to spend ten to fifteen minutes getting oriented to the situation before categorizing. The observer stops classifying whenever the classroom activity is inappropriate as, for instance, when there is silent reading or when various groups are working in the classroom, or when children are working in their workbooks.

A modification of the Flanders system of ten categories is a system developed by Hough and used by Bondi and Ober in research studies.[14, 15] That system provides three more categories of behavior than the Flanders system. In the thirteen-category system, teacher statements are classified as either indirect or direct. This classification gives central attention to the amount of freedom a teacher gives to the student. In a given situation, the teacher can choose to be indirect, that is, maximizing freedom of a student to respond, or she or he can be direct, that is, minimizing the freedom of a student to respond. Teacher response is classified under the first nine categories.

Student talk is classified under three categories and a fourth category provides for silence or confusion where neither a student nor the teacher can be heard. All categories are mutually exclusive, yet totally inclusive of all verbal interaction occurring in the classroom. Table 5.5 describes the categories in the thirteen-category modification of the Flanders System of Interaction Analysis.

Verbal Patterns of Teachers in the Classroom

Utilizing the Flanders system and other modifications of that system, teachers and supervisors can begin to isolate the essential elements of effective teaching by analyzing and categorizing the verbal behavioral patterns of teachers and students.

Four classroom patterns that particularly affect pupil learning are thrown into sharp relief when verbal patterns are identified and revealed by these techniques.

Table 5.5
Description of Categories for a Thirteen-Category Modification of the Flanders System of Interaction Analysis

	Category Number	Description of Verbal Behavior
T E A C H E R — **I N D I R E C T**	1.	*Accepts Feeling:* Accepts and clarifies the feeling tone of students in a friendly manner. Student feelings may be of a positive or negative nature. Predicting and recalling student feelings are also included.
	2.	*Praises or Encourages:* Praises or encourages student action, behavior, recitation, comments, ideas, etc. Jokes that release tension not at the expense of another individual. Teacher nodding head or saying "uh-huh" or "go on" are included.
	3.	*Accepts or Uses Ideas of Student:* Clarifying, building on, developing, and accepting the action, behavior, and ideas of the student.
	4.	*Asks Questions:* Asking a question about the content (subject matter) or procedure with the intent that the student should answer.
	5.	*Answers Student Questions (Student-Initiated Teacher Talk):* Giving direct answers to student questions regarding content or procedures.
T A L K — **D I R E C T**	6.	*Lecture (Teacher-Initiated Teacher Talk):* Giving facts, information, or opinions about content or procedure. Teacher expressing his or her own ideas. Asking rhetorical questions (not intended to be answered).
	7.	*Gives Directions:* Directions, commands, or orders to which the student is expected to comply.
	8.	*Corrective Feedback:* Telling a student that his answer is wrong when the correctness of his answer can be established by other than opinions (i.e., empirical validation, definition, or custom).
	9.	*Criticizes Student(s) or Justifies Authority:* Statements intended to change student behavior from a nonacceptable to an acceptable pattern; scolding someone; stating why the teacher is doing what he is doing so as to gain or maintain control; rejecting or criticizing a student's opinion or judgment.

Table 5.5
(continued)

	Category Number	Description of Verbal Behavior
	10.	*Teacher-Initiated Student Talk:* Talk by students in response to requests or narrow teacher questions. The teacher initiates the contact or solicits student's statements.
S T U D E N T T A L K	11.	*Student Questions:* Student questions concerning content or procedure that are directed to the teacher.
	12.	*Student-Initiated Student Talk:* Talk by students in response to broad teacher questions which require judgment or opinion. Voluntary declarative statements offered by the student, but not called for by the teacher.
	13.	*Silence or Confusion:* Pauses, short periods of silence, and periods of confusion in which communication cannot be understood by an observer.

Indirect-Direct Ratio = categories 1, 2, 3, 4, 5
                        categories 6, 7, 8, 9

Revised Indirect-Direct Ratio = categories 1, 2, 3
                                categories 7, 8, 9

Student-Teacher Ratio = categories 10, 11, 12
                        categories 1, 2, 3, 4, 5, 6, 7, 8, 9

The first pattern can be labeled "the excessive teacher-talk pattern." This occurs when teachers talk two-thirds or more of the time in the classroom. Obviously, if teachers are talking that much, there is very little time for students to get in the act. In classrooms where teachers talk at least two-thirds of the time, pity the curriculum approaches that emphasize extensive student participation in learning. Yet the two-thirds percentage of teacher talk is found in many classrooms today. Teachers can become aware of and able to control the amount of time they spend in the classroom through the use of feedback from interaction analysis.[16] This finding alone makes interaction analysis an effective teaching and supervisory tool.

A second verbal pattern is recitation. Arno Bellack, a pioneer in describing verbal behavior of teachers and pupils, has noted that despite differences in ability or background, teachers acted very much like one another.[17] They talked between two-thirds and three-quarters of the time. The majority of their activity was asking and reacting to questions that called for factual answers from students. Bellack and others presented an elaborate description of the verbal behavior of teachers and students during a study of fifteen New York City area high school social studies classrooms.[18] They summarized the results of their analysis in a set of descriptive "rules of the language game of teaching." Among their observations were the following:

1. The teacher-pupil ratio of activity in lines of typescript is 3 to 1. Therefore, teachers are considerably more active in amount of verbal activity.
2. The pedagogical roles of the classroom are clearly delineated for pupils and teachers. Teachers are responsible for structuring the lesson and soliciting responses. The primary task of the pupil is to respond to the teacher's solicitations.
3. In most cases, structuring accounts for about ten lines spoken; soliciting, responding, and reacting each account for twenty to thirty percent of the lines.
4. The basic verbal interchange in the classroom is the solicitation-response. Classes differ in the rate at which verbal interchanges take place.
5. By far, the largest proportion of the discourse involved empirical (factual) meanings. Most of the units studied were devoted to stating facts and explaining principles while much less of the discourse involved defining terms or expressing or justifying opinions. The core of the teaching sequence found in the classrooms studied was a teacher question, a pupil response, and more often than not, a teacher's reaction to that response.

William Hoetker studied junior high English classes in 1967 and his findings were much the same as Bellack's.[19]

Hoetker compared his findings in a report found in the *American Educational Research Journal.* Those comparisons are found in Table 5.6.

The findings of Bellack and Hoetker hardly seem earth-shaking to those who have observed teaching over the years. As a pedagogical method, the question-answer sequence was fully recognized fifty years ago when teacher education consisted of considerable training in the skill of asking questions. Unfortunately, it is still with us, despite the fact that successive generations of otherwise quite disparate educational leaders have condemned the rapid-fire question-answer pattern of instruction. This leads us to question the efficiency, or, in this case, the inefficiency of teacher training institutions in affecting the classroom behavior of teachers. If recitation is indeed a poor pedagogical method, why have teacher educators not been able to deter teachers from using it? Is recitation of textbook facts still to be the representative method of teaching pupils in American schools?

A classroom where recitation predominates suggests not only that a teacher is doing most of the work, but is giving little attention to individual needs of students. Moreover, the educational assets of role recitation are only verbal memory and superficial judgment.[20]

A third verbal pattern of teachers that affects student learning is teacher acceptance of student ideas. There is ample evidence that

Table 5.6

Comparisons Between Selected Mean Measures of Classroom
Verbal Behavior in Bellack (1966) and Hoetker (1967)

Measure	Bellack	Hoetker
A. Percentage of teacher talk, moves	61.7	65.7
B. Percentage of teacher talk, lines of typescript	72.1	74.5
C. Distribution of teacher moves, as percentage of all moves		
STRUCTURING	4.8	3.6
SOLICITING	28.8	32.3
RESPONDING	3.5	1.8
REACTING	24.3	27.0
D. Distribution of pupil moves, as percentage of all moves		
STRUCTURING	0.4	0.3
SOLICITING	4.4	2.0
RESPONDING	25.0	30.4
REACTING	5.7	1.1
E. Distribution of teacher moves, as percentage of total lines of typescript		
STRUCTURING	14.5	22.4
SOLICITING	20.3	20.6
RESPONDING	5.0	4.3
REACTING	24.8	31.4
F. Distribution of pupil moves, as percentage of total lines of typescript		
STRUCTURING	3.0	3.4
SOLICITING	2.5	1.2
RESPONDING	15.6	13.1
REACTING	5.1	0.6
G. Percentage of teacher questions calling for memory processes	80.8*	87.9

*Estimated from data on pages 74–75, Bellack (1966)

Source: Short, Edmund C., "Knowledge Production and Utilization in Curriculum: A Special Case of the General Phenomenon." *Reveiw of Educational Research,* Summer 1979, pp. 237–301. Copyright 1979, American Educational Research Association, Washington, D.C.

teachers who accept the ideas and feelings of students enhance learning in the classroom. A number of observational systems have been used to identify teacher acceptance. In a large-scale study, Flanders isolated junior high school teachers whose students learned the most and the least in social studies and mathematics. He found teachers of higher achieving classes used five to six times as much acceptance and encouragement of student ideas than teachers in lower achieving classes. Teachers in higher achieving classes were also less directive and critical of student behavior.[21] Findings similar to Flanders were found by Amidon and Giammatteo when they compared thirty superior teachers with one hundred fifty randomly selected teachers in elementary schools.[22]

The fourth pattern of teachers that affects pupil learning uncovers a teacher's flexibility—or inflexibility. Arno Bellack, in his "Rules of the Classroom Game," dramatically points up the power of the teacher. The teacher structures the game, asks the questions, evaluates the responses, and speaks "the truth" while students don't structure the game, respond to questions, keep their own questions to a minimum, and depend upon the teacher to decide whether or not they have spoken the truth.[23]

Hughes, in a study of classroom behavior, found the most frequent teaching acts were controlling ones.[24] Teachers in her study who were considered "good teachers" were those well-organized and generally attentive. Control meant goal-setting and directing children to the precise thing to which they gave attention. Not only is content identified for pupils, but they are held to a specific answer and process of working. The teacher wants one answer. As long as the question or statement that structures the class requires but one answer, the teacher is in absolute control.

Classroom Questions

In the Flanders or Modified Flanders System of Interaction Analysis, only one category of behavior deals with questions. That category concerns a teacher asking questions about content or procedure in order to elicit a student response. For a teacher to obtain greater understanding of her or his questions, other types of feedback instruments must be used.

Questioning is probably the most ancient pedagogical method. The dialogues of Socrates and dialectics of Plato have been used throughout history as models for teachers. As pointed out earlier in the section on recitation, unfortunately most of the questions asked by teachers require little thinking on the part of students. A number of reports in recent years have confirmed the high frequency of questions asked by teachers that require little more than the recall of memorized material.[25]

Perhaps these reports of the low level of teachers' questioning are the result of a tradition of teachers asking set questions requiring memorized answers. In improving classroom instruction, we must examine ways teachers' questioning ability can be developed. One of the most frequently used guides to the cognitive level of teachers' questions has been Bloom's *Taxonomy of Educational Objectives,* 1956.[26] A report of studies conducted by Farley and Clegg indicated that training in the knowledge and use of Bloom's taxonomy helps teachers increase their use of questions at higher cognitive levels.[27]

Table 5.7 illustrates how Bloom's taxonomy can be used in classifying teacher questions.

Another guide to cognitive level of teachers' questions has been Norris Sanders' taxonomy of questions.[28] Sanders has classified questions into the following seven categories:

Memory Questions—These are questions that ask students to recall or recognize ideas previously presented to them.

Translation Question—This occurs when students are presented with an idea and asked to restate the same idea in a different way.

Interpretation Questions—Students are asked to compare certain ideas or use ideas studied previously to solve problems that are new to them.

Application Questions—Application questions are similar to interpretation questions in that a student has to use an idea learned previously to solve a new problem. However, in application a student has to use an idea when not told to do so, but when the problem demands it. This involves transfer of training to a new situation.

Analysis Questions—Analysis questions ask students to solve problems through logical processes such as induction, deduction, cause and effect.

Synthesis Questions—Students put ideas together to create something. This could be a physical object, a communication, or even a set of abstract relations.

Evaluation Questions—Students must make a value judgment based on certain considerations such as usefulness, effectiveness, etc.

Inquiry or discovery methods of teaching have focused attention on questioning techniques. Richard Suchman has reported on a system of inquiry training to help teachers ask the appropriate "why" questions to get students to hypothesize about the relationship of events to explain phenomena.[29] Suchman's studies suggest that children can learn to develop a questioning style that will lead them to form testable hypotheses and procedures for verifying hypotheses.

Another approach to questioning has been developed in Taba's system of cognitive processes or tasks.[30] Taba developed a set of eliciting questions for use with each of the cognitive tasks of concept formation, development of generalizations, and application of principles to new situations. The teacher questions were formulated to elicit certain essential behaviors by students that are necessary to the accomplishment of cognitive tasks. Teachers in preservice or inservice programs might apply this approach to gain experience in a particular learning process before she or he begins to analyze it as a teaching process.

Table 5.7
Classifying Classroom Questions

Category	Key Word	Typical Question Words
1. *Knowledge* (Any question, regardless of complexity, that can be answered through simple recall of previously learned material.) e.g., "What reasons did Columbus give for wanting to sail west to find a new world?"	Remember	1. Name 2. List; Tell 3. Define 4. Who? When? What? 5. Yes or No questions: e.g., "Did...?" "Was...?" "Is...?" 6. How many? How much? 7. Recall or identify terminology. 8. What did the book say...?
2. *Comprehension* (Questions that can be answered by merely restating or reorganizing material in a rather literal manner to show that the student understands the essential meaning.) e.g., "Give the ideas in your own words."	Understand	1. Give an example... 2. What is the most important idea? 3. What will probably happen? 4. What caused this? 5. Compare. (What things are the same?) 6. Contrast. (What things are different?) 7. Why did you say that? 8. Give the idea in your own words.
3. *Application* (Questions that involve problem solving in new situations with minimal identification or prompting of the appropriate rules, principles, or concepts.) e.g., "How big an air conditioner?"	Solve the problem	1. Solve 2. How could you find an answer to ...? 3. Apply the generalization to ...

Table 5.7
(continued)

Category	Key Word	Typical Question Words
4. *Analysis* (Questions that require the student to break an idea into its component parts for logical analysis: assumptions, facts, opinions, logical conclusions, etc.) e.g.,. "Are the conclusions supported by facts or opinion?"	Logical Order	1. What reason does he give for his conclusions? 2. What method is he using to convince you? 3. What does the author seem to believe? 4. What words indicate bias or emotion? 5. Does the evidence given support the conclusion?
5. *Synthesis* (Questions that require the student to combine his ideas into a statement, plan, product, etc., that is new for him.) e.g., "Can you develop a program that includes the best parts of each of those ideas?"	Create	1. Create a plan . . . 2. Develop a model . . . 3. Combine those parts . . .
6. *Evaluation* (Questions that require the student to make a judgment about something using some criterion or standard for making his judgment.)	Judge	1. Evaluate that idea in terms of . . . 2. For what reasons do you favor . . . 3. Which policy do you think would result in the greatest good for the greatest number?[22]

The Gallagher-Aschner system of analyzing and controlling classroom questioning behavior has been widely used in preservice and inservice teacher training programs.[31]

This system is derived from intensive analyses of human mental abilities done by J.P. Guilford and his associates. Although there are many subcategories in the system, the use of just four of the major categories of classifying levels of questions can give a teacher strong clues as to the level of thinking demanded of students by that teacher.

Table 5.8 lists four of the major categories of the Gallagher-Aschner system with examples of types of questions used in each of the categories.

Table 5.8
The Gallagher-Aschner System: A Technique for Analyzing and Controlling Classroom Questioning Behavior

1. *Cognitive-Memory:* calls for a specific memorized answer or response; anything which can be retrieved from the memory bank.

   1a. What is 2 × 3?
   1b. When did Florida become a state?
   1c. What is a noun?
   1d. At what temperature Centigrade does water boil?

2. *Convergent:* calls for a specific (single) correct answer which may be obtained by the application of a rule or procedure; normally requires the consideration of more than a single quantity of information and/or knowledge.

   2a. What is 30.5 × 62.7?
   2b. How many years was the U.S. under the Prohibition Law?
   2c. Diagram this sentence.
   2d. How many calories are required to melt 160 grams of ice at 0 C?

3. *Divergent:* allows the student a choice between more than one alternative or to create ideas of his own; more than a single answer is appropriate and acceptable.

   3a. What is 10 to three other bases?
   3b. What might have been the effects on the growth of the United States had there not be a Civil War?
   3c. Write a short story about Halloween.
   3d. Design an apparatus that will demonstrate the Law of Conservation of Matter.

4. *Evaluative:* the development and/or establishment of relevant standard of criteria of acceptability involving considerations as usefulness, desirability, social and cultural appropriateness, and moral and ethical propriety, then comparing the issue at hand to these; involves the making of value judgments.

   4a. Is 10 the best base for a number system?
   4b. Was the Civil War defensible?
   4c. Is English the best choice for a universal language?
   4d. Should we continue our space program now that we have landed on the moon?

In their work with their system, Gallagher and Aschner found that a majority of teacher behavior falls in the first level, cognitive memory, but that even a slight increase in divergent questions leads to a major increase in divergent ideas produced by students. Sanders' work indicated that for teachers not acquainted with a system of looking at questioning, very few questions asked by those teachers fell above category one. The Florida Taxonomy of Cognitive Behavior, used at the University of Florida and the University of South Florida, parallels the Gallagher-Aschner system. It is based on Bloom's Taxonomy of Educational Objectives and the Sanders system. Use of the Florida taxonomy with teachers has produced findings that indicate extensive teacher use of low levels of questioning.

The need for helping teachers analyze classroom questions and developing appropriate strategies of questioning indicates that systematic training in the use of questions be made available to teachers. A number of systems of analyzing and controlling classroom questioning behavior has been presented in this chapter. These and other systems should be used in helping train teachers to stimulate productive thought processes in the classroom.

Nonverbal Communication in the Classroom

The importance of analyzing and controlling verbal behavior of teachers has been well documented. Another dimension of teaching that has drawn the attention of researchers is nonverbal communication. Nonverbal communication is often referred to as a silent language. Individuals send messages through a variety of conventional and non-conventional means. Facial expressions, bodily movements, and vocal tones all convey feelings to students. A student may be hearing a teacher verbally praise her work while the teacher's facial expression is communicating disapproval of that work. If a teacher fails to understand the nonverbal message being conveyed to his pupils, he may not be able to comprehend their responses to him. In analyzing a classroom, then, it is just as important to examine *how* the teacher says what she has to say, how she behaves and expresses feelings, as *what* the teacher says, does, and feels. How teachers communicate their perceptions, feelings, and motivations can be identified with facial expressions, gestures, and vocal tones. Such expressions determine in large measure how pupils perceive those teachers.

In examining the significance of nonverbal communication, it is important to understand that teaching is a highly personal matter and prospective inservice teachers need to face themselves as well as to acquire pedagogical skills. Teachers need to become more aware of the connection between the messages they communicate and the consequences that follow. Teachers also need to capitalize on the nonverbal cues expressed by students as keys to their clarity and understanding. While nonverbal interaction in the classroom is less amenable to systematic objective inquiry than verbal interaction, the meanings pupils give to a teacher's nonverbal message have significance for learning and teaching.

Through continued study of nonverbal behavior, teachers can sharpen, alter, and modify their nonverbal messages they transmit to students. The advantage of adding nonverbal analysis in a study of teaching is that teachers can look at their behavior in two ways—what their behavior means to pupils, and how their behavior is being interpreted by their pupils.

Classroom Management

Another aspect of teaching, and one that is becoming increasingly important in today's classrooms, is classroom management. The changing family structure and increased conflict found in all elements of our society have led to concern about a general breakdown of school discipline and the need for better classroom management. There are a number of techniques to help a teacher maintain an effective learning environment in the classroom.

Kounin* has developed a system for analyzing classroom management that deals with transitions from one unit to another. The following are examples:

Group alerting. The teacher notifies pupils of an imminent change in activity, watches to see that pupils are finishing the previous activity, and initiates the new one only when all of the class members are ready. In contrast, *thrusting* is represented when the teacher "bursts" in on pupil activity with no warning and no awareness, apparently, of anything but his own internal needs.

Stimulus boundedness is represented by behavior in which the teacher is apparently trapped by some stimulus as a moth by a flame. For example, a piece of paper on the floor leads to interruption of the on-going activities of the classroom while the teacher berates the class members for the presence of the paper on the floor or tries to find out how it got there.

Overlappingness is the teacher's ability to carry on two operations at once. For example, while the teacher is working with a reading group, a pupil comes to ask a question about arithmetic. The teacher handles the situation in a way which keeps the reading group at work while he simultaneously helps the child with his arithmetic.

A dangle occurs when the teacher calls for the end of one activity, initiates another one, then returns to the previous activity. For example, "Now pupils, put away your arithmetic books and papers and get out your spelling books; we're going to have spelling." After the pupils have put away their arithmetic materials and gotten out their spelling materials the teacher asks, "Oh, by the way, did everybody get problem four right?"

If the teacher never gets back to the new activity which he initiated (for example, if he had never returned

*For a detailed report of Kounin's work, see Jacob S. Kounin, *Discipline and Group Management in Classrooms* (New York: Holt, Rinehart & Winston, Inc., 1970).

to the spelling in the previous example) this would be a *truncation.*

With-itness is the teacher's demonstration of his awareness of deviant behavior. It is scored both for timing and for target accuracy. Timing involves stopping the deviant behavior before it spreads, and target accuracy involves identifying the responsible pupil. If, for example, an occurrence of whispering in the back of the room spread to several other children, and at this point the teacher criticizes one of the later class members who joined in, this would be scored negatively both for timing and for target accuracy.

The Kounin examples illustrate the ways teachers can maintain the group and not hinder learning in the classroom. In analyzing classrooms, we must not ignore the techniques of group management teachers must utilize daily. Teachers must be provided feedback of their own behavior if they are to improve instruction.

Improving the Skills of Teaching

Teachers are almost universally expected to evaluate, revise, and improve the methods they follow in their teaching. The improvement of teaching involves a behavioral change on the part of teachers. That change comes after careful analysis and feedback of information. Feedback may come from any number of sources including observational systems such as the Flanders system, the analysis of a microteaching lesson, or simply from peer comments.

Evaluation of teaching performance has numerous meanings and connotations ranging from a rating or grading to a gathering of information to assess the effects of program and teaching.

In this chapter, a number of different instruments and systems were identified that look at classroom instruction and provide teachers with feedback about teaching performance. The use of evaluation instruments involves appropriate procedures and techniques. The following guideline should be used by professional personnel in using evaluation instruments:

1. Evaluation instruments should be as objective as possible.
2. Evaluation instruments should be relatively simple, understandable, and convenient to use.
3. Evaluation criteria should focus on performance.
4. All personnel should be familiar with the instruments used and procedures followed in evaluating effectiveness.
5. Personnel should be encouraged to make self-evaluations prior to formal evaluations by others.

The accountability movement with its emphasis on student performance has resulted in increased data from researches linking pupil performance to a number of variables, most of which are not directly controlled by the teacher. Changing social patterns have resulted in increased numbers of schoolchildren coming from broken homes. The trauma of a breakdown in the family structure has placed an additional burden on the schools which must provide additional instruction in the "basics" and still provide an atmosphere of attention, affection, and stability so needed by school-age youngsters. The human quality of teaching then becomes an important dimension in today's schools.

A feedback model that attempts to assess the unique human quality of teaching is the Tuckman Teacher Feedback Form.[32]

The Tuckman Form shown in Figure 5.3 involves an observer rating a teacher in each of twenty-eight categories of behavior describing a human element in teaching.

Figure 5.3 Tuckman Teacher Feedback Form (TTFF)

Teacher Observed _____ Observer _____ Date _____

Place an X in that one space of the seven between each adjective pair that best indicates your perception of the teacher's behavior. The closer you place your X toward one adjective or the other, the better you think that adjective describes the teacher.

1.	original __:__:__:__:__:__:__	conventional
2.	patient __:__:__:__:__:__:__	impatient
3	cold __:__:__:__:__:__:__	warm
4.	hostile __:__:__:__:__:__:__	amiable
5.	creative __:__:__:__:__:__:__	routinized
6.	inhibited __:__:__:__:__:__:__	uninhibited
7.	iconoclastic __:__:__:__:__:__:__	ritualistic
8.	gentle __:__:__:__:__:__:__	harsh
9.	unfair __:__:__:__:__:__:__	fair
10.	capricious __:__:__:__:__:__:__	purposeful
11.	cautious __:__:__:__:__:__:__	experimenting
12.	disorganized __:__:__:__:__:__:__	organized
13.	unfriendly __:__:__:__:__:__:__	sociable
14.	resourceful __:__:__:__:__:__:__	uncertain
15.	reserved __:__:__:__:__:__:__	outspoken
16.	imaginative __:__:__:__:__:__:__	exacting
17.	erratic __:__:__:__:__:__:__	systematic
18.	aggressive __:__:__:__:__:__:__	passive
19.	accepting (people) __:__:__:__:__:__:__	critical
20.	quiet __:__:__:__:__:__:__	bubbly
21.	outgoing __:__:__:__:__:__:__	withdrawn
22.	in control __:__:__:__:__:__:__	on the run
23.	flighty __:__:__:__:__:__:__	conscientious
24.	dominant __:__:__:__:__:__:__	submissive
25.	observant __:__:__:__:__:__:__	preoccupied
26.	introverted __:__:__:__:__:__:__	extroverted
27.	assertive __:__:__:__:__:__:__	soft-spoken
28.	timid __:__:__:__:__:__:__	adventurous

Figure 5.4 Tuckman Teacher Feedback Form Summary Sheet

A scoring system for the twenty-eight items is shown in Figure 5.4.

Person observed _____ Observer _____ Date _____

A. Item Scoring

    I. Under the last set of dashes on the sheet of 28 items, write the numbers 7–6–5–4–3–2–1. This will give a number value to each of the seven spaces between the 28 pairs of adjectives.

    II. Determine the number value for the first pair, Original-Conventional. Write it into the formula given below on the appropriate line under Item 1. For example, if you place an X on the first dash next to "Original" in Item 1, then write the number 7 on the dash under Item 1 in the summary formula below.

    III. Do the same for each of the 28 items. Plug each value into the formula.

    IV. Compute the score for each of the four dimensions in the summary formula.

B. Summary Formula and Score for the Four Dimensions

    I. Creativity

        Item (1 + 5 + 7 + 16) – (6 + 11 + 28) + 18

           (__ + __ + __ + __) – (__ + __ + __) + 18 = _____

    II. Dynamism (dominance and energy)

        Item (18 + 21 + 24 + 27) – (15 + 20 + 26) + 18

           (__ + __ + __ + __) – (__ + __ + __) + 18 = _____

    III. Organized Demeanor (organization and control)

        Item (14 + 22 + 25) – (10 + 12 + 17 + 23) + 26

           (__ + __ + __) – (__ + __ + __ + __) + 26 = _____

    IV. Warmth and Acceptance

        Item (2 + 8 + 19) – (3 + 4 + 9 + 13) + 26

           (__ + __ + __) – (__ + __ + __ + __) + 26 = _____

The Tuckman Form is a system for providing feedback in the affective domain. Teaching can be improved by an efficient program of supervision and through the use of systems such as the Tuckman Form that provide effective feedback to teachers. Modern teachers must make use of the feedback provided them whether that feedback comes from formal observations of outside observers or from instruments used by teachers themselves in the classroom.

Summary

Instructional considerations in curriculum development require planners to move beyond the theoretical framework of curriculum to the implementation of such plans in a classroom setting. Teachers are the ultimate determiners of the curriculum.

Goals and objectives serve to guide the selection of learning experiences in the classroom. Special care must be taken to provide for culturally diverse students, a rational process for selecting content, and maintaining relevance in the curriculum.

The organization of instruction should be an orderly process. The degree of individualization, the formality of instruction, grouping patterns, scheduling patterns, and the question of homogeneity vs heterogeneity should follow from the goals and objectives of the programs. Likewise, teaching strategies, the selection of resources, and the means of delivery should all be rationalized in terms of the intent of the curriculum.

Curriculum planners should involve themselves with teachers and their behaviors to insure that instruction complements the curriculum plan. Verbal patterns, classroom questions, non-verbal behaviors of the teacher, and classroom management are all instructional variables that affect the delivery of the curriculum. Where needed, the curriculum planner should become involved in improving the skills of the classroom teacher as they contribute to an effective curriculum.

Notes

1. Ernest F. Garcia, "Chicano Cultural Diversity: Implications for Competency Based Teacher Education," *ERIC Documents*, ED 901375 (May, 1974): 15.
2. A.S.C.D. Multicultural Education Commission, "Encouraging Multicultural Education," *Educational Leadership* 34, No. 4 (January, 1977): 291.
3. Joseph Watras, "The Textbook Dispute in West Virginia: A New Form of Oppression," *Educational Leadership* 33, No. 1 (October, 1975): 21-23.
4. Hilda Taba, *Curriculum Development, Theory and Practice* (New York: Harcourt, Brace and World, Inc., 1962), p. 40.
5. Joseph C. Bondi, Jr., *Developing Middle Schools: A Guidebook* (Wheeling, Illinois: Whitehall Company, Publishers, 1977), p. 87.
6. Robert H. Anderson, "Individualization—The Unfulfilled Goal," *Educational Leadership* 34, No. 5 (February, 1977): 323-24.
7. Herbert Klausmeir, Richard Rossmiller, and Mary Saily, *Individually Guided Elementary Education* (New York: Academic Press, 1977), p. 1.
8. George Weber, "The Cult of Individualized Instruction," *Educational Leadership* 34, No. 5 (February, 1977): 326-29.
9. B. Frank Brown, *The Nongraded High School* (Englewood Cliffs, New Jersey: Prentice-Hall, 1963).
10. James Popham and Eva Baker, *Planning an Instructional Sequence* (Englewood Cliffs, New Jersey: Prentice-Hall, 1963), pp. 2-3.
11. George Counts, "Some Notes on the Foundations of Curriculum Making," 26th Yearbook, National Society for the Study of Education (Bloomington, Indiana: Public School Publishing Co. 1926): 80.
12. Joseph C. Bondi, *Developing Middle Schools: A Guidebook* (Wheeling, Illinois: Whitehall Company, 1977) p. 72.

13. Ned A. Flanders, *Teacher Influence—Pupil Attitudes and Achievement* (Washington: Research Monograph 12, H.E.W., 1965).

14. John B. Hough, "A Thirteen Category Modification of Flanders' System of Interaction Analysis," mimeographed (Columbus, Ohio: The Ohio State University, 1965).

15. Joseph Bondi and Richard Ober, "The Effects of Interaction Analysis Feedback on the Verbal Behavior of Student Teachers." A paper presented at the annual meeting of the American Educational Research Association, Los Angeles, February, 1969.

16. Joseph C. Bondi, Jr., "Feedback in the Form of Printed Interaction Analysis Matrices as a Technique for Training Student Teachers." A paper read at the annual meeting of the American Educational Research Association, Los Angeles, February, 1969.

17. Arnold A. Bellack et al., *The Language of the Classroom* (New York: Teachers College Press, 1966).

18. Ibid.

19. Ibid., pp. 84–86.

20. William J. Hoetker, "An Analysis of the Subject Matter Related Verbal Behavior in Nine Junior High English Classes." (Ed. D. diss., Washington University, 1967).

21. Joseph C. Bondi, Jr., "Verbal Patterns of Teachers in the Classroom," *National Elementary Principal* 50, 5 (Washington, D.C., April, 1971): 90–91.

22. E. Amidon and M. Giammatteo, "The Verbal Behavior of Superior Teachers," *Elementary School Journal* 65 (February, 1965): 283–85.

23. Bellack, *The Language of the Classroom*, p. 13.

24. Marie Hughes, "What is Teaching? One Viewpoint," *Educational Leadership* 19, no. 4 (January, 1962): 37.

25. Ambrose A. Clegg, Jr., et al., "Teacher Strategies of Questioning for Eliciting Selected Cognitive Student Responses," (A Report of the Tri-University Project, University of Washington, 1970), p. 1.

26. Benjamin S. Bloom, ed., *Taxnomy of Educational Objectives: Handbook I— Cognitive Domain* (New York: David McKay, 1956).

27. George Farley and Ambrose Clegg, Jr., "Increasing the Cognitive Level of Classroom Questions in Social Studies." (A paper read at the annual meeting of the American Educational Research Association, Los Angeles, February, 1969).

28. Norris Sanders, "Synopsis of Taxonomy of Questions" mimeographed, n.p., n.d. See also Sanders' excellent text, *Classroom Questions, What Kinds* (New York: Harper & Row, 1966) 176 pages.

29. J. Richard Suchman, "Inquiry Training: Building Skills for Autonomous Discovery," *Merrill-Palmer Quarterly of Behavior and Development* 7 (1961): 154–155.

30. Hilda Taba, *Teaching Strategies and Cognitive Functioning in Elementary School Children.* (Washington, D.C.: H.E.W., U.S. Office of Education, Cooperative Research Project No. 2404, 1965).

31. J.J. Gallagher and Mary Jane Aschner, "A Preliminary Report: Analyses of Classroom Interaction," *Merrill-Palmer Quarterly of Behavior and Development* 9 (1963): 183–194.

32. Bruce Wayne Tuckman, "Feedback and the Change Process," *Kappan* 57, No. 5 (January, 1976), pp. 341–344.

Suggested Learning Activities _____

1. Prepare a checklist of the teaching skills you think are most important. Try to identify instruments or systems available that would provide you with feedback on how those skills are being demonstrated in the classroom.

2. Develop an instructional plan in your own teaching field. Consider the differences it will make if the focus is on (a) content, or (b) student interests.

3. Conduct a panel discussion on the pros and cons of homogeneous and heterogeneous grouping.

4. You are on a curriculum committee to examine formal systems for individualizing instruction such as IGE, IPI, or PLAN. What criteria would you use for appraising such approaches?

5. Summarize the research on nongraded vs. graded instruction.

Books to Review _____

Bellon, Jerry J., et al. *Classroom Supervision and Instructional Improvement: A Synergetic Process.* Dubuque, Iowa: Kendall-Hunt Publishing Co., 1976.

Gael, Meredith. *Handbook for Evaluating and Selecting Curriculum Materials* (Boston: Allyn and Bacon, 1981).

Graves, Norman. *Curriculum Planning in Geography* (London: Heinemann Educational Corporation, 1979).

Henning, Dorothy Grant. *Mastering Classroom Communication—What Interaction Analysis Tells the Teacher.* Pacific Palisades, California: Goodyear Publishing Co., Inc., 1975.

Howson, Geoffrey. *Curriculum Development in Mathematics* (Cambridge: Cambridge University Press, 1981).

Hunkins, Francis P. *Questioning Strategies and Techniques.* Boston: Allyn and Bacon, Inc., 1972.

Kissock, Craig. *Curriculum Planning for Social Studies Teaching* (New York: John Wiley & Sons, 1981).

Kounin, Jacob S. *Discipline and Group Management in Classrooms.* New York: Holt, Rinehart & Winston, Inc., 1970.

Leeper, Robert R., ed. *Supervision: Emerging Profession.* Washington, D.C.: Association for Supervision and Curriculum Development, 1969.

Ober, Richard L.; Bentley, Ernest; and Miller, Edith. *Systematic Observation of Teaching.* Englewood Cliffs, New Jersey: Prentice-Hall, Inc., 1971.

Sanders, Norris M. *Classroom Questions: What Kinds?* New York: Harper and Row Publishers, 1966.

Sergiovanni, Thomas J., ed. *Professional Supervision for Professional Teachers.* Washington, D.C.: Association for Supervision and Curriculum Development, 1975.

Travers, Robert M.W., ed. *Second Handbook of Research on Teaching.* Chicago: Rand McNally and Company, 1973.

Wallis, Nevada. *The Library Media Specialist in Curriculum Development* (McCutchan, 1980).

Chapter Six
Leadership and Change in Curriculum Development

Leadership represents a critical element in the curriculum development process. Without strong leadership in instructional improvement, values and goals are not clarified, plans are not drawn, and activities are not implemented. Leadership is the intangible driving force in planned educational change. Despite its importance, leadership remains one of the least understood concepts in educational program development.

Over the years, considerable thought and research has been directed toward understanding leadership behavior. Yet, despite extensive writings and a large body of empirical research, leadership remains a rather mysterious concept to most school curriculum personnel. Part of the problem is that, rather than possessing a scarcity of information on the subject, students of leadership are overwhelmed by a wide range of expert opinion and conflicting research reports. While most conceptions of leadership are broad, empirical studies are narrow due to the need to work in areas with existing samples and measurable variables. The overall picture for the reader is something of a mixed message that does not clearly differentiate the essentials of leadership from the more peripheral interests.

There are in today's literature over 130 formal definitions of leadership.[1] Some of those definitions are shown below to illustrate the breadth of the samples available:

> A leader is best when people barely know he exists. When our work is done, his aim is fulfilled, they will say, "We did this ourselves." Lao-Tzu, *The Way of Life*, Sixth Century, B.C.

> Love is held by a chain of obligation . . . but fear is maintained by the dread of punishment which never fails. . . . A wise prince must rely on what is in his power and not on what is in the power of others. Niccolo Machiavelli, *The Prince*, 1500 A.D.

> Leadership is the art of imposing one's will upon others in such a manner as to command their obedience, their respect, and their loyal cooperation. *G-I Manual*, Staff College, United States Army, 1947.

> Leadership is the ability to get a man to do what you want him to do, when you want it done, in a way you want it done, because he wants to do it. Dwight Eisenhower, 1957.

> Leadership is the human factor which binds a group together and motivates it toward a goal. K. Davis, *Human Relations at Work*, 1962.

> Leadership is the process of influencing the activities of an individual or group in efforts toward goal achievement in a given situation. Hersey and Blanchard, *The Management of Organizational Behavior*, 1977.

In his major study, *Handbook of Leadership*,[2] Stogdill identified seven families of definitions or conceptions of leadership which also serve to illustrate the range of inquiry into the subject:

Leadership as the focus of group process
> The leader is the nucleus of social movement. By control of social processes (structure, goals, ideology, atmosphere) the leader becomes the primary agent for group change.

Leadership as personality and its effects
> The leader possesses the greatest number of desired traits. Using these, the leader exerts a degree of influence over those about him.

Leadership as the art of inducing compliance
> The leader, through face-to-face control, causes the subordinate to behave in a desired manner.

Leadership as the exercise of influence
> The leader establishes a relationship and uses this interpersonal influence to attain goals and enforce behavior beyond mechanical compliance.

Leadership as a power relationship
> The leader is perceived as having the right to prescribe behavior patterns for others. Sources of power include referent power (liking), expert power, reward power, coercive power, and legitimate (authority) power.

Leadership as the initiation of structure
> The leader originates and structures interaction as part of a process to solve problems.

Leadership as goal achievement
> The leader is perceived as controlling the means of satisfying needs as the group moves toward definitive objectives.

The formal study of leadership has evolved through three distinct stages in the past century: a traits or "great man" approach, a study of leadership in situations or environments, and a study of leadership transactions or exchange. Each of these major avenues to understanding leadership as a concept is reviewed below.

Studies attempting to define leadership in terms of traits or characteristics of an individual were prevalent in the nineteenth and early twentieth century. A benchmark in such personality research was the 1933 list developed by Smith and Krueger:[3]

Personality Traits

Knowledge	Initiative
Abundance of physical and nervous energy	Imagination
	Purpose
Enthusiasm	Persistence
Originality	Speed of decision

Social Traits	Physical Characteristics
Tact	Some advantage as to height,
Sympathy	weight, and physical attrac-
Faith in others and self	tiveness
Prestige	
Patience	
Ascendance-Submission	

These so-called "great man" theories studied leaders and were an extension of Aristotle's notion of a "born leader." Such studies were supported by the early work of psychology that focused on individual differences. In general, trait theories held that there were certain identifiable qualities which separated leaders from non-leaders, and that these inherent traits were transferable from situation to situation.

Arguments for the trait theories tended to be circular since most of the leaders studied to identify traits were chosen by the position they already held. From an empirical viewpoint, the studies of traits were plagued by unreplicable conditions and a lack of control populations. Stogdill's 1948 review of some 124 studies organized around leadership traits was not able to substantiate a "trait theory." Another study by Sanford (1952) concluded:[4]

> From all of these studies of the leader, we conclude that: a) there are either no general leadership traits or, if they exist, they are not described in any of our familiar psychological or common sense terms, b) in a specific situation, leaders do have traits which set them apart from followers, but what traits set what leaders apart from what followers will vary from situation to situation.

The work of Stogdill, Sanford, and others closed the door on a long-standing belief—a leader is born and leadership is limited to those possessing certain desirable traits. By the same token, inquiry during the first half of this century produced new avenues for further inquiry. Writing about leaders in 1948, Stogdill observed:

> The findings suggest that leadership is not a matter of passive status, or the mere possession of some combination of traits. It appears rather to be a working relationship among members of a group, in which the leader acquires status through active participation and demonstration of his capacity for carrying cooperative tasks through to completion.[5]

Stogdill later defined this "situational" factor in terms of things like needs and interests of the followers, objectives, and mental level.

A second avenue for the study of leadership revolved around the situation (environment) in which leadership is exerted. In general, it was hypothesized that a person does not become a leader because of the possession of certain traits, but rather because of the relationship of those traits to the characteristics, goals, or activities of the followers.

Seeing a leader as a person who, due to a situation, emerges to help a group attain certain goals, broadened the scope of leadership research and theory. For one thing, being a leader now appeared apart from exerting leadership. Such an active definition of leadership also helped to explain why leadership was sometimes lost—when the leader ceased the critical function of helping a group to attain its goals. From the social sciences came the contribution that leadership was actually a process of producing change.

Attempts to define leadership wholly in terms of situational factors met with the same general rejection as did the earlier trait theories. There were simply too many situations observable where the leader with the correct set of skills or traits did not assume or maintain the leadership role. During the late 1960s, a third piece of the puzzle began to emerge with the development of transactional or exchange theory. This third effort continues today.

Leadership exchange theory focuses on how leaders initially motivate groups to accept their influence, the processes that undergird prolonged exertion of such influence, and the ways in which the leader makes real contributions to group goals.[6] In short, exchange theory seeks to learn and explain how leaders work within their groups to establish and maintain influence. Leadership, by this definition, is an exchange or transaction which occurs (acceptance of influence) when needs are present (until satisfaction is achieved) between the leader and the follower. The following generalizations about leadership in school environments, where multiple group needs are present, are offered by Wiles and Lovell:[7]

1. Leadership is a group role . . . he [the leader] is able to exert real leadership only through effective participation in groups.
2. Leadership, other things being equal, depends upon the frequency of interaction between the leader and the led.
3. Status position does not necessarily give leadership.
4. Leadership in any organization is widespread and diffused . . . if a person hopes to exert leadership for everybody, he is doomed to frustration and failure.
5. The norms of the group determine the leader.
6. Leadership qualities and followership qualities are interchangeable.
7. People who give evidence of a desire to control are rejected for leadership roles.
8. The feeling that people hold about a person is a factor in whether they will use his behavior as leadership.
9. Leadership shifts from situation to situation.

As leadership exchange theory emerges in the 1980s, it becomes clear that the "follower perceptions" of leadership are a critical ingredient for successful leadership practice. If the leader possesses skills or traits that will facilitate group attainment of goals, but is not perceived as possessing those attributes, leadership cannot and will not be exerted. For this reason, understanding patterns or "styles" of leadership is important for an educational leader in training.

Styles of Leadership

The serious studies of leadership style emerged in the 1930s from industry. A critical question for industrial leaders was how to match the organizational tasks of a bureaucracy with the human needs of the worker. Finding a compatible style of leadership to match organizational task requirements presented a research problem that is still being explored today.

The classic work in leadership styles categorized leaders into three groups: democratic, autocratic, and laissez-faire.[8] These styles were determined by a "field observation" approach which viewed the relationship of the leader to those being led. Later approaches to the study of styles tended to conceptualize the style in terms of tasks. Cartwright and Zander, for instance, saw leaders as either helping a group attain a specific goal (change) or maintaining the group itself (maintenance).[9] Katz and Kahn continued this orientation by categorizing leadership according to function: introducing structural change, interpreting organizational structure, or using structure to keep an organization in motion.[10] By far the most influential conception of leadership style, however, was provided by Douglas McGregor who described leader style in terms of the leader's view of the follower.[11]

McGregor presented two conflicting conceptions of managerial tasks which were based upon a number of assumptions about people in an organization (see Table 6.1). A traditional view, which he labeled "theory X," saw leadership stemming from the position of the leader and viewed subordinates as unwilling partners in group or organizational tasks. Since the "theory X" leader viewed followers as innately lazy or unreliable, a stern form of leadership had to be employed to guarantee organizational achievement. McGregor contrasted this view of the role of leadership with another, "theory Y," which began with a different set of premises. Theory Y leaders assumed that leadership was given by the group to the leader and that people, who are basically self-directed and creative, will produce if properly motivated. McGregor's models of leadership saw the relationship between the leader and followers as involving four key variables: the characteristics of the leader; the characteristics of the organization; the nature of the tasks to be performed; and the social, economic, and political milieu.

Table 6.1
Organizational View of People (McGregor)

Theory X Assumptions	Theory Y Assumptions
People by nature:	People by nature:
1. Lack integrity	1. Have integrity
2. Are fundamentally lazy and desire to work as little as possible	2. Work hard toward objectives to which they are committed
3. Avoid responsibility	3. Assume responsibility within their commitments
4. Are not interested in achievement	4. Desire to achieve
5. Are incapable of directing their own behavior	5. Are capable of directing their own behavior
6. Are indifferent to organizational needs	6. Want their organization to succeed
7. Prefer to be directed by others	7. Are not passive and submissive
8. Avoid making decisions whenever possible	8. Will make decisions within their commitments
9. Are not very bright	9. Are not stupid

Source: Douglas McGregor, "The Human Side of Enterprise," *The Management Review* 46 (1957): 22–28, 88–92.

McGregor's contrasting conceptions of leadership style were further developed in the work of Blake and Mouton who devised a grid on which to "plot" leadership style.[12] Using McGregor's "concern for production" and "concern for people" vantage points, Blake and Mouton constructed a "grid" for plotting leadership styles. While some 81 positions are possible in the managerial grid, only five (the corners and center) were analyzed by Blake and Mouton. The value of the grid, as a model of style, is to make the individual aware of various styles that can fit various situations (see Figure 6.1).

Blake and Mouton describe five primary styles that can be used to describe the grid:

1.1 *Impoverished Management* Effective production is unobtainable because people are lazy, apathetic, and indifferent. Sound and mature relationships are difficult to achieve, because human nature being what it is, conflict is inevitable.

1.9 *Country Club Management* Production is incidental to lack of conflict and good fellowship.

5.5 *Middle of the Road Management* Push for production but don't go "All Out," give some but not all. "Be fair but firm."

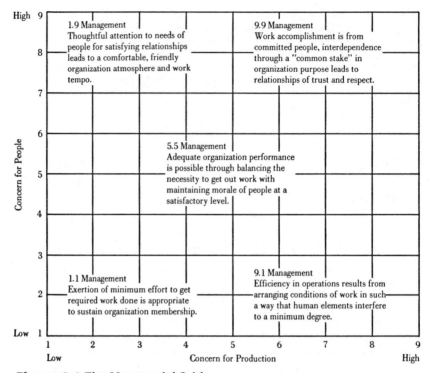

Figure 6.1 The Managerial Grid

9.1 *Task Management* Men are a commodity just as machines. A manager's responsibility is to plan, direct, and control the work of those subordinate to him.

9.9 *Team management* Production is from integration of task and human requirements into a unified system of interplay towards organizational goals.

Roles and Tasks

Leadership in curriculum development is not a function of title or appointed position. Titles may legitimize formal authority, but they do not insure leadership capacity. Leadership is a function of four complex variables: the character of the leader, the character of the followers, the character of the organization, and the character of the environment.

Leadership in educational organizations is a situational phenomenon. It is determined by the collective perceptions of individuals, is related to group norms, and is influenced by the frequency of interaction among members of the organization. Before leadership can be

effective in an open organization such as a school, it must be acknowledged as a group activity.

To some extent, leadership is a product of the leader's vision. The
way in which the leader conceives of the group's tasks, and the policies
and practices to successfully achieve those ends, defines leadership. In
the words of management specialist Douglas McGregor, "The theoretical assumptions management holds about controlling human resources
determines the whole character of the enterprise."[13]

The way in which the leader sees the organization and its needs,
when formalized, sets the foundation for a theory of leadership. Without such a theory, leadership behaviors will be little more than a series
of activities and projects that have little relationship to one another.
Most often, conceptions of leadership are developed in terms of what
the leader is to be and do, in terms of roles and tasks.

Leadership roles in curriculum development activities are multiple due to the numerous environments in which the curriculum
specialist operates and due to the supportive role of most curriculum
positions. Some leadership styles are shown in Table 6.2. A monolithic
perception of what a curriculum worker is to do is not applicable in
most school environments.

Havelock and associates have identified nineteen roles which may
be applicable to the work of curriculum development:

> **Expert**—sometimes the consultant is the source of knowledge or
> skill in an area.
>
> **Instructor**—the consultant may take the role of instructing about
> an area of knowledge.
>
> **Trainer**—a trainer goes beyond instruction in that he helps peo-
> ple master "do it" behavioral skills in performing actions.
>
> **Retriever**—the retriever brings what is needed to the client
> system.
>
> **Referrer**—the referrer sends the client system to a source where
> it can find what it needs.
>
> **Linker**—the linker provides a bridge to parties, or parts of a
> system, that need to be in contact.
>
> **Demonstrator**—the demonstrator shows the client system how
> something is done, but does not necessarily show him how
> to do it for himself.
>
> **Modeler**—the modeler provides an example of how to do, or
> be, something by evidencing it in his (the consultant's)
> own behavior.
>
> **Advocate**—there are times when a consultant can best facilitate
> an intention by taking the role of advocate for a goal, value,
> or strategy.
>
> **Confronter**—when the client system needs to be confronted with
> awareness of a discrepancy.

Table 6.2
Leadership Styles

1. "TELLS" Leadership
   A. Seeks unquestioning obedience
   B. Sometimes relies on fear, intimidation
   C. Gives orders
   D. Relies heavily on authority
   E. Sets all goals and standards
   F. Makes all decisions without consulting the group

2. "SELLS" Leadership
   A. Work assignments are alloted to workers
   B. Assignments are sometimes arbitrary
   C. Trys to persuade the group to accept assignments
   D. Seldom builds teamwork
   E. Does not motivate worker involvement
   F. Makes decisions without consulting the group

3. "CONSULTS" Leadership
   A. Does not rely on authority
   B. Develops considerable worker loyalty
   C. Does not hesitate to delegate
   D. Will usually explain "why" a task is to be performed in a certain way
   E. Takes time to inform his group what he thinks may be a solution

4. "JOINS" Leadership
   A. Builds teamwork by group involvement
   B. Accepts suggestions from the work group
   C. Treats each worker as an individual
   D. Helps workers believe their potential
   E. Uses the decision of the group

5. "DELEGATES" Leadership
   A. Turns the decision-making process over to the group
   B. Accepts all group decisions that fit within accepted parameters
   C. Encourages subordinate participation in many activities
   D. Stimulates creative thinking in employees

Source: John Wiles and Joseph Bondi, *Supervision: A Guide To Practice,* (Columbus, Ohio: Charles E. Merrill Publishing Company, 1980), 144. Reprinted by permission.

Counselor—the role of the counselor generally includes listening, acting as a sounding board, and raising awareness of alternatives. It is a nondirective effort in helping the client think through issues.

Advisor—the advisor role differs from the counselor in being more directive about what the client might do and how to do it.

Observer—the observer comments on the things that exist and how things are being done.

Data Collector—the data collector gathers information about what exists and how things are being done.

Analyzer—the analyzer interprets the meaning of data found in the system.

Diagnoser—the diagnoser uses analyses, data, and observations in determining why things happen the way they do in the system.

Designer—the designer develops action strategies, training programs, and management models for use by the system.

Manager—the manager takes charge of the development process by ordering events to achieve accountability.

Evaluator—the evaluator serves to feed back information that will make the system more effective in its task.[14]

These roles, and others, are all legitimate leadership actions given the correct conditions and needs of followers.

Leadership Tasks

The tasks of curriculum leadership, like roles, are numerous. The exact tasks required to be a leader vary from organization to organization and work situation to work situation. However, some generic tasks are found in most curriculum leadership opportunities.

Developing an Operating Theory. Leaders must be able to conceptualize tasks and communicate the approach to those tasks to others in the organization. The pattern of task identification and response forms the basis of an operating theory.

Developing Organization and a Work Environment. Curriculum tasks are often nonpermanent responses to needs. In such cases, the way in which people, resources, and ideas are organized is left to the leader. An important task is to structure an organization and work environment that can respond to those needs.

Setting Standards. Because curriculum problems often involve diverse groups of individuals with different needs and perceptions, an important task for a curriculum leader is to set standards and other expectations that will affect the resolution of problems. Such standards may include work habits, communication procedures, time limitations, or a host of related planning areas.

Using Authority to Establish an Organizational Climate. Persons assigned to leadership positions generally are able to structure organizations by suggesting changes and initiating policies. One of the most important tasks for a curriculum leader is using such authority to establish a desirable work climate. Such a climate, discussed later in this chapter, is made up of the collective perceptions of persons affected by the structure of the organization.

Establishing Effective Interpersonal Relations.   Since leadership is a product of human exchanges or transactions within organizations, it is essential that interpersonal relationships contribute to the attainment of desired ends. The way in which a curriculum leader interacts with others in the organization can assist in the establishment of a pattern of effective interpersonal relationships.

Planning and Initiating Action.   The curriculum leader is sometimes the only person with the authority to plan and initiate actions. Deciding when and how to initiate action is a strong leadership activity. Failure to lead planning or initiate action can undermine other leadership functions.

Keeping Communication Channels Open and Functioning. Many times the curriculum leader is in a unique position of being able to communicate with others in an organization when lateral and horizontal communication is limited for most members. The leader can use his or her position to facilitate the matching of persons who need to communicate with one another. The leader can also make changes in communication patterns, where necessary, to insure that such communication channels are functioning.

These tasks, in combination, are used to promote planned change for improving curriculum in schools.

Change as a Function of Curriculum Improvement

Curriculum improvement is almost always a case of curriculum change. For this reason, persons preparing for positions of leadership in curriculum should have a clear understanding of the change process in educational environments. There are a number of pressing questions in the area of change that need to be addressed. Among these are:

1. What causes a school to change?
2. Why do innovations nearly always fail in some schools?
3. Why do some schools never attempt to make changes?
4. What factors are significant in making a school either a high risk or a low risk for an innovation attempt?
5. What is the profile of an innovative school?

The answers to such questions as these will not come easily because change in school environments is a highly complex process with an interplay of many multifaceted variables.* Still, a review of existing literature on change as it interacts with educational environments can greatly increase understanding and make curriculum leaders more effective in their jobs. The study of change in schools, while not new, is being pursued vigorously by researchers. Rogers and Shoemaker observed in 1971: "There are about three times as many publications on the subject as there were eight years ago, which means more diffusion research has been done in the past few years than in the previous thirty years."[15]

Part of the difficulty in understanding change in school settings, then, results from the sheer volume of data and the constant nature of change in education. To clarify the topic for the reader, several key "lenses" for looking at change are presented below under the categories of types of change, models of change, strategies of change, and barriers to change:

Types of Change

Change is not synonymous with innovation. According to Miles, change is "any alteration in someone or something."[16] An innovation, by contrast, has unique qualities such as novelty or deliberateness. It is the specific application of change that distinguishes an innovation from random change. Such a distinction is underscored by the two types of change identified by Goodson: planned change and evolutionary change.[17]

More specific typologies of change have been developed by Bennis and Guba. Bennis[18] presents seven types of change commonly found in organizations:

1. planned change
2. indoctrination
3. coercive change
4. technocratic change
5. interactional change
6. cumulative change
7. natural change

Guba[19] reduces all change to three basic types: evolutionary or natural change, homeostatic or reactive change, and neomobilistic or planned change.

Models of Change

In addition to types of change, the literature on change contains numerous models that consider the process from a variety of perspectives. Among some of the most interesting to educational planners

*For a complete set of generalizations about the diffusion of innovations see Appendix A of Everett M. Rogers and F. Floyd Shoemaker, *Communication of Innovations: A Cross-Cultural Approach* (New York: Free Press, 1971).

are those institutional models that reveal how other areas of society approach the concept of planned change. Here are four stereotypic models of other institutions:

Agriculture—uses a *change agent* approach by having county agents go into the field to demonstrate new techniques of farming.

Medical—uses *action research* in approaching change. The diffusion of medical change proceeds from clinical research to development to dissemination.

Business—uses the *incentive approach* of rewards to encourage change. In organizations, sometimes this approach is used to pull persons toward change.

Military—uses *authority* to enforce change. This is a pushing strategy.

The emphasis in change models that appears to have captured the greatest concern and attention in education has been the process approach. The tremendous advances that the application of systems concepts have produced in science and technology are now being employed in education with promising results.

Kurt Lewin is generally acknowledged to be the intellectual forebearer of process models in change. His three-step change model has become a classic.[20] The process basically involves (1) unfreezing an old pattern, (2) changing to a new one, and (3) refreezing the new pattern. Lewin's model is based on the notion of the opposing forces that create varying amounts of pressure on situations. When forces are equal, the situation does not change. However, by the addition or subtraction of forces the pressure becomes unequal and change occurs.

Another popular model is one that conceptualizes the change process in terms of five stages leading to adoption:[21]

1. awareness
2. interest
3. evaluation
4. trial
5. adoption

Another approach to the change process has been offered by Lippitt, Watson, and Wesley in their pioneer work, *The Dynamics of Planned Change.*[22] They focus on the relationship between the change agent and the client system and identify seven stages:

1. the development of a need for change
2. the establishment of a change relationship
3. the diagnosis of the client system's problem
4. the examination of goals and alternative routes of action
5. the transformation of intentions into action

6. the generalization and stabilization of change
7. the achievement of a terminal relationship

Strategies of Change

Another area of research on change in organizations is that of strategy. Chin offers three general headings of change strategies: (1) rational-empirical, (2) normative-reeducative, and (3) power-coercive.[23] The first is based on the assumption that people are rational and that they will follow their rational self-interests once they are revealed to them. The second is founded on different assumptions about human motivation. The rationality of people is not denied; however, behavior is recognized as a sociocultural phenomenon reinforced by values and attitudes of individuals in the system. The third group of strategies is based on the application of power in some form, political or otherwise.

Barriers to Change

The barriers to change that are set forth in the literature are innumerable. Many authors, telescoping particular segments of the process, have identified countless barriers that impede change. Further, such barriers are described with varying amounts of specificity. Most common in the literature are lists of the potential barriers that affect educational change.

Such lists give an overview of the barriers. Here are eight barriers as compiled by McClelland:

1. Despite rapid social change, forces favoring the status quo in education remain strong as ever.
2. There are no precise goals for educational institutions.
3. There is no established systematic approach in the educational process.
4. Teacher education programs have failed to develop the skills and knowledge needed for innovations.
5. Teachers have failed to develop in themselves the habits of scholarship necessary to stay abreast of the knowledge explosion.
6. Evaluation and revision based on feedback are absent in educational institutions.
7. Many educators are reticent, suspicious, and fearful of change.
8. Complex management and funding problems always cost more than simple divisible problems.[24]

Rogers depicts the barriers in this manner:

1. There is no profit motive for being an innovator in education.
2. There is no corps of change agents in education comparable to extension agents in agriculture.

3. Educational innovations are less clear cut in their advantage over the existing ideas they are to replace.
4. Innovation decisions in education may not be an individual matter and the norms, statuses, and formal structure of the systems affect the process of diffusion.[25]

Even though there are many barriers to change in schools, such resistance may have a functional effect. Klein, for instance, notes that resistance

1. protects the organization against random change, which may be harmful;
2. protects the system from take-over by vested interests; and
3. may insure that unanticipated consequences of a change be spelled out and thus possibly avoided.[26]

The Promotion of Planned Change

While the literature on change in educational environments can outline some of the models, strategies, and barriers likely to be encountered, it is not yet sophisticated enough to serve as an absolute guide to practice. It is up to the individual curriculum leader to discover a means of reaching the desired goals.

One of the first realities that must be acknowledged by a curriculum leader is that change is often a political process. It is this political activity that activates the variables in an educational community. If there were no planning and maneuvering within school districts, there would be no change. According to Iannaccone and Lutz, ". . . politics is recognized as probably the single most important question in determining the course, present and future, of American education."[27] This topic is addressed comprehensively in chapter 11. Rather than being perceived as evil or undemocratic, the use of political influence can be seen as a means of altering the rate of change in school settings. Educators who seek the support of those interest groups that coincide in social intent with the school can legitimately do so in the name of better programs of education for children. Intellectual choices in planning are, inevitably, social choices with political implications.

Carlson found that in some communities schools are essentially tame, domesticated organizations controlled by local forces.[28] Under such circumstances, improved school programs cannot occur without an agent of change. As curriculum leaders acknowledge political reality they will be more effective in promoting planned changes.

The second important idea related to change in schools is that resistance to change is not unnatural. Individuals strive to bring order to their world and most change involves the realignment of roles and relationships. In the words of Warren Bennis: "Change will be resisted to the degree that the target has little information or knowledge of the change, has little trust in the source of change, and has little influence in controlling the nature and direction of the change."[29]

The third idea about change in school environments, which is supported by case studies, is that change is not an isolated event. Change in any complex organization involves interrelated events.

An awareness of the political dimensions of change, the natural tendency of individuals to resist change, and the awareness of change as a continuing process suggest that desired change is not a haphazard process but one which is the result of a concerted effort to influence the educational environment. Such influence is most effective when the curriculum leader possesses the concept of the change environment and an organizational structure.

While directing a project concerning the analysis of planned change in Florida schools, one of the authors attempted to develop such a concept in terms of the potential of innovation targets. The result of this effort was a probability chart, shown in Table 6.3, that roughly indicates the degree of readiness for innovation within a school. This construct has proven useful as a way of looking at change in schools.

Curriculum leaders need a structure for promoting planned alterations of the school environment. As Miles has observed: "This review of innovative processes shows clearly that innovative attitudes are not enough. Structures which permit design, adaptation, evaluation, trial, and routinization of innovations are essential. Without them, innovative motivation simply leads to 'dithering' quasi-random perturbations of practice."[30]

The long-term goal of any immediate change effort is to construct an institution that becomes capable of updating the renewing of itself as the environment changes. What is called for is the complex interweaving of continuity and change. Such a task is the central theme of John Gardner's book, *Self-Renewal:* "Over the centuries the classic question of social reform has been, 'how can we cure this or that specific ill?' Now we must ask another kind of question. How can we design a system that will continuously reform (renew) itself, beginning with presently specifiable ills and moving on to ills that we cannot now foresee?"[31]

The Act of Leading Curriculum Change

In schools, due to the open nature of the organization, curriculum development is basically a process in which organization members interact to produce improved school programs. While curriculum *planning* can produce philosophy statements, goals, objectives, syllabi, and

Table 6.3
Educational Innovations Probability Chart

	Higher Risk →			← Lower Risk	
Source of Innovation	Superimposed from outside	Outside agent brought in	Developed internally with aid	External idea modified	Locally conceived, developed, implemented
Impact of Innovation	Challenges sacrosanct beliefs	Calls for major value shifts	Requires substantial change	Modifies existing values or programs	Does not substantially alter existing values, beliefs, or programs
Official Support	Official leaders active opposition	Officials on record as opposing	Officials uncommitted	Officials voice support of change	Enthusiastically supported by the official leaders
Planning of Innovation	Completely external	Most planning external	Planning processes balanced	Most of planning done locally	All planning for change done on local site
Means of Adoption	By superiors	By local leaders	By Reps	By most of the clients	By group consensus
History of Change	History of failures	No accurate records	Some success with innovation	A history of successful innovations	Known as school where things regularly succeed
Possibility of Revision	No turning back	Final evaluation before committee	Periodic evaluations	Possible to abandon at conclusion	Possible to abort the effort at any time

Role of Teachers	Largely bypassed	Minor role	Regular role in implementing	Heavy role in implementation	Primary actor in the classroom effort
Teacher Expectation	Fatalistic	Feel little chance	Willing to give a try	Confident of success	Wildly enthusiastic about chance of success
Work Load Measure	Substantially increased	Heavier but rewarding	Slightly increased	Unchanged	Work load lessened by the innovation
Threat Measure	Definitely threatens some clients	Probably threatening to some	Mild threat resulting from the change	Very remote threat to some	Does not threaten the security or autonomy
Community Factor	Hostile to innovations	Suspicious and uninformed	Indifferent	Ready for a change	Wholeheartedly supports the school

Source: Adapted from Jon Wiles: PLANNING GUIDELINES FOR MIDDLE SCHOOL EDUCATION. Copyright © 1976 by Kendall/Hunt Publishing Company, Dubuque, Ia. Used with permission.

evaluation guidelines, curriculum *implementation* usually requires face-to-face interaction. Leading curriculum improvement in a human organization like a school calls for thoughtful and well-planned change; understanding the interpersonal dimension of leadership is essential.

Earlier in this chapter real leadership was shown to be a transactional process. School leaders must somehow "link" the needs of individuals with the tasks of the organization and while doing so there is, in schools, a dependence upon those being led: An executive decision is only a moment in the total process of the solution of the problem. It is the final statement of policy that the official leader is asked to administer. The solution begins with a clear definition of the problem, involves analysis of the factors of the situation, is based on procedure formulated by the group, is stated as an official decision, and is implemented by activities agreed upon by the group members as their responsibility in carrying out the decision.[32]

With this statement in mind, it is possible to view the dependence of the curriculum leader in each of the basic steps as shown in Figure 6.2. Because of this dependence and the effect of interaction on the quality of the curriculum development process, curriculum leaders can benefit from an analysis of various interpersonal factors.

Interpersonal relationships in school environments can be thought of as having the following six levels:

1. **Individual**—a personality system that is made up of many parts organized to enable the individual to respond to both internal and external conditions.
2. **Dyad**—a social unit of two individuals who develop patterns of response to each other as well as response to other levels of the human system.
3. **Group**—a small social system of individuals with fairly well-defined purpose, able to respond to itself and to external conditions.
4. **Organization**—a social unit of individuals with clearly defined and specialized functions requiring a disciplined and systematic relationship among members, able to respond to internal needs and external conditions.
5. **Community**—a social unit composed of a large number of individuals who form a variety of interacting sub-parts which are likely to respond more frequently to situations internal to itself.

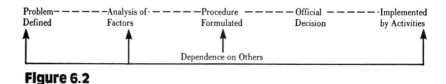

Figure 6.2

6. **Society**—a social unit including all previous levels interacting, related by some common norms of political, economic, and cultural coordination that together form an observable identity.

At each of these levels the curriculum specialist is interacting to facilitate the development of school programs. Such interaction is carried out through the following standard development functions:

Human Systems	Functions	Interactions
Individuals	Diagnosing	Perceiving
Dyads	Deciding	Valuing
Groups	Planning	Communicating
Organizations	Managing	Influencing
Communities	Producing	Cooperating
Society	Evaluating	Belonging

Understanding the exact relationship of interaction in curriculum development functions, human systems, and interpersonal relations is aided by a study of communication in organizations, individual personality theory, small group work, and group leadership.

Communication in Organizations _____

Communication among individuals in organizations is a delicate art requiring, among other things, self-discipline and a cooperative spirit. Spoken English is a complex language which is full of subtleties. Superimposed on these language patterns are a host of nonverbal clues that can alter the meaning of speech. Add to these dimensions an environmental context, and the result is a communication system that operates at varying levels of effectiveness.

Various social sciences have developed entire languages to describe the intricacies of communication in the American culture. Galloway has provided a model of foci in three such social sciences:[33]

Anthropology	Sociology	Psychology
Cultural behaviors	Role behaviors	Personal behaviors
Acculturation	Interaction	Personality
Implicit meanings	Empathetic meanings	Inferred meanings

Collectively, social science inquiry in the area of interpersonal communication has added immeasurably to our understanding of this complex and important dimension of curriculum improvement.

In any pattern of communication among humans there are at least the following nine elements:

1. What the speaker wants to say
2. What the speaker wants to conceal
3. What the speaker reveals without knowing it

4. What the listener wants or expects to hear
5. What the listener's perception of the speaker will let him hear
6. What the listener's experiences tell him the words mean
7. What the listener wants to conceal
8. What the emotional climate of the situation permits the persons to share
9. What the physical structure of the situation permits the persons to share[34]

Various models have shown communication to be a process of encoding and decoding. A source encodes a message and tries to transmit it to a receiver who tries to receive it and decode the message. Such a transmission between sender and receiver is often distorted by various barriers to communication and by defensive behaviors. Gibb has defined such communication defense:

> Defensive behavior is defined as that behavior which occurs when an individual perceives a threat or anticipates threat in the group. The person who behaves defensively, even though he gives some attention to the common task, devotes an appreciable portion of his energy to defending himself. Besides talking about the topic, he thinks about how he appears to others, how he can be seen more favorably, how he may win, dominate, impress, or escape punishment, and/or how he may avoid or mitigate a perceived or an anticipated attack.[35]

Berlo, in a study of human communication, has identified the following four major predictors of faulty communication that can be used by curriculum leaders to anticipate possible communication breakdown:

1. The amount of competition messages have.
2. The threats to status and ego which are involved.
3. The uncertainty and error in what is expected.
4. The number of links there are in the communication chain.[36]

Other barriers to effective communication among people might include any of the following:

1. People use words and symbols that have differing meanings.
2. People have different perceptions of problems being discussed.
3. Members of communication groups possess different values.
4. People bring to discussions varying levels of feeling or affect.
5. Words are sometimes used to prevent real thinking.
6. A lack of acceptance of diverse opinion is present in some communication.
7. Vested interests can interfere with genuine communication.
8. Feelings of personal insecurity can distort communication.
9. Tendencies to make premature evaluations are a barrier to communication.
10. Negative feelings about situations block effective communication.

Group Work _____

While relationships exist at the dyad, organizational, community, and societal levels, most curriculum development work proceeds at the group level. For this reason, curriculum leaders need to be particularly attentive to group work as a means of promoting better school programs.

Groups can generally be described as two or more people who possess a common objective. As groups interact in pursuit of an objective, their behavior is affected by a number of variables, including: the background of the group, participation patterns, communication patterns, the cohesiveness of the group, the goals of the group, standards affecting the group, procedures affecting the group, and the atmosphere or climate surrounding the group.

Groups perform various tasks that are important to the development of school programs. Among these group tasks are:

1. Initiating activities: suggesting new ideas, defining problems, proposing solutions, reorganizing materials.
2. Coordinating: showing relationships among various ideas or suggestions, pulling ideas together, relating activities of various subgroups.
3. Summarizing: pulling together related data, restating suggestions after discussion.
4. Testing feasibility: examining the practicality or feasibility of ideas, making preevaluation decisions about activities.

Group work in educational environments is often ineffective due to various types of nonfunctional behaviors. Leaders should be aware of some of the more common forms of nonfunctional actions:

1. Being aggressive—showing hostility against the group or some individual, criticizing or blaming others, deflating the status of others.
2. Blocking—interfering with group process by speaking tangentially, citing personal experiences unrelated to the problem, rejecting ideas without consideration.
3. Competing—vying with others to talk most often, produce the best idea, gain favor of the leader.
4. Special pleading—introducing ideas or suggestions that relate to one's own concerns.
5. Seeking recognition—calling attention to oneself by excessive talking, extreme ideas, or unusual behavior.
6. Withdrawing—being indifferent or passive, daydreaming, doodling, whispering to others, physically leaving the discussion.

As a group leader, the curriculum specialist should be able to differentiate between those roles and actions that contribute to group effectiveness and those roles that are basically negative and do not contribute to the effectiveness of the group. The following can be thought of as productive and contributing to group effectiveness:

1. Person brings the discussion back to the point.
2. Person seeks clarification of meaning when ideas expressed are not clear.
3. Person questions and evaluates ideas expressed in objective manner.
4. Person challenges reasoning when the soundness of logic is doubtful.
5. Person introduces a new way of thinking about topic.
6. Person makes a summary of points.
7. Person underscores points of agreement or disagreement.
8. Person tries to resolve conflict or differences of opinion.
9. Person introduces facts or relevant information.
10. Person evaluates progress of the group.

Roles that can be thought of as negative or nonproductive are:

1. Person aggressively expresses disapproval of ideas of others.
2. Person attacks the group or the ideas under consideration.
3. Person attempts to reintroduce idea after it has been rejected.
4. Person tries to assert authority by demanding.
5. Person introduces information which is obviously irrelevant.
6. Person tries to invoke sympathy by depreciation of self.
7. Person uses stereotypes to cover own biases and prejudices.
8. Person downgrades the importance of group's role or function.

Sensitivity to such roles allows the group leader to analyze the flow of group work and head off potential distractions to group progress.

Group Leadership

While working with groups, the curriculum leader does not have to restrict his or her role to that of passive observer. It is possible to take steps that will encourage greater group productivity (see Figure 6.3). In any group discussion, the leader has at least six roles which, if pursued, will lead the group toward accomplishment of its objectives. These areas are: presentation of the topic, the initiation of discussion, guiding the discussion, controlling discussion, preventing side-tracking, and summarizing the discussion.

In presenting the topic to be discussed, the leader should suggest the importance of the problem, place the general purpose of the discussion before the group, suggest a logical pathway for the discussion to follow, and define any ambiguous terms to remove misunderstanding. It is useful, where possible, to relate the current discussion to previous meetings or other convenient reference points.

Figure 6.3 Productivity in Group Work

If a group is to be productive, the individuals in question must first become a group in a psychological sense through acquiring the feeling of group belongingness which can come only from a central purpose which they all accept.

If a group is to be productive, its members must have a common definition of the undertaking in which they are to engage.

If a group is to be productive, it must have a task of some real consequence to perform.

If a group is to be productive, its members must feel that something will actually come of what they are expected to do; said differently, its members must not feel that what they are asked to do is simply busywork.

If a group is to be productive, the dissatisfaction of its members with the aspect of the status quo to which the group's undertaking relates must outweigh in their minds whatever threats to their comfort they perceive in the performance of this undertaking.

If a group is to be productive, it members must not be expected or required to attempt undertakings which are beyond their respective capabilities or which are so easy for the individuals in question to perform that they feel no sense of real accomplishment.

If a group is to be productive, decisions as to work planning, assignment, and scheduling must be made, whenever possible, on a shared basis within the group, and through the method of consensus rather than of majority vote; in instances in which these decisions either have already been made by exterior authority or in which they must be made by the group leader alone, the basis for the decisions made must be clearly explained to all members of the group.

If a group is to be productive, each member of the group must clearly understand what he is expected to do and why, accept his role, and feel himself responsible to the group for its accomplishment.

If a group is to be productive, its members must communicate in a common language.

If a group is to be productive, its members must be guided by task-pertinent values which they share in common.

If a group is to be productive, it is usually necessary for its members to be in frequent face-to-face association with one another.

If a group is to be productive, its members must have a common (though not necessarily a talked-about) agreement as to their respective statuses within the group.

If a group is to be productive, each of its members must gain a feeling of individual importance from his personal contributions in performing the work of the group.

If a group is to be productive, the distribution of credit for its accomplishments must be seen as equitable by its members.

If a group is to be productive, it must keep on the beam and not spend time on inconsequential or irrelevant matters.

If a group is to be productive, the way it goes about its work must be seen by its members as contributing to the fulfillment of their respective tissue and social-psychological needs, and, by extension, of those of their dependents (if any) as well.

If a group is to be productive, the status leader must make the actual leadership group-centered, with the leadership role passing freely from member to member.

If a group is to be productive, the task it is to perform must be consistent with the purposes of the other groups to which its members belong.

If a group is to be productive, the satisfactions its members expect to experience from accomplishing the group's task must outweigh in their minds the satisfactions they gain from their membership in the group *per se.*

In initiating the discussion, the leader provides advanced thinking for the group. Major questions to be answered are identified and relevant facts and figures are cited. A case in point may be drawn for purposes of illustration. In some cases, it may even be useful to purposefully misstate a position to provoke discussion.

The leader's job in guiding the discussion involves keeping the discussion goal-directed, assisting members in expressing themselves through feedback, and providing the transition from one aspect of the discussion to another. In fulfilling this role, the leader may use direct questions, stories, illustrations, or leading questions to maintain the flow of interaction.

In controlling the discussion the leader is concerned with the pace of progress and the involvement of the participants. Among techniques which can be used to keep discussion moving are purposeful negative statements, drawing contrasts between positions of participants, and regularly calling attention to the time remaining.

The discussion leader in a small group can deal with side-tracking in a number of ways. He can restate the original question or problems. He can secure a statement from a reliable group member to head off a rambler. He can request that side issues be postponed until main issues are settled.

Finally, the leader summarizes the discussion. This involves knowing when to terminate discussion and reviewing the high points that have been talked to.

Three situations in particular are troublesome to persons new to leading discussions in small groups; the dead silence, the over-talkative member, and the silent member. Any of these three conditions can sabotage an otherwise fruitful discussion period.

A most anxiety-producing situation is one in which there is a complete absence of participation resulting in an awkward silence among group members. While the natural response in such a situation is to speak to fill the conversational vacuum, the leader must do just the opposite. Silence in discussions sometimes means that real thinking is occurring, and this assumption must be made by the leader. Another common impulse is to seek out a member of the group and prod him or her for a contribution. Such a tactic will surely contribute to less participation. When the silent period is convincingly unproductive, the leader should try an encouraging remark such as, "There must be some different points of view here." Failing response, the leader should turn to the process involved with a comment such as "Let's see if we can discover what's blocking us."

Another situation that can ruin a group discussion is an over-talkative member. Such a person, if permitted, will monopolize discussion and produce anxiety among group members. The best strategy in such a situation is to intervene after a respectful period of time with a comment such as, "Perhaps we can hear from other members of the group." In the event that the dominating member still doesn't get the message, the leader can initiate an evaluation of the process and draw attention to the fact that a way must be found to gain input from all members.

A final situation that can be awkward occurs when a member of the group is regularly silent. The leader should recognize that some persons are fearful of being put on the spot and will resent being spotlighted. The leader can, however, observe the silent member and look for signals that he or she is ready to participate. If the member seems to be on the verge of speaking, an encouraging glance or nod may be all that is needed.

In cases where the leader becomes convinced that a member's silence is the result of boredom or withdrawing, it may be useful to confront the member away from other group members with a provocative or challenging question. Whether a member should be forced into a discussion, and whether such an act is productive for the entire group, is a matter of judgment and discretion.

Leaders of small groups should regularly evaluate their own performance following a discussion by asking themselves a series of questions such as the following:

1. Did members contribute to the discussion?
2. Did some people do more talking than others?
3. Are the most talkative persons, and the silent ones, sitting together?
4. Do members talk mostly to the leader or to each other?
5. Was there evidence of cliques or interest groups in the discussion?

Group leaders can sometimes retard creative thinking by regulating discussions in nonproductive ways. Among the most common errors in this respect are:

1. A preoccupation with order throughout the discussion.
2. Stressing too often "hard evidence" or factual information.
3. Placing too much emphasis on history or the way things have been done.
4. Using coercive techniques to insure participation.
5. Suggesting that mistakes are not acceptable.

Two skills that are useful for all small group leaders to possess are that of paraphrasing and brainstorming. In paraphrasing, the leader attempts to restate the point of view of another to his satisfaction prior to continuing discussion. This technique is especially useful in argumentative situations, and often sets a pattern which is followed by other group members.

In brainstorming, the leader introduces a technique that frees the group discussion from previous barriers to speaking. Here the leader sets ground rules which include the following: no criticism of others is allowed, the combining of ideas is encouraged, quality ideas are sought, wild ideas are encouraged. In introducing a brainstorming session the leader hopes to have members "spark" each other and have one idea "hitch-hike" upon another. Brainstorming, as a technique, is recommended when discussions continually cover familiar ground and little or no progress toward a solution to problems is forthcoming.

Finally, leaders of small groups should work to become better listeners. Numerous studies have identified poor listening skills as the biggest block to personal communication. Nicholas has identified ten steps to better listening:

1. While listening, concentrate on finding areas of interest that are useful to you.
2. Judge the content of what is said rather than the delivery.
3. Postpone early judgment about what is being said. Such a posture will allow you to remain analytical if you favor what is being said or to keep from being distracted by calculating embarrassing questions should you disagree with the speaker's message.
4. Focus on the central ideas proposed by the speaker. What is the central idea? What are the supporting "planks" or statements?
5. Remain flexible in listening. Think of various ways to remember what is being said.
6. Work hard at listening. Try to direct all conscious attention on the presentation being made.
7. Resist distractions in the environment by making adjustments or by greater concentration.
8. Exercise your mind by regularly listening to technical expository material that you haven't had experience with.
9. Keep your mind open to new ideas by being aware of your own biases and limited experiences.
10. Capitalize on thought speed. Since comprehension speed exceeds speaking speed by about 3:1, the listener must work to keep his concentration. This can be done by anticipating what is to be said, by making mental summaries, by weighing speaker evidence, and by listening between the lines.[37]

Approaches For Curriculum Leaders ─────────

Clearly, educational environments call for special leadership styles and approaches in order to promote positive curricular change. At the building level, in particular, an interactive and personal approach to leadership is needed. Two comprehensive approaches to leading change that have emerged in the past twenty years, organizational development and climate engineering, are worthy of study.

Organizational Development — Systems

Systems theory, a product of the physical sciences, provides the concept of interdependence in organizations and explains how one part of an organization affects the other parts or whole of the organization. A system is simply a grouping of objects which are treated as a unit. From an educational viewpoint, systems approaches allow leaders to see a school or school district holistically. Relationships, in particular, are clarified:

> [The conceptual skill is] the ability to see the organization as a whole; it includes recognizing how . . . the various functions of the organization depend on one another, and how changes in any one part affects all the others. Recognizing these relationships and perceiving the significant elements in any situation, the administrator should then be able to act in a way which advances the overall welfare of the organization.[38]

In school settings, a system might be defined as any set of components which are organized in a manner which constrains action toward the accomplishment of a goal. Thus, school programs which are established to educate children are comprised of facilities, materials, funds, teachers, testing, and a host of other contributing variables. The real value of a systems perspective for administrators is as a means of identifying noncontributing conditions or bottlenecks in the flow of activity. Once identified, these systems deficiencies can be targeted for redesign. Systems can also help the leading educator build models of preferred conditions for learning.

Perhaps the high watermark in the study of organization processes is the concept of Organization Development (O.D.), a planned and sustained effort to apply behavioral science for systemic improvement.[39]

The process of organizational development consists of data gathering, organizational diagnosis, and action intervention. The fulfillment of an OD program is, in a real sense, changing the school's way of working.

There are three elements of organization that appear particularly important for curricular changes: the roles various people play, the goals of the department or school, and the operational procedures of the organization being studied.

Organizational Development is a people-involving approach to systemic planning. The importance of sharing system goals and control by personnel can hardly be overstressed. Without such sharing, personnel will not be committed to the efficacy of system function, and it becomes correspondingly difficult to motivate action in accordance with system needs.

Individuals hold membership in groups when they show by some means that they have taken upon themselves those norms, values, beliefs, etc. that are most cherished by the group. During OD inquiry, what comes into the picture are long and strongly held organizational norms concerning such things as decision-making patterns, communication networks, work relationships, interpersonal relations, and attitudes about collaboration. Organizational Development concerns itself with tracing the contextual fabric of the organization, and discovering and modifying the interlocking programs, roles, norms, and procedures.

Generally, the first stage of OD work involves some form of diagnosis of the situation. Data are gathered by some means (questionnaire, interview, observation) and analyzed to determine those aspects of the organization which seem to warrant some corrective action. The hoped-for outcomes are building an understanding of the situation and gaining a commitment for taking some action.

It is important to realize that there are two kinds of leadership roles that seem important in discussions of curricular reform. The first is intellectual leadership, the leadership that provides insight into what is of worth. The second is political leadership, which offers guidance in how to make things happen.

The second major stage of any OD program will involve goal-setting and organization for achieving those goals. Techniques which have proven effective in linking individual and organizational goals are (1) capitalizing of teacher autonomy, (2) the use of democratically formed councils, and (3) the idea of decision-making by consensus. The first strategy plays heavily on the professional competence and conscience of the teacher. The second strategy seeks to move the decision-making apparatus closer to the source of information. The third strategy realigns responsibility, and to some extent authority, by allowing treachers to "develop" curriculum.

The third stage in an Organizational Development program is concerned with implementing changes and establishing reliable self-correction measures to insure continued self-renewal.

If the process of self-analysis and goal-setting succeeds, what occurs is that the goals . . . assuming the people have been honest in setting them . . . act as motivators in their own right. People will support the organizational goals because those goals *are a composite of individual goals*. The teacher, rather than seeing the school as an organization in which he teaches, comes to see the school as an organizational setting within which he channels his contributive efforts.

The fulfillment of the O.D. program is, in a real sense, changing the way a school works. There are three elements of organization (processes) that appear important for changes: the roles people play, the goals of the organization, and the operational procedures in place. In effect, Organization Development is a people-involving approach to systemic analysis. Through analysis, it is hoped, the members of the organization will become committed to the efficacy of the system function.

The other key to the success of the Organization Development methodology of improving institutional process is the commitment to deal with change over an extended period of time and to use some of the resources of the organization to maintain, rebuild, and expand the structure of the organization. Organization Development technology approaches the goal of a self-renewing school.

While Organization Development approaches school improvement systematically, another approach, climate engineering, focuses on the individual organization members and their personal motivation. The climate approach culminates fifty years of research on human motivation.

Motivation

Research indicates that the success of any form of social influence depends upon altering the ability of others to achieve their goals or satisfy their needs. Leaders in the curriculum development process can have increased success if they keep such research in mind.

In order to exert influence on the process of program development, the leader must have an understanding of the factors that motivate individuals. The work of two social scientists, Abraham Maslow and Frederick Herzberg, provides insight on motivation and points the way to entry into the transactional process.

Maslow theorized that experienced needs are the primary influences on an individual's behavior. When a particular need emerges, it determines the individual's behavior in terms of motivations, priorities, and actions taken.

Maslow placed all human needs into five need systems. He believed that there is a natural process whereby individuals fulfill needs in an ascending order from primitive to sophisticated, and he therefore developed a hierarchical model thought common to all persons. According to this model, people ascend upward toward more complex needs only after successfully fulfilling lower order needs. The needs are, in order of importance, survival, safety, belonging, status, and self-actualization.

The value of the Maslow model for understanding individual motivation in an organization is that it sensitizes leaders to the complexity of motives and provides a rough analytic tool for estimating the type of motivation which is appropriate for any individual.

A second major contribution to the understanding of human motivation in organizations has been provided by Frederick Herzberg. Herzberg, following on the work of Maslow and others, stressed that the factors which truly motivate workers are those "growth" experiences which give the worker a sense of personal accomplishment through the challenge of the job itself—in the internal dynamics that the worker experiences in completing a task.

Although it is the job itself that provides satisfaction in work, Herzberg also observed that poor environmental (hygiene) factors can be the source of unhappiness and dissatisfaction in work. In the following list, the Herzberg findings give leadership some variables by which to assess an organization and individual patterns of motivation.[40]

MOTIVATION FACTORS	**HYGIENE FACTORS**
(Job Content)	*(Job Environment)*
SATISFIERS	DISSATISFIERS
Work Itself	Company Policy & Administration
Achievement	Supervision
Recognition	Working Conditions
Responsibility	Interpersonal Relations
Growth and Advancement	Salary

Shown side-by-side, the Maslow and Herzberg conceptions of motivation provide a leader with a new perspective of follower needs. (See Figure 6.4.)

In light of these understandings, it soon became apparent that if a leader was aware of individual needs and structured an organization around such needs "motivation" might be incorporated in the way in which an organization operated. Specifically, if the leader could selectively apply roles, encourage desired communication patterns, assign tasks, and tailor rewards to the individual needs of the organization members, then effective leadership would flourish. It was believed possible for the leader to influence the organization by establishing an environment to control transactions. From these foundations, climate engineering emerged as an approach to leadership.

Research by Litwin and Stringer shows that the development of a transactional climate can be purposeful activity. In their work, Litwin and Stringer outline a climate theory that consists of the following:

1. Individuals are attracted to work climates that arouse their dominant needs.
2. Such on-the-job climates are made up of experiences and incentives.
3. These climates interact with needs to arouse motivation toward need satisfaction.
4. Climates can mediate between organizational tasks requirements and individual needs—it is the linkage.

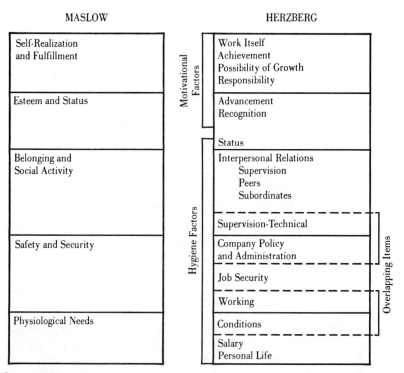

Figure 6.4

Source: K. Davis, *Human Relations at Work* (New York: McGraw-Hill, 1967), p. 37. Reprinted with permission.

5. Climates represent the most powerful leverage point available to managers to bring about change.

Leadership can, by its actions, affect the perceptions of individuals in the organization. The collective perceptions of leadership form a climate that influences change in the organization.

In their research, Litwin and Stringer identified nine organizational variables which can be manipulated to influence the climate of an organization:[41]

1. **Structure**—the feelings that employees have about the constraints in the group, how many rules, regulations, procedures there are; is there an emphasis on red tape and going through channels, or is there a loose and informal atmosphere.
2. **Responsibility**—the feeling of being your own boss; not having to double-check all of your decisions; when you have a job to do, knowing that it is your job.
3. **Reward**—the feeling of being rewarded for a job well done; emphasizing positive rewards rather than punishments; the perceived fairness of the pay and promotion policies.

4. **Risk**—the sense of riskiness and challenge in the job and in the organization; is there an emphasis on taking calculated risks, or is playing it safe the best way to operate.
5. **Warmth**—the feeling of good fellowship that prevails in the work group atmosphere; the emphasis on being well-liked; the prevalence of friendly and informal social groups.
6. **Support**—the perceived helpfulness of the managers and other employees in the group; emphasis on mutual support from above and below.
7. **Standards**—the perceived importance of implicit and explicit goals and performance standards; the emphasis on doing a good job; the challenge represented in personal and group goals.
8. **Conflict**—the feeling that managers and other workers want to hear different opinions; the emphasis placed on getting problems out in the open, rather than smoothing them over or ignoring them.
9. **Identity**—the feeling that you belong to a company and you are a valuable member of a working team; the importance placed on this kind of spirit.

Variables such as these allow the leader to make input into the flow of events and influence the perceptions of individuals and groups that make up the organization. To the degree that such input and influence serves organizational members, a successful transaction will be accomplished and leadership will be strengthened.

Issues In Curricular Leadership

While there are many leadership styles which are situationally appropriate for bringing about purposeful change to improve schools, some issues exist to "color" these approaches. While the authors do not expect the reader to gain cloture on these questions in the near future, the issues do illustrate how curriculum development is ultimately a normative experience.

School Mission as an Issue

Americans differ greatly in their opinions about what schools are for. While specific arguments may revolve around buzz words such as basics or open education, the issues underlying these concerns are foundational. Historically, schools in the United States adopted an educational pattern found in Europe in the 16th century; a system of education based on the mastery of specific content. By the 19th century a different conception of educating was borrowed from Europe; a child-centered program drawing its rationale from the needs of growing children. Both of these threads of educating have been preserved in the American system and exist in schools of the 1980s.

An important philosophical question underlying the design of school curriculums, however, is whether the intention of the program is to round out the student so that all graduates possess common knowledge and attributes, or whether the schooling experience should accentuate the uniqueness of the individual in an effort to gain the full potential of the student for society. This issue of the school's mission is best seen in the competition between goals of the school; learning competencies and graduation requirements on the one hand, efforts to serve special students and find unique characteristics (gifted, talented, special education) on the other.

While both of these ends are worthy, a school would be organized in different ways to accomplish these different ends. To encourage sameness and uniformity of the graduate, the school would employ high degrees of structure so that students would experience a near-alike program. To encourage uniqueness, flexibility would be encouraged so that each student could have the freedom to develop to his capacity, whatever that capacity is. Arguments over course materials, teaching methods, building designs, etc., spring from this key difference in the intention of the program. Curriculum leaders need to have some understanding of which purposes seem dominant to them as educators who will have an unusual degree of control over these variables.

Scope of Responsibility as an Issue

An issue which separates many curriculum leaders is the scope of their responsibility on the job. Few job descriptions are meant to be comprehensive or restrictive in nature, and the residual dimensions of school leadership will provide curriculum specialists with many choices beyond what is identified as their responsibility. Examples of such choices are whether they are obligated to help a teacher who is having personal problems outside of school, whether they are obligated to provide a quality school program for students who are beyond the benefit of the current offerings, and whether they should engineer change in the schools by leading the community toward novel programs and practices.

Exactly what constitutes the job of a curriculum leader, indeed what is meant by the term curriculum itself, will be decided by the person filling the position. The definition of what is curriculum will, of course, reflect a larger definition of the purpose of schooling.

Focus of Leadership as an Issue

The curriculum leader, clearly, has significant influence over how educational programs are organized and operate. By the control of task focus, communications, resource allocation and evaluation, the curriculum leader sets a tone for the organization and channels its activities.

One of the great differences among schools evolves from whether the leader defines his or her leadership as tractive or dynamic in its orientation.

The terms "tractive" and "dynamic" were suggested by Harris to differentiate between a leadership style which preserves and a leadership style which changes an organization. Tractive leaders gear their activities toward continuity, maintenance, and support of existing conditions. Dynamic leaders, by contrast, pursue activities designed to foster change, promoting discontinuity and the substitution of new practices for old.

While a balance between reinforcing activities and change-oriented activities is logical, school environments are characterized by constantly shifting pressures which encourage imbalances and instability. For the school leader to know, then, whether he or she is attempting to retain an existing pattern of operation or directing these ever-present pressures toward a new pattern of operation is important. Without such vision, leadership may be characterized as random or incongruous.

A corresponding subissue relating to tractive or dynamic leadership is the curriculum leader's definition of professionalism. Is professionalism the application of skills in operating a school or school district in an optimal fashion (engineer) or is professionalism the act of directing school operations toward an optimal form based on special knowledge (architect)? Each curriculum leader must know his own mind on this question.

Public Involvement as an Issue

One of the issues that commonly separates school leaders is whether the public should be fully involved in the operation of schools. While reason would seem to prevail on a case-by-case basis, the involvement or noninvolvement of citizens actually constitutes an entire strategy for survival of administrators in some cases.

For instance, in many districts assessments of need are conducted to gain information useful in making decisions about school programs. Whether the public should be involved in the gathering and analysis of such information, and whether the public should be involved in the actual decision-making resulting from that analysis, is an issue. On the one hand, there is the argument that the public sponsors the schools with their tax dollars and entrusts their children to the educational programs of the school. By this argument, involvement in decision-making is only natural and almost a right of each interested parent. On the other hand, many curriculum leaders feel that there is no clear consensus on many educational issues and that involvement of the public in decision-making only serves to polarize the many publics which support the schools. This position would draw an analogy to representative government, or would speak of professional judgment when declaring that the school administrator has no real obligation or mandate to involve the public in the daily decision-making or operation of the school.

In truth, this issue revolves around the concept of trust and the very democratic principles upon which this nation was founded.

Use of Influence as an Issue

Perhaps one of the most difficult issues for new curriculum leaders is that of dealing with use of influence. Most curriculum leaders like to think of public school leadership as a democratic process where they oversee the many competing forces as a professional. In reality, things are not always so simple.

A curriculum leader is a trained professional who is knowledgeable about the field of education. Such knowledge should mean that the school administrator has knowledge and skills not possessed by the average citizen. The issue of leadership relating to the use of influence arises when the public makes a poor choice from among limited alternatives and the school administrator knows it. At what point does the curriculum leader step in and share the professional knowledge or skills even though they have not been solicited? When does the sharing of knowledge cross over to become manipulation? An honest leader will acknowledge that even the medium (how decisions are made, committees formed, etc.) possess a degree of manipulation.

Obviously, to lead a public institution like a public school, the leader must have a clear conception of democratic principles and their use. It makes a great deal of difference whether the leader sees himself or herself as a controller of events due to position, or simply one more force in a sea of influencing factors around the school.

Moral Integrity as an Issue

School leaders, unlike leaders in other institutions, carry a special burden that might be termed "moral integrity." This extra responsibility stems from the value-laden nature of the schooling enterprise and the precious commodity which is the subject of educational influence. Stated bluntly, the public holds a special expectation for the moral integrity of school leaders.

When compared with business or political leaders, educational leaders clearly have a much narrower range of moral latitude in daily decision-making and operational procedures. The businessman, for whatever reason, is permitted great discretion in making decisions and in his method of operation: after all, business is business! The politician, too, is able to rationalize behavior under the banner of expedience or the fact that power corrupts absolutely. Even physicians and engineers are able to fall back on "professional judgment" when defending their acts or motivation. The school administrator can do none of these things. He or she must be exemplary in behavior, democratic in procedure, and responsive to the publics from which power is drawn.

The crux of the issue is that the school leader is in the business of human potential. Such potential is, by its complex nature, variable. Every act in educational programming which determines how children are to be nurtured is a value judgment. Curriculum leaders-in-training need to be aware of this fact and should realize that the special expectations for their behavior reflect the specific expectations for this role.

Summary ─────────────────────────────────

Leadership is a critical function in all curriculum development efforts. This intangible driving force is the linkage between theory and practice.

There are many conceptions of leadership, and research has evolved through three defined stages: a trait approach, a situation approach, and a transactional approach. In the 1980s it seems clear that to lead, an individual must possess useful skills for appropriate environments and be recognized by followers as a potential leader.

Being recognized as a leader is a matter of style, and many styles of leadership exist. The classic theory X and theory Y assumptions of McGregor in the 1960s have given way to the selective application of leadership roles and tasks in the 1980s. An understanding of change in educational environments undergirds the prolonged use of influence by leaders regardless of the practice conditions.

In leading change, two modern approaches are promising in the 1980s. One approach, organizational development, focuses on the systemic aspects of the organization and tries to increase efficiency by the assessment processes such as goal-setting, decision-making, and operating procedures.

A second approach, climate engineering, studies the motivational needs of individuals in the organization and directs key organizational variables to create an environment or climate. From this approach, when individual needs are attracted to supportive climates, the organization functions to the benefit of all.

Leadership, then, can accomplish its transaction by addressing structure in the organization or by manipulating processes (variables) in the organization.

Notes ──────────────────────────────────

1. J. M. Burns, *Leadership* (New York: Harper & Row, 1978).
2. Ralph M. Stogdill, *Handbook of Leadership* (New York: Free Press, 1974).

3. H. L. Smith and L. M. Krueger, "A Brief Summary of Literature on Leadership," 9, no. 4 (Bloomington: Indiana University, 1933), pp. 3–80.

4. F. H. Sanford, *Authoritarianism and Leadership* (Philadelphia: Institute for Research in Human Relations, 1952), p. 66.

5. R. M. Stogdill, "Personal Factors Associated With Leadership: A Survey of the Literature," *The Journal of Psychology* 25 (1948):64.

6. This approach was popularized in the best-selling book, *I'm O.K., You're O.K.*

7. Kimball Wiles and John Lovell, *Supervision for Better Schools*, 4th ed. (Englewood Cliffs, New Jersey: Prentice-Hall, 1975), pp. 65–67.

8. K. Lewin, R. Lippitt, and R. White, "Patterns of Aggressive Behavior in Experimentally Created Social Climates, *Journal of Social Psychology* 10 (1939): pp. 271–299.

9. D. Cartwright, and A. Zander, eds., *Group Dynamics: Research and Theory*, 2nd ed. (Evanston, Illinois: Row, Peterson & Co., 1960).

10. D. Katz and R. Kahn, *The Social Psychology of Organizations* (New York: John Wiley and Sons, Inc., 1966).

11. Douglas McGregor, *The Human Side of Enterprise* (New York: McGraw-Hill Book Co., 1960).

12. R. Blake, and J. Mouton, *The Managerial Grid* (Houston: Gulf Publishing Company, 1964).

13. Douglas McGregor, *The Human Side of Enterprise* (New York: McGraw-Hill Book Company, 1960), p. vii.

14. Ronald G. Havelock and Associates, Institute for Social Research, University of Michigan.

15. Everett M. Rogers and F. Floyd Shoemaker, *Communication of Innovations: A Cross-Cultural Approach* (New York: Free Press, 1971), p. xvii.

16. Matthew B. Miles, "Educational Innovation: The Nature of the Problem," *Innovations in Education* (New York: Teachers College Press 1964).

17. M. R. Goodson, "Models for Effecting Planned Educational Change" (Madison, Wisconsin: Research and Development Center for Training and Re-Education, 1966), ED 010214.

18. Warren G. Bennis, *Changing Organizations* (New York: McGraw-Hill Book Company, 1966).

19. Egon Guba, "The Role of Educational Research in Educational Change" (Bloomington, Indiana: National Institute for the Study of Educational Change, 1967), ED 012505.

20. Kurt Lewin, *Field Theory in Social Science* (New York: Harper-Torch Books, 1951).

21. H. Lionberger, *Adoption of New Ideas and Practices* (Ames, Iowa: State University Press, 1961) and E. M. Rogers, *Diffusion of Innovations* (New York: Free Press, 1962).

22. R. Lippitt, J. Watson, B. Westley, *The Dynamics of Planned Change* (New York: Harcourt, Brace and World, 1958).

23. W. Bennis, K. Benne, R. Chin, *The Planning of Change* (New York: Holt, Rinehart & Winston, 1969), pp. 34–35.

24. W. A. McClelland, "The Process of Effecting Change" (Washington, D.C.: George Washington University Human Resources Office, 1968).

25. E. M. Rogers, *Innovations: Research Design and Field Studies* (Columbus, Ohio: Research Foundation, Ohio State University, 1965). ED 003120.

26. D. Klein, "Some Notes on the Dynamics of Resistance to Change: The Defender's Role," in G. Watson, ed., *Concepts for Social Change,* COPED, NTL, Washington, D.C., 1967.

27. L. Iannaccone and F. Lutz, *Politics, Power, and Policy: The Governing of Local School Districts* (Columbus, Ohio: Charles E. Merrill, 1970), p. v.

28. R. O. Carlson, "Barriers to Change in Public Schools," in *Change Processes in the Public Schools* (Eugene, Oregon: Center for the Advanced Study of Educational Administration, 1965), pp. 3–8.

29. Bennis, Benne, and Chin, *The Planning of Change.*

30. Matthew Miles, *The Development of Innovative Climates in Organizations* (Menlo Park, California: Stanford Research Institute, 1969), p. 7.

31. J. W. Gardner, *Self-Renewal: The Individual and the Innovative Society* (New York: Harper & Row, 1964).

32. Kimball Wiles, *Supervision For Better Schools,* 3rd ed. (Englewood Cliffs, New Jersey: Prentice-Hall, 1967), pp. 39–40.

33. Charles Galloway, speech to the Ohio State Association of Student Teaching, Columbus, Ohio, October, 1968.

34. Wiles, *Supervision for Better Schools,* p. 53.

35. J. R. Gibb, "Defense Level and Influence Potential in Small Groups," in L. Petrullo and B. M. Bass, eds., *Leadership and Interpersonal Behavior* (New York: Holt, Rinehart & Winston, Inc., 1961), p. 66.

36. D. Berlo, "Avoiding Communication Breakdown," BNA Effective Communication film series.

37. Ralph Nicholas, "Listening is a Ten-Part Skill," in *Managing Yourself* compiled by the editors of *Nation's Business.*

38. Robert Katz. "Skills of an Effective Administrator," *Harvard Business Review* (January–February, 1955): 35–36.

39. See Richard Schmuck and Matthew Miles, *Organization Development in Schools* (Palo Alto, California: National Press Books, 1971).

40. Frederick Herzberg, *Work and the Nature of Man* (Cleveland: World Publishing Company, 1966).

41. George H. Litwin and Robert A. Stringer, Jr., *Motivation and Organizational Climate* (Boston: Division of Research, Harvard University, 1968), pp. 81–82.

42. Ben Harris, *Supervisory Behavior in Education* (Englewood Cliffs, New Jersey: Prentice-Hall, 1963), pp. 18–19.

Selected Learning Activities

1. Develop an operational definition of leadership in curriculum development efforts.

2. Outline specific behaviors identified by the authors that would allow curriculum leaders to be more effective in transactions.

3. Using Litwin and Stringer's categories, outline a plan for affecting the climate of a school involved in curriculum development.

Books to Review

Combs, Arthur, and Snygg, Donald. *Individual Behavior: A Perceptual Approach to Behavior*. New York: Harper & Row, 1949.

Denys, John. *Leadership in the Schools*. London: Heinemann Educational Corporation, 1980.

Giamatteo, Michael, and Giamatteo, Delores. *Forces on Leadership*. Reston, Virginia: National Association of Secondary School Principals, 1981.

Havelock, Ronald. *Planning for Innovation Through Dissemination and Utilization of Knowledge*. Institute for Social Research, University of Michigan, 1971.

Homans, George. *The Human Group*. New York: Harcourt, Brace & Co., 1950.

Jacobs, T. O. *Leadership and Exchange in Formal Organizations*. U. S. Office of Naval Research, HumRRO, 1970.

Katz, Daniel and Kahn, Robert. *The Social Psychology of Organizations*. New York: John Wiley & Sons, 1966.

Litwin, George and Stringer, Robert. *Motivation and Organizational Climate*. Harvard University: Division of Research, Graduate School of Business Administration, 1968.

Speiker, Charles A. *Curriculum Leaders: Improving Their Influence*. Washington, D.C.: Association for Supervision and Curriculum Development, 1976.

Chapter Seven
Managing and Evaluating Curriculum Development

As the United States enters the last years of the twentieth century, schools as we have known them for fifty years face major challenges. Most school districts in the nation will be confronted with significant enrollment declines (see Table 7.1) and a corresponding draw-down of the basic curriculum offered to students. Superimposed on this natural shrinking of the school population, and program, is the nation's entry into a new technological age; events of the early 1980s including recession, a depressed business environment, and a greater base of unemployed workers all hint at the ending of an eighty-year-old industrial era. Finally, public and private education have experienced a steady erosion of support for nearly a decade. In many districts this lack of support has led to a real crisis in financing even basic school programs.

Table 7.1
Projected Enrollments in Grades K-12 in the United States for Selected Years, 1974-1990[1]

| Grade | Enrollment in Year (in thousands) | | | |
	1974	1980	1985	1990
K	2,672	2,431	2,950	3,172
1	3,527	3,179	3,783	4,200
2	3,540	3,194	3,579	4,095
3	3,691	3,416	3,462	4,074
4	3,793	3,546	3,250	3,902
5	4,036	3,611	3,226	3,879
6	4,045	3,485	3,124	3,677
7	4,092	3,447	3,181	3,519
8	4,108	3,487	3,330	3,353
Total K-8	33,504[2]	29,796	29,885	33,871
9	4,034	3,552	3,480	3,191
10	3,964	3,657	3,409	3,050
11	3,653	3,501	3,083	2,765
12	3,669	3,619	3,108	2,870
Total 9-12	15,320[2]	14,329	13,080	11,876

[1]Estimated on the basis of Series II projections of the U.S. Bureau of the Census and age-grade ratios from the U.S. Census of 1970. Series II is one of three Bureau of the Census population projection series. It is considered the most reasonable choice at this time.

[2]In the fall of 1974 there were an estimated 34.4 million enrollees in K-8 and 15.6 million in grades 9-12. See National Center for Education Statistics, *Digest of Educational Statistics* (Washington, D.C.: U.S. Government Printing Office, 1975), Table 1.

Source: Declining Enrollment: The Challenge of the Coming Decade, U.S. Department of Health, Education, Welfare (Washington, D.C.: 1978) 21.

These factors, in combination, mean that many school districts throughout the United States are actively engaged in the reassessment of their curriculum and in the renewal of curriculum designs for learning. Curriculum planners are central to this widespread process by assisting others in gaining goal focus, assessing the status of programs, identifying priorities, developing plans for accomplishing desired ends, and evaluating progress for the sake of accountability. The many pressures of the school environment are making curriculum development *the* central role for school leadership in the eighties.

In the late 1980s and early 1990s curriculum leaders will need to superimpose a "planning and management" function upon the traditional cycle of curriculum development to bring about desired change. Valuable resources must be carefully directed to achieve priority objectives and random changes must be controlled where possible. The overall goal for any curriculum worker in the future will be to introduce a degree of regularity and predictability into the rapidly changing and often political school environment.

Comprehensive School Planning

The past decade has witnessed major strides in the application of managerial techniques to the process of curriculum planning. An awareness of the interrelatedness of school functions such as administration, curriculum, supervision, and instruction has led to a "systems" view of change. With this awareness has come the natural tendency to be comprehensive in school planning efforts. Many of the documents found in this chapter are the products of the authors' work with school districts in such comprehensive planning.

Comprehensive school planning begins with an awareness of what purposes the school or school district will serve and a commitment to those purposes. In the 1980s, certain issues have divided school leaders (see chapter 6 for a treatment of this area): Do we serve all students equally? Do we involve the public in planning and development of programs? Should professsional opinion be exerted over public will in some areas? These questions present school leaders with real choices, both in terms of strategy and tactics of operating, and districts throughout the United States differ in their stand on such questions. The most common position to be found on a host of value questions, however, is no position. A traditional academic curriculum with numerous unrelated satellite programs that have been initiated for non-educational reasons flourishes in too many districts. In the event of an economic squeeze, there must be some "criteria" for measuring the value of programs and courses. Without such clarity, curriculum development cannot be effective or efficient.

A number of methods are available to curriculum leaders to gain a clearer picture of a school district's goals. In some cases, documents can be analyzed for common themes. In other instances, possible goals can be suggested and prioritized in the search for consensus. Phi Delta Kappa, a professional education fraternity, provides school districts with a "card-sort" of possible goals. A third approach might be to conduct a pre-needs assessment in selected areas to determine what results are being gained from existing programming. Ultimately, there must be a shared opinion about the purposes of educating if planning and management are to occur.

When goals are stated explicitly in an organization such as a school, at least three benefits occur immediately. First, the management of personal, social, and intellectual development becomes easier to direct. Second, such goals assist members of an organization in feeling a sense of momentum and accomplishment since all activities are related to a fixed pattern of achievement. Third, and perhaps most important, a process begins whereby organizational resources are used more effectively in relation to an end product.

The following five criteria can be applied to any set of goals and help the curriculum leader assure their usefulness to the organization.

1. Are the goals realistic? If goals are attainable they possess a quality that allows members of the organization to relate to them in daily work.
2. Are the goals specific? Specific goals imply behaviors that need to be changed.
3. Are the goals related to performance? Goals that are developed in an organizational context suggest patterns of interaction.
4. Are the goals suggestive of involvement? To be effective, goals must be stated in such a way as to allow individuals in the organization to see themselves as being able to achieve the objective.
5. Are the goals observable? Can people in the organization see the results of their efforts and monitor progress toward the desired condition?

Once clarity has been accomplished, it is vital that such agreement about purpose be documented in a formal way. Reality in school districts today is often that superintendents and school boards come and go, unions change leadership, and public interests vary as conditions change in the society. To the degree that written commitments can be gained from school boards, superintendents, administrators, or union representatives (see Figures 7.1 and 7.2), then continuity is "built-in" to any subsequent planning effort. Without such formal endorsements, the goals of most school districts swing wildly and change is haphazard.

Curriculum leaders must work hard to insure that school goals reflect the needs of the clients—students. While many valuable lessons can be learned from the study of the past and present (adult focus), we must never forget that students in today's schools will be active citizens

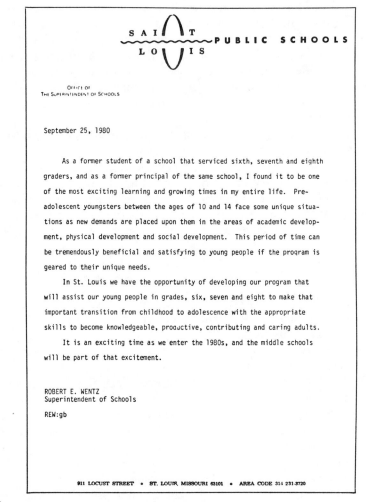

Figure 7.1 Superintendent's Endorsement

until the middle of the 21st century. The curriculum should reflect our changing society as basics are defined and endorsed. In this sense, all curriculum leaders must be advocates for the students who are dependent upon the school for preparation for adult living.

When clear goals are in place, a second step is to assess present conditions in the school or school district. This vital step is often omitted by leaders in a hurry to improve school programs and such an omission, ultimately, will bring failure to change efforts. Since American public education is an open system in which everyone participates, there is a tendency for goals to be general or even purposefully nebulous. Who, for instance, could argue with the goal of preparing citizens

St. Louis Teachers Union · AFT · AFL-CIO · 420

The attached questionnaire provides you with a chance to express your feelings about some important issues relating to education in the middle school year. You will also be able to indicate your own individual classroom needs which you believe are important in teaching children.

Your response will be tabulated and read. They will be used as basic information in an overall program of school improvement aimed at supporting, in every way, your own instructional efforts.

I urge you to help us in this effort by taking time out, of what I know is an already busy schedule, to complete this questionnaire.

Your help is very much appreciated.

Sincerely,

Evelyn H. Battle

Figure 7.2 Union Endorsement

for a democratic society. In the application of that goal, however, there can be many interpretations of citizenship and of a democratic society. By assessing present conditions, *curriculum leaders translate philosophy to decision-making data.*

There are many ways in which school districts accomplish such an assessment. The most common method is through the regular accreditation of schools within a district. Other methods regularly used are the school survey and the internal needs assessment.

The establishment of standards for school accreditation began in 1885 with the organization of select colleges in various regions of the country. The goal of these institutions was to deal with the persistent problem of entrance requirements. Following the establishment of the College Entrance Examination Board in 1901, youthful associations of colleges and schools took up the task of raising educational standards. The process of accreditation was the initial thrust in this effort and the product was a set of standards for membership in the associations. Eventually, six regional accrediting associations have been formed and serve today to assist schools in assessing their conditions.

School surveys are generally less formal than accreditation visits, and are more concerned with organization and structure in schools. Like the accreditation process they utilize a set of external standards, but are more oriented to internal consumption of the data gathered than a judgmental assessment of quality control. School districts enter into the survey process when they wish to prepare for accreditation or to conduct a periodic status check.

Unlike accreditation visits and surveys, the needs assessment focuses primarily on school *programs* and the clients of that program. The needs assessment is usually prescriptive, rather than descriptive, and is often conducted internally by members of the organization. Needs assessments are just that; they identify problems or needs and tie changes to the remediation of those conditions.

In Table 7.2, the three methods of determining the status of the curriculum are compared for the reader's study.

Once the current conditions of the school program are known, it is possible to compare and contrast the philosophy or beliefs of the

Table 7.2
Methods of Assessing School Conditions

Accreditation	Survey	Needs Assessment
Organizational orientation	Administrative orientation	Programmatic orientation
Concern with structure, organization	Concern with structure and management	Concern with clients and corresponding programs
Analysis of what actually exists (descriptive)	Analysis of what actually exists (descriptive)	Assessment of what should be in existence (prescriptive)
Scheduled	Self-contained	Ties to remediation
Comprehensive	Quasi-comprehensive	Focused on client needs
Validation emphasis	Judgmental	Objective with design
	Data	
Pupil-teacher ratio	Community background	School-community history
Number library books	Administration and organization	Achievement patterns
Statement of purpose	Instructional patterns	Attitudes toward school
Quality of buildings	Finance	Motivation, self-concepts
Financial patterns	Extracurricular	Student interests
Pupil-personnel services		Teacher perception
Standards	*Standards*	*Problems*
External	*External*	*Internal*
Post-evaluation	Post-evaluation	Pre-evaluation

school or district with these data. Such a comparison may warrant further study, and most school districts will use a committee structure to conduct further data-gathering procedures. The rationale for such an approach is: the more people who have studied the needs and problems, the more people who will understand projected changes to correct such conditions.

A typical organization will have two types of study committees: a central steering or coordinating committee whose function it is to organize and assess the inquiry and specific "ad hoc" (temporary) committees who gather specific data and disband. A sample chart of committee organization with three tiers of planning is shown in Figure 7.3.

As the study of the school or district's status continues and discrepancies between the intended program and the actual program as it is operated surface, a "desired" program begins to take shape. This "forming" process may take the shape of objectives, checklists of needs, standards of quality, or simple priorities for action. At this point the curriculum cycle moves from an analysis stage to a design stage.

One promising method of setting the curriculum design is through the use of "standards" such as those shown in Figure 7.4. In the example given, a mathematics program in the St. Louis City School System is defined by certain characteristics or standards of quality. Sometimes such standards are defined by outcomes such as scores on standardized tests. A status check on each standard is reported by a percentage of attainment (some 13 percent of the middle schools have a unit in computer science). Additionally, the resources needed to upgrade the program to meet the standard are identified as well as the relative priority of the standard according to instructional leaders in the district. Using such data for design purposes, the school board can now allocate resources selectively to bring the actual program into compliance with the desired program.

The type of data collected by the committee structure will vary from district to district. Table 7.3 suggests some of the more obvious data that might be reviewed, as well as regularly monitored, by school districts in order to improve their school programs.

The use of data gathered by schools or districts can help answer important questions about the current status of school programs. In viewing the program comprehensively, as in Figure 7.5, it is possible to "look across" all programs for areas of need. In this example, students in one city school system are compared to national norms in mathematics and language arts. What is obvious from this comprehensive vantage point is that students in the district begin school below national norms, work hard in these skill areas and approach national norms by the end of the eighth grade, and then "fall off" dramatically in the early high school years. Obviously, curriculum development work needs to be directed toward articulation between the eighth and ninth grades in these subject areas.

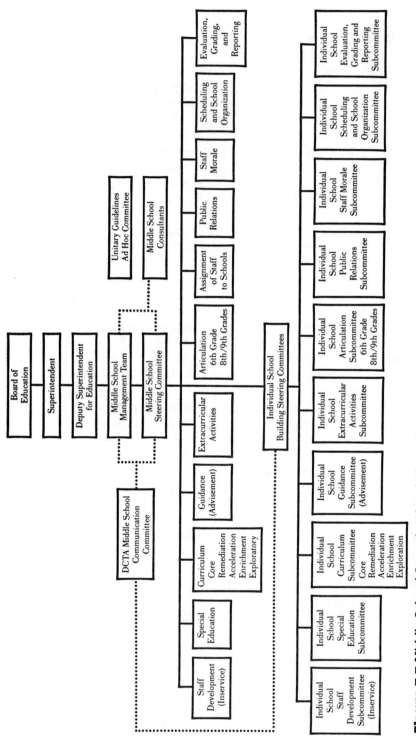

Figure 7.3 Middle School Organizational Chart for Planning

Source: School District One, Denver (Colorado) Public Schools. Used with permission.

Figure 7.4 School Standards Checklists

Program Standards	Status					Needs (Mark all that apply)						Specifics	Priority		
	Exceeded	Reached	Slightly	Far	Not Present	Personnel	Facilities	Equipment	Supplies	Inst. Prog.	Other-specify		High	Moderate	Low
3. Mathematics															
Provides sequential development of skills that enable students to comprehend our number system, to perform mathematical calculations, and to use mathematical thinking in solving problems.															
• Sufficient classroom quantity of durable, accurate, manipulative materials	—	46	33	13	13	—	4	17	—	4	4		63	17	—
• Developmental program provided	—	88	13	—	—	—	—	—	—	4	4		67	17	—
• Remedial program provided	—	71	13	—	13	8	4	4	—	8	—		67	8	—
• Enrichment program provided	—	29	20	13	20	29	13	17	—	29	4		67	13	—
• Opportunities to apply computation skills in daily living situations	—	79	17	4	—	—	—	—	—	4	4		71	4	4
• Variety of practice materials for basic skills	—	63	38	4	—	—	—	8	—	8	4		58	13	4
• Supplemental materials	—	67	25	8	—	—	—	—	—	4	—		58	20	4
• Opportunity to practice creative problem-solving	—	71	20	8	—	4	4	—	—	8	—		71	17	4
• Opportunity to practice solving word problems	—	79	17	4	—	—	—	—	—	—	8		71	4	4

Figure 7.4 (continued)

Program Standards	Status					Needs (Mark all that apply)						Specifics	Priority		
	Exceeded	Reached	Below			Personnel	Facilities	Equipment	Supplies	Inst. Prog.	Other-specify		High	Moderate	Low
			Slightly	Far	Not Present										
3. Mathematics															
Provides sequential development of skills that enable students to comprehend our number system, to perform mathematical calculations, and to use mathematical thinking in solving problems.															
• Includes basic geometric knowledge	—	79	8	8	4	—	4	4	—	13	4		54	25	4
• Includes abstract thinking	—	63	25	8	—	4	—	4	—	17	—		50	29	4
• Includes interdisciplinary tie-ins with science, practical arts, and social studies	—	42	38	17	—	8	4	13	—	20	—		71	17	4
• Introduction to computer science as a unit	—	13	4	—	75	33	29	42	—	38	—		42	20	33
• Consumer math as a unit	—	71	25	—	—	—	4	—	—	13	—		67	8	—

Table 7.3
Sources of Data About an Instructional Program

A. Pupil performance
   1. Standardized tests—teacher-made tests
   2. Pupil grades
   3. Dropout data
   4. Pupil attendance
   5. Observation of pupil performance
   6. Inventories—skill continuums
   7. Observations of teaching-learning situations in the classroom
   8. Degree of student attention and involvement
B. Questionnaires—polls of opinions of pupils, teachers, parents
   1. Polls of parents regarding the success of certain school programs
   2. Group interviews with students, parents, teachers about the success of curriculum innovations
   3. Attitude surveys of students about certain programs
   4. Comparison of attitudes of pupils and teachers toward contrasting programs
   5. Systematic questionnaires, rating sheets, and interviews with small random samples of students
C. Follow-up studies of learners
   1. Success at the next grade level
   2. Continuation of schooling
   3. College success
   4. Success at work
   5. Application of skills learned, interests generated in school—e.g., participation in lifetime sports, the arts
D. Examination of learning materials
   1. Examining learning materials to see if they are feasible and practical for use by teachers in the schools—accuracy and soundness of materials
   2. Determining if costs of materials are too great.
   3. Checking materials to see if they are at the right level for students
   4. Determining whether teachers get special retraining in order to understand and use new materials
   5. Matching materials to students' interests, needs, and aspirations—relevancy of materials

In yet another example, Table 7.4, a single class is followed for progress and a pattern emerges which illuminates certain skill growth. This might suggest the further identification of specific skills in reading or math that could be targeted by teachers of those subjects in the seventh and eighth grades.

In the design stage of curriculum development, the concept of "systems" is most evident. Philosophy and goals and objectives have now been tested against data that indicate real conditions. Standards at a program level have been established and resources needed to attain such standards identified. In designing this system, curriculum planners proceed through five basic stages:

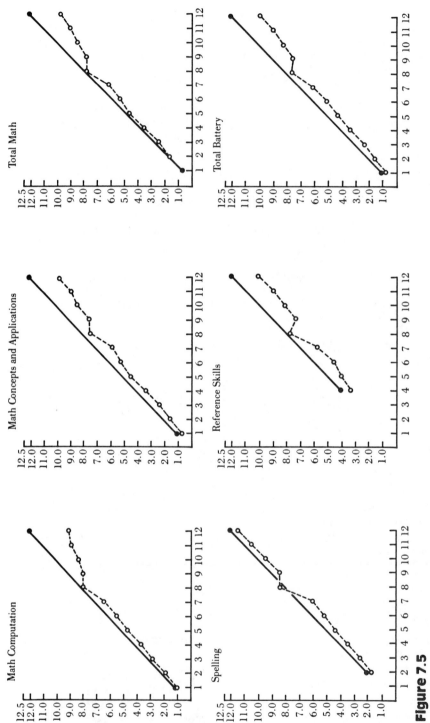

Figure 7.5

Source: St. Louis (Missouri) Public Schools.
o---o Citywide mean grade equivalent score
—— National norm

Table 7.4
Metropolitan Achievement Test: Mean Percentile by Subtest in Reading and Math

	Reading			Math			
	Word Knowledge	Reading Comprehension	Total Reading	Math Computation	Math Concepts	Math Problem Solving	Total Math
Table 1	**Growth of 1978 Sixth Grade Class Through the Eighth Grade**						
1978 (6)	46	50	46	48	40	46	50
1979 (7)	52	48	50	46	40	40	44
1980 (8)	44	48	48	50	48	40	48
Table 2	**Growth of 1978 Seventh Grade Class Through the Eighth Grade**						
1978 (7)	50	44	46	46	40	46	44
1979 (8)	40	40	40	44	48	36	46
Table 3	**Growth of 1979 Sixth Grade Class Through the Seventh Grade**						
1979 (6)	46	50	50	48	40	46	46
1980 (7)	56	50	54	46	40	40	44

Source: East Baton Rouge Parish School District.

1. A description of the desired end product, uncontaminated by means, is drawn.
2. Objectives are analyzed to find preconditions needed to produce the desired end product.
3. Analysis proceeds downward, describing in greater and greater detail what is to occur.
4. When the smallest components are outlined, the process to produce the desired result is constructed.
5. The process is activated.

At some point in the design stage the curriculum specialist must translate planning data into conceptualizations of a desired program. Such a conceptualization would include a brief description of the desired program, learning objectives to be addressed, the organization of the program, organization of the staff and staffing requirements, teaching strategies, and resources needed. Below, the reader can review a plan for a kindergarten program:

Plan for Establishing a Kindergarten

Population—Approximately 300 students, ages 3–5, and 6-year-olds who do not have the readiness for the first grade.

Program Concept—The kindergarten program will be divided into two distinct components. An A.M. program will be provided with a basic instructional format that will match the individualized and continuous progress concepts. The major focus of the A.M. program will be readiness for the more formal education program to follow, while the specific objectives will be to develop social skills, motor skills, self-direction, self-esteem, and communication. During the P.M. program, a child care service will be provided for those students who need the service because both parents work away from the home. The program will follow an action format that will have little structure. Focus will be primarily on socialization.

Areas of Learning—Socialization, school readiness, independence, motor skills, communication.

Program Organization—The student population will be divided into instructional units of thirty students each and will be comprised of students of varying ages, but with similar maturation characteristics. The formal program will be scheduled from 8:00 A.M. to 12:00 noon, with a breakfast and lunch program provided. Students that are eligible for the child care program will remain at school until 3:00 P.M. The kindergarten program will operate five days a week, twelve months of the year when school is in session.

Staff Organization—The staff will be organized to complement the instructional unit approach. For each unit, there will be one teacher and three instructional aides who will work as a team.

Staff Requirements—The kindergarten school staff will consist of one program coordinator, ten teachers, thirty instructional aides, one school nurse, and one secretary/bookkeeper.

Teaching Strategies—Some examples of teaching strategies to be used by the kindergarten staff are: role playing, field trips, working with educational games, regular planned rest, rhythmical activities, positive reinforcement, creative expression, peer teaching, exploration of self, school, and community.

Facilities—The kindergarten school will utilize the cafetorium and the auditorium located on the current high school site. Both buildings need remodeling in order to be adequate for an early childhood program. Floors and restrooms of the auditorium need remodeling, and lighting, controlled air, and carpeting should be updated.

Using such a complete plan, curriculum development teams can assess the scope and cost of desired programs and make decisions about priorities based on factual information. In Table 7.5 and Figure 7.6, the cost of the proposed kindergarten program is computed, and district-wide staffing requirements have been plotted.

As curriculum planners translate program components into action steps, the curriculum development cycle enters a third stage of implementation or management. This management stage is what differentiates curriculum development in the 1960s from the 1980s because much has been learned about the management of change in schools. The first large tasks leading to implementation are to develop a holistic picture of the effort and place the change effort in some sort of timeframe. Figure 7.7 shows how one curriculum leader outlined the tasks with a checklist.

In another example of seeing the overall effort (Table 7.6), the Denver Public Schools outlined some twenty-six steps leading to the conversion of junior high schools to middle school programs. As the reader will note, each of the steps is tied to the four-part curriculum development cycle.

It is important that, at some point, those persons involved in the improvement of the school program be able to see all the parts or the "system of management." Often each stage of change is documented by some form of report and the sum of these reports indicates how and where change is to occur. Figure 7.8 outlines such a management system and its parts.

Table 7.5
Cost of Proposed Kindergarten

Item	Cost	
	Start Up	Continuing
1. *Personnel*		
a. 10 Regular Teachers		$150,790
b. 30 Instructional Aides		200,000
c. 1 Program Coordinator		15,000
d. 1 Secretary/Bookkeeper		9,000
2. *Fixed Charges*		
Social Security and Teacher Retirement		
@ 15% of $374,790		56,218
3. *Materials*		
Continuous Cost—10 teachers @ $500/teacher	$10,000	5,000
4. *Equipment*		
Cots, chairs, tables, learning center equipment,		
playground equipment	20,000	2,000
5. *Facilities*		
Renovation of the cafeteria and auditorium on		
the present high school site	68,750	
6. *Maintenance and Operation of Plant*		
10 Teachers @ $2,200/teacher		22,000
7. *Staff Development*		
a. Consultant honorarium and travel	1,800	15,000
b. Materials		400
Total	$100,500	$461,908
Total Cost of Kindergarten School Program	$562,458	

Activation of these outlines for action is dependent upon the direct identification of action and responsibility for the attainment of goals. School planners use a variety of technical aids to accomplish this "delegation" of responsibility and such aids have in common that they spell out what is to occur, who is responsible, when the event is to be completed, and, in some cases, evidences that the action has been taken. Sometimes the technical aid is simply a schedule of activities (Table 7.7), sometimes the aid identifies objectives or milestones (Table 7.8), and sometimes the technical aid displays workload distribution (Figure 7.9). In Figure 7.10, needs, goals, and strategies are shown along with the timeframe and the responsible agents. Whatever their form, technical aids "propel" desired changes from one point to another and assist the curriculum planner in monitoring the many on-going events.

	Kindergarten	Elementary School	Middle School	High School	Adult School	System-wide Special Services	Totals
Driver Education				1			1
Vocational/Occupational				6			6
Reading				2			2
Special Education		2	4	2			8
Music Teacher		1	1	1			3
Art Teacher		1	1	1			3
Physical Education Teacher		1	2	3			6
Regular Teachers	10	25	24	11			70
Part-time Teachers					6		6
Instructional Aides	30	27	26	18			101
Secretary/Bookkeeper	1	1	1	1			4
Bookkeeper						1	1
Secretary						1	1
Program Coordinators	1	1	4	1	1		8
Counselors		½	1	2			3½
Media Specialists		1	1	1			3
Career Awareness Coordinators		½	1				1½
Vocational/Occupational Coord.				1			1
Language Arts Coordinator						1	1
Registered Nurse						1	1
Social Worker						1	1
Curriculum Director						1	1
Director Pupil Services						1	1
Principals		1	1	1			3
Superintendent						1	1

Figure 7.6 Staff Requirements

Figure 7.7 Planning Checklist

_____ *Needs Assessment Completed*	Formal—survey, interview, question-naire Informal—discussion, belief, etc. Directive—necessary mandate Other
_____ *Goals Developed* **Start Date Established** **Target Date Projected** (most likely time)	Goals Identified Goals Synthesized Mission Identified Mission Clarified Mission Accepted
_____ *Major Activities Delineated*	All Possible Mission Objectives Synthesize All Objectives Convert to Product Statements Activities (Product Statement) Agreed Upon
_____ *Responsibility Charted*	Activities Stated Personnel (Human Resources) Identified Responsibility Allocated
_____ *Activities Assigned*	Supervision Responsibility Accepted Work Accepted
_____ *Tasks Identified*	Work Detailed Target Date Set
_____ *Events Delineated*	Work Assigned Target Dates Set

_____ *Time Scheduled*	Event, Task, Activity, Time
	  Combined
	Combined Time and Target Date
	  Compared
	Time Adjusted When Necessary

_____ *Manual Completed and Distributed*	Mission, Activity, and Task Sheets Collated and Tabbed Responsibility Chart Entered Manual Duplicated
_____ *Time Schedules Completed*	Time Charts Developed Time Charts Centrally Posted

Table 7.6
Comprehensive Plan of the Denver Public Schools

ANALYSIS STAGE	1. Identify Denver Public Schools' philosophy.
	2. Identify Board Policy relative to Middle Schools.
	3. Superintendent (public) statement on Middle Schools.
	4. Outline timeframe for implementation.
	5. Formation of centralized coordinating group.
	6. Delineation of tasks + appointment of sub-committees.
	7. Develop "definition" of Denver Middle Schools.
	8. Structure Awareness/orientation campaign.
	    a. Administrators
	    b. Teacher groups

DESIGN STAGE	9. Translate philosophy into goal statements. 10. Project preliminary budget/resource base. 11. Prioritize goal statements. 12. Translate goal statements to objectives format. 13. Block out 3–5 year plan for implementation. 14. Establish management/information system to monitor progress of implementation (external audit). 15. Establish evaluation targets, time, responsibilities, resources; identify baseline data needed. 16. Conduct needs assessment. 17. Develop final management system (PERT).

IMPLEMENTATION OR MANAGEMENT STAGE	18. Provide advanced organizers (simple plan) to all interested persons.
	19. Provide each school with resource kits, glossaries, data bank from needs assessment (local planning/decision-making data).
	20. Formation of teams in each school to serve as:
	    1. study group for mapping curriculum/skills
	    2. planning group/house plan
	    3. team/cooperative teaching unit.
	21. Provide preliminary staff development (demonstration teaching) in all schools on:
	    1. advisor/advisee program
	    2. continuous progress curriculums
	    3. team planning and teaching.
	22. Require school-by-school development plan including curriculum, staff development, evaluation, community involvement.
	23. Provide local budget supplement based on plan.

EVALUATION STAGE	24. Conduct formative evaluation (external audit) every six weeks to monitor management outline. 25. Conduct major review after 6 months—revise timeline, goals, needs, etc. 26. Develop master evaluation plan (sum of all schools) for 3-year period.

Source: Author's notes, Denver, Colorado, 1980.

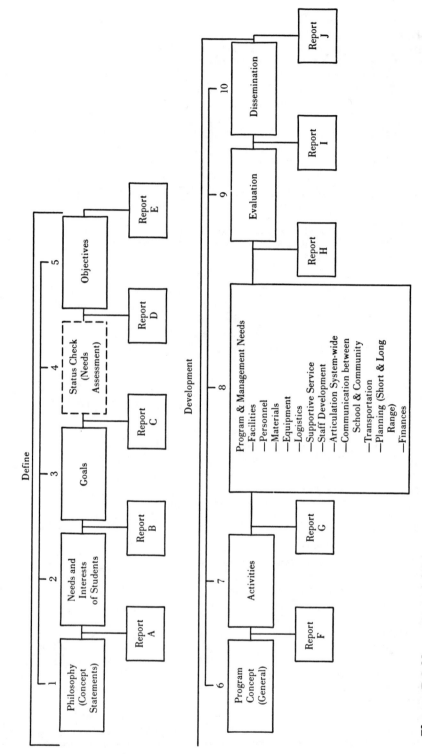

Figure 7.8 Management System

Table 7.7
Schedule of Activities

Major Event	Starting Date	Completion Date
Hiring administrative staff (Project Director and secretary)	Notification of Funding Date	August 1
Overall planning	August 1	May 23
Recruiting three lead teachers and two counselors	Notification of Funding Date	August 1
Recruiting 12 teacher aides and 12 student tutors	August 1	August 17
Evaluating and selecting instructional materials	Notification of Funding Date	August
Purchasing instructional materials	August	August 17
Purchasing office supplies	August 1	June 30
Concentrated training of instructional staff	August 20	August 24
In-service training of instructional staff	September 4	May 24
Pretesting of students in program	September 10	September 14
Posttesting of students in program	April 22	April 26
Interim testing of students in program	September	May
Working with parents and community groups	September 17	May 24
Disseminating information about program	August 1	June 29
Developing and implementing instructional program	August 1	May 24
Replicating project activities in other schools within LEA	August	Indefinitely
Demonstrating the project to interested observers and making available staff members as well as materials, equipment, and facilities which are relevant to the project.	January	Indefinitely

Table 7.8
Milestone Chart

Milestones	Completion Date						
	1983				1984		
	Sept.	Oct.	Nov.	Dec.	Jan.	Feb.	Mar.
1. Review guidelines with State Department of Education June 7							
2. Identify the criteria for selecting a representative group of the school, community to serve as a task force	△13						
3. Identify the Education Task Force	△20						
4. Orientation for Education Task Force to guidelines and intent		△4					
5. Design a management system for processing the development of a plan		△6					
6. Identify special groups representing the school and community for involvement		△7					
7. Describe the scope and depth of the plan		△7					
8. Plan task for completing the philosophy stage		△7					
9. Appoint Task Force committees		△7					
10. Orientation for all special groups to guidelines, intent and management system		△11					
11. Collect data for the philosophy stage		△18					

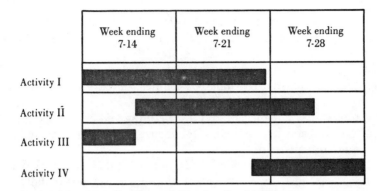

	Week ending 7-14	Week ending 7-21	Week ending 7-28
Activity I			
Activity II			
Activity III			
Activity IV			

Figure 7.9 The Distribution of Work—Gantt Chart

Figure 7.10 Program Evaluation Review Technique

PERT charts employ symbols and formulas for assisting planners in establishing a long-range plan. Some of those symbols are as follows:

Definition	**Symbol**
Event—the start or completion of a task. There is always a sequential relationship between events.	(1)
Flow—the order of events is indicated by arrows, not event numbers.	
Activity—the performance of a task. The time-consuming portion of the PERT network. An activity always requires resources.	a, b, c
Time—the estimated performance time is an average of "optimistic," "most likely," and "pessimistic" estimates in weeks or months.	$Te = \dfrac{a + 4m + b}{6}$

a = optimistic time
b = most likely time
c = pessimistic time

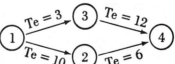

In the example, event 4 shows a dependence on both events 2 and 3. Since the largest time-consuming path (in this case 1–2–4) represents the earliest possible time to begin event 4, Te for event 4 is 16 weeks.

Perhaps the most complicated technical aid used in schools today is the Program Evaluation and Review Technique (PERT). Although PERT was initially a management system designed and used by the Department of Defense to accelerate the development of the Polaris submarines, it holds far-reaching possibilities for assisting educators in planning complex changes in school programs. PERT does two things for planners: it is a manager's tool for defining and coordinating what must be done, and it is a method of focusing attention on problems that require decisions (see Figure 17.10).

The *Gantt Chart,* developed by Henry Gantt during World War I, is a linear calendar on which future time is spread horizontally and work to be accomplished is displayed vertically in bar graph fashion. Using the Gantt Chart, planners can view activities in terms of the only constant in planning procedure—time. The Gantt Chart, shown in Figure 7.9, is useful in avoiding an overload of organizational activity during any single period of time.

Evaluation—The Critical Step

Evaluation is the fourth step in the curriculum development cycle and, from the author's experience, evaluation is *the* critical step in program renewal. The syndrome of endless and random change in American education cannot be broken until school leaders develop a means of measuring progress toward an identifiable goal. In many states, the development of such ends is mandated by specific legislation. The landmark piece of legislation was the 1971 "Stull Bill" passed by the California Assembly:

> Each school district is required to adopt specific evaluation and assessment guidelines which shall include but not necessarily be limited to (a) the establishment of standards of expected student progress in each area of study and of techniques for the assessment of that progress (b) the assessment of certified personnel competence as it relates to the establishment standards. (Bill 293, Ch. 361, Sec. 13403–13489, Education Code).

In the years since the first "accountability" legislation a great deal of effort has been devoted to identifying the goals of education. In some states, like Florida (see Figure 7.11) and Connecticut, complex state-level systems have been designed and developed to "direct" education. In other districts, national achievement tests have become the measure of excellence and curriculums have been streamlined to facilitate the performance of students on these measures. Almost every school and school district has responded to the pressing need for more evaluation.

Figure 7.11 Florida's Accountability Act

Education accountability acts have done much more than just establish minimum competency requirements. The Florida Educational Accountability Act of 1976, for instance, is a very detailed act that is designed to establish the framework for a totally integrated system of accountability for the public schools in Florida. The stated intent of the act is to:

1. Provide information for educational decision makers at the state, district and school levels in order to appropriately allocate resources and meet the need of the system in a timley manner.

2. Provide public information on the costs of educational programs and the differential effectiveness of various types of instructional activities.

3. Guarantee to each student the availability of instructional programs which meet minimum performance standards consistent with the state plan for education.

4. Provide thorough analyses of various programs costs and the degree to which school districts meet the state-established minimum performance standards.

5. Provide information to the public about the performance of the state system in meeting established goals, and in providing effective, meaningful, and relevant educational experiences designed to give students at least the minimum skills necessary to function and survive in today's society.

Purposes of Evaluation

The general purpose of evaluation is to improve the educational program by facilitating judgments about its effectiveness based on evidence. Specific purposes include:

1. To make explicit the rationale of the instructional program as a basis for deciding which aspects of the program should be evaluated for effectiveness and what types of data should be gathered.
2. To collect data upon which judgments about effectiveness can be formulated.
3. To analyze data and draw conclusions.
4. To make decisions which are based on the data.
5. To implement the decisions to improve the instructional program.

There are some existing guidelines found in most curriculum texts which indicate the type of concerns general to all programs. Saylor and Alexander provide one such list in their "marks of a good curriculum":

1. The program should be systematically planned and systematically evaluated.

2. Learning opportunities should reflect the aims of the school.
3. Balance should be maintained among all of the goals of the school.
4. Continuity among learning experiences should be promoted.
5. Flexibility in the curriculum should be both encouraged and utilized.
6. Each learner should be provided for adequately.[1]

In order to check on such criteria, the curriculum leader needs to establish various evaluation programs and initiate research in numerous areas. Examples of such areas are student performance, staff development patterns, parent-community feedback, policies and regulations, utilization of facilities and resources, design of specific programs, effectiveness of instruction, and administrative procedures. Collectively, research in these and other areas will lead to a comprehensive evaluation program for the school, as illustrated in Figure 7.12.

Criteria for Evaluating Instructional Programs _____

1. The first consideration in the evaluation of instructional programs has to be the purposes for which the instructional program is being planned. Whether it is the objectives stated for a particular lesson in a classroom or the general educational goals for a school or district, planning occurs on the basis of the purposes defined. As stated early in this text, the authors believe a good instructional program must adequately reflect the aims of the school or agency from which they come. At the school level, the faculty, students, and parents need to define comprehensive educational goals and all cur-

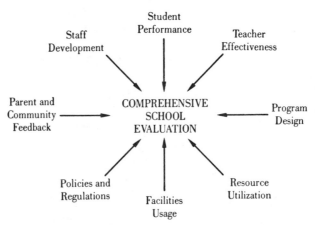

Figure 7.12

riculum opportunities offered at the school should be planned with reference to one or more of those goals.

2. A good instructional program must provide for continuity of learning experiences. Students should progress through a particular program on the basis of their achievement, not on the basis of how much time they have spent in the program. Instructional programs in a school that are planned over several years lend themselves to better vertical progress. Continuity of learning experiences within a program dictates that a relationship between disciplines be established. Core or interdisciplinary programs allow students to see purpose and meaning in their total instructional program.

3. All principles of learning need to be drawn upon in selecting an instructional program. Programs that rely solely on operant conditioning as a psychological base for teaching neglect the important theories of Combs, Piaget, and others. All those associated in education understand the difficulty of putting psychological principles into practice. A careful analysis of new programs can reveal the psychological bases of those programs.

4. Programs selected should make maximum provision for the development of each learner. Any program selected should include a wide range of opportunities for individuals of varying abilities, interests, and needs. Each child is characterized by his or her own pattern of development. Youngsters are curious, explorative, and interested in many things. An instructional program must promote individual development in students rather than making them conform to a hypothetical standard.

5. An instructional program must provide for clear focus. Whether a program is organized around separate subjects such as history or science, or around related subjects such as social studies, it is important that the one selecting the program know which dimensions to pursue, which relationships of facts and ideas should stand out, and which should be submerged. The problem for those who are reviewing programs is to decide which element of the program is the center of organization. Instructional programs may be organized around life problems, content topics, interests, or experiences. In selecting instructional programs, however, the organizing focus must also be examined to see which topics are emphasized, which details are relevant, and which relationships are significant.

6. A good instructional program should be well planned and must include a built-in process for evaluation. Steps need to be defined that would include a periodic assessment of the success of the program and a continuous process for reviewing and updating the program.

Types of Evaluation

Daniel Stufflebeam has developed an outline or evaluation structure that is general to all types of evaluation:

A. Focusing the Evaluation
    1. Identify the major level (s) of decision-making to be served e.g., local, state, or national.
    2. For each level of decision-making, project the decision situations to be served and describe each one in terms of its locus, focus, timing, and composition of alternatives.
    3. Define criteria for each decision situation by specifying variables for measurement and standards for use in the judgment of alternatives.
    4. Define policies within which the evaluation must operate.

B. Collection of information
    1. Specify the source of the information to be collected.
    2. Specify the instruments and methods for collecting the needed information.
    3. Specify the sampling procedure to be employed.
    4. Specify the conditions and schedule for information collection.

C. Organization of Information
    1. Specify a format for the information which is to be collected.
    2. Specify a means for coding, organizing, storing, and retrieving information.

D. Analysis of information
    1. Specify the analytical procedures to be employed.
    2. Specify a means for performing the analysis.

E. Reporting of Information
    1. Define the audiences for the evaluation reports.
    2. Specify means for providing information to the audiences.
    3. Specify the format for evaluation reports and/or reporting sessions.
    4. Schedule the reporting information.

F. Administration of the Evaluation
    1. Summarize the evaluation schedule.
    2. Define staff and resource requirements and plans for meeting these requirements.
    3. Specify means for meeting policy requirements for conduct of the evaluation.
    4. Evaluate the potential of the evaluation design for providing information which is valid, reliable, credible, timely, and pervasive.

5. Specify and schedule means for periodic updating of the evaluation design.

6. Provide a budget for the total evaluation program.[2]

Another useful resource for curriculum leaders responsible for designing evaluation systems is a classification outline developed by the Phi Delta Kappa National Study Committee on Evaluation. This outline presents the following four types of evaluation commonly found in schools according to their objective, method, and relationship to the decision-making process:

1. **Context Evaluation**

Objective: To define the operation context, to identify and assess needs in the context, and to identify and delineate problems underlying the needs.

Method: By describing individually and in relevant perspectives the major sub-systems of the context; by comparing actual and intended inputs and outputs of the subsystems; and by analyzing possible causes of discrepancies between actualities and intentions.

Relation to DM Process: For deciding upon the setting to be served, the goals associated with meeting needs and the objectives associated with solving problems, i.e., for planning needed changes.

2. **Input Evaluation**

Objective: To identify and assess system capabilities, available input strategies, and designs for implementing strategies.

Method: By describing and analyzing available human and material resources, solution strategies, and procedural designs for relevance, feasibility, and economy in the course of action to be taken.

Relation to DM Process: For selecting sources of support, solution strategies, and procedural designs, i.e, for programming change activities.

3. **Process Evaluation**

Objective: To identify or predict, in process, defects in procedural design or its implementation, and to maintain a record of procedural events and activities.

Method: By monitoring the activity's potential procedural barriers and remaining alert to unanticipated ones.

Relation to DM Process: For implementing and refining the program design and procedure, i.e., for effecting process control.

4. **Product Evaluation**

Objective:	To relate outcome information to objectives and to context, input, and process information.
Method:	By defining operationally and measuring criteria associated with the objectives, by comparing these measurements with predetermined standards or comparative bases, and by interpreting the outcome in terms of recorded input and process information.
Relation to DM Process:	For deciding to continue, terminate, modify, or refocus a change activity, and for linking the activity to other major phases of the change process, i.e., for evolving change activities.[3]

Assessing Educational Research

Another task for curriculum workers that is related to school evaluation activities is to assess educational research. In some cases such research will be conducted external to the school district while in other cases the research will be "in-house" evaluation. The curriculum specialist should be able to identify good research and be able to assess research reports.

Good research possesses a number of characteristics which, while seemingly obvious, distinguish it from mediocre research. The following guidelines will assist the review of research efforts:

1. The problem should be clearly stated, be limited, and have contemporary significance. In the proposal the purpose, objectives, hypotheses, and specific questions should be presented concisely. Important terms should be defined.
2. Previous and related studies should be reported, indicating their relationship to the present study.
3. The variables, those which are controlled and those to be manipulated, should be identified.
4. A description of procedures to be used should be clear enough to be replicated. Details such as the duration of the study and the treatments utilized should be spelled out in depth.
5. The groups being studied should be defined in terms of significant characteristics.
6. The report should note the school setting, describing among other things organization, scale of operations, and any special influences.
7. The evaluation instruments should be applicable to the purpose of the study. Growth in self-concept, for instance, is not measured by standardized achievement tests in reading, Evidence of validity (is this test the correct one) and reliability

(measures what it is supposed to) should be given for all evaluation instruments used.

8. Scoring of measures should be done by the most appropriate method whether it be means, medians, percentages, quartiles, rank, or whatever.

9. Results or findings should be clearly stated in the report in a prominent location.

10. Limitations on findings, and there usually are limitations, should be clearly stated.

In addition to understanding what goes into "good research," the curriculum specialist may sometimes be asked to assess specific research reports which have application to the schools with which they work. The following questions will help in such an assessment:

1. *Problem presentation*—Is the question being asked an important one? Will the question being asked add to further understanding? Will the question being asked aid in decision making? Is the problem explained well in light of limitations in the research area? Are the concepts presented reasonable and testable?

2. *Methodology*—Are the hypotheses stated in a manner which will reveal expected differences? Can this research be replicated? Is the sampling adequate and representative? Is the study designed to show evidence of causation or correlation? Will the results be generalizable to other groups with similar characteristics?

3. *Results*—Are the observational categories used relevant to the purpose of the study? Are the statistical treatments appropriate to the data presented? Are the reported differences statistically significant? (Significance at the .01 level of confidence, for instance, means that there is only 1 chance in 100 that differences as observed occurred by chance.) Are the results presented in a manner that makes them understandable?

4. *Conclusions*—Are logical inferences drawn from the findings? Are inferences of any use to decision making? Are the limitations of the research identified?

It is useful for those considering research to understand conceptually how it is organized and where the major decision points are in research proceedings. The following diagram by Roberts describes those relationships (Figure 7.13).[4]

In conclusion, then, the role of evaluation is to complete the curriculum development cycle by returning leaders to the analysis stage. If we know what we want from schools, and if we set up and activate a school to accomplish those ends, and if the school is not accomplishing those purposes originally envisioned, then it is time to

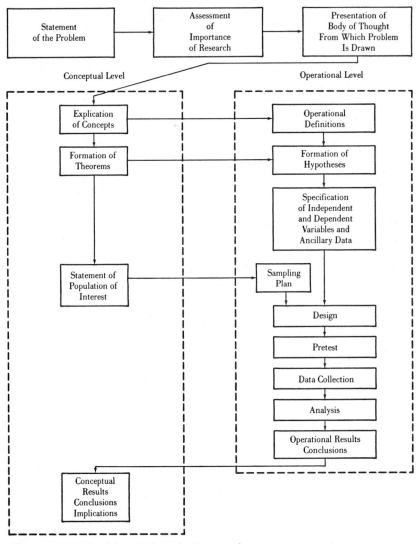

Figure 7.13 Decision Points in Research

reconsider what more the school can do. This never-ending cycle of curriculum development is shown in Figure 7.14.

Finally, there is some nomenclature or terms which will confront any new curriculum leader in the area of evaluation. Some of these important terms are defined below for the reader's review.

Curriculum

Affective: A term that describes behavior or objectives of an attitudinal, emotional, or interest nature; discussed in *The*

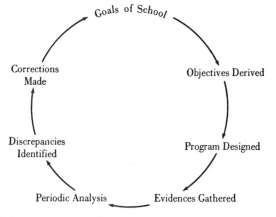

Figure 7.14

Taxonomy of Educational Objectives: Handbook II, The Affective Domain by David Krathwohl and others.

Behavior Objectives: This term describes what the learner should be able to do at the conclusion of an instructional sequence.

Cognitive: An adjective referring to learner activities or instructional objectives concerned with *intellectual* activities; discussed in *The Taxonomy of Educational Objectives: Handbook I, The Cognitive Domain* by Benjamin S. Bloom and others.

Course of Study: A guide prepared by a professional group of a particular school or school system as a prescriptive guide to teaching a subject or area of study for a given grade or other instruction group.

Criterion: The measure used to judge the adequacy of an instructional program. Ordinarily, it would be a test, broadly conceived, of the program's objectives.

Curriculum: A structured series of intended learning outcomes.

Lesson Plan: A teaching outline of the important points of a lesson for a single class period arranged in the order in which they are to be presented. It may include objectives, points to be made, questions to ask, references to materials, and assignments.

Psychomotor: This refers to learner activities or instructional objectives relating to physical skills of the learner, such as typing or swimming.

Resource Unit: A collection of suggested learning and teaching activities, procedures, materials, and references organized around a unifying topic or learner problem; it is designed to be helpful to teachers in developing their own teaching units.

"So much for curriculum development this school year. I hear you asking yourself, 'What about 1982, 1983, 1984, 1985, and 1986?'"

Source: Phi Delta Kappan. September 1981. Used by permission of Ford Button.

Scope: The extent of content or objectives (or both) covered by a course or curriculum.

Sequence: The order in which content or objectives are arranged in the curriculum.

Subject: A division or field of organized knowledge, such as English or mathematics.

Syllabus: A condensed outline or statement of the main points of a course of study.

Teaching Unit: The plan developed with respect to a particular classroom by an individual teacher to guide the instruction of a unit of work to be carried out by a particular class or group of learners for a period longer than a single class session.

Evaluation

Content Validity: The degree to which a measuring device is *judged* to be appropriate for its purpose; for example, the degree to which it is congruent with a set of instructional objectives.

Criterion-Referenced Measurement: A measurement designed to assess an individual's status with respect to a particular standard of performance, irrespective of the relationship of his performance to that of others.

Criterion Validity: Characteristically, the degree to which a particular measure, such as a test of intellectual ability, correlates with an external criterion such as subsequent scholastic performance in college.

Formative Evaluation: The evaluation of an instructional program before it is finally completed—that is, the attempt to evaluate a program in order to improve it.

Item Analysis: Any one of several methods used in revising a test to determine how well a given item discriminates among individuals or different degrees of ability or among individuals differing in some other characteristic.

Item Sampling: The procedure of administering different forms of a test (characteristically, shorter forms), to different individuals, thereby reducing the time required for testing.

Norm-Referenced Measurement: A measurement designed to assess an individual's standing with respect to other individuals on the same measuring device.

Summary

Schools throughout the United States face a challenge in redefining school programs under the pressure of declining enrollments, changing technology, and diminished resources. The management and evaluation of curriculum will become a central function of school leadership for the remainder of this century.

Comprehensive school planning will mean seeing all areas of school operations as a system. All planning, in a system, must begin with a clear conception of purpose. The formalization of that purpose is important for the sake of continuity in program development. Assessing present conditions, usually through a needs assessment, provides planning data to support philosophic goals.

The design phase of curriculum development proceeds deductively from goals previously identified and endorsed. Broad conceptualizations of the programs desired are projected and plans for specific components of the program are developed. Placing these plans into one holistic understanding of the desired change leads to the management or implementation stage of the cycle.

A management system can be used to tie together the many activities needed to accomplish the planned change. Activation of this system is dependent upon the identification of responsible agents to carry out tasks and upon setting a timeframe for the planned change. Various technical aids can assist the curriculum leader in managing the many variables.

Evaluation, a fourth step of the curriculum development cycle is the critical stage for the 1980s and 1990s. School leaders are being held accountable for their performance and must be both effective and efficient in their work to develop quality school programs. Historic criteria for curriculum quality, plus sound educational research, will guide curriculum leaders in their evaluation of school programming.

Notes

1. J. Galen Saylor and William M. Alexander, *Curriculum Planning for Modern Schools* (New York: Holt, Rinehart & Winston, 1966), p. 243.
2. D.L. Stufflebeam, "Toward a Science of Educational Evaluation," *Educational Technology* (July 30, 1968).
3. In *Educational Technology*, July 30, 1968, p. 8.
4. Karlene H. Roberts, "Understanding Research: Some Thoughts on Evaluating Completed Educational Projects." An occasional paper from ERIC at Stanford, 26, ED 032 759.

Suggested Learning Activities

1. Develop a checklist for selecting new instructional programs in your school.
2. What sources of data would you use for a follow-up study of students leaving an elementary school? middle school? high school?
3. You are chairing a committee to suggest an evaluation design for a new science program at your school. What things would you consider in the design?
4. What is the role of an accrediting agency? Which association of colleges and secondary schools represents your area?
5. You have been asked by your PTA to explain the accountability movement. Outline in detail what you would say.
6. Develop a program for the continuing evaluation of your school.
7. Describe the relationship between educational research and educational evaluation. Can you reduce this relationship to a model or outline?

Books to Review

A Programmed Introduction to PERT. Federal Electric Corporation, ITT. London: John Wiley and Sons, 1963.

AASA. *Educational Management: Tools For the Practicing School Administrator.* Arlington, Virginia: American Association of School Administrators, 1979.

Glaser, Barney and Strauss, Anselm. *The Discovery of Grounded Theory: Strategies for Qualitative Research.* Chicago: Aldine-Atherton, 1967.

Lien, Arnold. *Measurement and Evaluation of Learning.* Dubuque, Iowa: W.C. Brown Publishers, 1976.

NSSE. *Educational Evaluation: New Roles, New Means.* Chicago: 68th Yearbook of National Society for the Study of Education, Part I, 1969.

Owen, Robert. *Organizational Behavior in Education.* Englewood Cliffs, New Jersey: Prentice-Hall, 1980.

Payne, David. *Curriculum Evaluation: Commentary on Purpose, Process, Product.* Lexington, Massachusetts: D.C. Heath and Company, 1974.

Reddin, William. *Managerial Effectiveness: Leaders or Managers.* Berkeley, California: University of California Press, 1977.

Selltiz, C. Wrightsman, L. and Cook, S. *Research Methods in Social Relations.* New York: Holt, Rinehart & Winston, 1976.

Storey, Arthur. *The Measurement of Classroom Learning.* Science Research Associates, 1970.

Tanner, Kenneth. *Educational Planning and Decision Making: A View Through the Organizational Process.* Lexington, Massachusetts: Lexington Books, 1981.

Thorndike, R. and Hagen, E. *Measurement and Evaluation in Psychology and Education.* New York: John Wiley & Sons, 1969.

Wiles, David. *Changing Perspectives in Educational Research.* Worthington, Ohio: Charles A. Jones, 1972.

Part Three
Curriculum
Practices

Chapter Eight
Elementary School Programs and Issues

Introduction ────────────────────────────────

During the 1970s, a pervasive mood in American education was expressed by the slogan, "Let's get back to the basics." The elementary school, perhaps more than any other level of schooling, responded to basic education demands. Those demands were usually identified with testing and evaluation and attempts were made to identify minimal competencies to determine whether students at each grade level had attained minimal skills in reading, writing, and computation. Legislators and political groups, rather than professional educators, led the charge in demanding that "basic skills" be taught. Although the attention was focused on exit skills for high school students to make sure they were not deficient in basic literacy and mathematical competency, the major changes in curriculum and instruction occurred at the elementary level. By the mid-1980s, the elementary curriculum was characterized by:

1. A return to single series texts in reading.
2. An emphasis on mastery of skills in reading, grammar, and computation.
3. Established writing programs for all students.
4. Mandated instructional time for reading and mathematics, e.g., one hour daily for reading, 45 minutes for writing, and one hour for mathematics.
5. Pupil progression plans (often dictated by legislation) that required diagnosis, instruction in certain skills, and evaluation of each student before promotion to the next grade level.
6. A reduction in time devoted to science and social studies instruction. In many cases, instructional time in art and music has been reduced.
7. Curriculum management plans that include the use of skill continuums and instructional activities designed to teach identified skills in a systematic and sequential manner.
8. Extensive skill grouping within individual classrooms and across classes within a grade level.
9. Less emphasis on affective activities.
10. A "packed" school day, especially for students requiring remediation. Almost every minute of the day is devoted to direct instruction designed to improve test scores.

The elementary school, which represents the first chance at formal schooling for most children, has thus become a more rigid and standardized school in the 1980s. Gone are the days of experimentation and innovations in program, time schedules, and organizational patterns. As we prepare for a new generation of elementary students (one that will reflect increased enrollment for the first time in a decade), it will be useful for the reader to examine the history and purposes of the elementary school and to study the major components of the elementary curriculum.

Basis of the Elementary School Curriculum _____

The modern elementary curriculum has evolved over the past 200 years from a narrow curriculum devoted to the teaching of reading, writing, and arithmetic to a broad program encompassing not only basic skills, but a variety of learning experiences. Because schools in the United States, as in other countries, are mechanisms for social change, schools often become battlegrounds for diverse groups with conflicting interests. The history of the elementary school during the past quarter century has been one of continuous change. Schools in the United States, like the nation itself, are in transition. Gone, at least for the present, are experimentations such as nongradedness, open classrooms, and a variety of elective activities. By examining the history of the elementary school, one can see that elementary schools have been responsive to the needs of our expanding and diverse society.

History of the Elementary School

The establishment of free elementary schools for all children by state legislation was a grand and unique experiment in this country. Free elementary schools became associated with the highest ideals of our citizens.

Unlike most other countries, the United States has no national system of education. Under our Constitution, control of schools has been delegated to the states. Precedents were established early in the history of our country for the exercise of state legislative authority in educational matters. As early as 1642, the colonies were enacting legislation concerning educational matters. The Colonial Assembly of Massachusetts enacted compulsory education laws in 1642 and 1647. The 1647 legislation compelled communities above a certain size to set up grammar schools. That legislation, known as the "Old Deluder Satan" Act, passed by the General Court of the Massachusetts Bay Colony, required towns to establish common schools and grammar schools so men could read the Scriptures and escape the clutches of Satan. The Act was not only the first law in America requiring that schools be established, but was also the first example in history requiring that children be provided an education at the expense of the community.

By 1693, legislation was passed allowing selectmen authority to levy school taxes with the consent of the majority of the townspeople. Previously, each town could determine how buildings, salaries, and other matters were handled.

Elementary teachers relied heavily on the *New England Primer*, a book used for more than one hundred years. That book utilized Bible verses and books to teach reading and number skills. Disciplinary practices also followed religious lines with floggings and other measures designed to "drive the devil out of children."[1]

In addition to religious purposes, early elementary schools served another purpose—rallying support for the new American political system. James Madison and Thomas Jefferson both spoke out against ignorance and in favor of an educated populace. Elementary schools were established not only for the maintenance of society by inculcating religious doctrine, but also to maintain society by inculcating political doctrines.

As the nation expanded westward with new states admitted to the Union, the elementary school experienced reforms. Many of the reforms were influenced by European examples. Perhaps the person most responsible for building the base for the modern elementary school was the educational reformer, Johann Heinrich Pestalozzi (1746–1827). Pestalozzi viewed child growth and development as organismic rather than mechanistic. He recognized that the narrow curriculum, consisting mainly of mechanical exercises in reading, was inadequate to prepare children for intelligent citizenship. Through teacher training programs he helped prepare elementary teachers to provide a variety of learning experiences for children. His ideas were best expressed in his book, *How Gertrude Teaches Her Children.*

In the early 1800s, Prussian educators borrowed many of Pestalozzi's methods to build a national system of education. Horace Mann and other educators of the day visited Prussia and returned to the United States with glowing reports of the Prussian-Pestalozzian system. That system, imitated in this country, included grading students on the basis of ability, better methods of instruction and discipline, setting up a state agency for education, and developing special teacher training institutions.

Public education became more and more popular in the first half of the 1800s. The first state board of education was established in Massachusetts in 1837 with Horace Mann as its first secretary. By 1876, the principle of public elementary education had been accepted in all states. The period from 1826–1876, known as the public school revival, led to a new American conscience in respect of educating children. Legislators were pressured to provide more money for elementary schools and the curriculum was enriched.

Expansion and Continued Reforms of Elementary Schools

From 1876 to the mid-1930s, the United States became a great industrial nation. As America moved from a simple agricultural society to an industrial power, schools as instruments of society became instruments of change. Elementary enrollments doubled, many new subjects were added to the curricula, and the school day was lengthened. World War I had resulted in demands for new skills on the part of youth, and curriculum change included a "back to the basics movement" in 1918 to make sure all children could read and write. Teacher education is an influence in curriculum change, and because new courses in psychology and methods were introduced in teacher training institutions the elementary curriculum began to change. By the 1930s, standardized tests were used to determine achievement in school subjects and individual and group intelligence tests were administered. Efforts were made to differentiate instruction for slow, average, and above average elementary children.

During the 1920s and 1930s, educational philosophers like John Dewey had a great influence on the elementary curriculum. Dewey and other "progressive" educators saw schools as agencies of society designed to improve our democratic way of life. Dewey believed that schools should be a reflection of community life with students studying about the home, neighborhood, and community. By studying what is familiar to them, students become more curious about the disciplines of science, geography, and mathematics. "Learning by doing" is a principle of learning that was central to Dewey's ideas about schools. Active children will learn more. Thus, learning in the elementary school should not include simply rote, mechanistic learning activities, but a variety of creative activities where students are active participants in the learning process. Dewey maintained the curricula of the elementary school should build on the interest of students and should represent real life by taking up and continuing the activities with which the child is already familiar at home.

The progressive education movement, led by John Dewey, George Counts, Harold Rugg, and others, heavily influenced the elementary curricula until 1957 when Sputnik forced a reexamination of the purpose of the elementary school. Critics like Admiral Rickover and Arthur Bestor censured progressive education as failing to provide students with the necessary skills and knowledge to compete in a scientific world. Congressional acts establishing the National Science Foundation (NSF) and the National Defense Education Act (NDEA) pumped millions of dollars into the development of science and mathematics programs and materials. The elementary curriculum began to reflect a growing emphasis on science and mathematics in student courses such as "Science: A Process Approach" and inservice programs designed to improve teachers' skills in teaching science and mathematics.

The 1960s began an era of innovation in the elementary curriculum. Many of the innovations dealt with organizational changes such as nongradedness, open classrooms, and team teaching. Elementary school buildings were designed to facilitate those organizational changes. As with other innovations involving organizational changes, teachers were often ill-prepared to cope with such new ideas. Lack of inservices and continued turnover of elementary staffs resulted in growing resistance to nongradedness, open space, and teaming. Moreover, elementary leaders who jumped on bandwagons confused organizational *means* with *ends*. Although their schools were advertised as "open and nongraded," little change occurred in teaching methods or in curriculum substance. Process had been confused with product, and results of the innovations were disappointing.

Educators in the 1970s and 1980s, for the first time in the history of American education, saw a decline in elementary enrollment. Retrenchment, funding problems, and dissatisfaction with the experimentation of the 1960s led to legislated accountability measures and increased testing programs in the elementary school. Another "back to basics movement" began, with demands for an elementary curriculum emphasizing reading, writing, and arithmetic. By the mid-1980s, the elementary curriculum had expanded to include a variety of learning experiences, but it had narrowed its focus to the basic skills of written and oral communication and mathematics.

Organizing the Curriculum

The curriculum of the elementary school is organized around the bases of knowledge, the needs of society, and human learning and development. As seen in the previous section, the early elementary school was concerned simply with the transmission of knowledge. Later, schools were seen as an instrument of society to foster religious views and the political doctrine of early America. In the first half of the 1900s the elementary school was seen as serving an emerging industrial society and as an instrument for the improvement of democratic institutions. Human learning and development did not influence the curriculum until the late 1920s and 1930s when psychologists began to introduce educators to research on student learning and child growth and development. Not until the 1960s did major changes in curriculum and training of curriculum leaders result from research studies of learning and development. From 1960 to the 1980s, many new programs were introduced into the elementary program to accommodate young learners and those learners with special needs. Free public kindergarten programs were implemented for five-year-olds in all states along with a variety of other programs such as *Head Start* for disadvantaged young children. Special education programs for physically and mentally handicapped elementary students were greatly expanded and gifted programs were made available to more elementary students.

Individualizing Instruction in the Elementary Grades

A consistent theme of elementary school learning for twenty years has been that of individualizing instruction to accommodate differences among students. Owing to the complexity of the concept, the term individualization is often misunderstood. Individualization has other dimensions than the rate of progress. Among the variables that may be manipulated to individualize instruction are:

1. materials for study—prescribed or individually chosen. Various levels of difficulty and with varying purposes.
2. method of study—prescribed or chosen methods of learning
3. pace of study—timed or untimed, structured or fluid
4. sequence of study—ordered or providing the option for personal coverage of material
5. learning focus—factual, skill-based, process or values
6. place of learning—classroom, school, environment or optional
7. evaluation of learning—exam-based, product-based, open-ended or student-evaluated
8. purpose of learning—mastery, understanding, application or experiential

In most elementary programs students work with similar materials at about the same pace in the same spaces, and they usually have similar if not identical learning criteria for evaluating their progress. Some widespread techniques are used to accommodate differences, however, including grouping, use of materials with differing levels of reading difficulty, and special programs for students at the greatest range from group norms.

Grouping

Flexibility is the key in any grouping arrangement. The major reason for employing grouping as an instructional technique is to provide more effectively for students' individual differences. Some common groups found in the elementary school are:

1. *A class as a whole* can function as a group. Teachers sometimes have guilt feelings about whole class activities, but there are occasions when the teacher can address the whole class as a single group. New topic or unit introductions, unit summaries, and activities such as reports, dramatizations, and choral reading may be effectively conducted with the total class.
2. *Reading level groups* formed according to reading achievement levels are commonly found in classrooms. These groups are not static and must accommodate shifts of pupils from group to group as changes in individual achievement occur.
3. *Reading need groups* are formed to assist students in mastering a particular reading skill such as pronouncing a phonic element or finding the main idea in a paragraph.
4. *Interest groups* help students apply reading skills to other language arts and other content areas. Storytelling, recreational reading, writing stories and poems, and dramatization are activities that can be carried out in interest groupings.

5. *Practice or tutorial groups* are often used to allow students to practice oral reading skills, play skill games, and organize peer teaching situations.
6. *Research groups* allow for committee work, group projects, and other research activities. Learning centers in the classroom and research areas in the media center are often developed for research groups.
7. *Individualization* allows a student to work as an individual in selecting books and references for learning projects. Developmental programs provide for individual progress through a series of lessons.

Two common terms used in grouping in the elementary school are heterogeneous (mixed) and homogeneous (like) groups. Usually, these two types of groups are used interchangeably during a school day. Teachers who organize skill groups in the classroom are using homogeneous grouping. The key is flexibility. Students are moved from group to group as they achieve required skills. Also, the skill groups are organized only for a portion of the school day. The rest of the day, students are organized into heterogeneous groups where they can interact with students of varying abilities.

Reading Levels

Another common means of providing for student differences is in providing books of varying degrees of difficulty. Textbook publishers regularly provide grade specific texts (4th grade math, for example,) with several "leveled" versions. Teachers use the "readability" of the text as a means of tailoring instruction to the student.

Readability is the objective measure of the difficulty of a book or article, and usually involves the use of a specific formula with results reported in terms of grade level. Seven such formulas are listed below.

1. Flesch Reading Ease Score—Grades 5-12. Involves checking word length and sentence length. Source: Flesch, R. F. *How to Test Readability*. New York: Harper & Brothers, 1959.
2. Wheeler and Smith—Index Number. Involves determining sentence length and number of polysyllabic words. Grades: Primary-4. Source: Wheeler, L. R., and Smith, E. H. "A Practical Readability Formula for the Classroom Teacher in the Primary Grades." *Elementary English* 31 (November 1954): 397-399.
3. The Cloze Technique. The readability of two pieces of material can be compared by the Cloze technique. Measures redundancy (the extent to which words are predictable) while standard readability formulas measure the factors of vocabulary and sentence structure. It can be used to determine relative readability of material, but cannot predict readability of a new

sample. It does not give grade level designations. Source: Taylor, W. C. "Cloze Procedure: A New Tool for Measuring Readability." *Journalism Quarterly* 30 (Fall 1953): 415–433.

4. Lorge Grade Placement Score—Grades 3–12. Uses average sentence length in words, number of difficult words per 100 words not on the Dale 769-word list, and number of prepositional phrases per 100 words. Source: Lorge, l. *The Lorge Formula for Estimating Difficulty of Reading Materials*. New York: Teachers' College Press, 1959.

5. The Fry Graph. Method is based on two factors: average number of syllables per 100 words, and average number of sentences per 100 words. Three randomly selected 100 words samples are used. Source: Fry, Edward. "Graph for Estimating Readability."*Journal of Reading* (April 1968): 513–16, and *Reading Teacher* (March 1969): 22–27.

6. SMOG Grading Plan—Grades 4–12. Involves counting repetition of polysyllabic words. Source: McLaughlin, Harry G. "SMOG Grading—A New Readability Formula." *Journal of Reading* 12 (1969): 639–646.

7. Spache Grade Level Score—Grades 1–3. Looks at average sentence length and number of words outside Dale list of 769 words to give readability level. Source: Spache, G. "A New Readability Formula for Primary Grade Reading Materials." *Elementary School Journal* 53 (March 1953): 410–413.

Armed with such assessments, the teacher can provide students with reading materials tailored to their needs and abilities.

Special Programs for Handicapped Students

The 1970s represented an era of significant progress for special and handicapped students. Public concern resulted in laws guaranteeing their access to the curriculum and public dollars to insure implementation of special programs.

Although some 195 federal laws specific to the handicapped were enacted between 1927 and 1975, the National Advisory Committee on the Handicapped reported in 1975 that only 55 percent of handicapped children and youth were being served appropriately. Of the 195 acts passed, 61 were passed between March 1970 and November 1975. Public Law 93–380, passed in 1974, was the most important of the laws passed; it extended and amended the Elementary and Secondary Education Act of 1965 and established a national policy on equal educational opportunity.

The most far-reaching and significant federal act passed affecting the handicapped was Public Law 94–142, the Education for All Handicapped Children Act of 1975, which was an amendment to Public Law 93–380. PL 94–142 has been described by many educators as a "Bill of

Rights for the Handicapped." This law sets forth specific procedures that school districts must carry out to establish due process for handicapped students. The most important feature of the law is that all handicapped students between ages three and twenty-one must have available to them a free and appropriate public education. That includes an emphasis on the regular class as the preferred instructional base for all children.

It is the feature of reversing the historical method of referring handicapped *out* of regular classes that makes PL 94–142 unique. It also has major implications for classroom teachers and supervisory personnel who implement the act.

The right to education means that children with handicaps are eligible for all programs and activities sponsored by the school. This includes cheerleading, athletics, and other extracurricular activities. Children with handicaps can no longer be excluded from course offerings, most notably vocational courses.

PL 94-142 also prohibits discriminatory evaluation. Testing and evaluation materials must be selected and administered so as to not be culturally discriminatory. No single test or procedure can be used as the sole criterion for determining educational placement in a program.

Working with children with handicaps requires an individualized instructional plan much like a plan used for all children in a regular classroom. It requires a substantial amount of diagnostic information about present and past academic and social performance. Finally, it requires teachers and supervisory personnel to project what specific needs each handicapped child may have and prescribes special programs to meet those needs.

The Individual Education Plan (IEP) provision of PL 94–142 that became practice on October 1, 1977 was really a model for instruction that all good teachers should follow. Collecting diagnostic data, setting goals and objectives, selecting instructional materials, and evaluating student performance are all steps in the instructional process. There are in the instructional process important activities that teachers must consider for handicapped students. Table 8.1 outlines these major steps for the reader's study. Table 8.2 indicates some of the groups who serve as advocates for the handicapped student in school.

Mainstreaming has been defined in many ways, most of which center on moving handicapped children from segregated special education classes into "normal" classrooms. Since the implementation of special education classes in the United States, segregated classroom environments have been the most popular method of educating handicapped children. Because children were labeled according to the severity of their handicaps and grouped into uniform categories in special classes, they were removed from what educators titled the "mainstream."

PL 94–142 mandates that the most appropriate education for handicapped children should be the least restrictive setting. This means

Table 8.1
Developing IEP for Handicapped Students

SETTING GOALS
Basic, life-oriented, attainable goals are more important than global, unrealistic goals.

SELECTING SPECIFIC OBJECTIVES
Teachers should take into consideration such factors as the child's attention span, level of cognitive functioning, level of written and verbal communication, and ability to participate in various academic and nonacademic activities of the school.

SELECTING INSTRUCTIONAL MATERIALS
A variety of curriculum materials are needed for handicapped children—both teacher-made and commercial. Those materials must be appropriate if they are to help implement the objectives set for each child. Materials should be selected or constructed to fit the child's level of proficiency.

EVALUATING STUDENT PERFORMANCE
Models of norm-referenced tests rarely apply to handicapped students. Evaluation should be skill-based and continuous. A diagnostic profile of skills should be used to determine whether or not a student should move on to the next objective or receive further instruction on the same objective.

Source: Jon Wiles and Joseph Bondi, *Supervision: A Guide to Practice* (Columbus, Ohio: Charles E. Merrill Publishing Company, 1980), p. 97. Reprinted by permission.

that handicapped students should be integrated into, not segregated from, the normal program of the school. It does *not* mean the wholesale return of all exceptional children in special classes to regular classes.

Mainstreaming means looking at educational needs and creative programs that will help general educators serve handicapped children in a regular setting. It does not imply that specialists will no longer be needed, but that they and other classroom teachers must be willing to combine efforts and work cooperatively to provide the most appropriate program for all children.

Legal decisions and legislation have made it clear that the rights of all children must be respected in our schools. Unfortunately, legal decisions and legislation won't insure the development of adequate or appropriate programs. Inservice education will be necessary to provide teachers with more specialized skills to deal with specific behavioral and academic problems. Mainstreaming can succeed only with a strong partnership of curriculum specialists, teachers, and supervisory persons working cooperatively to provide the most appropriate education for all children.

Table 8.2
National Organizations and Agencies
Concerned with Special Needs Children

ACLU Juvenile Rights Project
22 East 40th Street
New York, NY 10016

**American Academy for Cerebral
  Palsy**
University Hospital School
Iowa City, IA 52240

**American Association for the
  Education of Severely and
  Profoundly Handicapped**
1600 West Armory Way
Garden View Suite
Seattle, WA 98119

**American Association
  for Gifted Children**
15 Gramercy Park
New York, NY 10003

American Epilepsy Society
Department of Neurology
University of Minnesota
Box 341, Mayo Building
Minneapolis, MN 55455

**American Foundation
  for the Blind**
15 West 16th Street
New York, NY 10011

American Medical Association
535 North Dearborn Street
Chicago, IL 60610

**American Psychological
  Association**
1200 17th Street, NW
Washington, DC 20036

**Association for Children with
  Learning Disabilities**
2200 Brownsville Road
Pittsburgh, PA 16210

**National Committee for Multi-
  Handicapped Children**
239 14th Street
Niagara Falls, NY 14303

**Association for the Aid of
  Crippled Children**
345 East 46th Street
New York, NY 10017

**Association for Education of the
  Visually Handicapped**
919 Walnut
Philadelphia, PA 19107

**Bureau for Education of the
  Handicapped**
400 6th Street
Donohoe Building
Washington, DC 20202

Council for Exceptional Children
1920 Association Drive
Reston, VA 22091

**Institute for the Study of Mental
  Retardation and Related
  Disabilities**
130 South First
University of Michigan
Ann Arbor, MI 48108

**Muscular Dystrophy Association
  of America**
810 7th Avenue
New York, NY 10019

**National Association for
  Retarded Citizens**
2709 Avenue E, East
P.O. Box 6109
Arlington, TX 76011

**National Association of
  Social Workers**
2 Park Avenue
New York, NY 10016

**President's Committee
  on Employment
  of the Handicapped**
U.S. Department of Labor
Washington, DC 20210

Table 8.2
(continued)

National Institutes of Health	**President's Committee on**
United States Department of Health	**Mental Retardation**
and Human Services	Regional Office Building #3
Washington, DC 20014	Room 2614
National Rehabilitation	7th and D Streets, SW
Association	Washington, DC 20201
1522 "K" Street, NW	
Washington, DC 20005	

Special Programs for the Gifted Student

It has been estimated that over 2.5 million young Americans are endowed with academic, artistic, or social talents far beyond the talents of their peers. These "gifted" children come from all levels of society, all races, and both sexes.[2]

Until recently, gifted children received little attention in public schools. Parents had to seek out costly private schools, which many parents could not afford. Most American educators and the supporting public felt the poor and handicapped desperately needed extra attention and balked at singling out an "elitist" group of bright children in public schools.

In 1972, Congress established the Federal Office for the Gifted and Talented. That office was charged with helping identify and develop talented youngsters. With funding increased in 1978, the Office for the Gifted and Talented has fostered a resurgence of interest in gifted children.

All fifty states have programs for the gifted, but there are still problems of identifying and providing for talented youngsters. For instance, many gifted children cannot be identified by IQ tests alone. New yardsticks for identifying the gifted have to be used including creativity, advanced social skills, and even exceptional physical aptitude such as the kind that marks fine surgeons, watch repairers, or engineers.

As a group, talented and gifted children tend to learn faster and retain more than their peers. A gifted child is also a divergent thinker. All of these characteristics can be unsettling in a class, and sometimes gifted and talented children have been seen as "troublemakers." Other gifted children are turned off by boring classes and become alienated from school.

Teachers, faced with increased demands to improve low achievers' basic skills and to also provide for handicapped and special education students, often find little time to work with the gifted and talented.

A number of instructional models have been proposed for helping classroom teachers develop curricular plans for gifted students in regular classrooms. Two of these are the Enrichment Triad Model[3] and the Self-Directed Learning Program.[4]

In addition, an exemplary longitudinal research study has been conducted at Johns Hopkins University dealing with mathematically gifted junior high school students. The results of this study have provided information on facilitating the learning of gifted students in the areas of creativity, achievement, productivity, and motivation.[5]

The models and research on the gifted and talented have helped provide a sound basis for differentiating instruction and evaluating programs for the gifted.

Differentiating instruction, fostering creativity, allowing for independent study, and encouraging peer learning are all important tasks of teaching. They are expecially important for nurturing the diverse aptitudes and abilities of gifted and talented children. Organizational procedures such as cluster grouping, mainstreaming, and part-day grouping have all been used with the gifted and talented.

Other Students with Needs

Between the special education student, who is categorically identified, and the gifted student who is provided for by a special program, are all other students. Most of these "normal" students have needs too, particularly during the elementary years. Figure 8.1 provides the reader with a checklist of needs for students who are not served by special programs but who may need assistance.

The Influence of the Middle School On the Elementary Curriculum

The growing middle school movement in the 1960s and 70s resulted in curricular and organizational changes in the elementary school. Early in the middle school movement, grades 5 and 6 were taken from the elementary curriculum and combined with grades 7 and 8 of the junior high school or high school. The ninth grade went to the high school. Later, fifth grades were returned to the elementary school in most districts resulting in a grades K–5, 6–8, 9–12 structure in many districts. By losing the sixth grade, the elementary school was left with two developmental groups, early childhood youth in grades K–3, and late childhood youth in grades 4 and 5. Not having to cope with emerging adolescents in grade six allowed elementary schools to better match their curriculum with the developmental levels of the youth served by the elementary school. Table 8.3 illustrates the developmental levels and curricular implications for students in elementary, middle, and high schools.

Figure 8.1 Checklist for Identifying Students
Who May Need Educational Therapy

1. Gross motor and motor flexibility
   _____ incoordination and poor balance
   _____ difficulty with jumping—skipping—hopping (below age 9)
   _____ confusion in games requiring imitation of movements
   _____ poor sense of directionality
   _____ inept in drawing and writing at chalkboard
   _____ inaccuracies in copying at chalkboard
   _____ eyes do not work together
   _____ eyes lose or overshoot target

2. Physical fitness
   _____ tires easily
   _____ lacks strength

3. Auditory acuity, perception, memory—speech
   _____ confuses similar phonetic and phonic elements
   _____ inconsistent pronunciation of words usually pronounced correctly
   by peers
   _____ repeats, but does not comprehend
   _____ forgets oral directions, if more than one or two

4. Visual acuity, perception, memory
   _____ complains that he cannot see blackboard
   _____ says that words move or jump
   _____ facial expression strained
   _____ holds head to one side while reading

5. Hand-eye coordination
   _____ difficulty in tracing—copying—cutting—folding—pasting—
   coloring at desk
   _____ lack of success with puzzles—yo-yos—toys involving targets, etc.

6. Language
   _____ has difficulty understanding others
   _____ has difficulty associating and remembering
   _____ has difficulty expressing himself

7. Intellectual functioning
   _____ unevenness of intellectual development
   _____ learns markedly better through one combination of sensory
   avenues than another

8. Personality
   _____ overreacts to school failures
   _____ does not seem to know he has a problem
   _____ will not admit he has a problem

9. Academic problems
   _____ can't tolerate having his routine disturbed
   _____ knows it one time and doesn't the next
   _____ writing neat, but slow
   _____ writing fast, but sloppy

Figure 8.1 (continued)

_____ passes the spelling test, but can't spell functionally
_____ math accurate, but slow
_____ math fast, but inaccurate
_____ reads well orally, but has poor comprehension
_____ does poor oral reading, but comprehends better than would
be expected
_____ lacks word attack skills
_____ has conceptual—study skill—organizational problems in content
areas

10. Parents
_____ seemingly uninformed about nature of learning problem
_____ seemingly unrealistic toward student's problems

Table 8.3
Developmental Levels of Students in the Elementary,
Middle, and High School

Program

Elementary School	_Middle School_	_High School_
Introduction to School	Personal Development	Comprehensive
Socialization	Refinement of Skills	Vocational Training
Beginning Skills		College Preparatory
Beginning Learnings	Continued Learnings	In-Depth Learnings
Introduction to Disciplines	Education for Social Competence	Chemistry
Social Studies		Algebra
Science		World History
_____		American Literature
_____		
	Interdisciplinary Learnings	Career Planning

Organization
Developmental Skills

Elementary School		_Middle School_	_High School_
K–5		6, 7–8	9–12
K–3	4–5	6–8	
Early Childhood	Late Childhood	Transescence	Adolescence

Selection of Content ———————————————————————

Content in the elementary school is selected from the basic disciplines of language arts, mathematics, social studies, science, the arts, and health.

Curriculum developers at the national, state, and local levels help select content. Since we do not have a national system of education, the work of curriculum developers and researchers must fit a variety of learning needs and expectations of students in the 14,500 school districts of this country. Although textbook series and curriculum projects may be designed to accomplish that task, ultimately the classroom teacher has the final choice on selection of content. So, although geography may be taught in grade seven and American history in grade eight in most school districts, how those courses are taught, and what materials and texts are used are left up to the teachers in local school districts. Indeed, the sequence of courses may be altered in some districts to allow the teaching of American history before geography.

Determining What Content is Appropriate for Elementary Students

Determining what content is appropriate for elementary school children is not always easy. Testing programs today often dictate the selection of content. "Teaching for the test" has become a common practice in many classrooms.

Another problem facing elementary educators is the changing nature of our society. Divorce, mobility of families, and pressures brought on by the economy have influenced the achievement of elementary students. Testing programs and accountability legislation in many states have resulted in demands to teach more reading, writing, and mathematics.

The first "R," reading, is perhaps the most controversial area of the elementary program. Reading is not only an emotional issue, but a political one in many districts. Reading becomes the concern of parents long before their children enter school. Reading has also become the center of national rage, the focus of numerous research studies, and a federal crusade in the past quarter-century. In recent decades, millions of dollars have been poured into the development of reading programs. There are scores of reading programs that all work, yet we still have millions of nonreaders in our schools. It is debatable whether we are any closer to solving the mysteries of reading. We do know that reading has engaged the time of more teachers and received a larger share of the school dollar than any other subject in the curriulum.[6]

The second "R," writing, has again become a center of focus in today's elementary schools. Responding to demands of colleges that students know how to write better, elementary and secondary schools have devoted more time in the day to the teaching of writing skills. It is ironic that after a decade of the back-to-the-basics movement in the 1970s, the National Assessment of Educational Progress reported that there was no major change in the writing abilities of most American students in the decade between 1970 and 1980.[7]

Curricular Areas in the Elementary School

As with other areas of schooling, the curriculum of the elementary school must be designed for a variety of learner needs. Major areas include language arts, mathematics, science, social studies, health and physical education, and the arts.

Language Arts includes all the communication skills of reading, writing, listening, and speaking. These four modes of learning are interrelated in a developmental sequence. From listening to speaking to reading to writing, children begin to comprehend and use language skills. The reciprocal relationship between all four of the communication areas implies a need for those areas to be taught in a holistic approach.

The reading component of a total language arts program must include development of skills in decoding and comprehension in order to utilize functional and literary written material. Although reading educators differ on approaches to learning reading, students who fail to master these skills will likely face a lifetime of underachievement. Table 8.4 compares and contrasts seven common approaches to reading found in American elementary schools.

Mathematics instruction in the elementary school, as with language arts, is more effective if it is carefully adapted to the developmental characteristics of children. Early in the history of our schools, objectives of mathematics instruction centered on the development of computational skills. By the 1920s and 1930s, objectives shifted to a more practical application of mathematics. Today, mathematics educators are concerned with providing a balanced program in mathematics where students not only attain computational skills but have an understanding of mathematics concepts and reasoning. The rapid increase in the number of microcomputers in the elementary school has resulted in the need for elementary students to perceive and understand structure in mathematics including concepts, relationships, principles, and modes of mathematical reasoning.

Science in the elementary school has also been influenced by the rapid advancements in technology in this country. During the 1960s, there was a reform movement in science to shift the emphasis from the learning of "facts" in science to an understanding of the processes of science. More recently, there has been an emphasis on the technological applications of science.

Learning scientific concepts, principles, and generalizations allows an elementary child to better understand the universe in which he lives

Table 8.4
Seven Basic Approaches to Teaching Reading

Basals

Advantages	Disadvantages
1. Comprehensive and systematic	1. Stereotyped: uncreative
2. Reading skills presented in order	2. Limit one reading book
3. Flexible	3. Overabundance of material
4. Well-established basic vocabulary	4. Geared to middle class whites
5. Equipped with diagnostic tools	5. Very expensive
6. Themes built around familiar situations	6. Overdependent on visual or sight word methods
7. Well-rounded reading choice	7. Leaves little time for creativity
	8. Little transfer from skill to functional reading.

Language Experience

Advantages	Disadvantages
1. Integrates all listening and speaking skills	1. Materials limited
2. Student's own language utilized	2. No sequencing of skills
3. Develops sensitivity to child's environment	3. No concrete evaluative process
4. Useful with the culturally different	4. Limits word attack skills
5. Encourages sharing of ideas	
6. Develops confidence in language usage	
7. Develops self-expression	

Individualized Approach

Advantages	Disadvantages
1. child has the ability to select appropriate books	1. insuffucient skill development
2. greater opportunity to interact with other children	2. large amount of recordkeeping required
3. child progresses at his own rate—self-confidence	3. a vast amount of books and supplementary materials required
4. one-to-one relationship established through conferences with the teacher	4. children tend to limit their own selection
5. Diminishes competition and comparison	5. little provision for readiness
6. Flexible	6. no advance preparation for words or concepts
	7. teacher must have a wide knowledge of books

Table 8.4
(continued)

Linguistic Approach

1. begins with familiar words that are phonetically regular
2. words are presented as wholes
3. letters become a function by arrangement in the words
4. develop sentence order early

1. there are many different linguistic approaches
2. not greatly field-tested
3. vocabulary too controlled
4. word-by-word reading is encouraged
5. little emphasis on reading for meaning

Phonics

1. develops efficiency in word recognition
2. helps the child become independent in word recognition
3. creates interest because of immediate success of child
4. child can see association between print and sounds

1. tends to isolate speech sounds in an unnatural manner
2. too much repetition—boring
3. sounding out of word is slow process
4. too many exceptions to the rules

Alphabetic Approach

1. simpler
2. child can express himself more freely
3. more enthusiasm to read because success comes quickly
4. learns words more rapidly

1. the techniques and materials need better clarification
2. transition from ITA is difficult
3. very expensive
4. confusing because children would see ITA only at school
5. has not been around long enough to know its validity

Programmed Instruction

1. child proceeds at his own pace
2. reinforcement after each step
3. complete program with records to show progression
4. self-instructional
5. helps teacher to understand sequencing

1. research is limited
2. attention span of student limited
3. becomes repetitious
4. bypasses comprehension because it is difficult to program
5. little room for child to develop his own interests or tastes in reading
6. expensive

by enabling him to see orderly arrangement in the natural world and to explain the continual change in the world. A functional competency with the tools of science must also be developed to help students live in a highly technological society.

Social Studies instruction in the elementary school focuses on the interaction of people with each other and with their natural and human environments. Although there has been less reform in the social studies area than in the other major areas of the elementary curriculum, there have been a number of recent efforts on the part of educators to develop a more relevant program for elementary school students.

Of prime importance today is utilizing social studies in the elementary school to teach critical thinking, develop civic responsibility, build self-concept, and improve human relationships.[8]

Health and Physical Education are core components of a complete elementary school curriculum. Health education includes learning all aspects of healthful and safe living. Physical education includes adaptive and developmental activities that lead to better coordination and psychomotor skills.

Since one cannot separate the physical from the mental or social being, health and physical education programs must include activities designed to interrelate all three areas of physical, mental, and social.

The *Arts* in the elementary school include visual and performing arts. Aesthetic education brings together cognitive, affective, and psychomotor areas of learning and includes experiences in music, art, dance, literature, and other artistic modes of expression.

Until recently, mathematics and language were assumed to be cognitive in nature; the arts, on the other hand, dealt with feelings and emotions and were in the affective domain. Reading, writing, and arithmetic, moreover, were assumed to be essential skills that made information processing possible; the ability to "read" or to produce in the arts was an end in itself, leading to nothing more than inner satisfaction. Recent research indicates that the basic distinction between intellect and emotion can no longer be rationalized. It is now more clearly understood that the mind's activities always involve both intellect and feelings, that we communicate in a rich variety of modes of symbolization, and that each art medium contributes a "language" and experience which adds cognitive data to our functioning brain.[9]

In the push for basic skills in the elementary school, the arts must not be left out of the curriculum. The arts are a necessary part of human experience. Nothing could be more basic.

Balance in the Elementary Curriculum

The elementary school is designed to serve all children. Many elementary children come to school with physical, mental, or social handicaps. Others will come to school at a low readiness level for learning and will immediately fall behind in skill development. A curriculum that is narrowly defined will eliminate many youngsters from the services they need.

The scope and uniqueness of each student in the elementary school should cause us to realize that we must have a balanced curriculum—balanced in the sense that all relevant areas of education are represented and all types of learning are included.

Organization and Grouping in the Elementary School

Vertical and Horizontal Organizational Patterns

Organizational patterns in elementary school may include self-contained classrooms, grade level teams, cross-grade teams, or a total ungraded structure. In some schools there may be a combination of the above patterns. For instance, the primary grades may be nongraded while the upper elementary grades are graded. Also, teams may operate at certain grade levels while other grade levels are self-contained. Classes may also be self-contained or departmentalized.

There are two basic types of organization groups for instruction, *vertical* and *horizontal* organization. Vertical organization refers to the movement of students from grade to grade or level to level. Horizontal organization refers to the grouping of students within a grade or level and the assignment of teachers to a grade or level. Self-contained classes and departmentalized classes, with a separate teacher for each discipline, fall within a horizontal organization. Vertical organization may include both graded and nongraded plans.

Team teaching allows for teachers' special competencies though the cooperation of two or more teachers is the joint responsibility for providing instruction for a group of students. Members of a team may teach all of the disciplines, or they may have lead teachers in each discipline who take the major responsibility for the teaching of a subject area. Teams may be organized within a grade level or across grade levels. Teams may employ self-contained departmentalized and inter-disciplinary instruction during a school year.

Organization and grouping, however, should be flexible. A single pattern of organization or grouping arrangement should not be used in a school. A sound approach is to organize and group according to the needs of students, abilities of teachers, and availability of facilities and resources. No single pattern fits all situations.

Figure 8.2 illustrates an elementary scheduling pattern that includes both a graded and nongraded grouping arrangement. The school is organized into two schools within a school. School A includes grades K–3 and School B, grades 4–6. A block of time is allowed for both

Figure 8.2

SCHOOL A (K-3)	SCHOOL B (4-6)	
Homeroom (Non-Graded/Reading Level)	Homeroom (Non-Graded/Reading Level)	
		9:15–9:30
		9:30–9:45
Language Arts	Language Arts	9:45–10:00
(Nongraded)	(Nongraded)	10:00–10:15
		10:15–10:30
Mathematics		10:30–10:45
(Nongraded)	Mathematics	10:45–11:00
	(Nongraded)	11:00–11:15
Lunch		11:15–11:30
(Nongraded)	Physical Ed.	11:30–11:45
	(Nongraded)	11:45–12:00
		12:00–12:15
	Social Studies	12:15–12:30
	(Graded)	12:30–12:45
		12:45–1:00
Social Studies	Lunch	1:00–1:15
(Graded)	(Graded)	1:15–1:30
Science		1:30–1:45
(Graded)	Science	1:45–2:00
Physical Ed.	(Graded)	2:00–2:15
(Graded)		2:15–2:30
Enrichment	Enrichment	2:30–2:45
Program	Program	2:45–3:00
		3:00–3:15

graded and nongraded courses, thus allowing for time-frames for instruction in the discipline to be used. Enrichment classes are taught by all faculty members and are nongraded within School A and School B.

The governance of the school illustrated in Figure 8.2 includes the principal, curriculum assistant who also chairs the curriculum committee, and chairman of the steering committee. The steering committee consists of the chairman of School A, chairman of School B, a representative from the specialists group (P.E., art, EMR, media, music), and one other teacher from School A and from School B (total of five members). The chairman of each school is selected yearly by staff members of that school. The chairman of the steering committee is also selected by that group on a yearly basis. This governance structure is shown in Figure 8.3.

In concluding this chapter on elementary education, the authors present the reader with some curriculum problems that are common and recurrent:

Figure 8.3 Governing Structure of Oakleaf Elementary School

	Principal	
	Curriculum Assistant	
	Steering Committee	
	2 members of School A	
	2 members of School B	
	1 Specialist	
	Curriculum Committee	
	Language Arts Chairman	
	Math Chairman	
	Science Chairman	
	Social Studies Chairman	
School A	Specs. Chairman	School B
13 Teachers	Specialists	11 Teachers
1 Chairman	Special Education	1 Chairman
	Physical Education	
	Etc.	

1. With 20 percent of all American families moving each year, how can elementary programs deal with in-migration and out-migration?
2. Elementary children watch up to six hours of television each day. How can teachers compete with the influence of this medium?
3. School consolidations and bussing have ended the century-old pattern of the neighborhood school in many communities. How can school identity and school spirit be maintained?
4. With only one family in six having a two-parent family where the mother is home during the day, how can the school gain family support for achievement at school?
5. With fewer new teachers being hired and many staffs "aging in place," how can the school maintain a spirit of growth and an openness to new ideas?
6. With so many special learning programs in the elementary school, how can a regular program be maintained in the face of students being "pulled-out"?
7. How can curriculum leaders promote a balanced school experience for learners in the face of accountability laws and policies that focus solely on student achievement of basic skills?

Summary

The elementary curriculum in the 1980s has been impacted dramatically by demands brought on by testing and evaluation. Legislators and political groups have led the change in insighting that "basic skills" of reading, writing, and arithmetic be the focus of teaching in the elementary school. Single series texts in reading, mandated instructional time for reading and mathematics, and minimum competency testing at various grade levels have resulted.

In looking at the history of the elementary school, we can see how various reform movements have affected the elementary curriculum. Examining lessons from the past, we can see that the elementary curriculum must include a variety of learning experiences for a variety of learners. A balanced program must be available for all elementary children if the elementary school is to meet the needs of students in the 1980s and beyond.

Although most elementary programs in the 1980s are not fully individualized to meet the diverse needs of learners, many programs do accommodate differences through grouping, use of varied reading materials, and providing for extreme ranges with special programs.

Notes

1. William Ragan and Gene Shepherd, *Modern Elementary Curriculum* (New York: Holt, Rinehart & Winston, 1977).
2. Merrill Sheils et al., "The Gifted Child," *Time Magazine* 92 (October 23, 1978): 108.
3. Joseph Renzulli, *The Enrichment Triad Model: A Guide for Developing Defensible Programs for the Gifted and Talented* (Wetherfield, Conn.: Creative Learning Press, 1977).
4. Donald Treffinger and J. F. Feldhusen, *Teaching Creative Thinking and Problem Solving* (Dubuque, Iowa: Kendall/Hunt, 1977).
5. J. C. Stanley, D. P. Keating, and Lynn Fox, *Mathematical Talent: Discovery, Description, and Development* (Baltimore, Maryland: Johns Hopkins University Press, 1974).
6. Ben Brodinsky, *Defining the Basics of American Education,* Phi Delta Kappa Fastback #95 (Bloomington, Indiana), 1977, pp. 21–22.
7. *National Assessment of Educational Progress Newsletter,* XIII, 4 (Winter, 1980–81).
8. See *Social Studies in the 1980s,* Irving Morrissett, editor (Alexandria, Virginia: Association for Supervision and Curriculum Development, 1982).
9. Elliot E. Eisner, "The Arts As a Way of Knowing," *Principal,* 60, 1 (September, 1980): 12.

Suggested Learning Activities

1. Identify the major events in the evolvement of the elementary school in the United States.

2. Analyze the curriculum of your elementary school to determine if there is a "balanced curriculum" available.

3. A group in your community has called for the abolishment of all art and music programs in the elementary school. Prepare a paper defending the inclusion of art and music in the elementary curriculum.

4. Develop a schedule for an elementary school that will include provisions for both graded and nongraded classes.

5. Prepare evaluative criteria for a committee charged with developing guidelines for the selection of content in the major areas of language arts, mathematics, science, and social studies.

Books to Review

Association for Supervision and Curriculum Development. *Fundamental Curriculum Decisions,* 1983 Yearbook. Alexandria, Virginia: Author, 1983.

Bloom, Benjamin. *All Our Children Learning: A Primer for Parents, Teachers, and Other Educators.* New York: McGraw-Hill, 1981.

Eisner, Elliot W. *The Educational Imagination—On Design and Evaluation of School Programs.* New York: Macmillan, 1979.

Goldstein, Herbert. *Mainstreaming.* Guilford, Connecticut: Special Learning Corporation, 1978.

Lautelli, Celia; Moore, Walter; and Kaltsounis, Theodore. *Elementary School Curriculum.* New York: Holt, Rinehart & Winston, 1972.

Michaelis, John; Grossman, Ruth; and Scott, Lloyd. *New Designs for Elementary Curriculum and Instruction.* New York: McGraw-Hill, 1975.

Ragan, William, and Shepherd, Gene. *Modern Elementary Curriculum,* 6th ed. New York: Holt, Rinehart & Winston, 1982.

Weham, Paul. *Program Development in Special Education: Designing Individualized Education Programs.* New York: McGraw-Hill, 1981.

Chapter Nine
Middle School
Programs and Issues

Introduction ——————————————————————————

The middle school and its predecessor the junior high school were
developed to provide a transitional school between the elementary school
and the high school.

The junior high school, originated in 1910, was intended to move
the secondary program into the elementary grades. The familiar bulletin,
Cardinal Principles of Secondary Education, recommended that a school
system be organized into a six-year elementary school and a six-year
high school designed to serve pupils twelve to eighteen years of age.[1]
The *Bulletin* also suggested that secondary education be divided into two
periods designated the junior and senior periods. Thus, junior high
schools were thought to be a part of the high school and for fifty
years the curriculum of the junior high tended to parallel that of the
high school. Activities such as varsity athletics, marching bands, and
even cap-and-gown graduation exercises tended to exert considerable
pressures on junior high students. Teacher training institutions also
prepared "secondary" teachers for positions in the junior high schools.
Most junior high schools were organized with grades 7–9.

By 1960, a number of factors led to the emergence of a new
school known as the middle school. Critics of the junior high school
were beginning to try to reform the junior high school in the 1940s and
1950s but could not break the junior high from the high school mold.

Four factors led to the emergence of the middle school. First, the
late 1950s and early 1960s were filled with criticisms of American
schools, classroom and teacher shortages, double and triple sessions,
soaring tax rates, and books such as *Why Johnny Can't Read* triggered
new concerns about the quality of schooling in the United States. The
successful launching of Sputnik in 1957 led to a new wave of criticism
about the curriculum of elementary and secondary schools. Sputnik
created an obsession with academic achievement especially in the areas
of science, foreign languages, and mathematics. A renewed interest in
college preparation led to a call for a four-year high school where
specialized courses could remain under the direction of the college
preparatory school—the high school. Likewise, the inclusion of grades
five and six in an intermediate school could strengthen instruction by
allowing subject area specialists to work with younger students. Many of
the first middle schools were organized with grades five through eight.

A second factor leading to the emergence of the middle school
was the elimination of racial segregation. *The Schoolhouse in the City*
stated that the real force behind the middle school movement in the
larger cities (New York City, for example) was to eliminate de facto
segregation.[2]

A third factor leading to the emergence of the middle school was
the increased enrollments of school age children in the 1950s and
1960s. The shortage of buildings resulted in double and even triple

school sessions in school districts. Because older students in high schools were able to cope with overcrowding better than younger students, the ninth grade was moved to the high school to relieve the overcrowded junior high school. The same rationale was used to relieve the elementary school by moving the fifth or sixth grade to the junior high school.

A fourth factor resulting in middle schools was the "bandwagon effect." Because one middle school received favorable exposure in books and periodicals, some administrators determined that the middle school was "the thing to do."

All of these factors may not have been the most valid reasons why middle schools should be organized, but regardless of the "wrong reasons," educators seized the right opportunities to develop programs designed for the pre- and early adolescent learner.

It is ironic that in the late 1970s and early 1980s the same four factors influencing middle school development exist except for two changes. The criticism of schools is not directed toward language, science, and mathematics excellence, but toward basic skill in reading and mathematics. Also, the increased enrollment of the 1950s and 1960s has become declining enrollment in the 1970s and 1980s.

Today, junior high schools are being reorganized into middle schools to eliminate segregation, to alleviate population and building problems brought on by declining enrollment, to improve basic skills programs in the middle grades, and because "other districts have middle schools and we should too."

The authors believe the following reasons related to providing a more relevant and appropriate program and learning environment for "transescent" learners are easier to justify:

1. To provide a program especially designed for the ten to fourteen-year-old child going through the unique "transescent" period of growth and development. There is recognition that students ten to fourteen constitute a distinct grouping—physically, socially, and intellectually.
2. To build upon the changed elementary school. Historically, the postSputnik clamor to upgrade schools prepared the way for elementary school personnel to accept the middle school concept. The introduction of the "new" science, the "new" social studies, the "new" mathematics, and the "new" linguistics in elementary schools eroded the sanctity of the self-contained classroom. As part of the reorganization of curriculum that followed Sputnik, elementary teachers tended to cultivate a specific content area in the curriculum. This led to a departure from the self-contained classroom toward more sharing of students among teachers.

3. Dissatisfaction with the existing junior high school. The junior high school, in most cases, did not become a transitional school between the elementary and senior high school. Unfortunately, it became a miniature high school with all the sophisticated activities of the high school. Instruction was often formal and discipline-centered with insufficient attention given to the student as a person.

4. The middle school through a new program and organization provides for much needed innovations in curriculum and instruction. By creating a new school, the middle school, rather than by remodeling the outmoded junior high school, educators have provided an atmosphere for implementing those practices long talked about but seldom effected.

Functions of the Middle School _____

Middle schools in both recognition and numbers have become a separate, intermediate institution in America. Cumulative experience, research, and the fact that "the middle school works" have resulted in widespread acceptance of the middle school by children, teachers, administrators, and parents. The middle school is defined by the authors as a transitional school concerned with the most appropriate program to cope with the personal and educational needs of emerging adolescent learners. The middle school should be an institution that has:

1. A unique program adapted to the needs of the pre- and early-adolescent student.
2. The widest possible range of intellectual, social, and physical experiences.
3. Opportunities for exploration and development of fundamental skills needed by all, with allowances for individual learning patterns. An atmosphere of basic respect for individual differences should be maintained.
4. A climate that enables students to develop abilities, find facts, weigh evidence, draw conclusions, determine values, and that keeps their minds open to new facts.
5. Staff members who recognize and understand the student's needs, interests, backgrounds, motivations, goals, as well as stresses, strains, frustrations, and fears.
6. A smooth educational transition between the elementary school and the high school that allows for the physical and emotional changes of transescence.
7. An environment where the child, not the program, is most important and where the opportunity to succeed is ensured for all students.

8. Guidance in the development of mental processes and attitudes needed for constructive citizenship and the development of lifelong competencies and appreciations needed for effective use of leisure.

9. Competent instructional personnel who will strive to understand the students whom they serve and will develop professional competencies that are both unique and applicable to the transescent student.

10. Facilities and time to allow students and teachers an opportunity to achieve the goals of the program to their fullest capabilities.

Table 9.1 illustrates the unique and transitory nature of the middle school.

The middle school, then, represents a renewed effort to design and implement a program of education that can accommodate the needs of the pre-adolescent population. It is a broadly focused program of education drawing its philosophy and rationale from the evolving body of knowledge concerned with human growth and development. The middle school represents a systematic effort to organize the schooling experience in a way that will facilitate the maximum growth and development of all learners.

The middle school program consists of arrangements and activities that attempt to tie formal learning directly to the developmental

Table 9.1
School in the Middle

	Elementary	Middle	High
Teacher-Student Relationship	Parental	Advisor	Random
Teacher Organization	Self-contained	Interdisciplinary Team	Department
Curriculum	Skills	Exploration	Depth
Schedule	Self-contained	Block	Periods
Instruction	Teacher Directed	Balance	Student Directed
Student Grouping	Chronological	Multi-age Developmental	Subject
Building Plan	Classroom Areas	Team Areas	Department Areas
Physical Education	Skills & Games	Skills & Intramurals	Skills & Interscholastics
Media Center	Classroom Groups	Balance	Individual Study
Guidance	Diagnostic/ Developmental	Teacher Helper	Career-Vocational
Teacher Preparation	Child-Oriented Generalist	Flexible Resource	Disciplines Specialist

needs of the students who are served. To date, identified "developmental tasks" represent the most promising criteria for curriculum development that will intersect school activity with learner growth and development.

Establishing an Identity for the Middle School ___

Education for emerging adolescents has received an intensive reexamination over the past decade. One result has been the verification of a need for a school with a differentiated function for the age group of 10–14. That need for a distinct school unlike the elementary, high school, or even the junior high school, is more defensible than ever in light of recent information about growth and development of emerging adolescents. Changing social conditions have also helped establish the need for a school in the middle with an identity of its own. As middle schools have grown in number and quality, a number of common elements have helped establish an identity for the middle school. Some of these are:

1. Absence of the "little high school" approach.
2. Absence of the "star system" where a few special students dominate everything, in favor of an attempt to provide success experiences for greater numbers of students.
3. An attempt to use instructional methods more appropriate to this age group: individualized instruction, variable group sizes, multimedia approaches, beginning independent study programs, inquiry-oriented instruction.
4. Increased opportunity for teacher-student guidance. May include a home base or advisory group program.
5. Increased flexibility in scheduling and student grouping.
6. At least some cooperative planning and team teaching.
7. At least some interdisciplinary studies, where teachers from a variety of academic areas provide opportunities for students to see how the areas of knowledge fit together.
8. A wide range of exploratory opportunities, academic and otherwise.
9. Increased opportunity for physical activity and movement, and more frequent physical education.
10. Earlier introduction to the areas of organized academic knowledge.
11. Attention to the skills of continued learning, those skills which will permit students to learn better on their own or at higher levels.
12. Accent on increasing the student's ability to be independent, responsible, and self-disciplined.
13. Flexible physical plant facilities.

14. Attention to the personal development of the student: values clarification, group process skills, health and family life education when appropriate, career education.
15. Teachers trained especially for, and committed to, the education of emerging adolescents.

The Middle School Student

The middle school espoused the same goals as did the junior high. Those goals were to provide a transition school between the elementary and the high school and to help students bridge the gap in their development between childhood and adolescence.

Emerging adolescent learners in the middle school represent the most diverse group of students at any organizational level of schooling. As ninth graders moved to the high school and sixth graders came into the middle school, the middle school became a real transitional school with students found at all levels of physical, social, and intellectual maturity. Middle schools, unlike junior high schools that tended to treat all students as adolescents, have attempted to develop programs to help students bridge the gap in development between childhood and adolescence.

Pre– and early adolescents experience dramatic physical, social, emotional, and intellectual changes resulting from maturational changes. More biological changes occur in the bodies and minds of youngsters between the ages of ten and fourteen than at any other period in their lives except the first nine months of their development.

Because the transitional years between childhood and adolescence are marked by distinct changes in the bodies and minds of boys and girls, the success of the middle school depends on teachers and administrators understanding each learner and his or her unique developmental pattern.

Table 9.2 will help the reader study in detail characteristics of emerging adolescent learning and their implications for the middle school.

The Middle School Teacher

The middle school teacher, more than any other factor, holds the key to realization of the type of effective middle school required for emerging adolescents.

The middle school teacher must have all those characteristics that research indicates are good for all teachers. However, because of the ages embraced in the middle school, he or she is responsible for children who are striking in their diversity. What confronts a teacher in the middle school is a rapidly changing group of children in different stages of development.

Table 9.2
Development of Emerging Adolescents and Its Implications
for the Middle School

Characteristics of Emerging Adolescents	Implications for the Middle School
Physical Development	

Accelerated physical development begins in transescence marked by increases in weight, height, muscular strength. Boys and girls are growing at varying rates of speed. Girls tend to be taller for the first two years, and tend to be more physically advanced. Bone growth is faster than muscle development and the uneven muscle/bone development results in lack of coordination and awkwardness. Bones may lack protection of covering muscles and supporting tendons.	Provide a curriculum that emphasizes self-understanding about body changes. Health and science classes should provide experiences that will develop an understanding about body growth. Guidance counselors and community resource persons such as pediatricians can help students understand what is happening to their bodies.
	Adaptive physical education classes should be scheduled for students lacking physical coordination. Equipment should be designed for students in transesence to help them develop small and large muscles.
In the pubescent stage for girls, secondary sex characteristics continue to develop with breasts enlarging and menstruation beginning.	Intense sports competition, especially contact sports, should be avoided.
	Schedule sex education classes, health and hygiene seminars for students.
A wide range of individual differences among students begins to appear in pre-pubertal and pubertal stages of development. Although the sequential order of development is relatively consistent in each sex, boys tend to lag a year or two behind girls. There are marked individual differences in physical development for boys and girls. The age of greatest variability in physiological development and physical size is about age 13.	Provide opportunities for interaction among students of multi-ages, but avoid situations where one's physical development can be compared with others (e.g., gang showers).
	Intramural programs rather than interscholastic athletics should be emphasized so that each student will have a chance to achieve regardless of physical development. Where interscholastic sports programs exist, the number of games should be limited and games played in the afternoon rather than evening.
Glandular imbalances occur resulting in acne, allergies, dental and eye defects—some health disturbances are real and some are imaginary.	Regular physical examinations should be provided all middle school students.

Table 9.2
(continued)

Characteristics of Emerging Adolescents	Implications for the Middle School
Physical Development	
Displays change in body contour— large nose, protruding ears, long arms—has posture problems and is self-conscious about the body.	Health classes should especially emphasize exercises for good posture. Students shall be led to understand through self-analysis that growth is an individual process and occurs unevenly.
A girdle of fat often appears around the hips and thighs of boys in early puberty. A slight development of tissue under the skin around the nipples occurs for a short time and boys may fear they are developing "the wrong way." Considerable anxiety arises during this natural phase of development which quickly passes.	Films, talks by doctors and counselors can help students understand the changes the body goes through in the period from childhood to adolescence. A carefully planned program of sex education developed in collaboration with parents medical doctors, and community agencies should be developed.
Students are likely to be disturbed by body changes. Girls especially are likely to be disturbed about the physical changes that accompany sexual maturation.	
Receding chins, cowlicks, dimples and changes in voice result in possible embarrassment to boys.	Teacher and parental reassurance and understanding are necessary to help students understand that many body changes are temporary in nature.
Boys and girls tend to tire easily but won't admit it.	Parents should be advised to insist that students get proper rest— overexertion by students should be discouraged.
Fluctuations in basal metabolism may cause students to be extremely restless at times and listless at others.	The school should provide an opportunity for daily exercise by students and a place where students can be children by playing and being noisy for short periods of time.
	Activities such as special interest classes, "hands on" exercises should be encouraged. Students should be allowed to physically move around in their classes and avoid long periods of passive work.

Table 9.2
(continued)

Characteristics of Emerging Adolescents	Implications for the Middle School
Physical Development	
Shows ravenous appetite and peculiar tastes, may overtax the digestive system with large quantities of improper foods.	Snacks should be provided to satisfy between-meal hunger. Guidance should be provided about nurtition as it applies to emerging adolescents.
Social Development	
Affiliation base broadens from family to peer group. Conflict sometimes results due to splitting of allegiance between peer group and family.	Teachers should work closely with the family to help adults realize that peer pressure is a normal part of the maturation process. Parents should be encouraged to continue to provide love and comfort to their children even though they may feel their children are rejecting them.
	All teachers in the middle school should be counselors. Home-base, teacher advisor house plan arrangements should be encouraged.
Peers become sources for standards and models of behavior. Occasional rebellion on the part of child does not diminish importance of parents for development of values. Emerging adolescents want to make their own choices, but authority still remains primarily with the family.	The school can sponsor activities that permit the student to interact socially with many school personnel. Family studies can help ease parental conflicts. Involvement of parents in the school should be encouraged. Students should know their parents are involved in the school program but parents should not be too conspicuous by their presence.
	Co-curricular activities should be encouraged. An active student government will help students develop guidelines for interpersonal relations and standards of behavior.
Mobility of society has broken ties to peer groups and created anxieties in emerging adolescent youth.	"Family grouping of students and teachers can be encouraged to provide stability for students moving to a new school. Interdisciplinary units can be structured to provide interaction among various groups of students. Clubs and special interest classes should be an integral part of the school day.

Table 9.2
(continued)

Characteristics of Emerging Adolescents	Implications for the Middle School
Social Development	
Students are confused and frightened by new school settings.	Orientation programs and "buddy systems" can reduce the trauma of moving from an elementary school to a middle school. Family teams can encourage a sense of belonging.
Shows unusual or drastic behavior at times—aggressive, daring, boisterous, argumentative.	Debates, plays, playdays, and other activities should be scheduled at the middle school to allow students to "show off" in a productive way.
"Puppy love years"—shows extreme devotion to a particular boy or girl friend, but may transfer allegiance to a friend overnight.	Role playing, guidance exercises can provide students the opportunity to act out feelings. Opportunities should be provided for social interaction between the sexes—parties, games, but not dances in the early grades of the middle school.
Feel the will of the group must prevail—sometimes almost cruel to those not in their group. Copies and displays fads of extremes in clothes, speech, mannerism, and handwriting, very susceptible to advertising.	Set up an active student government so students can develop their own guidelines for dress and behavior. Adults should be encouraged not to react in an outraged manner when extreme dress or mannerisms are displayed by young adolescents.
Strong concern for what is "right," and social justice. Shows concern for less fortunate others.	Activities should be planned to allow students to engage in service activities. Peer teaching can be encouraged to allow students to help other students. Community projects such as assisting in a senior citizens club or helping in a child care center can be planned by students and teachers.
Is influenced by adults—attempts to identify with adults other than their parents.	Flexible teaching patterns should prevail so students can interact with a variety of adults with whom they can identify.
Despite a trend toward heterosexual interests, same sex affiliation tends to dominate during transescence.	Large group activities rather than boy-girl events should be scheduled. Intramurals can be scheduled so students can interact with friends of the same or opposite sex.

Table 9.2
(continued)

Characteristics of Emerging Adolescents	Implications for the Middle School

Social Development

| Desires direction and regulation but reserves the right to question or reject suggestions of adults. | The middle school should provide opportunities for students to accept more responsibility in setting standards for behavior. Students should be helped to establish realistic goals and should be assisted in helping realize those goals. |

Emotional Development

Erratic and inconsistent behavior is prevalent among emerging adolescents. Anxiety and fear contrast with reassuring bravado. Feelings tend to shift between superiority and inferiority. Coping with physical changes, striving for independence from family and becoming a person in his or her own right and learning a new mode of intellectual functioning are all emotion-laden problems for emerging adolescents. Students have many fears, real and imagined. At no other time in development is a student likely to encounter such a diverse number of problems simultaneously.	Students in the middle school should be led in self-evaluation. Activities should be designed to help students play out their emotions. School activity programs should provide opportunities for shy students to be drawn out and loud students to engage in calming activities. Counseling must operate as a part of the learning program rather than as an adjunct to it. Students should be helped to interpret superiority and inferiority feelings. Mature value systems should be encouraged by allowing students to examine options of behavior and study consequences of various actions.
	Students should be encouraged to assume leadership in group discussions and experience frequent success and recognition for personal efforts and achievements. A general atmosphere of friendliness, relaxation, concern, and group cohesiveness should guide the program.
Chemical and hormone imbalances during transescence often trigger emotions that are little understood by the transescent. Students sometimes regress to childlike behavior.	Adults in the middle school should not pressure students to explain their emotions, i.e. crying for no reason. Occasional childlike behavior should not be ridiculed by adults.
	The school program should provide numerous possibilities for releasing emotional stress.

Table 9.2
(continued)

Characteristics of Emerging Adolescents	Implications for the Middle School
Emotional Development	
Physical development is a source of irritation and concern. Development of secondary sex characteristics creates additional tensions about their rate of development.	Appropriate sex education should be provided. Utilizing parents and community agencies should be encouraged in the middle school. Pediatricians, psychologists, and counselors should be called on to assist students in understanding developmental changes.
Is easily offended and sensitive to criticism of personal shortcoming.	Sarcasm by adults should be avoided. Students should be helped to develop values in the solution of their problems.
Students tend to exaggerate simple occurrences and believe their problems are unique.	Sociodrama can be utilized to enable students to see themselves as others see them. Readings dealing with problems similar to their own can help students see that many problems are not unique.
Intellectual Development	
Emerging adolescents display a wide range of skills and abilities unique to their developmental patterns.	A variety of approaches and materials in the teaching-learning process should be utilized in the middle school.
Students will range in development from the concrete-manipulatory stage of development to the ability to deal with abstract concepts. The transescent is intensely curious and growing in mental ability.	The middle school should treat students at their own intellectual levels providing immediate rather than remote goals. All subjects should be individualized. Skill grouping should be flexible.
Middle school learners prefer active over passive learning activities, prefer interaction with peers during learning activities.	Physical movement should be encouraged with small group discussions, learning centers, and creative dramatics suggested as good activity projects. Provide a program of learning that is exciting and meaningful.

Table 9.2
(continued)

Characteristics of Emerging Adolescents	Implications for the Middle School
Intellectual Development	
Students in the middle school are usually very curious and exhibit a strong willingness to learn things they consider to be useful. Students enjoy using skills to solve "real life" problems.	Organize curricula around real life concepts such as conflict, competition, peer group influence. Provide activities in both formal and informal situations to improve reasoning powers. Studies of the community, environment are particularly relevant to the age group.
Students often display heightened egocentrism and will argue to convince others or to clarify emergence of independent, critical thinking.	Organized discussions of ideas and feelings in peer groups can facilitate self-understanding. Provide experiences for individuals to express themselves by writing and participating in dramatic productions.
There is growing evidence that there is a slowing of brain growth in transescents between the ages of 12 and 14.	Existing cognitive skills of learners should be refined and continued cognitive growth during the 12–14 years may not be expected.
	Opportunities should be provided for enjoyable studies in the arts. Self-expression should be encouraged in all subject areas.

Source: Jon Wiles and Joseph Bondi, *The Essential Middle School* (Columbus, Ohio: Charles E. Merrill Publishing Company, 1980), pp. 24–30. Reprinted with permission.

A number of key competencies have been identified for teachers in the middle school. Table 9.3 is presented for the reader's study.

A Program Design for the Middle School _____

A well designed middle school features a balanced program focusing on personal development, basic skills for continuous learners, and utilization of knowledge to foster social competence. The curriculum of a middle school thus follows closely the developmental stages represented in the students it serves.

Table 9.3
Selected Teacher Competencies for Middle School Teachers

1. Possesses knowledge of the pre–and early adolescent physical development which includes knowledge of physical activity needs and the diversity and variety of physical growth rates.

2. Commands knowledge of the pre–and early adolescent intellectual development with emphasis on the transition from concrete to formal levels of mental development.

3. Has a knowledge of a recognized developmental theory and personality theory which can be utilized in identifying appropriate learning strategies for the pre–and early adolescent.

4. Understands the socioemotional development including the need to adjust to a changing body.

5. Possesses the necessary skills to allow interaction between individual students as well as the opportunity to work in groups of varying sizes.

6. Understands the cultural forces and community relationships which affect the total school curriculum.

7. Has the ability to organize the curriculum to facilitate the developmental tasks of preadolescence and early adolescence.

8. Understands the transitional nature of grades 3–6 as they bridge the gap between the children of the lower elementary grades and late adolescents and early adults of the upper grades.

9. Possesses the skills needed to work with other teachers and school professionals in team teaching situations.

10. Has the ability to plan multidisciplinary lessons or units and teach them personally or with other professionals.

11. Commands a broad academic background, with specialization in at least two allied areas of the curriculum.

12. Possesses the skill to integrate appropriate media and concrete demonstrations into presentations.

13. Is able to develop and conduct learning situations that will promote independent learning, and maximize student choice and responsibility for follow through.

14. Possesses the knowledge and skills that will allow students to sort information, set priorities, and budget time and energy.

15. Is able to teach problem-solving skills and develop lessons that are inquiry-oriented.

16. Has the ability to teach students how to discover knowledge and use both inductive and deductive methods in the discovery of knowledge.

17. Possesses the knowledge and skills necessary to use role playing, simulation, instructional games, and creative dramatics in teaching the content as well as the affective domain in a middle grade classroom.

Table 9.3
(continued)

18. Commands the knowledge and skill needed to organize and manage a classroom that allows individuals to learn at a rate commensurate with their ability.

19. Possesses verbal behaviors that will promote student input in a variety of group settings.

20. Is able to write behavioral objectives and design lessons to effectively conclude the objectives.

21. Has the knowledge and skills needed to diagnose strengths and weaknesses, to determine learning levels of individuals, to prescribe courses of action, and evaluate the outcomes.

22. Has experiences in innovation and possesses the skill to experiment with teaching techniques to find ones that are most effective in given situations.

23. Is able to teach the communication skills of reading, writing, and speaking in all subject areas.

24. Commands knowledge of reading techniques that will enable students to progress and improve their reading in the subject areas.

25. Possesses the skills needed to diagnose reading problems and provide a remedial program in the regular classroom.

26. Has a knowledge of the techniques necessary to promote positive self-concepts and self-reliance.

27. Is able to help students clarify values, consider alternative values, and develop a personal and workable valuing system.

28. Possesses a knowledge of group dynamics and the ability to organize groups that will make decisions and provide their own leadership.

29. Has a knowledge of careers and the ability to help students explore careers.

30. Commands knowledge of several major learning theories and the learning strategies that emanate from the theories.

31. Has a knowledge of how to deal with unusual classroom problems.

32. Possesses skills necessary to effectively manage groups of students in activity settings.

33. Possesses the ability to recognize difficulties that may be emotionally or physically based.

34. Possesses the knowledge and skills needed to effectively manage abusive and deviant behavior.

35. Works with extracurricular activities in the school.

36. Gathers appropriate personal information on students using question-naires, interviews, and observation.

37. Provides frequent feedback to students on learning progress.

Table 9.3
(continued)

38. Functions calmly in a high-activity environment.

39. Handles disruptive behavior in a positive and consistent manner.

40. Builds learning experiences for students based upon learning skills (reading, math.) obtained in elementary grades.

41. Works cooperatively with peers, consultants, resource persons, and paraprofessionals.

42. Exhibits concern for students by listening or empathizing with them.

43. Selects evaluation techniques appropriate to curricular objective in the affective domain.

44. Utilizes value clarification and other affective teaching techniques to help students develop personal value system.

45. Provides an informal, flexible classroom environment.

46. Cooperates in curricular planning and revision.

47. Evaluates the teaching situation and selects the grouping techniques most appropriate for the situation, large group instruction (100+ students), small group instruction (15–25 students), or independent study.

48. Uses questioning techniques skillfully to achieve higher-order thinking processes in students.

49. Can move from one type of grouping situation to another smoothly.

50. Functions effectively in various organizational and staffing situations, such as team teaching, differentiated staffing, and multiage groupings.

51. Selects evaluation techniques appropriate to curricular objectives in the psychomotor domain.

52. The teacher establishes povitive relationships with the parents and families of students.

53. The teacher works at understanding, accepting and being accepted by members of the subcultures in the school and the community.

54. The teacher understands the middle school concept and attempts to apply it in the classroom, and in the school as a whole.

55. The teacher manages the classroom with a minimum of negative or aversive controls.

56. The teacher uses himself (herself) as a tool in promoting the personal growth of students and colleagues.

57. The teacher's relationships with colleagues, administrators, and supervisors are harmonious and productive.

58. The teacher is aware of the needs, forces, and perceptions which determine his (her) personal behavior.

59. The teacher maintains a balance between teacher-directed learning and student-directed learning.

Table 9.3
(continued)

60. The teacher's efforts in curriculum and instruction proceed from a problem-solving framework, involving the students in relevant inquiry.

61. The teacher possesses skill in asking questions which encourage student thinking beyond the level of "recall."

Source: Jon Wiles and Joseph Bondi, *The Essential Middle School* (Columbus, Ohio: Charles E. Merrill Publishing Company, 1980), pp. 53–56. Reprinted with permission.

There has been much progress in recent years in developing new and exciting programs for emerging adolescent learners, yet much still needs to be done. The retrenchment of the 1970s and 80s has brought new pressures to narrow the curriculum of the middle school to the teaching of rote skills and the transmission of knowledge. Exploratory programs, guidance services, and health and physical education programs are being cut back in many schools. Thus, the curriculum area of Personal Development is being shortchanged in many middle schools. This development has forced an imbalance in the middle school program and a return to the more content-centered junior high or imitation high school model. With sixth graders now being housed in many middle schools, the result has been the thrusting down of a high school program to an even younger group of students. Combined with a return to a seven period, departmentalized organizational model, the lack of emphasis on personal development signals a return to a secondary emphasis in the middle grades. The gains in program improvement won in the 1960s and early 1970s by middle school educators are being washed away in many places by a return to the high school or secondary model which is easier to schedule and administer. The lessons learned by the failure of the junior high school have been lost in the face of doing what is easier and less costly.

Because inservice programs for middle school teachers have not been sustained and preservice training has not changed from the old model of training secondary teachers, the high school program model and organizational pattern will meet with approval of teachers in many middle schools. Unless there are dramatic developments in the middle school movement in the late 1980s, middle schools will be characterized by aging staffs, departmental organizations, narrow programs, and high-school type instruction.

Curriculum leaders in the 1980s must not lose sight of the purpose of the middle school. The middle school is a transitional school and must not be an exact replica of the high school or elementary school. The need for balance in the program and organizational flexibility has never been greater. In addition to the normal developmental changes middle school students are experiencing, social changes have had a major impact on the lives of emerging adolescent learners between the ages of ten to fourteen. Consider the following:

1. The American family is breaking down. For every marriage today, there is a divorce. One of five children in public schools comes from a broken home.
2. More adults moonlighted last year than at any other time in the history of our country.
3. Only 16 percent of American homes today have the family pattern of a mother at home and a father working.
4. Alchoholism increased 800 percent among teenagers in the last ten years. By the end of the ninth grade, 20 percent of adolescents will suffer a serious drinking problem.
5. 43 percent of all persons arrested for serious crimes in the United States (rape, murder, robbery) are juveniles, yet juveniles make up only 20 percent of the population.
6. One in two Americans moved during the past five years.
7. Six hundred thousand girls between the ages of 10 and 18 gave birth to illegitimate babies in America last year. One of ten girls will be pregnant before age 18. There are an estimated 11 million teenage boys and girls that are sexually active.
8. The second leading cause of death among teenagers, after accidents, is suicide. The suicide rate among teenagers doubled in the decade between 1970 and 1980.
9. It is estimated that pre- and early adolescents spend one-third of their waking hours watching television.
10. 75 percent of all advertising is aimed at 10–18-year-olds.
11. Psychologists regard the lack of a stable home as the biggest contributor to delinquency.
12. The most impressionable age group are youngsters 12–14 years of age. It is no accident that the Hitler Youth, Red Guard, and even our Boy Scouts have age 12 as the starting point.

Dealing with emerging adolescents has become a national priority. In funding of the National Institute of Education (NIE) in 1980, Congress mandated that the number one priority of NIE be research on emerging adolescent learners.

(a) The middle grades years represent the last chance for students to master basic skills.
(b) The middle grades represent the last time for formal schooling for many of our youth. Low achievers drop out after the middle grades.

(c) The final attitude toward self and others, as well as a lasting attitude toward learning, occurs in the middle grades.

(d) Future school success, indeed future life success, can be predicted for most students in the middle grades.

Curriculum leaders must take a strong stance to prevent the middle school from becoming an imitation high school again. There are still many good models of middle schools and reformed junior high schools that offer promise for curriculum developers desiring to improve middle grades education.* In addition, the number of articles, texts, and research studies in the middle school area has grown both in quantity and quality in the last decade. Organizations such as The National Middle School Association, and Association for Supervision and Curriculum Development have organized numerous conferences and workshops for educators interested in middle school improvement.

Figure 9.1 illustrates the three major program elements needed in the middle school.

A balanced program needed to serve the diverse group of youngsters found in the middle grades should include the following:

1. Learning experiences for transescents at their own intellectual levels, relating to immediate rather than remote academic goals.

2. A wide variety of cognitive learning experiences to account for the full range of students who are at many different levels of concrete and formal operations. Learning objectives should be sequenced to allow for the transition from concrete to formal operations.

3. A diversified curriculum of exploratory and/or fundamental activities resulting in daily successful experiences that will stimulate and nurture intellectual development.

4. Opportunities for the development of problem-solving skills, reflective-thinking processes, and awareness for the order of the student's environment.

5. Cognitive learning experiences so structured that students can progress in an individualized manner. However, within the structure of an individualized learning program, students can interact with one another. Social interaction is not an enemy of individual learning.

6. A curriculum in which all areas are taught to reveal opportunities for further study, to help students learn how to study, and to help them appraise their own interests and talents. In addition, the middle school should continue the

---

*See "Miracle on Main Street—The St. Louis Story," *Educational Leadership,* November, 1982, pp. 52–53, for a description of the significant results of the middle school program in St. Louis.

Figure 9.1 Program Design for the Essential Middle School

I. *Personal Development*

Guidance—Physical Education—Intramurals—Lifetime Sports—Sex Education—Health Studies—Law Education—Social Services—Drug Education—Special Interests—Clubs—Student Government—Developmental Groupings—Programs for Students with Special Needs—Mainstreaming— Alternative Programs

II. *Education for Social Competence*

Basic Studies
   Science
   Social Studies
   Mathematics
   Language Arts

Exploratory Studies
   Practical Arts
     Home Economics
     Industrial Arts
     Business-Distributive
      Education
Fine Arts
   Music
   Art
   Foreign Language
   Humanities

Environmental Studies
   Outdoor Education

Career Exploration

Consumer Education

Media Study

III. *Skills for Continuous Learning*

Communication
   Reading
   Writing
   Listening
   Speaking

Mathematics
   Computation
   Comprehension
   Usage

Observing and Comparing

Analyzing

Generalizing

Organizing

Evaluating

Source: Jon Wiles and Joseph Bondi, *The Essential Middle School* (Columbus, Ohio: Charles E. Merrill Publishing Company, 1981), p. 84. Reprinted with permission.

developmental program of basic skills instruction started in the elementary school, with emphasis upon both developmental and remedial reading.

7. A planned sequence of concepts in the general education areas, major emphasis on the interests and skills for continued learning, a balanced program of exploratory experiences and other activities and services for personal development, and appropriate attention to the development of values.

8. A common program in which areas of learning are combined and integrated to break down artificial and irrelevant divisions of curriculum content. Some previously departmentalized areas of the curriculum should be combined and taught around integrative themes, topics, and experiences. Other areas of the curriculum, particularly those concerned with basic skills which are logical, sequential, and analytical, might best be taught in ungraded or continuous progress programs. Inflexible student scheduling, with its emphasis upon depart-mentalization, should be restructured in the direction of greater flexibility.
9. Encouragement of personal curiosity, with one learning experience inspiring subsequent activities.
10. Methods of instruction involving open and individually directed learning experiences. The role of the teacher should be more that of a personal guide and facilitator of learning than of a purveyor of knowledge. Traditional lecture-recitation methods should be minimized.
11. Grouping criteria which involve not only cognitive, but also physical, social, and emotional criteria.
12. As much consideration for who the student is and becomes, his or her self-concept, self-responsibility, and attitudes toward school and personal happiness, as for how much and what he or she knows.
13. Experiences in the arts for all transescents to foster aesthetic appreciations and to stimulate creative expression.
14. Curriculum and teaching methods which reflect cultural, ethnic, and socioeconomic subgroups within the middle school student population.[3]

There has been much progress in the past ten years in developing new and exciting programs for emerging adolescent learners, yet much needs to be done. Whether programs for students in the middle grades are housed in organizational structures called middle schools or are found in upper elementary grades, junior high schools, or secondary schools, the focus of such programs has to be the developmental characteristics of the emerging adolescent learner group itself.[4]

Organizing for Instruction in The Middle School _

Middle school educators, building on a philosophy and knowledge of the emerging adolescent learner, have structured a broad and relevant program for the varied needs of students found in the middle grades. To facilitate that program, the middle school must be organized to accommodate a flexible approach to instruction. Block schedules, teams of teachers with common planning periods teaching common groups of students, and special activity periods are essential elements of true middle schools. Inflexible, departmentalized high school organizational structures do not facilitate the broad program needed by middle grade students.

The interdisciplinary team approach to planning and implementing instruction has distinct advantages over a self-contained or departmentalized teaching pattern. Some of those advantages are:

1. More than one teacher with the knowledge of scheduling, use of instructional materials, grouping, and instructional methods benefits individual student learning.
2. Curriculums among subject areas can be coordinated so that the students can relate one subject to another. Leads to greater breadth of understanding for students, "sees" more relationships.
3. Teachers can better understand individual differences in students when more than one person is making observations and evaluations; can therefore "cope" with those differences more effectively; discipline problems are more easily handled; guidance for the student is discussed among the team.
4. The team approach enables teachers to contrast a student's behavior and ability from class to class, thereby helping them develop a systematic and consistent approach to helping the child.
5. Allows for closer work with guidance and other specialists.
6. Block scheduling allows the teachers a greater flexibility in uling to accommodate large and small group instruction, remedial work, and independent study.
7. Flexible time schedules can be made more conducive to children's developmental needs at this age level than are rigid departmentalized schedules.
8. A number of instructors can lend their individual expertise to a given topic simultaneously.
9. Large blocks of time are available for educational field trips, guest speakers, films, etc.; at the same time, scheduling is not disrupted. Less teaching time is lost to repetitious film showing.
10. Teachers can be more aware of what their students are learning in other classes—what assignments, tests, projects are making demands on their time.
11. Common planning time can lead to more creativity in teaching approaches and consistency in teaching strategies.
12. Interdisciplinary teaching leads to economy of learning time and transfer among students.
13. Student leadership is distributed among all the teams since each team's students are typical of the total school community.

14. Students are able to identify themselves with a smaller school within a school; with team representation on student council, they are more closely related to student government.
15. Correlated planning of content and project work is more easily carried.
16. Parent conferences can be arranged by the guidance counselor for times when all of a student's academic teachers are available.
17. Individual teams may rearrange completely time and period schedules without interference with the overall school program. For example, each team may individually manipulate their block of time so as to provide periods of various length. All students do not move in the hallways at the end of 55 minutes.
18. Field trips can now be planned by teams, and built-in chaperoning is thus provided. Longer times for such trips are now available without disrupting a multiple number of classes.
19. One of the greatest advantages of team teaching is the assistance provided to the beginning teacher.
20. Building utilization is improved; large and small group space is utilized as well as regular classrooms.
21. An interdisciplinary team scheduling arrangement promotes the professional growth of the teachers by encouraging the exchange of ideas among the members of their teaching team.

An example of block scheduling to facilitate interdisciplinary teaming is found in Figure 9.2. The Activity Period Schedule (Enrichment and Remediation) is explained in Figure 9.3.

Comprehensive Planning for Middle Schools _____

The curriculum of the middle school, with its concern for the special needs of pre- and early adolescents, with its comprehensive definition of education, with its promotion of continuity in learning and development, is more than a series of catch phrases and education innovations. The middle school is, in fact, a highly complex plan for educating a special learner. Owing to the complexity of the educational design, successful implementation of the program calls for a significant degree of advanced planning.

During the 1970s and early 1980s, the middle school movement entered a new era of maturity. However, developments such as declining enrollment (contrasted with the increased enrollment of the 1960s), court-ordered integration (in the large cities of the Midwest, Northeast, and West) continued to precipitate new middle schools. Unfortunately, numbers of students, bussing patterns, racial quotas, and building uses rather than identified student needs were reasons most given for the establishment of middle schools.

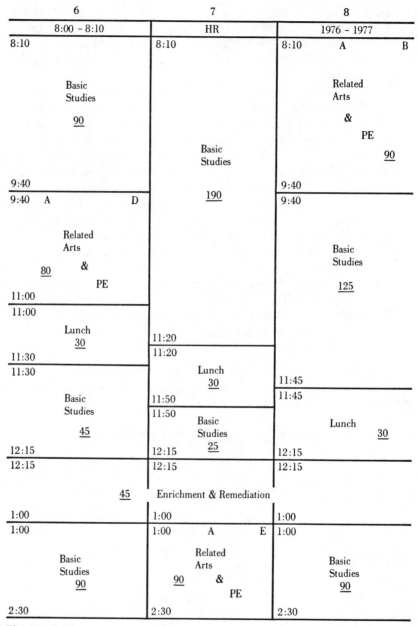

Figure 9.2

As in the 1960s and early 1970s, the authors have stated that although the wrong reasons may be advanced for developing middle schools, the right opportunity existed to really plan and implement the kind of middle grades curriculum so needed by American youth.

Figure 9.3 Enrichment and Remediation

This is a 45-minute period that meets after lunch, five days a week. The period serves three basic purposes: (1) We teach year-long advanced classes, and other single session elective classes that cannot be scheduled during the day; (2) We require remedial work for those students who are failing or who are identified as needing help; and (3) We offer enriching activities on a nine-week basis.

The following is a list of the advanced classes and the single session electives that we offer during Enrichment and Remediation period:

1. American Industry PV (8th)
2. Power and Training PV (8th)
3. Exploring Occupations to Homemaking (8th)
4. Orientation to Home Ec. Occupations (7th)
5. Creative Business Opportunities (8th)
6. Publications (7th and 8th)
7. Algebra (8th)
8. Pre-Algebra (7th and 8th)
9. Art (8th)
10. Chorus (7th and 8th)
11. Adaptive PE—males (6, 7, 8)
12. Adaptive PE—females (6, 7, 8)
13. Employability Skills (8th)
14. Speech

About 50 percent of our students are involved in the program. This allows us some flexibility in dealing with related arts and helps us to overcome some problems with scheduling; particularly with students who desire much academic involvement.

The following are the remedial classes we offer:

1. Remedial Reading (4 classes—7th and 8th)
2. Remedial Math (2 classes—6th, 7th, and 8th)
3. Remedial English (1 class—6th, 7th, and 8th)
4. Remedial Science (1 class—6th, 7th, and 8th)
5. Remedial Social Studies (1 class—6th, 7th, and 8th)

All children who fail a class are assigned to a Remediation class for nine weeks. The team teachers meet and decide on the students who will benefit from special help in the various subjects; and these students are also assigned to remedial help for nine weeks. Any student in the 7th or 8th grade who needs Reading help is moved into a special Reading class. (Sixth graders are not placed in these Reading classes as they have Reading every day with their team.) We also send a form home to the parents so that they may have the opportunity to request special help for their child during this period. We honor these requests by placing the child in the requested class.

The Enrichment classes we offer are as follows:

Figure 9.3 (continued)

1. Square Dancing	8. Crocheting
2. Embroidery-Jeans	9. Indoor Games
3. History of Bible Lands	10. Cheerleading
4. Baton Twirling	11. Country Music
5. Colonial Crafts	12. Photography
6. Exploratory Reading	13. Arts and Crafts
7. Creative Writing	14. Outdoor Games

About 40 percent of our student body is involved in the Enrichment classes. They are nine weeks in length. Basically, our sixth and seventh graders are involved in these classes.

In the realistic world of the 1980s, with continued decline in enrollment and financial support for schools, the key to successful implementation of middle school programs will be successful planning. Small, medium-sized, and large school districts have used comprehensive planning models to develop excellent middle school programs.[5]

The curriculum planning model suggested early in this text is necessary if middle schools are to succeed. In assisting in the development of middle schools across America, the authors have noted that planning often determines the fine line between success and failure. Such planning is necessary at the district, school, and classroom level. The following district-level planning steps, in sequence, are recommended for the establishment of middle schools.

Analysis

The middle school should arise from need. Ideally, school systems and communities will proceed through value-clarification processes that reveal the logic of the middle school design, and programs will be initiated on what is known about their students. Overcrowding, integration, or building availability are poor reasons for choosing the concept.

An important point in making such an analysis is not to allow the search to be focused only on problems. The analysis should also be projective—what kind of an educational experience do we want for students during this period of development?

Involvement

Preliminary investigations of the middle school should involve all parties with vested interests in intermediate education. A step often taken in planning the middle school is to explore the concept without involving those who will be most directly affected by its activation: students, teachers, parents, and the community. At a superficial level, the elimination of this stage will probably lead to future confrontations over both programs and policy (interscholastic athletics, social events, grading policies, community-based learning). More important from the planning standpoint, however, is the dedication and support that will be needed to put such a program in practice in the first place. The middle school cannot be implemented and maintained unless it is believed in by those involved.

Of the constituencies mentioned above, particular attention must be given to the community in which the middle school will reside. Unaccustomed to educational jargon, and unfamiliar with national trends in educational programs, many citizens will resist the middle school because of misunderstandings about the academic nature of the program and the necessary organizational arrangements. Without a clear understanding of the rationale of the program and the reason for these arrangements, community resistance will be high.

Involvement of community members representing all segments of the population in the initial analysis of student needs, in the investigation of the middle school concept, in the drafting of documents, and in the planning of implementation stages will build-in a means of communicating with the community at later times.

Commitment

Philosophical commitments to the middle school definition of education should be secured prior to activating the program. This book has repeatedly underscored the necessity of understanding and accepting the middle school's philosophic position on education as a prerequisite for successful implementation of such a program. An understanding or lack of understanding of the middle school concept represents the largest potential stumbling block to successful implementation. Without such understanding and a basic philosophic acceptance of the middle school concept, there can be no substantial rationale for practices and programs found in the middle school.

It is important to note that this understanding and acceptance must go beyond school board approval and superintendent acquiescence, although both are consequential. Such an understanding and commitment must be held by the building principal, the involved teachers, and the parents of involved students.

Funding

Appropriate monies must be earmarked for activation of the plan. An observable phenomenon in American education is that finance is the "fuel" of progress. Few major innovations of the past twenty years (middle schools being a notable exception) have really succeeded without substantial financial support.

Although it is not impossible for a building faculty to implement the middle school concept with sheer dedication, two simple facts about middle schools are worth noting: Middle schools are a more complex form of education than traditional programs; as such, they require more energy and money to operate.

Every deviation from standardized patterns of educating, such as the uniform textbooks, the classroom-confined learning experience, and the single-dimension instruction will require effort and expense. As school districts do commit themselves to the middle school concept, a pledge equal to their commitment for financing building conversion, materials acquisition, staff development, and so forth is called for.

Resources

Resources commensurate with the task must be allocated. One of the common pitfalls in establishment of middle schools is to assume they can operate on the same resource base as the traditional intermediate school. To rely on teacher-made materials exclusively, to overlook a consumable materials budget, to fail to allocate materials to build up the instructional resource center, to make no provision for off-campus experiences is to doom in advance the programs of the middle school. Middle schools, if properly operated, require substantial resources for instruction.

Personnel

There must be an attempt to staff middle schools with dedicated and enthusiastic teachers. There are several appropriate comments to note regarding the selection, training, and use of middle school staff. The middle school will be only as effective as its personnel in succeeding at new roles. With only several colleges in the nation training teachers and staff members exclusively for middle school positions, most teachers and support personnel will enter the middle school from other more traditional educational designs. Such persons, regardless of their belief in and allegiance to the middle school philosophy of educating, will need special assistance in adjusting to their new roles. Predictably, the middle school staff will need extensive assistance in assuming new roles.

A problem witnessed in many school districts is that middle school teacher behaviors are prone to return to traditional patterns if sufficient support is not maintained. Many middle schools open under the so-called Hawthorne effect (a term coming from the Hawthorne studies in which workers were found to be more productive regardless of work conditions if they first received sufficient attention as being special), and with such a condition, teacher enthusiasm and energy are understandably high. However, as program development slows or resource bases erode with the gradual lessening of attention, it is not unusual for old patterns of teacher-pupil interaction and learning to creep in. Such a condition would warn against a one short summer treatment for the middle school staff and would call, instead, for long-term, systematic training opportunities.

Detailed Planning

Prior to the development of a middle school, detailed planning is essential. From an administrative/organizational perspective, it is crucial that schools conduct detailed planning to smoothly implement the middle school concept. The past experience of many middle schools suggests that a "broken front" approach to this concept does not work. The middle school concept does not easily emerge because there are prerequisites for implementation. There must be an understanding of objectives; there must be a commitment to this definition of educating; there must be an involvement of those who support the school; there must be money and resources to implement its components; there must be personnel capable of willing to assume the required roles. The time-frame for opening a middle school must allow for the magnitude of the process proposed.

While the amount of preparation time required to open a real middle school is dependent upon environmental conditions in the community, a minimum period appears to be eighteen to twenty-four months. This estimate is based on several definable steps of planning:

1. Awareness and study phases.
2. Educating community and gaining commitments.
3. Budgeting for development.
4. Selection of staff, site.
5. Construction of detailed implementation plan.
6. Intensive training of staff.
7. Development of curriculum.
8. Construction or conversion of site.
9. Opening of middle school.

In some communities and school districts it would be possible to accomplish the above steps in six months or less because of central office organization and support from the community leaders. The experience of many middle schools, however, would suggest that to hasten through steps 2, 6, and 7, or to proceed with step 8 prior to step 7 leads to significant problems later on. Eroding community support, an ill-prepared staff, a superficially constructed curriculum, and a dysfunctional site all are causes of middle school failure.

The Middle School as a Part
of the Total Curriculum _____

As is true of the elementary and high school, the middle school does not stand alone. It must build on the curriculum of the elementary school and in turn form a solid educational base for students entering the high school. Although early in the middle school movement educational leaders fought for a separate identity for the middle school to prevent it from following the path of the "Jr." high school, more and more emphasis today is being placed on an articulated K-12 curriculum and less on building separate programs for elementary, middle, and high school students. The move toward developing a unified K-12 curriculum is a welcome one. Regardless of housing patterns or grade level organizations, students should be viewed as individuals progressing through definite stages of development. An articulated curriculum that accommodates the developmental needs of youngsters is more important than grade organizations of schools. The middle school, however, must be a strong bridge that holds together the total K-12 curriculum.

In concluding this chapter on middle grades education, the authors present the reader with some curriculum problems that are common and recurrent:

1. Absentee rates for students in the intermediate grades are generally higher than those at the elementary and secondary levels. What may be some of the factors causing this condition and how can curriculum leaders address this problem?
2. Because many educators view the high school as a distinctive level of specialized academic preparation, many students are retained at the eighth grade level. What price do we pay for such retention? What is a reasonable retention rate? What can curriculum personnel do about this problem?
3. Students in the intermediate grades have many interpersonal concerns related to growing up. Yet, the average student-to-counselor ratio for this age group is 1:450. What can be done in the curriculum to address this problem?
4. Declining achievement scores on national tests are a common phenomenon in the intermediate grades. What causes this to happen and what can curriculum teachers do about it?

Notes

1. Commission on the Reorganization of Secondary Education, *Cardinal Principles of Secondary Education.* Bulletin 1918, No. 35 (Washington, D.C.: U. S. Department of Interior, Bureau of Education, 1918), pp. 12–13.
2. Educational Facilities Laboratories, *The Schoolhouse in the City* (New York: Author, 1966), p. 10.
3. A.S.C.D. Working Group on the Emerging Adolescent Learner, *The Middle School We Need* (Washington, D.C.: Association for Supervision and Curriculum Development, 1975), pp. 11–12. Reprinted with permission of the Association for Supervision and Curriculum Development. Copyright © 1975 by the Association for Supervision and Curriculum Development. All rights reserved.

4. Joseph Bondi, "Programs for Emerging Adolescent Learners," in Robert Leeper, ed., *Middle School in the Making* (Washington, D.C.: Association for Supervision and Curriculum Development, 1974), pp. 17–18.

5. See "Miracle on Main Street—The St. Louis Story," *Educational Leadership* (November 1982): 52–53.

Suggested Learning Activities ⎯⎯⎯⎯⎯⎯⎯⎯

1. Write a philosophical statement defending the emerging middle school design. Identify the functions of the middle school that are the most important to you.

2. Prepare an oral presentation for parents that would make them aware of the developmental characteristics of middle school students.

3. Identify the ten more important teacher competencies of the selected teacher competencies identified in this chapter. Give reasons why you selected the ones on your list.

4. Develop an outline of an ideal curriculum design for middle school students.

5. Prepare an outline of a district plan for organizing a middle school.

Books to Review ⎯⎯⎯⎯⎯⎯⎯⎯⎯⎯⎯⎯⎯

A.S.C.D. Working Group on the Emerging Adolescent Learner, *The Middle School We Need*. Washington, D.C.: Association for Supervision and Curriculum Development, 1975.

Elkind, David, *A Sympathetic Understanding of the Child: Birth to Sixteen*. Boston: Allyn and Bacon, 1974.

Havighurst, R., *Developmental Tasks and Education*. New York: David McKay Co., 1972.

Wiles, Jon and Bondi, Joseph, *The Essential Middle School*. Columbus, Ohio: Charles E. Merrill, 1981.

Chapter Ten
Secondary Programs and Issues

Introduction ————————————————————————

The secondary school of today is receiving more attention than at any time since Sputnik in the late 1950s. As the exit school for a majority of American youth, the high school is viewed as the "finishing school" and as the means by which American society is renewed. Unfortunately, when the larger society experiences problems such as those plaguing the nation today, the secondary school is expected to find necessary solutions. When scientists, mathematicians, and technical workers are needed for a rapidly emerging high-tech society, for example, the schools draw criticism because the mathematics and science curriculum is not rigorous enough. Inflation and a stagnant economy mean the schools are not teaching enough economic education. Critics and reformers emerge each generation to undo the reforms of yesterday.

Secondary schools in America are closely wedded to local communities and therefore to public opinion. Because schools reflect the weaknesses as well as the strengths of the larger society, they are caught up in the ebb and flow of continual revitalization.

The secondary school of today is not perfect nor will it ever be in the eyes of society. We can learn from the past, however, and focus on those problems and issues that are important. We can also gain an increased knowledge of how the curriculum of the secondary school is developed and organized. Finally, we can attempt to chart a course for the future of the secondary school so that the secondary school can meet the great expectations society has for it. In the next sections of this chapter, we shall deal with each of the above topics.

Historical Development of the Secondary School —

Although elementary schools were developed for students at public expense from the mid-1600s, the public secondary school did not become a reality for a majority of American youth until late in the nineteenth century.

From the middle of the eighteenth century until the Civil War period the principal instrument of secondary education in the United States was the academy. Benjamin Franklin is credited with the establishment of the first academy, the Philadelphia Academy and Charitable School, opened in 1751.[1] The academy achieved great popularity in New England and the Middle Atlantic States. Although the academy was neither wholly private nor wholly public (unlike the Latin grammar school which was highly selective and private), it did not open the door to all youth in need of a secondary education.

In the mid-1800s, leaders in Massachusetts like Horace Mann were successful in obtaining strong support for public schools. The first high school in the United States was founded in Boston in 1821.

Known as the English Classical School, the school provided a three-year sequence of English, mathematics, history, and science.

The extension of secondary education in the United States was accomplished by state legislation and later by court cases. Again taking the lead, the commonwealth of Massachusetts enacted laws that required towns with five hundred or more families to establish high schools with a ten-month program. Earlier, Massachusetts had required the establishment of elementary schools in towns of fifty families or more and had reorganized the state's responsibility for the preparation of teachers by establishing under Horace Mann's leadership the first state normal school. Massachusetts also passed the first compulsory attendance law in 1852. Today, all states compel students to attend school until a certain age, usually sixteen.

As secondary schools emerged in more and more states, from the mid-1850s to the 1870s, there was great debate as to whether high schools should be provided at public expense. The high school coexisted for a long time with the academy. With a frontier spirit of increased democracy, more and more youth were enrolling in high schools; however, not until the famous Kalamazoo Case in 1874 was the concept of free high school education for all youth firmly established.

The Kalamazoo Case

The Kalamazoo Case resulted when a taxpayer in Kalamazoo, Michigan, challenged the right of the school board to establish a high school with public funds and to hire a superintendent. In 1874, the Supreme Court of Michigan ruled that a school district was not limited to the support of elementary schools but could establish whatever level of schools it wished so long as the voters were willing to pay the taxes. This historic decision affirmed the idea that secondary education was a legitimate part of the program of public schools.

After the Kalamazoo decision, public secondary schools grew in number. The most popular grade-level organization of schools was the eight-four pattern (eight years of elementary school and four of high school). Later, other patterns emerged including the popular six-six pattern (six years of elementary school and six years of high school or secondary school). Not until 1910 was the junior high school established, and a three-level organizational system emerged. The popular organizational pattern then became the grades 1–6 elementary school, 7–9 junior high school, and 10–12 high school. For almost fifty years the elementary, junior high, high school pattern dominated American schools. In the 1960s a new school emerged, the middle school, which was to force a realignment of grade levels in American schools. Although grade patterns vary in the middle school in many school districts, the most common pattern is the grades 6–8 pattern. In the early 1980s, some large school districts, the St. Louis District, for example, that had ignored the junior high school and were still organized in a grades K–8 elementary and 9–12 high school pattern, organized separate grades 6–8 middle schools.

Today, the secondary school is viewed as encompassing the junior high school and senior high school. The middle school, larger in number than the junior high school, has sought its own identity and is considered neither elementary nor secondary. The relaxing of college admissions requirements in the 1960s released many schools from strict adherence to Carnegie unit requirements, especially in the ninth grade, and helped spur the development of middle schools. Other developments in the 1960s, such as overcrowded schools and court-ordered desegregation, helped pave the way for shifting the ninth grade to the high school and bringing the sixth grade into a new grades 6–8 middle school.

It is ironic that in the 1980s, declining enrollment and a call for increased required numbers of courses for secondary students are forcing yet another realignment of grade levels and program change in the secondary school. As in the past, however, the secondary school will make adjustments to reflect changing social needs and emerge as an even stronger force in shaping future generations.

Problems and Issues in the Secondary School ____

High school reform has become a major political and social issue. Studies and commissions have been organized in recent years aimed at reforming the high school. Although people who work in high schools have never lacked advice on how to improve their performance, in the 1980s, reform of the high school became a growth industry.

The tradition of secondary school reform began in the 1890s with a number of committees and commissions organized to examine the high school curriculum, especially its effectiveness in preparing students for college. The Committee of Ten on Secondary Schools, the Committee of Fifteen on Elementary Education, and the Committee on College Entrance Requirements organized in 1893–94, endorsed the idea of pushing high school subjects down into the upper elementary grades (grades 7, 8, and 9).

In 1913, the National Education Association appointed the Commission on the Reorganization of Secondary Education whose report was five years in the making. Their report in 1918 resulted in the famous seven "Cardinal Principles of Education." The report recommended that every subject be reorganized to contribute to the goals expressed in the "Cardinal Principles." Most important, the Commission endorsed the division of secondary education into junior and senior high periods. The Commission recommended that vocational courses be introduced into the curriculum and that a comprehensive program be offered to both junior and senior high students.

The pushing down of the high school program into the upper elementary grades continued to be an issue even as school district after school district reorganized to include the junior high school. By the late 1970s, middle schools had all but replaced junior high schools as the dominant intermediate grade school in the United States.

The high school came under strong attack in the late fifties and early sixties following Sputnik. Although weaknesses in science and mathematics programs were attacked, other areas of the secondary school like foreign language instruction also came under attack. The problem of "why Johnny couldn't read" was perceived primarily to be a problem for the elementary school.

James Conant and others led a movement in the 1950s to expand the high school curriculum to include both vocational and academic courses for students in a unitary, multipurpose school—the comprehensive high school. Conant and others were finally developing the kind of unitary high school recommended in the 1918 report of the NEA Commission on the Reorganization of Secondary Education. Such a comprehensive school would serve as a prototype of a democracy in which various groups could be federated into a larger whole through the recognition of common interests and ideals.[2] The establishment of cooperative federal-state programs for vocational education in 1917 had resulted in separate specialized vocational schools, and that pattern (modeled after the European system) prevailed until the late 1950s.

Recommended Reforms in the 1970s _____

The 1970s proved to be a decade in which serious reforms of the American high school were recommended and, in some cases, attempted. Throughout the land prestigious commissions met to assess the needs of secondary education and to make suggestions for reform. Among those commissions were:

1. The National Association of Secondary School Principals whose report, *American Youth in the Mid-Seventies* (1972), recommended increased "action learning" programs in the community.
2. The President's Science Advisory Committee whose report, *Youth: Transition to Adulthood* (1973), advocated the creation of alternative high schools and occupational high schools.
3. The Institute for the Development of Educational Activities (IDEA) whose report, *The Greening of the High School* (1973), called for a new type of institution for modern students, with an emphasis on individual needs and student choice.
4. The U.S. Department of Education, HEW, whose report *National Panel on High Schools and Adolescent Education* (1975), recommended decentralization of the comprehensive

high school and reduction of the secondary school day to 2-4 hours.

Reflecting these observations and recommendations were a number of innovative secondary schools that emerged and then receded when primary leadership was withdrawn:

Nova High School (Ft. Lauderdale, Florida), an experiment with the application of technology to instructional processes.

Parkway Schools (Philadelphia Pennsylvania), an attempt to move learning out into the community—the "school without walls."

McGavok High School (Nashville, Tennessee), a truely comprehensive school with a broad range of occupational tracks under one roof and tied closely to business interests in the community.

Melbourne High School (Cocoa Beach, Florida), an academic high school with five tracks including "Quest," an advanced placement program in which students could progress to their limits.

Berkeley High Schools (Berkeley, California), employing the "public schools of choice" concept in which parents and students selected their high school by philosophy and purpose.

Adams High School (Portland, Oregon), an experimental school where students participated in the governance of the program thereby learning basic democratic procedures for citizenship.

Typical of the broad goals for education at this period were those advocated by Harold Spears, a long-time advocate of the comprehensive high school (Table 10.1). In addition to many special programs, the actual course offerings of high schools grew extensively as suggested by the English offerings of one high school (Table 10.2).

Around 1974, the picture in secondary education began to change dramatically, and proposals for the expansion of the role of the American high school were no longer heard. Among the major factors causing this reversal were the following:

Declining Enrollment. Between 1970 and 1980, secondary enrollment declined by a full 25 per cent. This decline, which is projected to last until 1992, meant falling teacher-pupil ratios and an increased cost per pupil.

Inflation. By 1974, the inflationary effects of the Vietnam War were in full bloom and taxpayers became painfully aware of the soaring cost of education in a time when the purchasing power of the dollar was shrinking.

Table 10.1
The Goals of Education

1. Learn how to be a good citizen.
2. Learn how to respect and get along with people who think, dress, and act differently.
3. Learn about and try to understand the changes that take place in the world.
4. Develop skills in reading, writing, speaking, and listening.
5. Understand skills and practice democratic ideas and ideals.
6. Learn how to examine and use information.
7. Understand and practice the skills of family living.
8. Learn to respect and get along with people with whom we work and live.
9. Develop skills to enter a specific field of work.
10. Learn how to be a good manager of money, property, and resources.
11. Develop a desire for learning now and in the future.
12. Learn how to use leisure time.
13. Practice and understand the ideas of health and safety.
14. Appreciate culture and beauty in the world.
15. Gain information needed to make job selections.
16. Develop pride in work and a feeling of self-worth.
17. Develop good character and self-respect.
18. Gain a general education.

Source: From a lecture by Harold Spears given at George Peabody College, 1972.

Unionization of Teaching Staffs. Between 1966 and 1977, the number of states recognizing the right of teachers to enter into collective bargaining rose from eleven to thirty. By 1977, eighty per cent of all teachers were members of either the NEA (National Education Association) or the AFT (American Federation of Teachers). Because high school teachers tended to be more senior and therefore more expensive to the taxpayer, they were often identified with the union movement.

Declining Achievement. Throughout the 1970s there were regular media reports of declining achievement as measured by nationally-normed standardized tests such as the SAT (Scholastic Aptitude Test). This was interpreted to mean, in the eyes of the public, that schools were failing.

Table 10.2
The English Curriculum in one Comprehensive High School

English IX	Practical Communication	Acting I
English X	Science Fiction (Depth)	Acting II
English X (AP)	Science Fiction (Survey)	Films—Communications
English XI (AP)	Speech	Creative Writing I
English XII (AP)	Sports Literature (Depth)	Creative Writing II
Secretarial English I	Sports Literature (Survey)	Film Making
Secretarial English II	Techniques of Research	Folklore
Humanities	Women in Literature	American Literature (Focus)
American Dream	Themes: Modern Life	American Literature (Images)
Your America	Eng. as a Second Lang.	Contemporary Literature
American Novel	Reading—Grade 9	English Literature (Past)
Basic English Skills	Reading—Grade 9	English Literature (Modern)
Directed Reading		Journalism

By the late 1970s and early 1980s, the curriculum of the American high school was under attack throughout the nation. School Boards in state after state called for legislation to "focus" the curriculum and eliminate the frills. Among the more conservative elements focused on education, Mortimer Adler's *Paideia Proposal* (1982) became a rallying post.[3] Adler called for a nationwide twelve-year, single-track academic program with virtually no electives and no vocational training.

Symptomatic of the rush to implement the "return to the basics" were the proposals of a special commission in the state of Florida.[4] This commission proposed narrowing the functions of the Florida high school to four tasks, and suggested structuring the graduation standards in the state so that more than 90 per cent of the experiences would be in required subjects (Figure 10.1 and Table 10.3).

Perhaps the greatest issue facing secondary schools in the 1980s is whether the American public is still committed to a system of free public schools. The call for tuition vouchers, and suggestions by business leaders that secondary education can better be offered by private enterprise, are strong evidence that public secondary education does not enjoy the same widespread support it once had. The high-tech society of the 1980s and 1990s will most certainly result in major changes in the secondary school curriculum. Curriculum leaders must not let those changes be dictated entirely by those outside our school systems.

Figure 10.1

The Purpose and Function of Florida's High Schools
Meeting Diverse Needs

(1) To offer an appropriate educational program designed to provide students with necessary skills for earning a living.

(2) To offer a quality general education with an emphasis on literacy, quantitative skills, and science for those students who are undecided about their future.

(3) To provide a strong academic program for students who plan to attend a college or university.

(4) To provide a program of remediation for those students deficient in the basic skills of mathematics, reading, and writing.

Florida's Secondary Schools
A Problem of Considerable Dimensions
The Direction of Changes

In Florida, four broad categories of change are necessary:

(1) The requirement of high standards of education which are dependent on a thorough revision of the high school curriculum.

(2) The enhancement of the incentives and rewards for attracting and retaining high caliber principals and teachers, and the upgrading of requirements for teacher training and certification.

(3) The strengthening of educational funding, with special emphasis on the major disciplines.

(4) The measurement and enhancement of school effectiveness.

Source: Secondary Education: A Report to the Citizens of Florida (Governor's Commission on Secondary Schools for the State of Florida, 1983).

The Curriculum of the Secondary School _____

The curriculum of the secondary school has changed little over the past seventy years. Basically, the high school curriculum consists of a number of courses that students must complete to graduate. "Credits" are given for successful completion of required courses. A student must earn a certain number of credits to graduate. To assure that each student receives a basic education during the high school years certain courses and credit hours are required. Some states and districts also require students to pass a proficiency test to receive a diploma. Recent pressures to tighten up the high school curriculum have resulted in some districts raising the number of required credits in certain disciplines for students to graduate; for example, from two years of required mathematics to three years.

Table 10.3
Proposed Graduation Requirements for Florida High Schools

Graduation Standards

		Credits
4 Years of English	Major concentration: composition and literature	4
3 Years of Mathematics	Including one semester in micro-computer literacy at the 9th grade level	3
3 Years of Science	Two courses must have a laboratory component	3
3 Years of Social Science	1 year-American History	1
	1 year-World History	1
	1 semester-Economics	½
	1 semester-American Government	½
1 Semester of Practical Arts	Selected from the following: typing, business, industrial arts, home economics, vocational education	½
1 Semester of Fine Arts	Selected from the following: music, dance, theater, painting, sculpture	½
1 Semester of Personal Health	Including nutrition, parenting, drug education	½
1 Semester of Physical Education		½
	Requirements	15
	Electives	7
	Total Credits	22

Source: Secondary Education: A Report to the Citizens of Florida (Governor's Commission on Secondary Schools for the State of Florida, 1983).

Since the high school is the last phase of formal schooling for a significant number of young people, the curriculum must include a salable skill for those not going on to higher education. Vocational programs have been introduced to train students for immediate employment. Unfortunately, only one-half of the jobs existing in the 1970s were still around in the 1980s. Moreover, those students with a general education find themselves in need of highly technical skills to work in even the simplest jobs. Secretaries, for instance, must know how to operate word processors, and machine operators and office workers must know how to read computers.

The traditional academic subjects of English, mathematics, science, social studies, and foreign language are still the core courses for preparation of college-bound students in the American high school. University entrance requirements are such that separate courses in each of the major subject divisions must appear on a high school diploma.

English

English instruction and content center on the various elements of communicating in the language: reading, writing, listening, and spelling. The fundamental skill of reading receives, deservedly, the most attention in the school curriculum. The ability to read leads to the ability to comprehend the mass of informational material produced in our modern society.

Writing has received increased attention in schools in recent years. Reports of the National Assessment of Educational Progress indicating that students lack writing skills, coupled with pressures of colleges and universities to improve writing skills, have resulted in new writing requirements for high school students in English classes.

Content in English education focuses on literary selections classified as "valuable" for students. Recently, selections have come under attack from self-styled censors who reject certain literary works for religious or moral reasons.

Social Studies

The term social studies refers to those courses that examine past and present social institutions and society. Geography, civics, American history, world civilization, and courses dealing with problems of democracy dominate the social studies curriculum. Reform in the social studies curriculum has been slow. Attempts at national curriculum projects and other reforms in the social studies have met with little success.

Mathematics

Mathematics in the secondary school has drawn almost as much attention as reading. The "new" math of the 1960s met with great criticism because of content change but apparently had little harmful effect on achievement. Although millions of dollars have been spent on the development of new mathematics programs through the National Science Foundation and National Defense Education Act, the results at improving the ability of American youth to compute and comprehend better in mathematics has not been encouraging. Like reading, the problem seems to stay with us generation after generation.

Science

The traditional program in science in the secondary school consists of a sequence of year-long courses including general science, biology, chemistry, physics, and physiology or advanced biology.

Science programs, like mathematics programs, have come under close scrutiny in recent years. Again, the needs of a high-tech society are dictating a more rigorous science program for American high school youth.

The Arts

The arts include visual arts, music, dance, and theater in the high school. As required credits in English, science, and mathematics are increased, a growing trend has been to eliminate the number of electives available in the arts. The need for well-rounded youth has never been greater, and the arts contribute to the total development of adolescent youth.

Physical Education

Physical education in the high schools has been required of most students, yet many districts are reducing the number of required physical education credits to accommodate the increased requirements in English, science, and mathematics. The need for lifelong sports and the working use of leisure time dictate a continuing need for required physical education programs in the secondary school.

Vocational Education

Vocational education and the practical arts, after two decades of amazing growth, have faced demands for a reassessment of their mission in the 1980s. Business and industrial leaders are calling for better prepared students in the basic academic areas and are suggesting that technical and vocational training be found outside the secondary school.

The Extracurricular Curriculum

The cocurricular or extracurricular curriculum has traditionally consisted of student clubs, sports, student government, and other activities. However, the landmark U.S. Supreme Court case of Tinker v. Des Moines Independent Community School District (1969) and other court cases and legislation have given students equal rights as adults in secondary schools. Rules and regulations must be reasonable. Student government and the student press are now more independent. All of these developments have ushered in a new era in developing the school's extracurricular program.

Organizational Practices in the Secondary School -

The organizational structure of a secondary school is designed to carry out the instructional program. The dominant pattern of organization in most secondary schools is departmentalization. Departmentalization operates under the assumption that the disciplinary construct is the purest form of organizing knowledge. The curriculum is organized around separate disciplines that are taught by teachers in a department such as the mathematics or social studies department.

Scheduling is fairly simple in a departmentalized school. Courses are taught in uniform lengths of time, e.g., 55-minute periods.

For years most secondary schools have operated under the assumption that:

1. The appropriate amount of time for learning a subject is the same uniform period of time, 50 to 60 minutes in length, six or seven periods a day, for 36 weeks out of the year.
2. A classroom group size of 30–35 students is the most appropriate for a wide variety of learning experiences.
3. All learners are capable of mastering the same subject matter in the same length of time. For example, we give everyone the same test on Chapter Five on Friday. We pass everyone from level one of Algebra to level two when June comes.
4. We assume that once a group is formed, the same group composition is equally appropriate for a wide variety of learning activities.
5. We assume that the same classroom is equally appropriate for a wide variety of learning activities. Conference rooms are not provided for teacher-student conferences. Large group facilities are not provided for mass dissemination of materials. Small group rooms are unavailable for discussion activities.
6. We assume that all students require the same kind of supervision.
7. We assume that the same teacher is qualified to teach all aspects of his or her subject for one year.

Operating on those assumptions, we have locked students into an educational egg-crate with thirty students to a cubicle from 8 A.M. to 3 P.M. five days a week. In short, schools operating under those assumptions have existed more for the convenience of teaching than for the facilitation of learning.

Secondary schools today are attempting to break this lockstep approach to instruction. Rigid class sizes, facilities, and fixed schedules are being challenged. Subject matter is also being organized in terms of more than single disciplinary instruction. Core or correlation of subjects, interdisciplinary instruction, and fusion (which provides for the merging of related subjects into a new subject) represent alternative patterns of curriculum organization.

The organizational structure in a secondary school must be flexible enough to allow for groups of different size to serve different functions of individualizing instruction. Scheduling in a secondary school should come after it is determined what kind of instrument is desired; for example, if departmentalization and interdisciplinary teaming are desired, then a flexible schedule should be developed to accommodate those goals. Arrangements should be made to accommodate individual teaching, small groups, large groups, and laboratory-study groups.

Teaming and variable grouping can be designed for a secondary school to build on student needs and teacher talents. Interdisciplinary teaming can facilitate the correlation of subject matter. Common groups of students shared by common groups of teachers with common planning time is necessary for interdisciplinary teaching to succeed.

William Bailey has suggested the following goals for a flexible scheduling pattern in a modern secondary school:[5]

1. variable class size
2. variable time allotments for classes and/or block time periods
3. maximum use of facilities, particularly resource centers, labs, and IMCs
4. selected students may elect seven courses or more
5. multiple teaching assignments, i.e., team or cooperative teaching
6. a weekly schedule is preferable to a routinized daily schedule that, for example, maintains the same class each afternoon during poor times for concentration
7. facilitate independent study and individual study courses
8. provide students with opportunities for individualized, continuous progress learning
9. maximize planning time for teacher and teaching teams— should be around 25 percent
10. enable band and chorus to be included in a regular school day
11. increase the degree to which students are responsible for their own education
12. provide for order in daily attendance
13. provide for orderly but rapid changes adaptable to pep rallies, assemblies, dismissals, and other interruptions
14. provide for proper sequencing of the various types of instruction, i.e., lab following demonstration, small groups following lectures, etc.
15. general flexibility
16. in addition to the intent to accommodate the above, the schedule should make it possible to carry forward present curriculum practices that have proven successful and are crucial to progress

Future Directions of the Secondary School _____

Many believe the high school will disappear before it will change to the dynamic school it should be in shaping young people. Today, many districts are experimenting with alternative secondary schools such as magnet schools and academic and performing arts high schools. Also, special schools have been organized for students who have discipline problems. Athletic programs are also coming under increasing review by school officials who fear interscholastic sports have gotten out of hand.

Perhaps the greatest challenge facing the secondary school today is the attempt to establish its real role in American education. In the early years, the secondary school was viewed as an academic school designed to prepare students for college. Later, the high school assumed a greater function, that of preparing students for the immediate work force. Fed by legislation after World War I, vocational programs were organized in school districts to train students who were not going on to higher education. By the 1950s, high schools assumed yet another function, i.e., to provide a comprehensive curriculum of academic and vocational courses for students under one roof.

By the mid-1980s, the functions of providing students for college and of training for jobs came under attack by numerous groups in the United States. Reeling under pressure to provide better trained and informed young people for high-tech jobs, colleges and secondary schools increased program requirements for their students. Because many vocational programs are training many young people for jobs that are rapidly becoming obsolete, the supporting public is questioning the value of any vocational programs at the secondary level. Since over one-half of our youth do not go on to higher education, large numbers of our youth may face the future with no salable skills and be unsuited for college or technical training. Our country can ill afford to write off one-half of our young people entering the greater society.

Compounding the problem is the increasing number of minority students found in large urban school districts who face language, cultural, family, and economic conditions that prevent them from learning. The experience of compensatory programs does not leave us with great optimism that more money and special programs will make a difference in the achievement of these youngsters.

We do know that we can obtain higher student achievement in secondary schools where the following variables exist:

1. Where there is a high degree of parent involvement.
2. Where there is order and sequence in the curriculum.
3. Where there are high expectations of teachers and the administrative staff.
4. Where maximum time is spent on instruction-time on task.

5. Where there is a strong guidance program and opportunities for tutorial help from peers, parents, and other adults.
6. Where there is structure and discipline existing in the school.
7. Where there are supporting teachers and positive reinforcement from teachers and support staff alike.

A Closing Note on the Secondary School _____

As curriculum persons, the authors are concerned about the trends of the 1980s as they relate to the American high school. In the rush to return to the basics, raise achievement scores, and legislate quality control, we seem to have forgotten a purpose for secondary education that underpinned most planning prior to 1955. That purpose for the secondary school is to foster democracy.

Democracy is a word that was used frequently by Dewey, Bode, Kilpatrick, and Rugg. In its context, these leaders spoke of democracy not as a system of government in which supreme power is vested in the people—although they understood these things—but rather as a way of life where no single group could dominate others on the basis of class distinction, heredity, or privilege. These educators, whom we cherish and whom we quote so often, perceived a danger in our way of life which pitted social equality against economic competition. If capitalism and competition became dominant, they reasoned, basic human rights might be trampled. Schools, according to Dewey, "were the institution best organized to serve Democracy's cause."

The point we are making is that we have lost sight of a very important value in recent times—Democracy. *Education throughout this century has been the key response to repressive social relations.*

> The educational system, perhaps more than any other contemporary social institution, has become the laboratory in which competing solutions to the problems of personal liberation and social equality are tested and the arena in which social struggles are fought out.[6]

In short, Democracy is *the* historic value or social ideal which has given direction to our educational aims. If education in public schools is our primary instrument to shape our destiny as a society, then should not our curriculum be planned with essentials first and refinements second?

What is the future of the secondary school? Perhaps the secondary school is destined to become less of a finishing school and more of a transitional school designed to send students on to higher education or to highly skilled technical jobs in a computer society. Redesigning a static curriculum to accomplish that task will be the greatest challenge facing curriculum workers in the last two decades of this century.

In concluding this chapter on secondary education, the authors present the reader with some curriculum problems that are common and recurrent:

1. Throughout the nation, secondary schools are attempting to define the essential "Core" of the curriculum. What process could be used to define this essential program?
2. Public pressure on the high schools to produce test scores (SATs) has meant that principals and curriculum leaders must organize for testing. What can be done to improve test scores in a school?
3. Nationally, about sixty percent of all students do *not* go on to a four-year college after high school graduation. How would you define the school program for that noncollege-bound majority?
4. Teacher unionism has increased dramatically during the past decade at the high school level. What should be the relationship between staff curriculum workers and union representatives in a building?

Summary

The secondary school today is receiving increased attention. Because it is the exit school for many American youth, the secondary school is expected to find solutions for many of the problems of society by training individuals to make necessary changes to improve society.

Secondary schools have experienced their share of reform movements in education. Tracing the development of the secondary school, one can see where numerous committees and commissions were established to improve the high school curriculum. Many of the reform movements, however, were aimed less at improving the high school, than in preparing high school youth for college or specialized jobs needed in society.

Although most secondary schools are organized in a uniform pattern (departmentalization), some secondary schools have tried different scheduling patterns to allow for more flexibility in the instructional program.

The future of the public secondary school is threatened by many forces in the 1980s. Educational leaders must begin to give direction to the secondary school. They must not leave decisions about that direction to politicians and special interest groups.

Notes

1. Peter Oliva, *The Secondary School Today,* 2nd ed. (Scranton, Pennsylvania: Intertext Educational Publishers, 1972), p. 15.

2. Daniel Tanner and Laurel Tanner, *Curriculum Development: Theory Into Practice,* 2nd ed. (New York: Macmillan, 1980), pp. 446–447.

3. Mortimer Adler, *The Paideia Proposal: An Educational Manifesto* (New York: Macmillan, 1982).

4. *Secondary Education: A Report to the Citizens of Florida* (Governor's Commission on Secondary Schools for the State of Florida, 1983).

5. William J. Bailey, *Managing Self-Renewal in Secondary Education* (Englewood Cliffs, New Jersey: Educational Technology Publications, 1975), pp. 154–155.

6. Samuel Bowles and Herbert Gintis, *Schooling in Capitalist America* (New York: Basic Books, 1970), p. 5.

Suggested Learning Activities ⎯⎯⎯⎯⎯⎯⎯⎯⎯⎯

1. Trace the development of the secondary school in the United States.

2. What are the major issues and problems facing secondary schools today? How do they compare with issues and problems found in secondary schools in the past fifty years?

3. The curriculum for the secondary school has often been described as dull and irrelevant. How would you reorganize the present curriculum of the secondary school to fit the needs of a rapidly emerging high-tech society in the United States?

4. Develop a flexible schedule for a medium-size high school that will include provisions for both departmentalization and team instruction.

5. Prepare a paper that will describe the high school found in the year 2000.

Books to Review ⎯⎯⎯⎯⎯⎯⎯⎯⎯⎯

Armstrong, David, and Savage, Tom. *Secondary Education: An Introduction.* New York: Macmillan, 1983.

Bolton, W. Warren. *History of Education and Culture in America.* Englewood Cliffs, New Jersey: Prentice-Hall, 1983.

Henson, Kenneth. *Secondary Teaching Methods.* Lexington, Massachusetts: D.C. Heath and Company, 1981.

Kim, Eugene, and Kellough, Richard. *A Resource Guide for Secondary School Teaching: Planning for Competence,* 3rd ed. New York: Macmillan Publishing Company, 1983.

Wiles, Jon, and Bondi, Joseph. *Principles of School Administration: The Real World of Leadership in Schools.* Columbus, Ohio: Charles E. Merrill, 1983.

Part Four
Curriculum
Prospectives

Chapter Eleven
Political Dimensions of Curriculum Development

Compared to the previous two decades, the remainder of this century will call for a different orientation by those persons in leadership positions in schools. The 1980s and 1990s will not be an extension of the 1960s and 1970s for a myriad of reasons. The overriding variable in this new mix, however, is that conditions of scarcity have increased the political dimensions of curriculum development to the point where such a factor must be acknowledged by planners. In many of the 14,000 school districts in this country there is a tendency toward random, in some cases even counterproductive, change and this tendency is a critical element in any effort to improve school programs.

The reader may wonder what is so new about the presence of random change in education. Certainly, such undirected change has always been a part of an open public education system where the public has direct access to the decision-making process. The real change in the condition, in the 1980s, is in the *degree* of political activity to be found rather than in the mere presence of influential change. The cause of this new increase in political change, if it can be clearly identified, lies in the growing discrepancy between what is expected of schools and what can actually be delivered by schools.

The Changing Environment _____

During the 1960s, particularly during the Great Society era of the Johnson administration, there was a belief in public education as a powerful tool for social improvement. The waterfall of money provided to public education during this period through "entitlement" programs seemed to indicate that (a) education could truly serve all learners in an equal manner, (b) that educational services should be comprehensive and "cradle to grave" if possible, (c) that any set of learners deemed not equal could be compensated for their deficiencies, and (d) that schools could serve as the primary vehicle for social adaptation to change and construction of desired social conditions. These hopeful assumptions placed public education in a central role in the American society and, in doing so, increased the value of the institution of the school. In the 1960s, the school was *the* basic vehicle for both personal and social improvement.

Events of the 1960s and 1970s challenged this new role for education in the American society. The Civil Rights movement challenged the previously held assumption that college was the universal extension of the twelve-year public education curriculum by presenting the school planners with a more diverse population to be educated. The Vietnam War raised serious questions about the purpose of a capitalist society in a world full of poverty. A long-range recession beginning in the early 1970s challenged the abilities of a society to support both a massive military capability and a universal education program. Finally, scandals in government, notably Watergate, undermined popular support for social planning and for public leaders in general. Politicians, law-enforcement officials, and even school leaders became suspect in their tactics and in their strategies of leading.

All of these events, and others, served to introduce a new condition into American education that has become characterized by financial scarcity, public suspicion of leadership, and an obscured mission for public schools. During the late 1970s this condition was perceived as a temporary phenomenon, one of the many recurring cycles in the history of public education. By the early 1980s, however, the scope and perversity of this new condition became more obvious. Eight years of recession and inflation, a declining birth rate, political conservatism, and an almost unbelievable simplicity in the public's vision of purpose in education provided educational planners with new parameters for curriculum development in the last years of this century.

If such conditions are to be with us for the next ten years, and the authors believe that they may, then developing school programs will be a different kind of activity than they were in past years. Added to the "if-then" logic of the curriculum cycle will be a political dimension that is not logical. Important questions about the development process must be asked by curriculum planners: Who is really in control of schools? What do we value for schooling and why? How are decisions to be made about the many choices available to us? How can planners access the "real" resources in education for the betterment of experiences for children? The authors feel that if conditions in public education have really changed, curriculum planners should understand these changes and play the "game" with a "full deck" of cards.

What Makes Curriculum Political?

It is competition that makes curriculum political; competition for authority and control, competition for scarce resources, competition for the primacy of values. In two short decades American education has gone from an era of abundance to an era of scarcity, and such scarcity has bred a new and fierce competition in education which is regularly "played out" in the curriculum arena.*

There are two brands of curriculum politics that vie for the control of schools: one occurs on the inside among professional educators, and the other is found outside of schools between professional educators and the public. An example of professional competition can be found in the continuing struggle to define purpose in education and

*For a full treatment of this topic see David K. Wiles, Jon W. Wiles, and Joseph C. Bondi, *Practical Politics for School Administrators* (Boston: Allyn and Bacon, 1981).

schools. Long an issue at the philosophical level, this concern has now become a judicial and legal issue. State legislatures mandate fixed curriculum, essential coursework, and skills; at the same time, courts define the access to that curriculum and the special conditions for the implementation of that curriculum. To speak in terms of traditional reference points, such as "liberal arts" education or "humanistic" curriculums, no longer accurately describes the essence of the curriculum development process or even the issues at stake.

During the 1980s, a special professional interaction can be anticipated between formal educational leaders like principals and curriculum personnel and spokespersons for teachers' organizations. Although the 1970s witnessed a phenomenal rise in the number of teachers belonging to a professional association, the coming decade will see the refinement of the management-union relations. Curriculum leaders, because they are in "staff" positions, should fully understand the concepts of management and union, especially the process of "collective negotiation" as the method of formalizing relationships in schools.

Collective negotiations in the 1980s will reflect the general type of relationship between school officials and teachers in classrooms. Specific bargaining issues will illuminate key aspects of personnel management as spelled out in the "contract." Typical items for such negotiation include salary, health benefits, sick leave policy, school calendars, and termination procedures. In the 1980s other items may include class size, compensation for committee work, duty-free work days, policies on teacher assignment, teacher involvement in textbook selection, and teacher participation in budget development and resource allocation. Obviously, the curriculum leader must know the "contract" to provide authoritative leadership.

The American Association of School Administrators in its monthly magazine, *The School Administrator,* provides the following recommendations for school leaders involved in the development of collective bargaining agreements:[1]

1. Retain self-control. Negotiation sessions can be exasperating. the temptation may come to get angry and fight back when intemperate accusations are made or when the straw that broke the camel's back is hurled on the table.
2. Avoid off-the-record comments. Actually nothing is off the record. Innocently made remarks have a way of coming back to haunt their author. Be careful to say only what you are willing to have quoted.
3. Don't be overcandid. Inexperienced negotiators may, with the best of intentions, desire to lay the cards on the table face up in the mistaken notion that everybody fully understands the other and utter frankness is desired. Complete candor doesn't always serve the best interests of productive negotiation. This suggestion is not a plea for duplicity; rather, it is a recommendation for prudent and discriminating utterances.

4. Be long on listening. Usually a good listener makes a good negotiator. It is wise to let your adversaries do the talking, at least in the beginning.

5. Don't be afraid of a little heat. Discussions sometimes generate quite a bit of heat. Don't be afraid of it. It never hurts to let the opposition sound off even when you may be tempted to hit back.

6. Watch the voice level. A wise practice is to keep the pitch of the voice down even though the temptation may be strong to let it rise under the excitement of emotional stress.

7. Keep flexible. One of the skills of good negotiators is the ability to shift position a bit if the positive gain can thus be accomplished. An obstinate adherence to one position or point of view, regardless of the ultimate consequences of that rigidity, may be more of a deterrent than an advantage.

8. Refrain from giving a flat "no." Especially in the earlier stages of negotiation it is best to avoid giving a flat "no" answer to a proposition. It doesn't help to work yourself into a box by being totally negative too early in the game.

9. Give to get. Negotiation is the art of giving and getting. Concede a point to gain a concession. That's the name of the game.

10. Work on the easier items first. Settle the least controversial things first. Leave the tougher items until later in order to avoid an early deadlock.

11. Respect your adversary. Respect those who are seated on the opposite side of the table. Assume that their motives are as sincere as your own, at least until proven otherwise.

12. Be patient. If necessary, be willing to sit out tiresome tirades. Time has a way of being on the side of the patient negotiator.

13. Avoid waving red flags. Some statements irritate teachers and merely heighten their antipathies. Find out what these are and avoid their use.

14. Let the other side win some victories. Each team has to win some victories. A shutout may be a hollow gain in negotiation.

15. Negotiation is a way of life. Obvious resentment to the fact that negotiation is here to stay weakens the effectiveness of the negotiator. The better part of wisdom is to adjust to it and become better prepared to use it as a tool of interstaff relations.

Competition between the professional educators and the public or community can occur in any number of arenas for any number of purposes. There may be controversy about cultural imprinting, the communist menace, teaching evolution, sex education in schools, the use of computers, or even specific curriculum materials. These types of concerns, in practice, go to the heart of professional policy-making autonomy and can be highly threatening to the real or perceived authority of school leaders. In the 1980s, political compromises resulting from such competition for control will often fail to address the real value issues at stake. A long-term process of challenge-controversy-compromise can lead to a hybrid curriculum; i.e., teaching evolution and a Bible-interpreted version of biology simultaneously to avoid conflict.

The upshot of this new and aggressive competition in curriculum development is a series of political behaviors that can detract from the school's program for children. As educators become "camps of opposing values," or align themselves with various lay groups for special purposes, the possibilities of finding an operational consensus for curriculum development diminishes. Emotional rhetoric tends to replace concrete meaning, and political compromise acts to deemphasize moral identification with any particular issue.

Resources

In addition to general competition over competing values, it is probable that many key educational and curricular decisions in the 1980s and 1990s will be restricted by a lack of resources. It is very important that curriculum leaders understand and acknowledge this general condition of availability of resources and the limits that such scarcity of resources can place on the process of curriculum development.

Limited resources can be described on a continuum ranging from abundance to nonexistence with five major intervals. Abundance might be represented by the "feast" days of the Great Society in the 1960s. Because of the abundance of resources, conflict or competition in such an environment was handled through simple diversification or by adding more resources (a program for everyone). Few school districts today can be characterized as abundant, but some still exist in the mid-1980s.

A second condition finds an initial shortage of resources that is thought to be critical. In such cases the school or district takes on an efficiency orientation; competition for resources, if it exists at all, is channeled through the process of deciding how things are to be accomplished because of the condition. Many school districts in the United States came to the growing awareness that things were changing in the early 1980s and assumed an efficiency coloration.

A third resource condition is one of drastic curtailment, a condition presently facing many school districts that have seen a rapid decline in enrollment. In such a situation, programs and even people are cut back (reduction in force) and competition becomes keen for basic resources and survival. In this stage, also, there is usually a great deal of attention given to what constitutes the "program core" or essentials.

A fourth condition is one of temporary unavailablity of resources. The school or district is asked to operate without resources for a short time (no more paper this year). Under such conditions there is a natural tendency to question the abilities of leadership since this change appears to have occurred because of faulty planning. Often, the environment in this condition is volatile with the rank-and-file workers wanting to assume self-governance or, at least, to replace their immediate supervisors.

Finally, there is the condition where no resource base exists. While a temporary shortage holds hope for a better day, this condition threatens the very existence of the organization. In private school education the school closes. In public schools (as in Michigan in the 1980s), there is a legal crisis and usually a very inadequate compromise for continued education. If a school district goes bankrupt or is unable to meet state law for a minimum number of required days, decision-making is irrational from an educational standpoint.

The danger for curriculum planners in the next fifteen years is that resource shortages, whether minor, temporary, or permanent, promote a simplicity of thinking about complex issues. Said in another way, it is possible that value issues can become a tinderbox in an environment of resource scarcity. Under such conditions, institutional concerns may avoid basic value issues and make educational decisions on the basis of economics alone. While such decisions definitely de-emphasize competition and potential conflict, they may not be in the best interests of schoolchildren served by the curriculum. The curriculum leader, in such cases, will face a severe test in deciding when and how to advocate the best interests of students for whom the curriculum is designed and implemented.

Understanding Budgets

In assessing the resource base of the school or district in which he or she works, the curriculum leader must become familiar with the budget. In many ways, budgets record the outcome of political struggles and curricular competition. An important task for any curriculum leader is to secure the resources needed to make program improvement a reality. Money is the fuel of modern curriculum development.

A strange phenomenon in American education is that educators think the budget is not their concern. Budgets, it seems, have something to do with boards of education, levy passings, and business managers. In fact, budgets are central to most decision-making in education and certainly reflect the values of schools and districts. Curriculum leaders should follow the budgeting process closely and understand the special language of this area.

Once budgets are established at the school site, only about five percent of the money is discretionary. Curriculum leaders need to understand, therefore, that the time to compete for monies is *prior* to the delegation of funds to the school level; budgets should never be tied to direct local school concerns but to ideas and programs implemented at the school site. A critical task for curriculum leaders is to transform abstract budget concepts into practical meanings *before* particular budget issues are decided.

The language of the budget is subtle but it reveals the political dimensions of the environment. Equality, for instance, speaks of a uniform distribution of monies. Equity, by contrast, speaks of "catch-up" compensatory distributions of funds. An "incremental" process of developing budgets means that, realistically, the budget base will not be altered and long-term inequities will remain. A "zero-based" budget, on the other hand, means that previously committed funds may be released for redistribution if they cannot be justified in terms of present needs. Lump sum allocations of money allow discretion by the curriculum leader to spend as needed in areas of choice. Categorical funding, by contrast, limits the ability of the leader to use funds except in pre-scribed ways.

A final point about budgets in a scarcity-oriented environment is that very careful accounting will be a political necessity. Not only is recordkeeping a means of communicating and building a case for future budgets, it can also prevent the curriculum leader from suffering the severe consequences of mismanagement of funds in hard times. A few guidelines would include:

1. Always issue receipts for money received.
2. Deposit all monies in a real bank account.
3. Expend all money by check if possible.
4. Keep receipts for all expenditures.
5. Prepare monthly and yearly financial statements.
6. Audit your accounts annually and share a "blind copy" of the audit with your administrative superior.

The Players

In times of resource scarcity it is important that curriculum leaders know the players and some possible problems with each signifi-cant group in the school district. Among the most important groups, from a political perspective, are the board of education, central office personnel, community groups, and teacher organizations. Each of these groups interacts with curriculum leaders in value-laden and potentially competitive areas of operation.

School boards, despite eloquent expressions of a desire to serve all, are typically representative of certain social, economic, or political groups. Boards are best thought of as a political interest group who have sought election for some purpose.* Time will be well spent reviewing

*For a thorough treatment of this topic see Jon Wiles and Joseph Bondi, *The School Board Primer* (Boston: Allyn and Bacon, 1984).

the voting positions on crucial issues before the board as well as voting coalitions on certain issues. From such an analysis it may be possible to determine what individual board members value and how consistent the total board has been in support of certain kind of issues. Finally, it is important for the curriculum leader to know how the board interacts with the superintendent, principals, and teacher representatives. Do board members, for example, intervene on behalf of individual teachers on certain kinds of value questions?

The central office, like the school board, bears watching and knowing in times of resource scarcity. In traditional districts the central office staff will operate as a bureaucracy with all personnel loyalty oriented upward to immediate superiors. Expect actions in such an environment to be mostly "by the book" and with a great deal of efficiency. There are, however, at least three other common patterns that would alter relationships: a paternalistic regime overseen by a father figure; a confederation where functions or turf have been divided and "feudal lords" reign; and a pluralistic administration where, due to change and stress, old organizations have broken down and coalitions form around specific issues. This last form is most common where severe resource shortages are present.

Obviously, each of these four central office patterns would call for different and unique tactics and strategies for successful communication about curriculum concerns. Curriculum leaders need to see the connection between personnel, organization patterns, and the ability to gain resources for school programs. Identifying key individuals, in certain contexts, and "reading" the organization in which one works is a necessary skill in the 1980s and beyond.

Community groups would include parents, students, and organized interest groups that interact with the school. These "noneducators" are regularly involved in school matters in a political way and tend to become more involved as resources become scarce.

Parents are important because they are the chief recipients of school programming through their children and because they are the opinion leaders for the school in the community. Additionally, because the home accounts for much of the variation in pupil achievement, parents must be considered partners in helping students benefit from the planned curriculum.

Students are not as vocal today as they were in the 1960s, but they have demonstrated their ability to resist changes and to advocate programs they favor. As a communication medium for building support for any program, students represent an unparalleled conduit. At a minimum, curriculum leaders should consider student opinion as a catalyst for criticism and negative opinion to prescribed curriculum changes in the 1980s and 1990s.

A new force in the 1980s is the political action committee (PAC) which represents an organized and highly aggressive community interest group. As resources become scarce, PACs lobby for special programs and perceived interests and these efforts are backed with substantial money and political influence. Look for community interest groups to take a stand on almost anything with a label: integration, sex education, minimal competencies. An important consideration for the coming fifteen years is that such groups will rarely be easy to understand by traditional criteria (liberal vs conservative); rather, they will select causes situationally and bring pressure to bear on school personnel as a primary tactic.

Promoting Change in an Era of Instability ————

Although the topic of change was addressed in Chapter 6, it is important to look at the subject in light of anticipated increases in political activity during the 1980s and beyond. If curriculum leaders are to promote improved instructional experiences for students, they must understand how such promotion can occur in an era of political and financial instability.

A general observation about promoting instructional change in the 1980s and 1990s is that curriculum leaders must have realistic expectations. Human nature being what it is, it is unlikely that many school personnel will be inclined to change during the first stage of a growing scarcity. To the contrary, the rational approach to change, if-then logic, will soon give way to a more political logic of "what's in it for me" or to a "trading mentality." Said in another way, under scarcity conditions most people will not "own" a proposal to change for fear that it might jeopardize existing resource bases. They may, however, respond to a "payback" or trading mentality to secure their position. Below are some reasons why people will regularly resist change:

1. Fear—the individual has had a previous experience with the change that was unpleasant, or the individual possesses a distorted knowledge about the change, or the individual fears failure in attempting the change.
2. Logical conservatism—the individual has learned from similar experience that such change is undesirable, or the individual is unable to see how the change will benefit him or her in light of his or her information about the change.
3. Previous obligations—the individual sees this change or growth opportunity in conflict with previous obligations or understandings.
4. High risk—the individual assesses that such change may have a price in terms of lost prestige, status, possession, or so forth that does not warrant the risk of trying.
5. Lack of identification—the individual may not be able to see that the change or experience has anything to do with his or her needs.

6. Awareness level—the individual may not be able to consider the change or experience because habit or tradition prevents the full analysis of the situation.[2]

Some specific observations about change in a political climate may help the reader envision how his or her role could be altered in times of resource scarcity:

1. Change seems to occur in distinct stages and people become involved in change efforts according to their willingness to change. Figure 11.1 outlines a bell-shaped curve for innovation adoption in school settings. The message for a curriculum leader in an era of instability probably, is: focus on those groups that hold promise of change and do not squander valuable resources on those most likely to resist any change.
2. The change process is always more effective when "showing" is used instead of "telling." The key to being persuasive with colleagues in an environment of scarce resources seems to be a demonstration of a better way through small-scale experiments or pilot efforts. Below, the reader will find a list of observations thought to improve the chances of overcoming resistance to change:

    1. Resistance will be less if administrators, teachers, board members, and community leaders feel that the project is their own— not one devised and operated by outsiders.
    2. Resistance will be less if the project clearly has wholehearted support from top officials of the system.
    3. Resistance will be less if participants see the change as reducing rather than increasing their present burdens.
    4. Resistance will be less if the project accords with values and ideals that have long been acknowledged by participants.

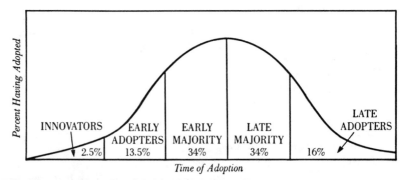

Figure 11.1 Stages of Adoption

Source: Reprinted by permission from *Adoption of New Ideas and Practices* by Herbert F. Lionberger © 1961 by The Iowa State University Press, Ames, Iowa 50010.

     5. Resistance will be less if the program offers the kind of new experience that interests participants.

     6. Resistance will be less if participants feel that their autonomy and their security are not threatened.

     7. Resistance will be less if participants have joined in diagnostic efforts leading them to agree on the basic problem and to feel its importance.

     8. Resistance will be less if the project is adopted by consensual group decision.

     9. Resistance will be reduced if proponents are able to empathize with opponents to recognize valid objections, and take steps to relieve unnecessary fears.

    10. Resistance will be reduced if it is recognized that innovations are likely to be misunderstood and misinterpreted, and if provision is made for feedback of perceptions of the project and for further clarification as needed.

    11. Resistance will be reduced if participants experience acceptance, support, trust, and confidence in their relations with one another.

    12. Resistance will be reduced if the project is kept open to revision and reconsideration if experience indicates that changes would be desirable.

    13. Readiness for change gradually becomes a characteristic of certain individuals, groups, organizations, and civilizations.[3]

3. A third point worthy of observation is that ownership must somehow be transferred from the curriculum leader to others by making a personal disassociation with the change. Curriculum leaders in the 1960s made their reputations by implementing new and innovative school programs. In the 1980s, any change effort identified with reputation-building or resource solidification will have a diminished chance of succeeding.

4. Finally, despite the new sophistication and heavy identification with professional organizations in the 1970s, most classroom teachers are still incapable of perceiving comprehensive curriculum change. A difficult task for the curriculum leader of the 1980s will be to "relate" any change to the anticipated benefits at the classroom level. Only in this manner, particularly in an era of scarcity, will a consensus for changing be achieved.

Curriculum Issues in a Political Era _____

While many basic curriculum issues have been present in American education for over a century, a new era of resource scarcity and increased political behavior may bring such issues to the forefront of curriculum planning. Even if curriculum leaders are unable to resolve these pressing issues, they should be aware of their personal and professional position on them; an inability to take a stand on critical issues could paralyze the instructional improvement efforts of a district and severely limit the leadership capacity of those in curriculum and instruction.

The sheer number of issues present in the 1980s and 1990s may prove challenging to those in leadership positions. While resource scarcity is driving a new competition between programs, older notions of mission and role are breaking down or being eroded by events. The traditional liberal arts preparation of the public school curriculum is presently caught between an economically-driven desire to teach "minimal competencies" and an opposing force to expand the curriculum to meet the changing environment of a technological society. While legislators contemplate laws to guarantee that all students possess the primary skills that are essential to social survival, teachers daily face students who have been raised with "outer space" in their heads and a comfortable acceptance of the coming "high tech" society of the next century. During the 1970s, environmental pressures of an economic and a political sense were great enough to prevent curriculum leaders from pursuing the wide horizons of the future. Instead, much attention in curriculum development was given to basic competencies and skills. In the final analysis, in the 1970s and early 1980s, cost became the final criterion for program development. In many respects, indeed, our computer-age children rode "the stagecoach" into the future in our schools.

During the later 1980s, the authors believe, this myopic posture will haunt curriculum planners in the public schools. Students and their parents, suffering under this fiscal stagnation and intellectual vise, will seek new outlets for learning. Some will join the regular flow to private education, enhancing the possibility of a new caste system in this nation. More probable, however, will be a growing dependence on the personal computer as a supplement, and perhaps even a substitute, to the regular school curriculum. According to a recent estimate, in 1982 some 100 companies sold nearly three million personal computers at a cost of nearly five billion dollars.[4] These marvelous instruments that can calculate, draw, sing, and even speak to students were purchased, in many cases, to give a son or daughter the "edge" in school. It is only a short step from this posture to seeing the basic curriculum in school as totally wasteful of the many hours devoted to it, thus breaking the monopoly of the school as "a learning place."

Curriculum planners, who have already experienced "computer" presure from the parents of "gifted" students in the 1980s, can expect more of the same from all parents as the realization grows that "computers are for real." However, the application of these wonderful devices to learning basic skills in school settings will not suffice for meeting public expectations. The personal computer is a potential socratic tutor for each child, not an extension of the typewriter and textbook! Ahead, in most school districts in this nation, is a growing debate between those wishing for a fixed curriculum with predictable (and controlled) outcomes and those wishing to individualize the learning process. The inability to clarify a position on this emerging issue will de facto be a "decision by indecision" for the curriculum leader.

Another key issue still to be decided by educators is the scope of their responsibilities to children in terms of the program offered. In the years of the Great Society, a tremendous commitment was made to provide all students with access and opportunity for learning. If students were unable to get to school, they should be transported. If students were hungry when they arrived, they should be fed. If students were not ready for learning, they should be compensated and enriched. These were lofty aspirations that have struggled to become programmatic realities during the past twenty years. The addition of special education legislation, notably P.L.94–142, completed the promise of a universal and comprehensive program of public education.

Fiscal realities and political priorities have badly undermined the implementation of such programs during the 1980s, yet the rationale for such programs remains unchallenged; there are people in our society who require assistance and the school is the natural vehicle for providing such help. Should the schools take up the societal "slack" to combat the disintegrating family, child abuse and neglect, or the basic provision of food and shelter? What are the consequences if the school fails to act? These are unresolved questions that will return for debate in the late 1980s and early 1990s. Educators, particularly curriculum planners, cannot abdicate professional opinion on such important issues.

Besides the redefining of the mission of the school, there will also be a redefinition of basic roles in education in the near future. As resource shortages bring political activity, it is unlikely that curriculum leaders can remain aloof from the debates and struggles. During the 1970s, for example, many teachers, principals, and curriculum leaders were challenged to define the nature of a "professional" during teacher strikes. To some, a sign of professionalism was to stay in school and "be with the kids." To others, professional behavior was defined as the courage to walk away from school buildings in order to "upgrade the profession." These kinds of issues, asking really whether school leaders can define the meaning of "professional" in education, will be commonplace in the 1980s.

One of the most difficult decisions for curriculum leaders will be the question of how much they should become involved in the politics of curriculum development. Are there areas of professional expertise that cannot be negotiated away or compromised? Should curriculum leaders actively "politic" for certain school programs and, if so, what limits are there on such behaviors? Is it acceptable for curriculum personnel to form coalitions of expedience in an effort to gain better programs for children?

There will probably be some very tough issues dealing with public involvement in education during the coming years. How can educators, and particularly curriculum leaders, combat the highly organized and well-financed political action committees? How can a representative input be gained from the parents of all children rather than from only those with the time and ability to bring pressure to bear on the school? How can public school leaders utilize the resources and expertise of industry without abdicating responsibility or adopting a "training for industry" mentality? How can schools attract and retain competent teachers who, for so long, have been shut out of the decision-making process in education?

Another set of issues will obviously revolve around the legislation and financing of education. The tug-of-war for control between state education agencies and local education agencies can be expected to continue into the 1980s and early 1990s. These battles are fiscal in nature and concern the results of fiscal effort. As states pick up more and more of the cost of schooling, it can be anticipated that they will press their constitutional right for control of education. Unfortunately, the past ten years have seen a series of poor and bad laws passed by state legislatures in an effort to regulate outcomes. Curriculum leaders can and should play a larger role in this legal–fiscal process. In many states in the 1980s and 1990s, curriculum leaders will stand at the "eye of the storm" in trying to rationalize either change or the status quo.

Finally, curriculum planners will be pressed by issues that reflect how change is to occur in schools. Certainly, there must be some easing of a "plan under pressure" environment. Such conditions not only foster a "reductionist" mentality in terms of curriculum experiences for children but, all too often, a win-at-all-cost pattern emerges as well. School districts that make dramatic test score gains in short periods should be highly suspect in light of the similarity of most school programs in the United States, and curriculum leaders who participate in such "scoring games" can expect a rapid decline in their professional status.

In summary, a political era will bring not only the opportunity for true professional behavior and leadership, but also excessive opportunism. The primary criterion for ethical concern is the open recognition of potential excesses and a continuous discussion of unethical possibilities by those involved in school governance. What is desirable in the next fifteen years is purposeful improvement of school programs, a continuation of a balanced program for school learners, a shared but not abdicated decision-making process, and an honest methodology for conducting school work. The political dimensions of curriculum development are real, the responsibilities of the position of curriculum leader are awesome.

Summary ―――――――――――――――――――――――――

The authors believe that a general resource shortage in education, begun in the 1970s, will continue until at least the turn of the next century. This condition will influence the process of curriculum development with the most notable change being an increase in political activity in schools. Overcoming random or unproductive changes and guiding purposeful improvement of school programs present leaders with a challenge for the 1980s and 1990s.

During the 1960s ambitious goals were established for the role of education in the American society. While events of the 1970s and early 1980s have sidetracked fulfillment of this role, aspirations for education remain high. A reduction of resources for education, coupled with such high aspirations, means increased competition among programs in schools for resources and even survival.

During this decade such competition will occur between educators and between educators and outside community groups. The relationship between formal (status) leaders and teacher groups will mark major internal competition, and competition between professional educators and outside groups will be highlighted by arrangements with political action committees.

Leaders in curriculum will need to acknowledge the realities of this resource shortage and understand how it will influence curriculum development. In particular, the language of the budget will provide clues about the relative position of various groups and programs.

New change strategies will be called for in this era. Change efforts will be limited, sometimes "trade" oriented, and focused on those who wish to see change occur. Curriculum leaders must work to disassociate their personal reputations from these professional efforts.

Political conditions in schools will push many historic issues to the forefront. Among the issues which may pressure curriculum leaders are the new technologies of learning, social conditions in the nation such as family support systems, maintaining a professional stance in a consistent manner on multiple issues, and rationalizing programs and change before the public.

The 1980s and 1990s will, undoubtedly, present persons in curriculum leadership roles with many opportunities for both ethics and excess while managing school programs.

Notes ―――――――――――――――――――――――――――

1. American Association of School Administrators, *The School Administrators and Negotiations* (Washington, D.C., AASA 1968), pp. 57–58.
2. David K. Wiles, Jon Wiles, and Joseph Bondi, *Practical Politics for School Administrators* (Boston: Allyn and Bacon, 1981), p. 72. Reprinted by permission.

3. Ibid., p. 69.
4. *Time*, 121, 1 (January 3, 1983).

Suggested Learning Activities ──────────

1. Develop a list of those events that are making the decision-making environment in schools political.
2. Of the promises made for education by Great Society programs of the 1960s, which have been most successful? Which have not been kept?
3. What authority and which responsibilities do you believe that curriculum leaders should not allow to be "negotiated" away during the 1980s?
4. Using the four central office patterns found in this chapter, develop a list of tactics and strategies that you believe would be most successful in gaining resources for the curriculum in each situation.
5. The challenge of the personal computer will bring changes in schools in the 1980s. Develop a list of the ways this tool might be applied to improve the curriculum.

Books to Review ──────────

Easton, David. *A Systems Analysis of Political Life*. New York: John Wiley and Sons, 1965.

Johns, Roe; Morphet, Edgar; and Alexander, Kern. *The Economics and Financing of Education*. 4th ed. Englewood Cliffs: Prentice-Hall, Inc. 1983.

Katz, Michael. *Class, Bureaucracy, and Schools*. New York: Praeger Press, 1971.

Kimbrough, Ralph. *Political Power and Educational Decision-Making*. Chicago: Rand-McNally, 1964.

Mosher, E. and Wagoner, J., eds. *The Changing Politics of Education*. Berkeley: McCutchan Publishing Co. 1978.

Sarason, Seymour. *The Culture of the School and the Problem of Change*. Boston: Allyn and Bacon, 1971.

Wildavsky, Aaron. *The Politics of the Budgetary Process*. 3rd ed. Boston: Little, Brown, 1979.

Wiles, David. *Energy, Weather, and Schools: Chronology of a Decision Crisis*. Lexington: Heath, 1979.

Wiles, David; Wiles, Jon; and Bondi, Joseph. *Practical Politics for School Administrators*. Boston: Allyn and Bacon, 1981.

Chapter Twelve
Curriculum Designs: Alternatives for the Future

During this century, differing opinions on fundamental questions concerning education have led to repeated efforts to change the form of the American school. Throughout this period, public schools have been able to sustain themselves despite challenges and criticism. Such stability, in the face of massive societal changes, is testimony to the soundness of the basic design of the public schools and to the ability of the American schools to accommodate change.

Differences of opinion are inevitable in an open and democratic society. Such variability in educational philosophy and programs is in stark contrast to the apparent consensus and purposefulness of educational opinion in totalitarian societies. Still, if history is an accurate indicator, the American school has benefited from the diversity of educational philosophy and attempts to reform public schools. An openness to ideas and a flexibility in meeting changing conditions have enriched our schools immeasurably. We live in a world which is constantly changing, and schools, to some extent, must change to maintain their utility.

In the early years of this century, attempts to introduce changes in our schools came from professional educators who were concerned with broad philosophical issues about the role of an education in society. Reform efforts, for the most part, had a philosophical base and evolved slowly over several decades. Only after considerable discussion and experimentation were educational reforms attempted.

Early attempts to reform the American school assumed a somewhat monolithic culture and aimed at developing programs that would serve the entire American society. In the latter half of this century, reform efforts have come more frequently, from more diverse sources, and without clear philosophical bases or records of controlled experimentation.

During the late 1950s and early 1960s, the American society experienced a cultural awakening. The diversity of the society, a pluralistic configuration of many subcultures, was revealed and the historic pattern of the public school was called into question. If the public school was to serve all members of the society, both the substance and the organization of the institution was open to review.

The frustrations and hopes of the numerous groups of the American public became linked to the schools, which are the social institutions for instilling values. The divergent norms and values of the subcultures suggested new ideas about what schools should be. Some of the ideas and concepts of these schools were incorporated by the public schools, but many were not.

Related to these attempts to reform the school, which came primarily from inside the ranks of education, were numerous reformation efforts by external groups. The importance of public education as an influence for social change led industry, foundations, and the federal agencies to introduce changes in the school. The sponsorship of such efforts continues today.

The implications of these trends for curriculum planners are multiple. First, it seems apparent that persons responsible for designing school programs should be able to view "forces of change" with some degree of perspective. Innovations and educational trends need to be seen in terms of some overriding framework and in light of historical precedence. An inability to categorize and order the multitude of curriculum changes found in today's public schools will result in short-range decisions and long-range chaos.

Second, it must be recognized that public sophistication concerning curriculum development has grown considerably during the past several decades. Seeing schools as purposeful agents of change has led to the development of many restricting designs with little or no concern for long-term social implications. Such educational focus has also led to the development of some relatively efficient public school programs.

Finally, recent changes in the design of school programs should suggest to curriculum leaders that schools are institutions with numerous possibilities. To be influential in the educational environment, curriculum designers must break away from the familiar and begin to be responsible to the changing needs and values of the society. The clients who support public schools must be responded to in imaginative ways.

This chapter looks at educational designs from a comprehensive vantage point, with the hope of leading the reader to see curriculum development as a means of working with young people in desired ways. Examples of school designs used in this chapter serve only as a reminder that such a role has been a consistent theme of curriculum development throughout the twentieth century.

Major Curriculum Designs

There are numerous ways in which the many forms of schooling in the United States might be classified. Each social science perspective would suggest a different set of variables and categorization. Perhaps the most useful existing classification available today is one developed by Lucas.[1] In this classification, school forms are separated by function. Six major types of school design, and their rationale, are presented:

1. Conservative liberal arts designs
2. Educational technology designs
3. Humanistic designs
4. Vocational designs
5. Social reconstruction designs
6. Deschooling designs

Conservative Liberal Arts Designs

The pervasive educational design found in the United States and throughout most of the world is one that has roots leading back to

Hellenistic Greece. It is based on a belief that a human being's unique and distinctive quality is intellect, and the quest for knowledge is the natural fulfillment of that intellect. In short, the highest purpose in life is to engage in the process of inquiry: to move from ignorance to truth, from confusion to enlightenment.

Historically, this quest for knowledge was seen as a reflection of a world whose laws and physical order were fixed properties. The process of education was concerned simply with the pursuit of objective knowledge for its own sake. A liberal education was suitable to free people who possessed the legal opportunity and means to devote themselves to cultural attainment.

In later times, after scientific revolutions and the loss of a shared culture had diminished the concept of *paideia* (the cultured man), the liberal arts approach to educating became a perspective. Liberal arts was not so much a mastery of subject matter as it was a way of looking at things. The human mind was trained so that the individual might live fully.

As this notion of education was translated into a public education format during the early American experience, such knowing was seen as a means of producing an enlightened citizenry. In the words of R. Freeman Butts: . . . the prime purpose of the public schools is to serve the general welfare of a democratic society by assuring the knowledge and understanding necessary to exercise the responsibilities of citizenship are not only made available but are inculcated.[2]

The curriculum design of the conservative liberal arts is familiar to most Americans as the program they experienced. Such a design was spelled out formally in a declaration of "permanent studies."[3]

1. Language and its uses (reading, writing, grammar, literature)
2. Mathematics
3. Sciences
4. History
5. Foreign languages

The program design of the liberal arts curriculum is also standard enough to warrant the omission of a descriptive program. Single resource texts, mastery learning, lecture format, and uniform blocks of time are dominant in most schools.

Educational Technology Designs

A second major curriculum design found in this century is one which is technological in nature, focusing on process and technique without equal regard for the goals or ends. Behavioristic in nature, this design has been used throughout the century to promote various school programs.

An early example of technological education was to be found in the much publicized Winnetka plan of the 1930s. In this program, students interacted with mimeographed assignment booklets to master essential skills and knowledge. Self-instructive practice exercises were monitored through a diagnostic-practice-remediation format that was the forerunner of much of today's programmed instruction. "Tests indicated whether the goal had been attained or whether further practice was necessary."*

Technological designs stress objectivity, precision, and efficiency. As a modern proponent B.F. Skinner has stated, "The traditional distinction comes down to this: when we know what we are doing we are training . . . any behavior which can be specified can be programmed."[4] Usually, goals and objectives of this design are described in terms of overt learner behaviors which may or may not last beyond the immediate treatment.

Modern applications of the technological approach have come in the form of electronic hardware and communication mediums: first generation television, programmed instruction, films, cassettes, and other visuals; second generation technology in the form of automatizing devices, computer-assisted instruction, air-beamed programming, microwave relays, and satellite transmissions.

Modern applications of the technological design have also employed "systems" technology in the form of concepts such as "delivery systems," cost-benefit analyses, and accountability. Organizationally, planning has been in the form of sophisticated programs like the Program Planning and Budgeting System (PPBS), using basic strategic planning, delineated procedures, and decentralized management techniques. Students in technological designs are "hooked-up and plugged-in" to the program.

Perhaps the best developed public school program to date which emphasized educational technology as the ultimate delivery system was the Ford Foundation-sponsored Nova Schools in Fort Lauderdale, Florida, In this program, students from preschool to high school interacted with hardware of all kinds in the pursuit of education.

Technological curriculum designs are usually characterized by high degrees of structure, but with greater student interaction with materials or equipment. Students in the Nova Schools, for instance, could be found with headsets on in video carrels, playing electronic musical instruments, or manipulating interactive games on the computer.

Humanistic Designs

A third curriculum design in the United States during the twentieth century has had as its main theme the "humanizing" of learning. Such designs generally feature student-centered curriculums and instructional patterns and a decentralization of authority and organization.

*As reported in J. Wayne Wrightstone's *Appraisal of Experimental High Schools,* Bureau of Publications, Teachers College, Columbia University, 1936.

Humane curriculum designs have deep roots in American education and have taken numerous forms in this century. In such programs there is a shift in atmosphere toward understanding, compassion, encouragement, and trust. Physical settings usually encourage freedom in the form of student mobility, increased choice of curricular activities, and a learning-by-doing format.

An early example of this design in the United States was the Dalton Plan, which was implemented in the Dalton, Massachusetts schools in the 1920s. The program featured freedom of movement and choice of materials by students, cooperation and interaction of student group life through a "house plan," and subject matter laboratories in the classrooms.

Another early version of a humanistic curriculum design was the organic method of education developed at the Fairhope, Alabama school around 1910. This program held that children are best prepared for adult life by fully experiencing childhood. Children were led "naturally" into more traditional areas of schooling only after experiencing a curriculum of physical exercise, nature study, music, field geography, storytelling, fundamental conception of numbers, drama, and games. General development rather than the amount of information controlled the classification of students.*

Contemporary versions of the humanistic design are to be found in open elementary schools, emerging middle schools, and student-centered programs such as Outward Bound. In such programs, the instruction is humane, personalized, and individualized. Curriculum is geared to the maturational levels of students, and teachers serve as guides to learning rather than authority figures or purveyors of knowledge. The problem-solving process of the instructional format borrows heavily from another humanistic design, the core curriculum.

The core curriculum, developed in the 1930s in schools such as the Denver public schools, attempted to present learning from a humane and holistic perspective. The following excerpt from an evaluation report outlines the program objectives:

> It is so named because it represents an attack upon those problems which are relatively common to the young people in the school and because it carries the chief responsibility for guidance, for general testing, and for record keeping. It is that part of the total school program which is planned for the development in boys and girls of the ability to solve common problems and of the power to think together and to carry on the democratic process of discussion and group decisions.**

*As reported in John and Evelyn Dewey's *Schools of Tomorrow* (New York: E.P. Dutton and Company, 1915).
**As reported in *Thirty Schools Tell Their Story*, vol. 5 (New York: Harper and Brothers, 1943), p. 166.

Core curriculums used a ten-point plan in organizing for instruction:

1. Continuity of teacher-pupil relationships
2. Greater teacher participation in formulating policies of the program.
3. Elimination of barriers to learning experiences through the attack on problems rather than through reliance upon the logical organization of subject matter in isolated courses.
4. Development of core courses based on student concerns.
5. Relating school activities to the community.
6. Pupil-teacher planning, emphasizing choice and responsibility.
7. Guidance by a teacher who knows the student in an intimate classroom setting.
8. Using a wide variety of sources of information.
9. Using a wide variety of means of expression—words, art, music.
10. Teacher-to-teacher planning.

Humanistic designs generally are characterized by highly flexible instructional areas, high degrees of student involvement, and an emphasis on the process of learning as opposed to a product orientation or a "preparation for life" outlook.

Vocational Designs

A fourth curriculum design present in the United States in this century has been one concerned with vocational and economic aspects of life. For years such designs were referred to as vocational education, and more recently have been identified by the broad phrase *career education*.

In the early years of this century, vocational programs were perceived as separate and parallel curriculum designs in public schools. These programs served the noncollege-bound populations and were strongest in highly industrialized and agricultural areas. The curriculum consisted of crafts and labor skills that had application in the immediate economic environment. More recently, there have been efforts to make work and the preparation for work a primary emphasis of the curriculum at all levels.

Sidney Marland Jr., former commissioner of the U.S. Office of Education, has stated the case for a vocational design in the following manner:

It is flatly necessary to begin to construct a sound, systematic relationship between education and work. This system will make it a standard practice to teach every student about occupations and the economic enterprise. A system that will markedly increase career options open to each individual and enable us to do a better job than we have been doing of meeting the manpower needs of the country.[5]

Efforts to implement a comprehensive vocational design have been increased during the past decade by a number of factors. First, there has been a growing recognition that the schools are an essential piece of the national economic condition. Welfare, unemployment, large segments of the population without useful skills, and the fact that only 40–45 percent of all high school graduates attend college have been given as reasons for an increased vocational emphasis in the schools.

Second, the entire relevancy movement of the 1960s revealed a condition of students who are bored and listless in senior high school, resentful of the holding pattern of formal schooling.

Third, vocational/career education has been promoted as a means of assisting minority groups and other disenchanted members of the society in breaking out of the cycle of poverty. Students experiencing such programs can escape the containment of environments and family backgrounds.

Finally, the whole concept of utilitarian education and no-frills curriculums has increased the awareness and demand for vocational designs. There is a growing opinion among the public that insufficient attention has been paid to the hard social reality that everyone must eventually seek gainful employment. Technological and political conditions demand a change in the basic definition of an education.

An interesting application of the vocational design is the number of large technical/vocational high schools being constructed in the United States such as McGavok High School in Nashville, Tennessee and Skyline High School in Dallas, Texas. The Skyline program features a 21.5 million dollar building, and over five million dollars worth of technological and scientific hardware. In the Center for Career Development complex, visitors will find airplane hangars, greenhouses, television studios, and computer terminals leading to careers in transportation services, horticulture, entertainment, and computer technology.

The Skyline curriculum takes the student through a series of steps enroute to employment: the development of a postive self-image, and understanding of economic structures, and expansion of occupational goals, perception of education as a means to goal attainment, and developing marketable skills.[6]

Proponents of vocational designs in the twentieth century have pictured them as a necessity: a means of serving all students in the public schools, a vehicle for making school useful and relevant, a contributor to the well-being of the American society. Vocational designs are practical. Critics of vocational designs, including career education, see them as static conceptions of life in the American society and insufficient preparation for life in an unknown future.

Social Reconstruction Designs

A fifth curriculum design found in the United States in this century has as its main theme social reconstruction. The conception of the school as a vehicle for social improvement is not new. Arguments for this type of school were made in the 1930s by members of the social reconstruction wing of the Progressive Education Association. Harold Rugg, for example, spoke of the changes impending in the American society and encouraged the schools to influence social changes. He outlined characteristics of a needed curriculum in the 26th National Society for the Study of Education Yearbook:

> A curriculum which will not only inform but will constantly have as its ideal the development of an attitude of sympathetic tolerance and critical open-mindedness . . . a curriculum which is constructed on a problem-solving organization providing constant practice in choosing between alternatives, in making decisions, in drawing generalizations . . . a curriculum in which children will be influenced to put their ideas sanely into action.[7]

The social reconstruction designs seek to equip students with tools to deal with the forces about them and to manage conditions as they meet them. They seek to alert students to social issues and choices and to equip them with attitudes and habits of action. Two recent educational programs approach a social reconstruction design in their curriculums as they work with students to become more self-sufficient in a rapidly changing society. These schools are Harlem Prep in New York City and the John Adams High School in Portland, Oregon.

Harlem Prep is a school started during the 1960s to assist students in a black ghetto to overcome social forces and succeed in a college preparatory program. The technique of the curriculum is to instill attitudes of racial pride which will allow the student to compete in academic circles. Using what Fantini and Weinstein refer to as a "contact curriculum," teachers start instruction where the student is and take him someplace else.[8] Ultimately, the goal of schools like Harlem Prep is to develop a cadre of educated inner-city leaders who can transform the Lower East Side of New York City.

The John Adams High School in Portland, Oregon, is an experiment in what has been termed a "clinical curriculum." School governance is carried out by the Adams Community Government which is modeled after the structure of the United States government. Students and teachers have control over such important areas as budget and the hiring and firing of teachers. The focus of study is on contemporary problems such as change in society, racial conflict, and street law. Working as a collective unit, "houses" within the school seek to design a more workable school society.

The major assumption of social reconstruction designs is that the future is not fixed, but rather is amenable to modification and improvement. The school, as an institution, cannot remain neutral in a changing world and can influence and direct social change.

Recent applications of the social reconstruction design have used "futurism" to justify the necessity of social intervention. Since the future will not be like the present, it is necessary to be flexible and develop the ability to make value decisions. In the words of Kirschenbaum and Simon: Unless one believes that the future is inevitable—that we have absolutely no control over our private and public destinies— the study of the future must include not merely possible and probable futures but preferable futures. This is why the broad movement aimed at shifting education into the future tense also brings with it a heightened concern with values.[9]

Social reconstruction designs generally combine classroom learning with application in the outer world. Teachers and students are partners in inquiry, and instruction is usually carried on in a problem-solving or inquiry format.

Deschooling Designs

The final curriculum design of the twentieth century in the United States is a rare and relatively new one. It seeks through its organization, or lack of, to de-emphasize or disestablish the formality of education, and the reliance on formal schooling. Most of the applications of this curriculum design have been found in alternative schools which, in a variety of ways, set the learner free to pursue knowledge and an education on his own.

According to its chief spokesman, Ivan Illich, schools are social tools which actually operate to deprive individuals of an education and real learning. Schools are not the panacea for social ills, but rather are rigid, authoritarian institutions which perpetuate the social order through a number of functions. Illich sees deschooling as an alternative design:

> Will people continue to treat learning as a commodity—a commodity that could be more efficiently produced and consumed by greater numbers of people if new institutional arrangements were established? Or shall we set up only those institutional arrangements that protect the autonomy of the learner—his private initiative to decide what he will learn and his inalienable right to learn what he likes rather than what is useful to somebody else? We must choose between more efficient education of people fit for an increasingly efficient society and a new society in which education ceases to be the task of some special agency.[10]

Problems of institutionalized education revolve around questions of power, leadership, and structure. Schools, by dominating the values and focus of organization, control the learner. Such control is often racist and sexist, and is always oppressive. Further, schools are undemocratic in their method of converting knowledge into power.

Reactions to formal schooling and its structure has been a continuous phenomenon of the twentieth century in the United States, but the free school movement of the late 1960s presents the best examples of the deschooling design. Glatthorn outlines the emergence of the free school movement during that period:

> The period of the late sixties, then, was a time ripe for radical change. The curriculum reform movement had run out of steam. The innovations in scheduling and staffing were proving to be only superficial tinkering. And there was acute dissatisfaction with all the public schools. This dissatisfaction was most keenly sensed by militant blacks and by radicals of the New Left. Each of these groups responded by opening their own schools, and these schools were the progenitors of the public alternatives that followed.[11]

Glatthorn identifies a number of ways in which free schools and alternative schools attempted to release the individual student from the institutional oppression of the school: travel-learn programs, work and apprenticeship programs, volunteer service, informal study in the community, and affective experiences. Collectively, these curriculum arrangements sought to define education as a personal act.

Efforts to break the monopoly of formal education and deschool learning continue today. They seek to downgrade the importance of accepting the functions of formal schooling, and to break the myth of a need for education. While on the decline, such curriculum designs are likely to emerge again in the future.

Together, these six curriculum designs outline the diversity of educational programs in the United States during the twentieth century. Curriculum leaders need to be aware that such diversity has always been present in American education and will continue to be present in the future.

The authors hope that these designs will suggest other possibilities to you. Curriculum leaders need to develop the intellectual freedom which will allow them to design the best possible school programs for children. As Lawrence Cremin has so eloquently stated in his *The Genius of American Education*, "Education is too significant and dynamic an enterprise to be left to mere technicians."[12]

A Look to the Future

To attempt to assess the possibilities for the future of curriculum development in America is to enter an area of inquiry which has seen great activity in recent years. Futurism in education is a topic of concern to all educators, and has been the subject of numerous commissioned studies and investigations by "think tanks" such as RAND,

Incorporated, and the Hudson Institute. You are encouraged to become familiar with resources such as those presented in the suggested readings section of this chapter.

In this chapter, we hope to stimulate thinking about the many possibilities for education which the future might hold, and present the process of curriculum development as the vehicle by which schools might arrive at that unknown future. Following a theme found throughout this book, the future of educational programs is presented in a format that suggests a trend toward either greater control in curriculum designs or greater flexibility in educational plans. It is entirely possible, of course, that other intellectual constructs may be more useful in addressing this highly complex topic.

A date of departure for this assessment is the year 1957, the date of the launch of Sputnik I. It was this event that jarred American education into a purposefulness which had been absent in the past and opened up fully the idea of using schools as an instrument of national policy. While the space race of the late 1950s has evaporated in scale to that of "just another federal program," the question of what role the schools shall play remains.

As we approach the twenty-first century, American education is faced with a bewildering array of alternatives concerning what it might become. The question that must be faced by all leaders in the field of curriculum is the primary question of all educational planning. What is the role of education in our society? Failure to consider this critical question is to abdicate a basic responsibility and decide by indecision.

Specifically, there are some questions that must be considered as we peer into the last years of the twentieth century. Among these are the following:

1. What directions seem to be most promising for the American society to pursue in planning for education?
2. Where and how do professional educators begin to assess educational alternatives?
3. Can the future be influenced by our actions or is it largely predetermined?
4. Where do we as planners gain the value structure to plan for the future?
5. How can we most effectively involve others in our society in planning for the future?

These questions present a challenge to all who are involved in developing educational programs.

The Future

In the final fifteen years of the twentieth century, the American society stands in awe of the possibilities of an unknown future. Developments during the third quarter of the century presented us with unprecedented changes in every aspect of social existence. Such changes were both substantive and superficial, and touched the lives of all citizens.

Harold Shane, well-known educational futurist, outlines some of the more substantial changes during the 1950–1975 period:

1. Human vision was extended a billion light years.
2. The molecule was made visible.
3. Low virus-like forms were created in the laboratory.
4. Men landed on the moon's surface.
5. The number of people on earth more than doubled.
6. Atomic and hydrogen bombs were exploded.
7. Biological cloning allowed the genetic reproduction of plants and animals.
8. Major organ transplants were made in human subjects.
9. Satellites internationalized television viewing on all continents.[13]

One decade later, Shane's list could be expanded tenfold. Each of the above events was bettered by modern technology, and new innovations continued to break a pattern of linear thinking about the future. Observing the scale of such change, economist Kenneth Boulding stated, "As far as any statistical series related to the activities of mankind are concerned the date that divides human history into two equal parts is well within the living memory."[14]

So pervasive and rapid was change during this period that prediction challenged projection as the most accurate indicator of future events. One writer in the mid-sixties went so far as to formulate this condition into the form of "Clark's Law" which read, "When a distinguished but elderly scientist states that something is possible, he is almost certainly right. When he states something is impossible, he is very probably wrong."[15]

The changes of the third quarter of the twentieth century had implications for all dimensions of the American society, introducing an element of "future shock" to all institutions. In his best-selling book by the same title, author Alvin Toffler cited numerous indicators of the scope of such change. A fact of great importance to an educational system still based on mastery of fundamental knowledge, for example, was that by the mid-1960s the output of books on a worldwide scale approached 1,000 titles per day or 30,000 titles per year in the United States alone.

Citing one study on the explosion of organized knowledge, Toffler stated, "At the rate at which knowledge is growing, by the time the child born today graduates from college the amount of knowledge in the world will be four times as great. By the time that same child is fifty years old, it will be 32 times as great and 97 percent of everything known in the world will have been learned since the time he was born."[16]

McDanield has identified seven factors that contribute to the type and scale of such changes:

1. *Demographic change*—sex and age patterns, death rates, life spans, etc.
2. *Technological innovation*—adaptive changes in machines and productivity
3. *Social innovation*—new arrangements, styles, and systems in education, politics, the economy, etc.
4. *Culture-value shifts*—changing preferences and ideas
5. *Ecological shifts*—scarcity of resources, catastrophic events, etc.
6. *Information-idea shifts*—the scope, quality, and manipulability of knowledge; new conceptions of how things work
7. *Cultural diffusion*—transfer of ideas, values and techniques from one culture to another via war, travel, advertising, etc.[17]

The changes experienced by the American society between 1950 and 1975 altered the social fabric of the society. Legal rulings, economic pressures, political intrigue, social upheaval, and information analysis and processing left basic institutions in a chaotic state. Schools, in particular, were beseiged by challenges of a social-economic-political nature. Such an experience greatly increased concern for the future and stimulated formal future planning in education.

Planning for the Future

One of the effects of too much change in too short a period of time in the United States has been the emergence of *transience*. Such transience, a mood or feeling of impermanence, is reflected in relationships among people, things, places, organizations, and information. Excessive transience threatens social stability by undercutting the framework of cultural preservation and transmission. The historic role of the school as the adaptive mechanism of the society is questioned in a culture where impermanence becomes a regular condition.

One of the roles of future planning in education, then, is to determine the exact purpose or purposes of the school as it relates to a changing society. This has proven to be difficult in the American culture due to the phenomenon of culture lag. The term culture lag refers to a condition where some sectors of the society exhibit different rates of change and therefore transform themselves more slowly. Since formal public school education represents the single largest institution in the United States, it has not kept pace with social and cultural evolution caused by technological and economic conditions. The result of culture lag in educational planning has been to have insufficient information with which to make critical decisions. Educational planners have regularly utilized linear thinking when necessary.

Futurists in education have recognized the problems of basic linear change. As Shane has observed:

> In all forms of planning, including educational planning, the assumption
> of linearity which leads to the passive, conformist policy of adapting to
> an inferred series of coming future events is an erroneous one . . .
> Actually, the future may be construed to be a fan-shaped array of
> possibilities of alternative futures which can be powerfully influenced or
> 'created' by man.[18]

The response of educational planners to conditions of transience, culture lag, and the need for nonlinear thinking has been to project educational goals and desired educational futures in a variety of ways. Early efforts at projection borrowed techniques from social science research including the use of scenario, think tanks, and Delphi technique.* One example, a study by Kahn and Wiener conducted in 1967, used "reasonable speculation" to identify conditions which might influence future educational planning. Among possible changes identified were:

1. Practical use of direct electronic communication with and stimulation of the brain
2. New and more reliable drugs for the control of personality and perceptions
3. Chemical methods for improving memory and learning
4. Home education via television and computerized learning
5. Genetic control over the "basic constitution" of the individual[19]

Such projective techniques, it was hoped, would provide educational planners in the public schools with preferences and options that would assist them in structuring decision making.

Another vehicle used by educators concerned with the future was the establishment of special commissions which would set standards and goals for long-range planning. An example of such a commission is the Commission on the Year 2000. Other similar groups of experts are to be found in the selected readings section of this chapter. By lending expert opinion to preferred futures in education, it was thought that education could be attracted to an improved state.

A third technique used by educational planners in moving toward the future is goal-reduction. In this procedure, agencies, professional groups, state departments of education, and others are asked to submit a list of their goals for the future of education. Then, through a ranking or sorting mechanism, the most desired goals are identified. These preferred goals will hopefully influence future decision-making in schools.

It should be noted that, in spite of considerable activity in professional education, dealing with the future is a primitive art in school circles. There is a heavy dependence on social science research for

---

*The Delphi technique, developed by Olaf Helmer, is a rounded questionnaire which uses reduction of opinion to gain consensus.

ideas and basic structures. There is also a problem, stemming from the affluence of education in the 1960s, of undue optimism in projecting goals. As Toffler has stated:

> Today in techno-societies there is an almost iron-clad consensus about the future of freedom. Maximum individual choice is regarded as a democratic ideal. Yet most writers predict that we shall move further and further from this ideal. They conjure up a dark vision of the future in which people appear as mindless consumers, surrounded by standard-ized goods, educated in standardized schools, fed a diet of standardized mass culture, and forced to adopt standardized styles of life.[20]

Whether educational planners can meld the idealism of futurology with the realism of social conditions remains to be seen. For all the rhetoric about the future, school planning remains dominated by quantified projections stemming from present conditions.

Alternatives and Ideas

There are numerous conceptions in existence about what schools should be like in the future. They represent the best thinking of individuals and professional organizations and come from all points on a philosophical continuum. Rather than trying to be comprehensive in presenting these models, the authors have chosen samples that project very different futures for the American public school.

One example is drawn from a working paper of the Research and Theory Group of the Association for Supervision and Curriculum Development, the largest professional association of curriculum special-ists in the United States. The task of this group was to develop and identify a set of valued learning outcomes that could guide curriculum development in the future. The result of their study was the develop-ment of a group of basic skills which would be attained by all students:

Self-Conceptualization
Understanding Others
Learning Skills
Capability for Continuous Learning
Responsible Member of Society
Mental and Physical Health
Creativity
Informed Participation in Economic World
Use of Accumulated Knowledge
Coping With Change[21]

The ASCD conception of the future of public education should be seen as an extension of previous global positions by the Educational Policy Commission of the National Education Association and other such groups. While each of the basic skills identified by the Research and Theory Work Group had accompanying subgoals, the projection is necessarily unfocused. Because ASCD represents curriculum leaders from all segments of public education, the vision of the future is necessarily broad-based and an extension of the present. Such a projected future illustrates the difficulty of melding theory with existing practice.

A second idea about the future of public education in the United States is presented by James S. Coleman who conducted a massive study of educational opportunity during the 1960s. Coleman's concern is with access to education and the question of who shall benefit from such a tax-based program:

> The relative intensity of the convergent school influences and the divergent out-of-school influences determines the proximity of the educational system in providing equality of educational opportunity. That is, equality of output is not so much determined by quality of the resource inputs, but by the power of those resources in bringing about achievement. The implication of the concept as I have described it here is that the responsibility to create achievement lies with the educational institution.
>
> I suggest that it may be realized through a change in the very concept of the school itself; from being an agency within which the child is taught to being the agent responsible for seeing that the child learns—a responsibility in which the school's own facilities may play only a part.[22]

Coleman's view that the school must be responsive to all learners represents the position of many minority groups in the United States. His definition of the responsibilities of the school would expand the operation of education into all walks of life, from cradle to grave.

A third conception of the future of public education is presented by psychologist B.F. Skinner. Skinner believes that we can no longer afford an educational system that does not control outcomes, and hopes for a school that contributes to "an improved society":

> We need to make vast changes in human behavior. . . . What we need is technology of behavior. . . . We can follow the path taken by physics and biology by turning directly to the relation between behavior and the environment and neglecting supposed mediating states of mind.
>
> We need to design contingencies under which students acquire behavior useful to them and their culture—contingencies that do not have troublesome byproducts. We must look to the contingencies that induce people to act to increase the chances that their culture will survive. We have the physical, biological, and behavioral technologies needed to save ourselves; the problem is how to get people to use them. The intentional design of a culture and the control of human behavior it implies are essential if the human species is to continue to develop.

What is needed is more intentional control, not less, and this is an important engineering problem.[23]

The Skinner blueprint for schools of the future acknowledges the many social problems faced by our society as we enter the final quarter of the twentieth century, and is representative of a host of positions which seek to manage education toward greater efficiency.

A final conception of the school of the future is offered by Alvin Toffler who concluded, after an intensive study of change in the American society, that what is needed is an education system that serves individuals:

> Every society has its own characteristic attitude toward the past, present, and future. This time-bias, formed in response to the rate of change, is one of the least noticed, yet most powerful determinants of social behavior, and it is clearly reflected in the way the society prepares its young in childhood.
>
> One hundred and fifty years ago Americans needed to learn to survive in a thinly settled frontier in the face of often threatening natural environments. Today there is a need to educate children to survive in a world made increasingly dangerous for man by man.
>
> No educational institution today can set sensible goals or do an effective job until its members subject their own assumptions about tomorrow to critical analysis. For their shared or collective image of the future dominates the decisions made in the institution.
>
> What we do in teaching depends on what we think people are like and what they can become.
>
> Learning for tomorrow includes learning to know one's own mind, so to speak, to understand one's own values clearly enough to be able to make consistent and effective choices.[24]

These four conceptions of the future in education, illustrated in Figure 12.1, present planners with very different alternatives. Do we develop an education program that helps each individual become

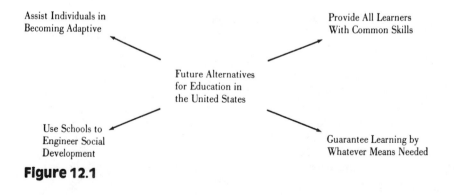

Assist Individuals in
Becoming Adaptive

Provide All Learners
With Common Skills

Future Alternatives
for Education in
the United States

Use Schools to
Engineer Social
Development

Guarantee Learning by
Whatever Means Needed

Figure 12.1

capable of adapting to a changing world as Toffler suggests? Do we provide all learners with a set of common adaptive skills and behaviors as the ASCD work group suggests? Do we construct an educational program that reaches out to serve all learners in society and guarantee, through whatever means necessary, that such learning occurs as Coleman recommends? Or do we begin to seriously engineer an educational program that will benefit the American society as Skinner suggests?

Even a cursory review of educational events in the United States since 1957 reveals that public schools are pursuing all of the above alternatives simultaneously.

Following the launching of Sputnik I there was a massive effort in the United States to "gear up" education so that our society might compete in a technological war with the Soviet Union. Heavy funding produced extensive curriculum renewal in the form of the so-called alphabet projects (BSCS, PSSC, etc.). The programs of the public schools were initially dominated by mathematics and hard sciences; curriculum improvement later spread to the social sciences and fine arts.

The reaction to this high pressure approach to curriculum development coincided with the awakening of cultural pluralism in the United States and the civil rights movements. Curriculum development efforts were sponsored to serve minority groups and divergent segments of the population.

As the American society entered the latter half of the 1960s, civil rights became individual rights. Numerous programs, in the public schools and outside the public schools, were developed to meet the needs of unique learners. Such alternatives raised important questions concerning the criteria for such program development, i.e., preparation for what?

Finally, into the 1970s the educational systems of the United States have attempted to define and refine the goals and objectives of programs. Diminishing levels of funding have created an accountability movement that seeks to maximize resources by engineering educational learning systems.

What the 1980s and beyond hold for public education in America is a matter of conjecture. History would suggest that economic prosperity and diminished social stress encourage increased flexibility and freedom in curriculum design. By the same token, social tension and economic problems have historically encouraged tight curriculum designs with greater degrees of control and structure.

Whatever the future holds for American public education in the remainder of the twentieth century, it is certain that the shape of education will be influenced by the thinking of those responsible for developing such programs: the curriculum development specialists. The challenge to all persons in the field of curriculum is to become aware of possibilities and develop models which present alternatives for the sponsoring public. To do so, we must overcome a historic reluctance to provide such leadership.

Charles Silberman, in his classic 1970 analysis of American education, posed the problem in the following manner:

> It simply never occurs to more than a handful (of educators) to ask why they are doing what they are doing . . . to think seriously about the purposes or consequences of education. This mindlessness—the failure or refusal to think seriously about educational purpose—is not the monopoly of the public school; it is diffused remarkably evenly throughout the entire educational system and indeed the entire society.[25]

To be aware of alternatives and to utilize opportunities to develop quality programs for our children is the mark of effective leadership in curriculum development.

Summary

Throughout this century, divergent opinions about education have led to efforts to reform the American public school. Because these efforts continue today, curriculum leaders should be aware of the multiple curriculum designs in existence, and be open to new thinking about the way schools and educational programs are organized.

Six designs have been prominent in the American experience: educational conservatism, technological designs, humanistic designs, vocational designs, social reconstruction designs, and deschooling designs. Such diversity has unquestionably enriched the programs of the American public school. The future holds multiple possibilities for education in the United States of America. Curriculum development is the vehicle by which schools will approach the unknown future in planning education.

Studies of the future reveal that we have experienced enormous changes in the American society during the third quarter of the twentieth century. It is probable that the rate and scale of change in our society will continue into the twenty-first century.

Planning for the future of education is made difficult by impermanence in our society, by cultural lag in educational institutions, and by the inefficiency of traditional linear projections of the future. Educational futurists have responded to these conditions by using projection and prediction techniques to attempt to attract schools to preferred futures.

There are numerous conceptions of what education should be like in the future. Some educators favor decentralized programs focused on the individual or specific publics in the American society. Others favor highly centralized programs which serve the state. School districts throughout the United States have responded to these options during the past twenty years by pursuing diverse and multiple ends for education.

The exact nature of educational programs in the United States during the final quarter of the twentieth century will be heavily influenced by the thoughts and work of curriculum specialists. The challenge to all curriculum workers is to think about the meaning of education in our society and present viable alternatives to the sponsoring public.

Notes _____

1. Christopher J. Lucas, *Challenge and Choice in Contemporary Education* (New York: Macmillan Publishing Company, 1976).

2. R. Freeman Butts, "Assaults on a Great Idea," *The Nation*, (April 30, 1973): 553–560.

3. Robert M. Hutchins, *The Restoration of Learning* (New York: Alfred A. Knopf, 1955).

4. B.F. Skinner, *Beyond Freedom and Dignity* (New York: Alfred A. Knopf, 1971), p. 169.

5. Sidney Marland, Jr., Working paper, U.S. Office of Education, 1972.

6. S. Marland, H. Lichtenwald, and R. Burke, "Career Education Texas Style: The Skyline Center in Dallas," *Phi Delta Kappan* (May, 1975): 616–620.

7. Harold Rugg in *The Foundation and Techniques of Curriculum Making*, 26th Yearbook of the National Society for the Study of Education (Bloomington, Indiana, 1927): 7–8.

8. Mario D. Fantini and Gerald Weinstein, *The Disadvantaged: Challenge to Education* (New York: Harper & Row. 1968).

9. Howard Kirschenbaum and Sidney Simon, "Values and the Futures Movement in Education," in *Learning for Tomorrow· The Role of the Future in Education*," Alvin Toffler, ed. (New York: Vintage Books, 1974), p. 257.

10. Ivan Illich, *After Deschooling, What?* in Alan Gartner, et al., eds, *After Deschooling, What?* (New York: Perennial Library, 1973), p. 1.

11. Allen A. Glatthorn, *Alternatives in Education: Schools and Programs* (New York: Dodd, Mead, and Company, 1975), pp. 117–136.

12. Lawrence A. Cremin, *The Genius of American Education* (Pittsburgh: The University of Pittsburgh Press, 1965), p. 75.

13. Harold G. Shane, "Future-Planning as a Means of Shaping Educational Change," in *The Curriculum: Retrospect and Prospect*, 70th Yearbook, Part I, National Society for the Study of Education (Chicago: University of Chicago Press, 1970), p. 191.

14. Kenneth Boulding, *The Meaning of the Twentieth Century* (New York: Harper & Row Publishers, 1964).

15. Arthur C. Clark, *Profiles of the Future* (New York: Harper & Row Publishers, 1963), p. 14.

16. Alvin Toffler, *Future Shock* (New York: Random House, 1970), pp. 157–158.

17. Michael M. McDanield, "Tomorrow's Curriculum Today," in Alvin Toffler, ed., *Learning for Tomorrow: The Role of the Future in Education* (New York, Vintage Books, 1974), pp. 115–116.

18. Harold G. Shane, "Future Planning as a Means of Shaping Educational Change," p. 187.

19. Herman Kahn and Anthony Wiener, *The Year 2000: A Framework for Speculating on the Next Thirty-Three Years* (New York: Macmillan Publishing Company, 1967).

20. Alvin Toffler, *Future Shock*, p. 263.

21. Preliminary draft of a 1978 report, "Valued Learning Outcomes," to the Executive Council of ASCD by the Research and Theory Working Group. Forthcoming.

22. James S. Coleman, "The Responsibility of the School: A Sociologist's Perspective," in Charles Tesconi and Emanuel Hurwitz, eds., *Education for Whom* (New York: Dodd Mead & Company, 1974), pp. 106–107.

23. B.F. Skinner, *Beyond Freedom and Dignity* (New York: Alfred A. Knopf, 1971), pp. 12, 149, 150, 167, 169.

24. Alvin Toffler, *Learning for Tomorrow*, pp. 4, 5, 20, 107, 196, 399.

25. Charles E. Silberman, *Crisis in the Classroom* (New York: Random House, 1970), pp. 6, 11.

Suggested Learning Activities _____

1. State in three sentences or less what you believe to be the purpose of formal education in the United States.

2. React to each of the six designs suggested by Lucas by developing a list of pros and cons for each position.

3. Develop arguments for and against the types of educational futures envisioned by the ASCD work group, James Coleman, B.F. Skinner, and Alvin Toffler. If you were required to do so, how would you rank these proposals as preferred futures in education?

4. Imagine the design of a new society on the planet Mars. What values should be dominant? How might education function in such a new society? What would be the consequences of such an education system?

5. Try to brainstorm likely changes in our society during the coming decade. How will such changes affect public school education? Which of your identified changes will have the greatest impact on educational planning?

6. Develop a list of ways in which the public schools might incorporate future thinking into their daily operations. How might curriculum specialists in public schools become more aware of alternatives in education?

Books to Review ───────────────

Association for Supervision and Curriculum Development. *Perspectives on Curriculum Development: 1776-1976*. Washington, D.C.: Author, 1976.

Bagdikian, Ben. *The Information Machines: Their Impact on Men and the Media*. New York: Harper & Row, 1971.

Bronwell, Alfred, ed. *Science and Technology in the World of the Future*. New York: John Wiley and Sons, 1970.

Commoner, Barry. *The Closing Circle: Nature, Man, Technology*. New York: Alfred A. Knopf, 1971.

Hipple, Theodore, ed. *The Future of Education 1975-2000*. Pacific Palisades, California: Goodyear Publishing Company, 1974.

Hyman, Donald. *Approaches in Curriculum*. Englewood Cliffs, New Jersey: Prentice-Hall, Inc., 1973.

Krug, Mark. *What Will be Taught—The Next Decade*. Itasca, Illinois: F.E. Peacock Publishers, Inc., 1972.

Lucas, Christopher. *Challenge and Choice in Contemporary Education*. New York: Macmillan, 1976.

Rubin, Louis, ed. *The Future of Education: Perspectives on Tomorrow's Schooling*. Research for Better Schools, Inc. Boston: Allyn and Bacon, 1975.

Wilhelms, Fred. *What Should the Schools Teach?* PDK Fastback #13, Bloomington, Indiana: Phi Delta Kappa Educational Foundation, 1972.

Appendixes

Appendix A
Training Paradigm for Curriculum Developers

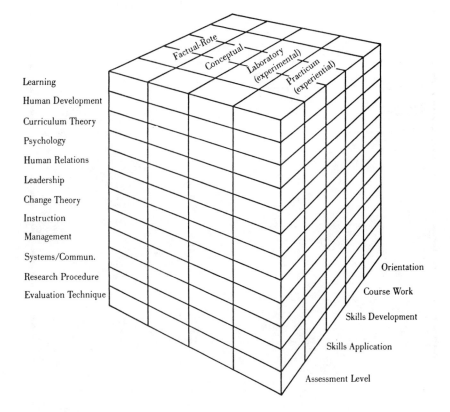

Learning
Human Development
Curriculum Theory
Psychology
Human Relations
Leadership
Change Theory
Instruction
Management
Systems/Commun.
Research Procedure
Evaluation Technique

Factual-Rote
Conceptual
Laboratory (experimental)
Practicum (experiential)

Orientation
Course Work
Skills Development
Skills Application
Assessment Level

Appendix B
Partial Listing of Organizations and Associations Affecting American Education

Citizens' Organizations

Council for Basic Education
725 15th Street, NW
Washington, D.C. 20005

National Coalition for Children
6542 Hitt Street
McLean, Virginia 22101

National Congress of Parents and Teachers
1715 25th Street
Rock Island, Illinois 61201

Educationally Related Organizations and Associations

American Association for Higher Education
One Dupont Circle, NW
Washington, D.C. 20036

American Association of School Administrators
1800 North Moore Street
Arlington, Virginia 22209

American Council on Education
One Dupont Circle, NW
Washington, D.C. 20036

American Educational Research Association
1126 16th Street, NW
Washington, D.C.

American Vocational Association, Inc.
1510 H Street, NW
Washington, D.C. 20005

Association for Supervision and Curriculum Development
(ASCD)
1701 K Street, NW
Washington, D.C. 20006

Childrens Television Workshop
One Lincoln Plaza
New York, New York 10023

College Entrance Examination Board
888 7th Avenue
New York, New York 10019

Council for American Private Education
1625 I Street, NW
Washington, D.C.

Council of Chief State School Officers
1201 16th Street, NW
Washington, D.C. 20036

International Reading Association
800 Barksdale Road
Newark, Delaware

Joint Council on Economic Education
1212 Avenue of the Americas
New York, New York 10036

National Art Education Association
1916 Association Drive
Reston, Virginia 22091

National Association for Education of Young Children
1834 Connecticut Avenue
Washington, D.C.

National Association of Elementary School Principals
1801 North Moore Street
Arlington, Virginia 22209

National Association for Public Continuing Adult Education
1201 16th Street, NW
Washington, D.C. 20036

National Association of Secondary School Principals
1904 Association Drive
Reston, Virginia 22091

National Council of Teachers of English
1111 Kenyon Road
Urbana, Illinois 61801

National Council of Teachers of Mathematics
1906 Association Drive
Reston, Virginia 22091

National Education Association
1201 16th Street, NW
Washington, D.C. 20036

National Middle School Association
P.O. Box 968
Fairborn, Ohio 45324

National School Boards Association
800 State National Bank Plaza
P.O. Box 1496
Evanston, Illinois 60204

National Science Teachers Association
1742 Connecticut Avenue, NW
Washington, D.C. 20009

Ethnic and Minority Organizations

Bilingual Education Service Center
500 South Dwyer
Arlington Heights, Illinois 60005

National Council of Negro Women, Inc.
1346 Connecticut Avenue, NW
Washington, D.C. 20036

National Indian Education Association
3036 University Avenue, SE
Minneapolis, Minnesota 55419

National Organization for Women (NOW)
1424 16th Street, NW
Washington, D.C.

General Associations

Committee for Economic Development
477 Madison Avenue
New York, New York 10022

National Association of Manufacturers
Economic Development Department
1776 F Street, NW
Washington, D.C. 20006

National Urban League
New York, New York

Labor Organizations

American Federation of Teachers
11 Dupont Circle
Washington, D.C.

Publishers

American Association of Publishers
One Park Avenue
New York, New York 10016

Association of Media Producers
1221 Avenue of the Americas
New York, New York 10020

Federal Bodies

House of Representatives
130 Cannon House Office Building
Washington, D.C. 20510

National Institute of Education
1200 19th Street, NW
Washington, D.C. 20208

National Science Foundation
5225 Wisconsin Avenue, NW
Washington, D.C. 20015

Office of Education
Office of the Assistant Secretary
Room 3153
400 Maryland Avenue, SW
Washinton, D.C. 20202

U.S. Senate
Senate Office Building
431 Russell
Washington, D.C. 20510

Author Index

Subject Index

The Authors

Jon Wiles and Joseph Bondi are professors of Educational Leadership at the University of South Florida at Tampa. Both have served in various educational roles—as classroom teachers, and as school and college administrators.

They have written together or coauthored with other writers *Curriculum Planning: A New Approach* (1974), *Curriculum Development: A Guide to Practice* (1979), *Supervision: A Guide to Practice* (1980), *The Essential Middle School* (1981), and *Practical Politics for School Administrators* (1981).

Both received doctoral degrees from the University of Florida, and reside in Tampa.